"What a great idea—*Managing Your Meals* will be a time and money saver for busy people everywhere. Winnifred Jardine, you've done it again!"

Dian Thomas
Food Specialist of NBC *Today* Show

"Think nutrition, think planning, think shopping, think cooking—getting it all together is the hard part. Doing so involves management of a very special order, and good management simplifies the job. *Managing Your Meals* is easy to follow, complete without finicky details, and has simple but good recipes."

Helen Thackeray
Cookbook Author and Former Manager
of General Foods Test Kitchen

"Who could ask for more? Carefully thought out menus, shopping lists, recipes, and the good information we have all expected from Winnifred through the years. Think of the major role she has already played in the upbringing and nurturing of countless families. . . . And now this superb addition—so practical!"

Carolyn Dunn
Customer Advisor to the President
Smith's Management Corporation

"Great guide and support for the busy homemaker. Winnifred has given us attractive, nutritious meals and saved us time in the process."

Janet Pittman
Cookbook Author and
Food Stylist

"Working from menu plans is a great saver, not only of time and money but of emotional energy. The 4:30 P.M. "What shall we eat?" panic attack is completely eliminated. There is a peace of mind that comes from knowing that your family will be eating nutritious meals that can be prepared in a short amount of time."

Marion Cahoon
Food Publicity Director and
Nutrition Specialist for the
Dairy Council

MANAGING
YOUR
MEALS

A Year's Worth of Menus,
Shopping Lists, and Recipes for
Delicious, Nutritious, and
Economical Meals.

Winnifred C. Jardine

SHADOW MOUNTAIN®
Salt Lake City, Utah

Recipe adaptations and their sources:

Baked Chicken with Sauerkraut, from *Country Gourmet Cooking*,
by Sherrill and Gil Roth, Workman Publishing, New York.
Kung Po Chicken, from *Sunset Oriental Cookbook*, Lane Publishing
Company, Menlo Park, California.
Zucchini Mushroom Pasta, from *Italian Family Cooking*, by Anne L.
Casale, Fawcett Columbine, New York.

Shadow Mountain is an imprint of Deseret Book Company

First printing April 1987
Second printing August 1987

Library of Congress Cataloging-in-Publication Data

Jardine, Winnifred C.
    Managing your meals.

    Includes index.
    1. Cookery   2. Menus.   I. Title.
TX715.J35 1987   641.5   86-29384
ISBN 0-87579-053-4

*To the families within our family who are
being nurtured by the meals and mealtimes
in their homes. And to my husband who has
come full circle to share, once again, meals
with only me.*

Contents

Acknowledgments

This endeavor, which has grown out of a lifetime of experience, requires many thanks:

To my husband, Stuart, who has given sustained encouragement and support.

To our children and their spouses—Jim and Jeanne, Stephen and Judy, Mark and Colleen, Ann and Brian—who have interacted on every level and given test to much of what has been written.

To Marion Jane Cahoon, a home economist of stature, who has been an invaluable resource.

To Eleanor Knowles, who has believed in this venture since its inception.

To Marci Chapman, who has served as a cheerful and meticulous editor and whose assignment has been bigger than I can comprehend.

To Michele Hansen, R. D., and Susan Ward, R. D., who gave appreciated guidance but on whom falls no responsibility for the final outcome.

To the Utah Heart Association, whose Eating Plan has contributed distinctly to the philosophy of meal patterns contained herein.

To many, many friends who have shared recipes and food ideas and who have helped in the important tasks of home-testing the theories.

To the home economics profession, which has directed my love and concern for family life.

To my angel mother, Winnifred Morrell Cannon, who was an abiding inspiration in the art of making a home.

And finally, my deep gratitude to The Giver of All Gifts, who provided inspiration and encouragement to me, and who provides so many of us with wondrous supplies of good food and a pattern for sharing what we have with those who have not.

Introduction

Planned menus are not for everyone. But for those who like the nutritional balance, the calorie control, the budget restraint, and the time management provided by preplanned meals, this book can be a household blessing.

From a Nutrition Point of View

The menus conform to the Daily Food Guide as recommended by the United States Department of Agriculture, the United States Department of Health and Human Services, the National Dairy Council, and the American Dietetic Association.

Since a basic tenet of good nutrition is to eat a wide variety of nourishing foods, the menus include many different kinds of fruits and vegetables; a variety of meat, poultry, fish, dried beans, and legumes; and a diversity of grains. Where food items are not available or where family tastes dictate, substitutions can be made. However, substitutions should be parallel. For example, one citrus fruit should be substituted for another, and one deep green or deep yellow vegetable or fruit should be used in place of another. Remember, however, that one key to nutritious eating is to include in the daily menu a wide variety of foods.

For the meal-planning novice, these menus can serve as a learning ground, giving sound guidance and providing excellent recipes for family use. Even if these menu plans are altered to accommodate family tastes and available produce, they still provide greater variety and eating adventure than most people ever get.

Daily Food Guide

Meat, Poultry, Fish, and Bean Group: Two servings. Dry beans and peas, soy extenders and nuts combined with animal protein (meat, fish, poultry, eggs, milk, cheese), or grain protein can be substituted for a serving of meat.

Milk and Cheese Group: Two servings for adults; four servings for teenagers; three servings for children. Foods made from milk (cheese, yogurt, ice cream) contribute part of the nutrients supplied by a serving of milk.

Vegetable and Fruit Group: Four servings daily. Dark green, leafy, or orange vegetables and fruit are recommended three or four times weekly for vitamin A. Citrus fruit is recommended daily for vitamin C.

Bread and Cereal Group: Four servings daily. Whole grain, fortified, or enriched grain products are recommended.

Fats and sweets complement but do not replace foods from the four basic groups. Amounts should be determined by individual caloric needs.

From a Money Management Point of View

Planned menus provide an excellent way to keep tab on the food budget. By knowing ahead of time what the menus include, one can purchase only those foods necessary, and there need be little waste.

Standardized servings in the home can help control costs just as they do in restaurants and institutions. One-half cup orange juice provides enough vitamin C for the day. Although a three-ounce portion of meat, poultry, or fish may seem skimpy to family members who are used to overeating (and, indeed, it may not be enough for the extremely active), for most Americans it is ample. Many are eating more protein than needed. Since protein foods are among the most expensive grocery items, cutting serving sizes can lower food costs, and increasing portions of such healthy complex carbohydrates as pasta, rice, potatoes, vegetables, and grains can satisfy appetites at less cost.

These menus with their recipes and shopping lists can be adjusted according to family size. Cut them in half for two people, increase them by half again for a family of six, or double everything to serve a family of eight. If you prefer, the adjustment of menus may be simply and accurately calculated to your particular family requirements by using the Family Survey Chart on page xv.

When doubling the recipes to serve two meals, you need to measure out and store the portions of food to be used for the second meal, *before serving your family*. Family members may react at first to having limits placed on their eating; for many the habit of eating is to continue until all the food is consumed, whether it is needed or not. A better habit is to eat only enough to satisfy the appetite rather than eating to the point of feeling very full. Both time and money are saved by controlling portions.

Menus can be dolled up or down depending upon the budget. If money is tight, cut down on or eliminate nuts, raisins, and other items that may be too costly for the budget. Most of the recipes can be made very basic, and still be tasty, by eliminating such frills as canned mushrooms or pimientos, using less expensive alternatives, and increasing the seasonings. For example, mild cheese (which is less expensive than medium or sharp) can be used in any recipe and zipped up in flavor with additional salt and a little mustard. I have often used chopped cabbage in place of celery, when we didn't have the latter on hand, in clam chowder. I also have had no problem substituting one vegetable for another in soup or stew. Low-cost, nonfat dry milk

can be kept on hand and used in many ways to cut food costs.

These menus do not make allowance for snacking. For health as well as for financial reasons snacks can be limited to vegetables, fruits, muffins, milk drinks, plain popcorn, and light sandwiches. Children and adults who are restrained in their snacking will bring heartier appetites to the meal table and will be more apt to enjoy the wide variety of foods offered.

From a Time Management Point of View

Shopping trips to the store can be drastically reduced. By combining weekly shopping lists, shopping can be limited to every two, three, or four weeks, with additional market stops only for fresh produce and milk. As most shoppers know, each additional trip to the market increases food costs and uses up precious time.

It is possible to look ahead at planned menus and prepare dishes when it is most convenient—then store them, covered, in the refrigerator for up to three days, or freeze them for later use. The peace of mind that comes from knowing in advance what's for dinner, and the relief of having it already prepared, is wonderful.

From a Weight Control Point of View

Planned menus are essential for effective weight control. The menus in *Managing Your Meals* limit the amount of fat, salt, and sugar that is used. Furthermore, for those individuals who are counting calories, vegetables and salads can be seasoned with only lemon juice, flavored vinegar, or seasonings. Syrups, jams, cookies, and desserts can be eliminated. Ice milk can replace ice cream, and skim milk can be used, as can low-fat cheeses: Mozzarella, Neufchâtel, and low-fat cottage cheese, for example. And, as mentioned previously, controlled portions of food are very conducive to weight control, as well as to good health. With this in mind, let me list for you the basic portions that should be allowed.

Basic Portions

Wherever milk is designated as the only beverage, both adults and children should drink one cup of milk in order to meet nutritional requirements. Where another beverage is designated along with milk, adults may have their choice of beverage while children should have milk. Milk used on cereal for breakfast is considered part of the beverage quota.

Whenever bananas are listed as being sliced, one-half banana is allowed per serving. Fruit toppings for cereals (for example, blueberries) or fruits cooked in cereal (for example, raisins) are used in the quantity of two tablespoons per serving or one-half cup for a family of four. Where fruit is served by itself either as a breakfast fruit or as a dessert, one-half cup per serving is allowed.

One-half cup serving of orange juice or grapefruit juice provides sufficient vitamin C for a person's daily needs. One cup of tomato juice is needed. Leftover juice should be stored in a tightly covered container in the refrigerator.

One-half cup cooked cereal or three-fourths cup prepared cereal is considered one serving. Two large pancakes are allowed per serving; one slice of toast or bread per serving; one sandwich made with two regular slices of enriched or whole grain bread is considered one serving. Enriched or whole wheat bread and enriched or whole wheat flour should be used.

Spreads per slice of bread include one-half teaspoon butter or enriched margarine, one tablespoon peanut butter, one-half tablespoon honey, or one-half tablespoon jam.

One-half teaspoon butter or enriched margarine is figured as enough spread per pancake; as is one tablespoon syrup.

One teaspoon butter or enriched margarine is allowed to flavor four servings of vegetables; bacon drippings are economical and delicious flavoring for vegetables.

For sandwiches, one 6½-ounce can tuna fish is allowed to make four sandwiches, and one ounce of luncheon meat and one ounce of cheese may also be used for individual servings.

Wherever soups or stews are designated for dinner, 1½ cups per serving are allowed. For luncheon or supper, 1 cup per serving is allowed.

Where cookies or cupcakes are designated for dessert, two cookies per person or one cupcake per person is allowed.

From a Family Enjoyment Point of View

Planned menus provide security, the security of knowing that dinner is planned and will be ready when it's time to eat. If menus are posted, family members can anticipate with pleasure the coming meals and, in fact, can help with their preparation and service. Through the use of these menus, families can learn to like new foods and new dishes, eat regular meals that are more nutritious, and enjoy the well-being that comes with planned menus.

Once menus have been tried, a homemaker may repeat some menus more than others, especially family favorites. And mixing and matching recipes from menu to menu is fun.

From the Author's Point of View

This book, if used well, can provide nutritious meals for more enjoyment. The preparation of it was in response to the needs of my four children and their families. Like most young families, they are on limited budgets, have constrained time and energy, and are novices in the art of meal preparation.

The philosophy behind the book includes cooking double-sized recipes, so that most cooking and baking efforts extend over more than one meal. The recipes are proven family favorites that are nourishing, easy to prepare, and tasty. Some food items on the menus may be purchased ready-to-eat—canned soups, bread sticks, and puddings, for example —but recipes for these things have been included for those whose finances are more limited than their time.

The menus provide quantities without excess so that family members are satisfied without stuffing themselves, and there are no leftovers except where planned. The ample and interesting meals outlined in *Managing Your Meals* assure your family of nourishment without waste or overeating. (If family members eat out, you may wish to shop for and follow menus for only five days in a week to avoid buying excess food.)

Your success in using these meals will be determined to a large degree by your sense of adventure—the will and enthusiasm to try new foods and to stay with planned menus until they become a habit. Children, by nature, are suspicious of unfamiliar dishes, but parents who accept them as standard fare provide a good example for children to follow.

While every family deals differently with individual food tastes, the following suggestions may prove valuable. Have a good time looking ahead and discussing the menus, and talk about the various dishes. Whenever possible, encourage your family to help with purchasing and preparing new foods and new dishes. Urge them to taste as they prepare and to make suggestions for improvement. If snacking is eliminated, or at least controlled, family members will come to the table hungry and more responsive to new and unusual foods. The best part of the adventure may be the new foods that will become treasured friends.

Family Survey Chart

The menus in *Managing Your Meals* have been planned for an average family of four: two adults and two elementary-school-age children. To adjust food purchases and meal preparation to meet the requirements of your individual family, you can fill in the following chart under the headings *Family Members, Age,* and *Units.* (Determine the units by using the information under *Description and Age Group.*) Add units together to find your *Family Total.*

The total units for the average family of four is around 100. If your family totals 150, or near there, you would increase the purchases of food by half again; and during recipe preparation, you would increase the amounts given by half again. Most recipes can be adjusted this way. If your family is larger and your total is somewhere around 200, then you would simply double everything. If, as in my own family now, there are only two of you, then cut everything in half. Freeze extra quantities of prepared foods and use them later.

Use a pencil often to make notations on recipes and menus as to what works best for your family. The menus and recipes are for *you* to use: change them, make substitutions, increase or decrease them, or make them serve more meals according to your own family needs. In other words, make them work for you!

Description and Age Group	Units	Family Members	Age	Units
For each infant	10			
For each child under 8	18			
For each boy 8 to 13	25			
For each girl 8 to 18	25			
For each boy 13 to 20	38			
For each adult female	25			
For each adult male:				
Sedentary	25			
Moderately active	38			
Very active	45			
		Family Total		

MENUS AND SHOPPING LISTS

Staples

Active dry yeast (store in refrigerator)
*Baking powder
*Baking soda
Beef bouillon cubes and/or instant granules
Bread crumbs, dry
Catsup
Cereal, a variety of prepared and uncooked, made from different grains
Chicken bouillon cubes and/or instant bouillon
Chocolate, unsweetened
Cocoa, unsweetened
Coconut
Cornmeal, yellow
Cornstarch
Corn syrup, light and dark
Cream of tartar
Evaporated milk
Flavoring extracts:
  almond
  lemon
  maple
  rum
  vanilla
*Flour, all-purpose unbleached white
Flour, whole wheat
French dressings, low calorie and/or regular
Garlic, fresh
Gelatin, unflavored
Horseradish (store in refrigerator)
Honey
Jam and/or marmalade and/or jelly

Mayonnaise or salad dressing
Molasses
Monosodium glutamate
Mustard, Dijon-style
Nonfat dry milk
Nuts:
  walnuts
  almonds
  pecans
  peanuts
Oil, vegetable
Onion, dried chopped
Parmesan cheese (store in refrigerator)
Peanut butter
Pickles and pickle relish:
  sweet
  dill
  mustard
Raisins
Rice, long-grain and/or brown
Rolled oats
*Salt
Shortening
Spaghetti
Soy sauce
Spices and herbs (store in tightly covered containers away from heat)
  Allspice, ground
  Basil, dried leaf
  Bay leaves, dried whole
  *Black pepper, ground
  Black peppercorns
  Caraway seeds
  Cardamom, ground
  Cayenne pepper
  Celery salt
  Chili peppers, dried red

Chili powder
Cinnamon, ground
Cinnamon sticks
Cloves, ground
Cloves, whole
Coriander, dried leaf
Cumin (or cominos), ground
Curry powder
Dill weed
Garlic salt
Garlic powder
Ginger, ground
Italian herb mixture
Mustard, dry
Marjoram, dried leaf
Nutmeg, ground
Onion powder
Onion salt
Oregano, dried leaf
Paprika
Parsley, dried flakes
Rosemary, dried leaf
Sage, dried leaf
Salt
Seasoned salt
Tarragon, dried leaf
Thyme, dried leaf
White pepper, ground
Sugar, brown (store in covered plastic container with piece of fresh bread)
*Sugar, granulated
Sugar, confectioners'
Syrup, maple-flavored
Tabasco
Tapioca, quick-cooking
Vinegar, cider
Vinegar, wine
Worcestershire sauce

*It is expected that staple cupboards will at all times include these items. They will not be included in staple lists for weekly menus.

	Breakfast	Lunch	Dinner
Sunday	Sliced Oranges French Toast (p. 256) Maple-Flavored Syrup (p. 253) Milk	Broiled Cheese and Tomato Sandwiches (p. 164) Spinach Bacon Salad (p. 219) Milk	Barbecued Chicken Thighs (p. 122) Baked Sweet Potatoes (p. 199) Buttered Broccoli (p. 192) Peach Cobbler (p. 288) Milk or Other Beverage
Monday	Grapefruit Halves Bran Flakes Whole Wheat Toast Milk	Tuna Salad Sandwiches (p. 217) Celery Sticks Apple Halves Soft Ginger Cookies (p. 269) Milk	Hamburger Vegetable Soup with Cheese (p. 150) Easy French Bread (p. 244) Peach Cobbler (leftover) Milk or Other Beverage
Tuesday	Orange Juice Oatmeal with Raisins Milk	Peanut Butter and Bacon Sandwiches (p. 161) Vegetable Sticks Bananas Milk	Barbecued Chicken Thighs (leftover) Steamed Rice (p. 257) Cabbage Stir-Fry (p. 197) Cornmeal Muffins (p. 250) Honey Milk or Other Beverage
Wednesday	Orange Juice Cold Cereal Mix with Nuts Milk	Hamburgers (p. 129) Waldorf Salad (p. 206) Soft Ginger Cookies (leftover) Milk	Zucchini Mushroom Pasta (p. 228) Cheese Slices Fresh Fruit Cup (p. 175) Soft Ginger Cookies (leftover) Milk or Other Beverage
Thursday	Fresh Fruit Cup (leftover) Cooked Wheat Cereal with Butter and Brown Sugar Milk	Creamed Hard-Cooked Eggs on Toast (p. 233) Vegetable Sticks Pears Milk	Hamburger Vegetable Soup (leftover) Cabbage Slaw (p. 214) Old-Fashioned Rice Pudding (p. 281) Milk or Other Beverage
Friday	Broiled Grapefruit (p. 175) Prepared Cereal Whole Wheat Toast with Jam Milk	Peanut Butter on Whole Wheat Toast Simple Carrot Slaw (p. 215) Old-Fashioned Rice Pudding (leftover) Milk	Zucchini Mushroom Pasta (leftover) with Shredded Cheddar Cheese Spinach Orange Salad (p. 220) Soft Ginger Cookies (leftover) Milk or Other Beverage
Saturday	Orange Juice Apple Pancakes (p. 253) Maple-Flavored Syrup (p. 253) Bacon Milk	Cream of Corn Soup (p. 149) Vegetable Sticks Whole Wheat Toast Soft Ginger Cookies (leftover) Milk or Beverage	Potato Frankfurters (p. 120) Parsleyed Carrots (p. 186) Sliced Tomatoes Chocolate Banana Shakes (p. 172)

Shopping List January First Week

	Product	Quantity	Variation for Your Family
Fresh Produce	Apples	6, including 3 red	
	Bananas	6	
	Broccoli	1 pound	
	Cabbage, green	1 head	
	Carrots	6 to 7 medium large (1 to 1½ pounds)	
	Celery	1 stalk	
	Fruits, assorted	1½ to 2 pounds (to make 4 cups, diced)	
	Grapefruit	4	
	Gingerroot	1 piece (peel to grate; freeze remaining)	
	Lemons	3	
	Lettuce, romaine	1 head	
	Mushrooms	1 pound (refrigerate in brown paper bag)	
	Onions, dry yellow	2	
	Onions, green	1 bunch	
	Oranges	7	
	Parsley	1 bunch (dry remaining parsley in oven)	
	Pears	4	
	Potatoes	4 to 5 (about 2 pounds)	
	Potatoes, sweet (or yams)	4 medium	
	Spinach	2 bunches or 1 cello bag (10 ounces)	
	Tomatoes	4 large	
	Zucchini	4 medium	
Canned Goods	Corn, cream-style	1 can (1 pound)	
	Mandarin oranges	1 can (11 ounces)	
	Peaches	1 can (29 ounces)	
	Tomatoes	1 can (29 ounces)	
	Tuna fish, chunk-style	1 can (6½ ounces)	
Frozen Foods	Orange juice, frozen concentrate	2 cans (6 ounces each)	
Dairy Products	Butter or margarine	1 pound	
	Cheese, Cheddar	1¾ pounds	
	Cheese, Monterey Jack	½ pound	
	Eggs	1½ dozen	
	Milk, low-fat	3½ gallons	
	Whipping cream	½ pint	
Bread and Cereal Products	Bread, French	1 loaf or homemade	
	Bread, whole wheat	2 large loaves	
	Buns, hamburger	4	
	Noodles	1 pound	
Meat, Poultry, and Fish	Bacon	1 pound	
	Beef, ground	2 pounds	
	Chicken thighs	8 (2½ to 3 pounds)	
	Frankfurters	1 pound	
Miscellaneous	Barbecue sauce	1 pint or homemade	

(Check staple supplies for active dry yeast, basil, bay leaves, brown sugar, catsup, celery salt, cider vinegar, cinnamon, dried red chili peppers, dried parsley, dry mustard, French dressing, garlic, ground cloves, ground ginger, honey, jam, maple-flavored syrup, mayonnaise, molasses, oil, paprika, Parmesan cheese, peanut butter, peanuts, poppy seeds, raisins, rice, soy sauce, Tabasco sauce, unsweetened cocoa, vinegar, walnuts, and yellow cornmeal.)

	Breakfast	Lunch	Dinner
Sunday	Grapefruit Halves Scrambled Eggs (p. 231) Whole Wheat Muffins with Jam (p. 251) Milk	Tuna Sandwiches Salad Greens with Tomatoes and French Dressing (p. 223) Banana Halves Milk	Halibut au Gratin (p. 139) Parsleyed New Potatoes (p. 178) Orange-Glazed Brussels Sprouts (p. 194) Lemon Surprise Pudding (p. 280) Milk or Other Beverage
Monday	Sliced Bananas Oatmeal with Butter and Brown Sugar Milk	Sliced Oranges with Cottage Cheese Raw Broccoli Sticks Raisin Nut Nibbles (p. 271) Milk	Chili (p. 154) Carrot Apple Slaw (p. 216) Lemon Surprise Pudding (leftover) Milk or Other Beverage
Tuesday	Grapefruit Halves Cornflakes Cinnamon Toast (p. 252) Milk	Hoagie Sandwiches on French Bread (p. l64) Carrot Sticks Fruit Shake (p. 172)	Halibut (leftover) Crisscross Salad (p. 212) Applesauce 'N' Dumplings (p. 177) Milk or Other Beverage
Wednesday	Applesauce 'N' Dumplings (leftover) Cheese Slices Milk	Fried Egg Sandwiches (p. 167) Vegetable Sticks Sliced Oranges Raisin Nut Nibbles (leftover) Milk	Oven-Fried Chicken (p. 121), double the recipe Baked Potatoes Baked Carrots Milk or Other Beverage
Thursday	Sliced Oranges Broiled Cheese on Toast Hot Chocolate	Peanut Butter Sandwiches Crisscross Salad (leftover) Banana Halves Milk	Chili (leftover) Cabbage Pineapple Slaw (p. 214) Raisin Nut Nibbles (leftover) Milk or Other Beverage
Friday	Orange Juice Cream of Wheat with Raisins Milk	Lettuce and Tomato Salad Broiled Cheese Sandwiches (p. 163) Apples Milk	Chicken a la King (p. 123), using leftover chicken Crisscross Salad (leftover) Baking Powder Biscuits (p. 249) Jam Milk or Other Beverage
Saturday	Orange Juice Prepared Cereal Toasted Biscuits (leftover) with Cinnamon and Sugar Milk	Chili (leftover) Steamed Rice (p. 257), 1/2 recipe Whole Wheat Bread with Butter Mixed Fruit Salad Milk	Creamed Tuna Fish on Toast (p. 136) Cabbage Apple Slaw (p. 215) Raisin Nut Nibbles (leftover) Milk or Other Beverage

Shopping List January Second Week

	Product	Quantity	Variation for Your Family
Fresh Produce	Apples	8	
	Bananas	5	
	Broccoli	1¼ pounds	
	Brussels sprouts	1 pound	
	Cabbage	1 small head	
	Carrots	1¼ pounds	
	Celery	1 stalk	
	Fruits, assorted	4 pounds	
	Grapefruit	4	
	Lemons	4	
	Lettuce, romaine	1 head	
	Onions, dry yellow	4 large	
	Onions, red	1	
	Oranges	13 (5 pounds)	
	Potatoes	3½ pounds, including 4 baking potatoes	
	Tomatoes	8 large	
Canned Goods	Applesauce	1 can (1 pound)	
	Beans, red kidney	1 can (8 ounces)	
	Pineapple, crushed	1 can (8 ounces)	
	Tomato juice	1 can (24 ounces)	
	Tomatoes	1 can (29 ounces)	
	Tuna fish, chunk-style	1 can (6½ ounces)	
Frozen Items	Orange juice, frozen concentrate	2 cans (6 ounces each)	
Dairy Products	Butter or margarine	1½ pounds	
	Cheese, Cheddar	1¾ pounds	
	Cheese, cottage	1 carton (8 ounces)	
	Cheese, Monterey Jack or Swiss	½ pound	
	Eggs	1½ dozen	
	Milk, low-fat	3½ gallons	
Bread and Cereal Products	Biscuits, refrigerated	2 packages (7½ ounces each) or homemade	
	Bread, French	1 loaf	
	Bread, whole grain	1 loaf (1½ pounds)	
	Rolls, French	4 6-inch	
Meat, Poultry, and Fish	Beef, ground	1 pound	
	Chickens, broiler-fryer	2 (3 pounds each)	
	Halibut or turbot, fresh or frozen	2 pounds	
	Pastrami	2 packages (2¼ ounces each)	
	Pork sausage, bulk	½ pound	
Miscellaneous	Beans, dry pinto or kidney	1 pound	

(Check staple supplies for bay leaves, brown sugar, catsup or chili sauce, chicken bouillon cubes, chili powder, cinnamon, cornflakes or other prepared cereal, cream of tartar, cream of wheat, curry powder, dill pickles, dried red chili peppers, evaporated milk, French dressing, garlic, ground cumin (cominos), ground nutmeg, jam, mayonnaise, nuts, oil, peanut butter, prepared mustard, raisins, rice, rolled oats, shortening, Tabasco sauce, unsweetened cocoa, vanilla, and whole wheat flour.)

	Breakfast	Lunch	Dinner
Sunday	Orange Juice Whole Wheat Pancakes (p. 254) Maple-Flavored Syrup Milk	Deviled Ham Sandwiches Sliced Tomatoes Hot Chocolate (p. 172)	Pot Roast of Beef with Vegetables (p. 103) Gingerbread with Lemon Sauce (p. 243) Milk or Other Beverage
Monday	Orange Juice Cold Cereal Mix Whole Wheat Toast Milk	Tuna Salad Sandwiches with Chopped Apple (p. 217) Vegetable Sticks Milk	Quick Chow Mein (p. 124) (leftover beef) Steamed Rice (p. 257) Shredded Carrot and Raisin Slaw (p. 216) Gingerbread (leftover) Milk or Other Beverage
Tuesday	Grapefruit Halves Oatmeal with Cinnamon and Sugar Milk	Egg Salad Sandwiches (p. 168) Tomato Wedges Applesauce Cupcakes (p. 267) Milk	Herb-Broiled Fish Fillets (p. 137) Honey-Glazed Acorn Squash (p. 190) Broccoli with Lemon Sauce (p. 192) Milk or Other Beverage
Wednesday	Sliced Bananas Prepared Cereal Milk	Cream Cheese and Jelly Sandwiches Carrot Sticks Applesauce Cupcakes (leftover) Milk	Split Pea Soup with Sausage Balls (p. 152) Rye toast Grapefruit Sections on Romaine, with French Dressing (p. 223) Milk or Other Beverage
Thursday	Sliced Oranges Prepared Cereal Cinnamon Toast (p. 252) Milk	Cheese Sandwiches Celery Sticks Pears Milk	Baked Chicken with Sauerkraut (p. 122) Parsleyed New Potatoes (p. 178) Basil Carrots (p. 186) Applesauce Cupcakes (leftover) Milk or Other Beverage
Friday	Orange Julius (p. 171) Cooked Cereal with Raisins Milk	Chicken (leftover), Sauerkraut, and Swiss Cheese on Rye Milk	Split Pea Soup (leftover) Crackers Waldorf Salad (p. 206) Milk or Other Beverage
Saturday	Banana Nog (p. 171) Whole Wheat Cinnamon Toast (p. 252)	Split Pea Soup (if any leftover) Frankfurters on Buns Vegetable Sticks Applesauce Milk	Broiled Cheese Sandwiches (p. 163) Sliced Tomatoes Sweet Pickles Hot Chocolate (p. 172)

Shopping List January Third Week

	Product	Quantity	Variation for Your Family
Fresh Produce	Apples	4, including 3 red	
	Bananas	5	
	Broccoli	1 pound	
	Carrots	2 ½ pounds	
	Celery	1 stalk	
	Grapefruit	5	
	Green peppers	1	
	Lemons	4	
	Lettuce, romaine	1 head	
	Onions, dry yellow	2 large	
	Pears	4	
	Potatoes	3 ½ pounds	
	Squash, acorn	2 medium or large	
	Tomatoes	8 large	
Canned Goods	Applesauce	2 cans (1 pound each)	
	Deviled ham	2 cans (4½ ounces each)	
	Sauerkraut	1 quart (32 ounces)	
	Tuna fish, chunk-style	1 can (6½ ounces)	
Frozen Foods	Orange juice, frozen concentrate	3 cans (6 ounces each)	
Dairy Foods	Butter or margarine	1½ pounds	
	Cheese, Cheddar	1 pound	
	Cheese, cream	2 packages (8 ounces each)	
	Cheese, Swiss	½ pound	
	Eggs	1 dozen	
	Milk, low-fat	3½ gallons	
Bread and Cereal Products	Bread, rye	1 loaf	
	Bread, whole wheat	2 large loaves	
	Buns, hot dog	8	
	Crackers, soda	1 small carton	
Meat, Poultry, and Fish	Beef, pot roast	4½ to 5 pounds	
	Chicken, broiler-fryer	1 (3 pounds)	
	Frankfurters	1 pound	
	Haddock fillets	1 pound	
	Pork sausage, bulk	1 pound	
Miscellaneous	Split peas, dried green	1 pound	
	Sweet pickles	1 small jar	

(Check staple supplies for beef bouillon cubes, cinnamon, cloves, cornstarch, crackers, dill pickles, dried parsley, dried red chili peppers, evaporated milk, garlic salt, ground ginger, honey, jam, jelly, maple-flavored syrup, marjoram, mayonnaise or salad dressing, molasses, nutmeg, oil, paprika, prepared cereal, prepared mustard, raisins, rice, rolled oats, rosemary, soy sauce, sweet pickles, Tabasco sauce, uncooked whole wheat cereal, unsweetened cocoa, vinegar, walnuts, and whole wheat flour.)

	Breakfast	Lunch	Dinner
Sunday	Orange Juice Prepared Cereal Grilled Sweet Rolls (p. 246) or Toast with Jam Milk	Pineapple and Cottage Cheese Salad Celery Sticks Bran Muffins (p. 250) Milk or Beverage	Oven Pork Chops (p. 116) Baked Potatoes Gingered Parsnips (p. 185) Baked Apple Tapioca (p. 282) Milk or Other Beverage
Monday	Applesauce Broiled Cheese on Whole Wheat Toast Milk or Beverage	Peanut Butter and Grated Carrot Sandwiches (p. 161) Fresh Pears Oatmeal Cookies (p. 272) Milk	Pork Chops (leftover) Stir-Fried Vegetables (p. 199) Baked Apple Tapioca (leftover) Milk or Other Beverage
Tuesday	Pears (fresh or canned) Cooked Oatmeal Toast with Honey Milk	Egg Salad Sandwiches (p. 168) Vegetable Sticks Orange Slices Milk	Sweet and Sour Tuna (p. 134) Steamed Rice (p. 257) Broccoli with Lemon Sauce (p. 192) Milk or Other Beverage
Wednesday	Orange Juice French Toast (p. 256) Maple-Flavored Syrup Bacon Milk	Tomato, Cheese, and Shredded Lettuce in Pocket Bread with Sour Cream Topping Chocolate Milk (p. 172)	Chicken Stew with Dumplings (p. 159) Pear and Grated Cheese Salad (p. 210) Milk or Beverage
Thursday	Grapefruit Halves Prepared Cereal Whole Wheat Toast Milk	Corned Beef and Cheese on Rye Vegetable Sticks Sliced Bananas Milk	Sweet and Sour Tuna (leftover) Chow Mein Noodles Sautéed Brussels Sprouts (p. 194) Custard Rice Pudding (p. 280), using leftover cooked rice Milk or Beverage
Friday	Orange Juice Puff Pancakes (p. 254) Maple-Flavored Syrup Corned Beef Slices, Fried Milk	Bacon, Lettuce, and Tomato Sandwiches Carrot Sticks Apples Milk	Chicken Stew with Dumplings (leftover) Cabbage Tomato Slaw (p. 214) Milk or Beverage
Saturday	Sliced Bananas Prepared Cereal Toast with Honey Milk	Cream of Mushroom (or other) Soup Cabbage Tomato Slaw (leftover) Whole Wheat Toast Applesauce (p. 176) Oatmeal Cookies (leftover) Milk	Zucchini Frittata (p. 236) Sliced Tomatoes Rye Toast Milk or Beverage

Shopping List January Fourth Week

	Product	Quantity	Variation for Your Family
Fresh Produce	Apples, tart	8	
	Bananas	6	
	Broccoli	1 pound	
	Brussels sprouts	³/₄ pound small	
	Cabbage	1 small head	
	Carrots	8 medium to large	
	Celery	1 large stalk	
	Gingerroot	1 piece	
	Grapefruit	2	
	Green peppers	2 large	
	Lemons	2	
	Lettuce, iceberg	1 head	
	Mushrooms	¹/₄ pound	
	Onions, dry yellow	3 small	
	Onions, green	1 bunch	
	Oranges	5 (about 2 pounds)	
	Parsnips	1	
	Pears	8 medium or 2 cans (29 ounces each)	
	Potatoes	6 medium	
	Tomatoes	7 large	
	Turnips	1	
	Zucchini	1 pound	
Canned Goods	Applesauce	2 cans (1 pound each)	
	Corned beef	1 can (12 ounces)	
	Chow mein noodles	1 can (3 ounces)	
	Pineapple chunks	1 can (20 ounces) in own juice	
	Pineapple slices	2 cans (8 ounces each) in own juice	
	Soup, cream of mushroom	2 cans (10 ³/₄ ounces each)	
	Tuna fish, chunk-style	2 cans (6¹/₂ ounces each), packed in water	
Frozen Foods	Orange juice, frozen concentrate	3 cans (6 ounces each)	
Dairy Products	Butter or margarine	1 pound	
	Cheese, Cheddar	1 pound	
	Cheese, cottage	1 carton (1 pound)	
	Eggs	2 dozen	
	Milk, low-fat	3¹/₂ gallons	
	Sour cream	1 carton (16 ounces)	
	Whipping cream	¹/₂ pint	
Bread and Cereal Products	Bread, French	1 loaf	
	Bread, pocket	2 round loaves (freeze extra)	
	Bread, rye	1 loaf	
	Bread, whole wheat	1 large loaf	
	Cereal, whole bran	1 small package	
	Sweet rolls, day-old	4	
Meat, Poultry, and Fish	Bacon	1 pound	
	Chicken, broiler-fryer	1 (3 pounds)	
	Pork chops	8 (1-inch) loin or rib chops	
Miscellaneous	Dried onion soup	1 package (1³/₈ ounces)	

(Check staple supplies for beef bouillon cubes, cheese, chicken bouillon cubes, cinnamon, garlic, ground nutmeg, honey, maple-flavored syrup, mayonnaise or salad dressing, oil, onion powder, Parmesan cheese, peanut butter, pickles, prepared cereal, prepared mustard, quick-cooking tapioca, raisins, rice, rolled oats, rosemary, shortening, soy sauce, Tabasco sauce, unsweetened cocoa, vanilla, vinegar, and walnuts.)

	Breakfast	Lunch	Dinner
Sunday	Citrus Fruit Cup (p. 175) Poached Eggs on Toast (p. 235) Milk	Cream of Tomato Soup (p. 148), canned or homemade Peanut Butter-Stuffed Celery Parmesan Toast (p. 252) Citrus Fruit Cup (leftover) Milk	Broiled Salmon with Cucumber Sauce (p. 140) Cauliflower with Browned Butter (p. 195) Broiled Tomato Halves (p. 188) Frozen Wheat Bread Rolls (p. 246) Carrot Cake (p. 267) Milk or Other Beverage
Monday	Orange Juice Prepared Cereal Milk	Peanut Butter and Grated Carrot Sandwiches (p. 161) Apple Halves Chocolate Milk (p. 172)	Salmon Salad (p. 216), using leftover salmon Frozen Wheat Bread Rolls (leftover) Milk or Other Beverage
Tuesday	Grapefruit Halves Oatmeal Cooked with Raisins Milk	Tomato, Cheese, and Lettuce Sandwiches Vegetable Sticks Grapes Milk	Pan-Fried Sausage Links (p. 115) Honey-Glazed Acorn Squash (p. 190) Tasty Brussels Sprouts (p. 194) Whole Grain Bread with Butter Baked Apples (p. 283) Milk or Other Beverage
Wednesday	Grapes French Toast (p. 256), with Honey Butter (p. 253) Milk	Pastrami and Pickle Sandwiches Carrot Cake (leftover) Milk	Barbecued Chicken Thighs (p. 122) Baked Potatoes (bake 8 potatoes) Oven-Cooked Carrots (p. 187) Broiled Grapefruit (p. 175) Milk or Other Beverage
Thursday	Applesauce Raisin Toast with Cream Cheese, Jelly, or Jam Milk	Egg Salad Sandwiches (p. 168) on Whole Wheat Vegetable Sticks Grapes Milk	Broccoli Cheese Soup (p. 149) Molded Citrus Salad (p. 210) Whole Grain Toast Milk or Other Beverage
Friday	Sliced Oranges Prepared Cereal with Nuts Milk	Tuna and Avocado Sandwiches (p. 217) Vegetable Sticks Chocolate Milk (p. 172)	Barbecued Chicken Thighs (leftover) Hash Brown Potatoes (p. 180), using leftover potatoes Buttered Broccoli (p. 192) Banana Pops (p. 289) Milk or Other Beverage
Saturday	Grapefruit Halves Apple Pancakes (p. 253) Maple-Flavored Syrup (p. 253) Milk	Tomato Juice Fried Egg Sandwiches with Lunch Meat (p. 167) Broccoli Sticks Milk	Cheesy Potato Soup (p. 153) Molded Citrus Salad (leftover) Crackers or Toast Banana Pops (leftover) Milk or Other Beverage

Shopping List February First Week

	Product	Quantity	Variation for Your Family
Fresh Produce	Apples, tart	8 large	
	Avocados	2	
	Bananas	6	
	Broccoli	1½ pounds	
	Brussels sprouts	¾ pound	
	Carrots	2 pounds	
	Cauliflower	1 5-inch head	
	Celery	1 stalk	
	Cucumber	1	
	Grapefruit	6	
	Grapes, green or red	2 pounds	
	Lemon	1	
	Lettuce, iceberg	1 head	
	Onion, dry yellow	1 large	
	Oranges	6	
	Parsley, fresh	1 bunch	
	Potatoes, baking	10	
	Squash, acorn	2 medium	
	Tomatoes	6 large	
Canned Goods	Applesauce	1 can (1 pound) or homemade (buy 4 additional apples)	
	Grapefruit	1 can (1 pound)	
	Mandarin oranges	2 cans (11 ounces each)	
	Soup, tomato	2 cans (10¾ ounces each) or 1 can (24 ounces) tomato juice for homemade soup	
	Tomato juice	1 can (24 ounces)	
	Tuna fish, chunk-style	1 can (6½ ounces)	
Frozen Foods	Bread dough, frozen whole wheat	1 loaf	
	Orange juice, frozen concentrate	2 cans (6 ounces each)	
Dairy Products	Butter or margarine	1½ pounds	
	Cheese, Cheddar	½ pound	
	Cheese, cream	2 packages (3 ounces each)	
	Eggs	2 dozen	
	Milk, low-fat	3½ gallons	
	Sour cream	1 carton (8 ounces)	
Bread and Cereal Products	Bread, French	1 loaf	
	Bread, raisin	1 loaf	
	Bread, whole wheat	3 loaves (1 pound)	
Meat, Poultry, and Fish	Chicken thighs	8 (1½ pounds)	
	Pastrami	3 packages (2¼ ounces each)	
	Pork sausage links	12 links (¾ pound)	
	Salmon steaks	2 pounds, including 4 small steaks or fillets	
Miscellaneous	Barbecue sauce	1 jar (8 ounces) or homemade	
	Milk chocolate	1 bar (8 ounces)	

(Check staple supplies for basil, brown sugar, chili sauce or catsup, cinnamon, confectioners' sugar, ground nutmeg, honey, maple-flavored syrup, marjoram, mayonnaise, oil, paprika, Parmesan cheese, peanut butter, peanuts, pickles, prepared cereal, prepared mustard, raisins, rolled oats, seasoned salt, Tabasco sauce, thyme, unsweetened cocoa, vanilla, and walnuts.)

	Breakfast	Lunch	Dinner
Sunday	Fresh Fruit Cup (p. 175) Scrambled Eggs (p. 231) Toast with Jam Milk	Tomato Corn Chowder (p. 156) Toast Stuffed Celery (p. 182) Milk	Roast Turkey (p. 130) Old-Fashioned Sage Stuffing (p. 132) Mashed Potatoes with Gravy (p. 202) Brussels Sprouts with Cream (p. 194) Orange Sherbet (p. 293) Snickerdoodles (p. 274) Milk or Beverage
Monday	Orange Juice Prepared Cereal Toast Milk	Reuben Sandwiches (p. 167), using leftover turkey Milk	Spanish Beef and Rice (p. 113) Tasty Broccoli (p. 192) Fresh Fruit Cup (leftover) Milk or Beverage
Tuesday	Sliced Oranges Breakfast Cottage Cheese Special (p. 252) Milk	Peanut Butter and Apple Sandwiches (p. 161) Celery Milk	Turkey Pineapple Salad (p. 213), using leftover turkey Buttered Peas (p. 190) Cinnamon Stack Biscuits (p. 249) Milk or Beverage
Wednesday	Orange Juice Cream of Wheat with Butter and Brown Sugar Cinnamon Biscuits (leftover) Milk	Spanish Beef and Rice (leftover) Vegetable Sticks Apple Halves Milk	Herb-Broiled Fish Fillets (p. 137) Hashed Brown Potatoes (p. 180) Glazed Carrots (p. 187) Snickerdoodles (leftover) Milk or Beverage
Thursday	Sautéed Apple Slices (p. 176) Puff Pancakes (p. 254) with Butter and Brown Sugar Milk	Tuna Sandwiches with Zucchini Slices on Rye Bread Oranges Milk	Turkey Vegetable Soup (p. 150) Easy French Bread (p. 244) Apple Crisp (p. 282) Milk or Other Beverage
Friday	Grapefruit Halves Cottage Cheese Pancakes (p. 255) Maple-Flavored Syrup (p. 253) Milk	Canned Corned Beef Slices Carrot Peanut Sandwiches (p. 164) Apple Crisp (leftover) Milk	Vegetables with Dill Dressing (p. 200) Broiled Cheese Sandwiches (p. 163) Snickerdoodles (leftover) Milk or Beverage
Saturday	Oranges French Toast (p. 256) with Cinnamon and Sugar Corned Beef Slices (leftover) Milk	Turkey Soup (leftover) Toast with Honey Sliced Bananas Snickerdoodles (if any left) Milk	Hot Spiced Tomato Juice (p. 170) Nut Waffles (p. 255) Maple-Flavored Syrup (p. 253) Bacon Milk or Other Beverage

Shopping List February Second Week

	Product	Quantity	Variation for Your Family
Fresh Produce	Apples, tart	7 large	
	Bananas	2	
	Broccoli	1 pound	
	Brussels sprouts	³/₄ pound	
	Carrots	1 pound	
	Celery	1 stalk	
	Grapefruit	2	
	Green peppers	1	
	Lemons	2	
	Lettuce, leaf	1 head	
	Mushrooms	1 pound	
	Onions, dry yellow	5 medium	
	Oranges	14	
	Parsley	1 bunch	
	Potatoes	3 pounds	
	Tomatoes	2 large	
	Zucchini	3 small	
Canned Goods	Applesauce	1 can (1 pound) or homemade	
	Beef broth (bouillon)	1 can (10¹/₂ ounces)	
	Corned beef	1 can (12 ounces)	
	Corn, cream-style	1 can (1 pound)	
	Pineapple slices	1 can (8 ounces) or 4 slices	
	Sauerkraut	1 can (8 ounces)	
	Tomato juice	1 can (24 ounces)	
	Tomatoes	3 cans (1 pound each)	
	Tuna fish, chunk-style	1 can (6¹/₂ ounces)	
Frozen Foods	Orange juice, frozen concentrate	3 cans (6 ounces each)	
	Peas	1 package (10 ounces)	
Dairy Products	Butter or margarine	1 pound	
	Buttermilk	1 carton (8 ounces)	
	Cheese, Cheddar	8 ounces	
	Cheese, cottage	1 carton (16 ounces)	
	Cheese, cream	1 package (3 ounces)	
	Cheese, Swiss	4 slices (4 ounces each)	
	Eggs	1¹/₂ dozen	
	Half-and-half	1 pint	
	Milk, low-fat	3¹/₂ gallons	
	Sour cream	1 carton (8 ounces)	
Bread and Cereal Products	Bread cubes, dry (for stuffing)	1 package (9 ounces) or 1¹/₂ quarts	
	Bread, French	1 loaf	
	Bread, rye	1 loaf	
	Bread, whole grain	1 large loaf	
	Noodles, egg	4 ounces	
Meat, Poultry, and Fish	Bacon	1 pound	
	Beef, ground	1 pound	
	Fish fillets, fresh or frozen	1 pound (haddock, cod, or perch)	
	Turkey, fresh or frozen	10 to 12 pounds	
Miscellaneous	Olives, stuffed green	1 small jar	
	Thousand Island dressing	1 jar (8 ounces)	

(Check staple supplies for basil, bay leaves, celery seed, chicken bouillon cubes, chili powder, cinnamon, cream of tartar, curry powder, Dijon mustard, dill weed, dried sage, evaporated milk, flour, garlic, gherkin sweet pickles, jam, maple-flavored syrup, marjoram, mayonnaise, monosodium glutamate, oil, onion powder, oregano, peanut butter, peanuts, pecans, poultry seasoning, prepared cereal, rice, thyme, unflavored gelatin, and walnuts.)

	Breakfast	Lunch	Dinner
Sunday	Apple Slices, Plain or Sautéed (p. 176) Whole Wheat Toast with Cinnamon and Sugar Milk	Corned Beef Omelet (p. 234) Raw Broccoli Sticks Parmesan Toast (p. 252) Fresh Apple Cake (p. 268) Milk	Sauerbraten (p. 104) Potato Pancakes (p. 182) Dilly Beans (p. 183) Green Salad and Orange Sections, with French Dressing (p. 223) Ice Cream Milk or Other Beverage
Monday	Orange Slices Cottage Cheese Wheat Toast with Jam Milk	Cream Cheese and Raisin Sandwiches Simple Carrot Slaw (p. 215) Banana Halves Milk	Curried Chicken (p. 126) Steamed Rice (p. 257) Tasty Brussels Sprouts (p. 194) Milk or Other Beverage
Tuesday	Grapefruit Halves Fried Egg Sandwiches (p. 167) on Whole Wheat Milk	Cream of Tomato Soup (p. 148) Croutons or Toast Cottage Cheese Apple Salad Carrot Sticks Gingersnaps (p. 269) Milk	Beef slices in Gravy (leftover) Parsleyed Noodles Buttered Peas (p. 191) Apple Cake (leftover) Milk or Other Beverage
Wednesday	Orange Juice French Toast (p. 256) Maple-Flavored Syrup (p. 253) Milk	Sliced Beef (leftover) Sandwiches Dill Pickles Celery Sticks Milk or Beverage	Stuffed Green Peppers (p. 110), using leftover curry and rice Orange Banana Salad, with French Dressing (p. 223) Milk or Other Beverage
Thursday	Grapefruit Halves Cooked Whole Wheat Cereal with Honey Toast Milk	Salmon Salad Sandwiches (p. 216) Celery Sticks Gingersnaps (leftover) Milk	Broccoli Cheese Soup (p. 148) Carrot and Raisin Slaw (p. 216) Saltines or Toast Milk or Other Beverage
Friday	Orange Juice Oatmeal with Cinnamon and Sugar Whole Wheat Toast Milk	Corned Beef Pickle Sandwiches Vegetable Sticks Apple Halves Milk	Tuna Pasta Salad (p. 227) Bread Sticks (p. 245) or Saltines Fresh Fruit Cup (p. 175) Milk
Saturday	Fresh Fruit Cup (leftover) Scrambled Eggs (p. 231) Whole Wheat Muffins (p. 251) Milk	Broccoli Cheese Soup (leftover) Toasted Whole Wheat Muffins (leftover) Milk	Beef Tacos (p. 112) Strawberry Sundaes Milk or Other Beverage

Shopping List February Third Week

	Product	Quantity	Variation for Your Family
Fresh Produce	Apples	10	
	Bananas	5	
	Beans, green	1 pound or 1 package (10 ounces) frozen	
	Broccoli	1 pound	
	Brussels sprouts	³/₄ pound	
	Carrots	1 pound	
	Celery	1 stalk	
	Grapefruit	4	
	Green peppers	5 large	
	Lemons	1	
	Lettuce, leaf	1 head	
	Mushrooms	¹/₄ pound	
	Onions, dry yellow	4 large	
	Oranges	8	
	Parsley	1 bunch	
	Potatoes	3	
	Tomatoes	5 large	
	Zucchini	1 small	
Canned Goods	Beef broth (bouillon)	1 can (10¹/₂ ounces)	
	Corned beef	1 can (12 ounces)	
	Green chilies	1 can (4 ounces)	
	Salmon	1 can (6³/₄ ounces)	
	Soup, tomato	2 cans (10¹/₂ ounces each) or homemade	
	Tomato juice	1 can (24 ounces)	
	Tomato sauce	1 can (15 ounces)	
	Tuna fish, chunk-style	1 can (6 ounces)	
Frozen Foods	Orange juice, frozen concentrate	2 cans (6 ounces each)	
	Peas	1 package (10 ounces)	
	Strawberries	1 package (10 ounces)	
Dairy Products	Butter or margarine	1 pound	
	Cheese, Cheddar	1 pound	
	Cheese, cottage	1 carton (16 ounces)	
	Cheese, cream	1 package (8 ounces)	
	Eggs	1¹/₂ dozen	
	Half-and-half	1 pint	
	Ice cream, vanilla	¹/₂ gallon	
	Milk, low-fat	3¹/₂ gallons	
	Sour cream	1 carton (8 ounces)	
Bread and Cereal Products	Bread, whole wheat	2 large loaves	
	Crackers, soda	1 small box	
	Noodles, egg	8 ounces	
	Tortillas, corn	8	
	Vermicelli or spaghetti	4 ounces	
Meat, Poultry, and Fish	Beef, ground	²/₃ pound	
	Beef, pot roast	5 pounds (shoulder, chuck, rump or round)	
	Chicken, broiler-fryer	1 (3 pound)	
Miscellaneous	Gingersnaps	1 small package	

(Check staple supplies for active dry yeast, black peppercorns, catsup, cayenne pepper, chili powder, cinnamon, curry powder, dill pickles, dill weed, dried parsley, dry mustard, garlic, ground cloves, ground ginger, ground nutmeg, honey, jam, maple-flavored syrup, mayonnaise or salad dressing, molasses, nuts, oil, paprika, Parmesan cheese, pickling spices, raisins, rice, rolled oats, uncooked whole wheat cereal, vanilla, vinegar, and whole wheat flour.)

	Breakfast	Lunch	Dinner
Sunday	Orange Juice Apple Pancakes (p. 253) Maple-Flavored Syrup (p. 253) Milk	Cottage Cheese and Pineapple Salad Vegetable Sticks Banana Nut Bread (p. 244) Milk	Easy Shrimp Newburg (p. 140) on Steamed Rice (p. 257) Broccoli with Orange Sauce (p. 192) Cider Fruit Salad Mold (p. 208), double the recipe Sponge Cake with Lemon Glaze (p. 265) Milk or Other Beverage
Monday	Grapefruit Halves Prepared Cereal with Honey Milk	Peanut Butter on Banana Nut Bread (leftover) Celery Sticks Milk	Oven-Fried Chicken (p. 121) Tomato Vegetable Spaghetti (p. 230) Sponge Cake (leftover) Milk or Other Beverage
Tuesday	Broiled Grapefruit Halves Cooked Cereal with Honey Milk	Hot Chopped Pork Sandwiches (p. 165) Vegetable Sticks Banana Nut Bread (leftover) Chocolate Milk (p. 172)	Baked Halibut with Lemon (p. 139) (double recipe) Baked Butternut Squash (p. 189) Buttered Peas (p. 191) Cider Fruit Salad Mold (leftover) Milk or Other Beverage
Wednesday	Applesauce Cooked Cornmeal with Raisins Whole Grain Toast Hot Chocolate (p. 172)	Broiled Cheese and Tomato Sandwiches (p. 164) Vegetable Sticks Cider Fruit Salad (leftover) Milk	Halibut (leftover) with Tomato Vegetable Spaghetti (leftover) Grapefruit Apple Salad Milk or Other Beverage
Thursday	Orange Juice Fried Cornmeal Mush (p. 256) Maple-Flavored Syrup (p. 253) Milk	Tuna Salad Sandwiches (p. 217) with Zucchini Slices Banana Halves Milk	Frankfurter-Vegetable Stew (p. 158) Green Salad with French Dressing Grapefruit with Apple Salad (leftover) Sponge Cake (leftover) Milk or Other Beverage
Friday	Fresh Fruit Cup (p. 175) Pigs in Blankets (p. 116) Milk	Hot Chopped Pork Sandwiches (leftover filling) Apple Slices Banana Nut Bread (leftover) Milk	Hamburgers (p.129) with Sliced Tomatoes and Pickles Sautéed Brussels Sprouts (p. 194) Chocolate Milk
Saturday	Sliced Oranges Cottage Cheese Cinnamon Rolls (p. 247) Milk	Hot Chopped Pork Sandwiches (leftover filling) Vegetable Sticks Fresh Fruit Cup (leftover) Milk	Pigs in Blankets (leftover) End-of-the-Week Fruit Salad (p. 205) Milk or Other Beverage

Shopping List February Fourth Week

	Product	Quantity	Variation for Your Family
Fresh Produce	Apples	8	
	Bananas	10, including 5 extra ripe	
	Broccoli	1 pound	
	Brussels sprouts	³/₄ pound	
	Cauliflower	1 medium head	
	Celery	1 stalk	
	Grapefruit	4	
	Green peppers	2	
	Lemons	4	
	Lettuce, romaine	1 head	
	Onions, dry yellow	3 large	
	Onions, green	1 bunch	
	Oranges	4	
	Squash, butternut	1	
	Tomatoes	3 large	
	Zucchini	6 small to medium	
Canned Goods	Apple cider or clear apple juice	1 quart	
	Applesauce	1 can (1 pound)	
	Pineapple slices	1 can (8 ounces)	
	Pork luncheon meat	1 can (12 ounces)	
	Shrimp, small deveined	2 cans (4¹/₂ ounces each)	
	Soup, cream of shrimp	1 can (10³/₄ ounces)	
	Soup, tomato	1 can (10³/₄ ounces)	
	Tomatoes, whole	1 can (1 pound) *and* 1 can (29 ounces)	
	Tuna fish, chunk-style	1 can (6¹/₂ ounces)	
Frozen Foods	Orange juice, frozen concentrate	2 cans (6 ounces each)	
	Peas	1 package (10 ounces)	
Dairy Products	Butter or margarine	1¹/₂ pounds	
	Cheese, Cheddar	6 ounces	
	Cheese, cottage	1 carton (16 ounces)	
	Cheese, cream	1 package (3 ounces)	
	Eggs	2 dozen	
	Milk, low-fat	3¹/₂ gallons	
	Sour cream	1 carton (8 ounces)	
Bread and Cereal Products	Bread, French	1 loaf	
	Bread, whole wheat	2 loaves (1¹/₂ pounds each)	
	Buns, hamburger	8	
	Cinnamon rolls	4 (or homemade)	
	Rolls, refrigerated crescent	1 can (8 ounces)	
	Spaghetti or pasta shells	1 pound	
Meat, Poultry, and Fish	Bacon	¹/₂ pound	
	Beef, ground	1 pound	
	Chicken, broiler-fryer	1 (3 pounds)	
	Halibut fillets, frozen or fresh	2 pounds	
	Frankfurters	1 pound	
	Pork sausage links	12 (³/₄ pound)	

(Check staple supplies for active dry yeast, basil, cinnamon, confectioners' sugar, cream of tartar, Dijon mustard, French dressing, garlic, honey, lemon extract, maple-flavored syrup, mayonnaise or salad dressing, nonfat dry milk, oil, oregano, paprika, peanut butter, prepared cereal, raisins, rice, shortening, soda, sweet pickles or relish, Tabasco sauce, uncooked cereal, unflavored gelatin, unsweetened cocoa, vanilla, walnuts, and yellow cornmeal.)

	Breakfast	Lunch	Dinner
Sunday	Grapefruit Halves Poached Eggs on Toast (p. 235) Milk	Broiled Cheese and Tomato Sandwiches (p. 164) Dill Pickles Vegetable Sticks Hot Chocolate (p. 172)	German Fish Skillet (p. 137) Tasty Brussels Sprouts (p. 194) Spinach Orange Salad (p. 220) Apple Kuchen (p. 283) Milk or Other Beverage
Monday	Orange Juice Cooked Oatmeal with Dates Milk	Tuna and Ripe Olive Sandwiches Vegetable Sticks Apple Oatmeal Cookies (p. 272) Milk	Chili Beef Soup (canned) Wheat Crackers and Cheese Crisscross Salad (p. 212) Apple Oatmeal Cookies (leftover) Milk or Other Beverage
Tuesday	Applesauce Whole Wheat Cinnamon Toast (p. 252) Milk	Peanut Butter and Bacon Sandwiches (p. 161) Stuffed Celery (p. 182) Oranges Milk	Pizza Hamburger (p. 107) Scalloped Potatoes (p. 181) Crisscross Salad (leftover) Milk or Other Beverage
Wednesday	Sliced Oranges Cooked Cereal with Honey Milk	Ground Nut and Raisin Sandwiches (p. 162) Carrot Sticks Banana Halves Milk	Skillet Macaroni and Cheese (p. 228) Tabboulah Salad (p. 220) Apple Oatmeal Cookies (leftover) Milk or Other Beverage
Thursday	Orange Juice French Toast with Blueberries Bacon Slices Milk	Hot Spiced Tomato Juice (p. 170) Pigs in Blankets (p. 116) Carrot Apple Slaw (p. 216) Milk	Luncheon Meat Salad (p. 221) Buttered Peas (p. 191) Blueberry Muffins (p. 251) Milk or Other Beverage
Friday	Grapefruit Sections Prepared Cereal with Butter and Brown Sugar Milk	Luncheon Meat Salad (leftover) Toasted Blueberry Muffins (leftover) Milk	Skillet Macaroni and Cheese (leftover) Baked Butternut Squash (p. 189) Broccoli with Buttered Crumbs (p. 192) Apple Oatmeal Cookies (leftover) Milk or Other Beverage
Saturday	Orange Juice Apple Puff Pancakes (p. 254) Pork Luncheon Meat Slices (leftover) Milk	Hot Dogs Carrot Peanut Slaw (p. 216) Chocolate Milk (p. 172)	Lazy Susan Dinner (p. 143) Milk

Shopping List March First Week

	Product	Quantity	Variation for Your Family
Fresh Produce	Apples	7 large	
	Bananas	2	
	Broccoli	2 pounds	
	Brussels sprouts	³/₄ pound	
	Cabbage, green	1 head	
	Carrots	1 pound	
	Celery	1 stalk	
	Cucumbers	1 large	
	Grapefruit	4	
	Green peppers	1 medium	
	Lemons	2	
	Lettuce, romaine	2 heads	
	Onions, dry yellow	4 large	
	Onions, red	1	
	Oranges	10	
	Parsley	1 bunch	
	Potatoes, Russets	8 medium	
	Spinach	2 bunches or 1 cello bag (10 ounces)	
	Squash, butternut	1 large	
	Tomatoes	8 large	
Canned Goods	Applesauce	1 can (1 pound)	
	Beans, kidney	1 can (8 ounces)	
	Dried onion rings	1 can (3 ounces)	
	Evaporated milk	1 can (13 ounces)	
	Pork luncheon meat	1 can (12 ounces)	
	Pimiento	1 jar or can (2 ounces)	
	Ripe olives, chopped or sliced	1 can (4¹/₂ ounces)	
	Soup, chili beef	2 cans (10¹/₂ ounces each)	
	Tomato juice	1 can (24 ounces)	
	Tuna fish, chunk-style	1 can (6¹/₂ ounces)	
Frozen Foods	Blueberries	1 package or 1 can (15 ounces) or 1 cup fresh	
	Orange juice, frozen concentrate	3 cans (6 ounces each)	
	Peas	1 package (10 ounces)	
Dairy Products	Butter or margarine	1¹/₂ pounds	
	Cheese, Cheddar	2 pounds	
	Cheese, Monterey Jack	¹/₄ pound	
	Eggs	1 dozen	
	Milk, low-fat	3¹/₂ gallons	
	Whipping cream	¹/₂ pint	
Bread and Cereal Products	Bread, French	1 loaf	
	Bread, whole wheat	2 loaves (1 pound each)	
	Buns, hot dog	8	
	Crackers, wheat	small box	
	Macaroni	7 ounces	
Meat, Poultry, and Fish	Bacon	1 pound	
	Beef, ground	1 pound	
	Fish fillets, fresh or frozen	1 pound (cod, perch, sole, or haddock)	
	Frankfurters	1 pound	
	Pork sausage links	12 (³/₄ pound)	
Miscellaneous	Bulgur wheat (from Middle East or other specialty food stores)	¹/₂ pound	
	Dates	¹/₂ pound	

(Check staple supplies for basil, cinnamon, dill pickles, dried parsley, evaporated milk, ground nutmeg, honey, Italian or French dressing, mayonnaise, oil, paprika, peanut butter, raisins, rolled oats, unsweetened cocoa, vinegar, and walnuts.)

	Breakfast	Lunch	Dinner
Sunday	Orange Juice Cinnamon Rolls (p. 247) Cheddar Cheese Slices Milk	Vegetable Soup (homemade or canned) Grilled Cinnamon Rolls (p. 246), using leftover cinnamon rolls Milk	Teriyaki Steak (p. 105) Steamed Rice (p. 257) Gingered Vegetables (p. 200) Pineapple Upside Down Cake (p. 268) Milk or Other Beverage
Monday	Grapefruit Halves Oatmeal with Raisins Whole Wheat Toast Milk	Steak (leftover) Sandwiches Vegetable Sticks Oatmeal Cookies (p. 272) Milk	Country Baked Beans (p. 259) Carrot Apple Slaw (p. 216) Pineapple Upside Down Cake (leftover) Milk or Other Beverage
Tuesday	Sautéed Apple Slices (p. 176) Oatmeal Cinnamon Toast Milk	Baked Bean (leftover) and Cheese Sandwiches Celery Sticks Fresh Grapes Milk	Hot Teriyaki Steak Slices (leftover) Fried Rice (p. 257), using leftover rice Sautéed Brussels Sprouts (p. 194) Ambrosia (p. 176) Milk or Other Beverage
Wednesday	Fresh Pear Slices French Toast (p. 256) with Cinnamon and Sugar Milk	Scrambled Egg Sandwiches with Chili Sauce Stuffed Celery (p. 182) Oatmeal Cookies (leftover) Milk	New England Fish Chowder (p. 157) Easy Bread Sticks (p. 245) Spinach Bacon Salad (p. 219) Ambrosia (leftover) Milk or Other Beverage
Thursday	Orange Juice Prepared Cereal with Raisins Milk	Lunch Kabobs (p. 119) Vegetable Sticks Bread and Butter Sandwiches Milk	Easy Baked Tarragon Chicken Thighs (p. 121) Baked Beans (leftover) Cabbage Apple Slaw (p. 215) Milk or Other Beverage
Friday	Sliced Bananas Broiled Cheese Sandwiches (p. 163) Hot Chocolate (p. 172)	Peanut Butter and Celery Sandwiches (p. 161) Apples Chocolate Milk (p. 172)	Fish Chowder (leftover) Bread Sticks (leftover) Cottage Cheese Orange Salad Milk or Other Beverage
Saturday	Orange Halves Whole Wheat Pancakes (p. 254) Jam Milk	Grilled Tuna Sandwiches (p. 217) Carrot Sticks and Pickles Milk	Hot Spiced Tomato Juice (p. 170) Waffles (p. 255) Maple-Flavored Syrup (p. 253) Pan-Fried Sausage Links Milk or Other Beverage

Shopping List March Second Week

	Product	Quantity	Variation for Your Family
Fresh Produce	Apples, red	8 large	
	Bananas	2	
	Brussels sprouts	³/₄ pound	
	Cabbage, green	1 head	
	Carrots	2 pounds	
	Celery	1 stalk	
	Gingerroot	1 piece	
	Grapefruit	2	
	Grapes, Tokay	1 pound	
	Green peppers	1	
	Lemons	1	
	Lettuce, leaf	1 head	
	Onions, dry yellow	4 large	
	Onions, green	1 bunch	
	Oranges	10	
	Pears	2	
	Potatoes, Russets	3 large	
	Spinach	2 bunches or 1 cello bag (10 ounces)	
	Sugar peas	4 ounces	
Canned Goods	Pineapple chunks	1 can (8 ounces)	
	Pineapple slices	1 can (8 ounces)	
	Soup, vegetable	2 cans (10¹/₂ ounces each)	
	Tomato juice	1 can (24 ounces)	
	Tuna fish, chunk-style	1 can (6¹/₂ ounces)	
	Vienna sausages	1 can (5 ounces)	
Frozen Foods	Orange juice, frozen concentrate	2 cans (6 ounces each)	
Dairy Products	Cheese, Cheddar	¹/₄ pound	
	Cheese, cottage, small curd	1 carton (16 ounces)	
	Cheese, cream	1 package (3 ounces)	
	Cheese, Swiss	¹/₂ pound	
	Eggs	1 dozen	
	Milk, low-fat	3¹/₂ gallons	
	Whipping cream	¹/₂ pint	
Bread and Cereal Products	Bread, whole wheat	3 loaves (1 pound each)	
	Cinnamon rolls	8 or homemade	
Meat, Poultry, and Fish	Bacon, lean	1 pound	
	Beef, sirloin tip roast	4 pounds	
	Chicken thighs	6 (1¹/₂ pounds)	
	Pork sausage links	8 (¹/₂ pound)	
	Fish fillets, fresh or frozen	1¹/₂ pounds (cod, perch, or haddock)	
Miscellaneous	Beans, dried	1 pound pinto or small white	
	Coconut	1 package (6 ounces)	
	Maraschino cherries	1 small jar	

(Check staple supplies for active dry yeast, bay leaves, brown sugar, catsup, chili sauce, cinnamon, dill pickles, dried parsley, dry bread crumbs, garlic salt, ground cloves, ground ginger, horseradish, jam, maple flavoring, mayonnaise, oil, peanut butter, prepared mustard, raisins, rice, rolled oats, soy sauce, tarragon, unflavored gelatin, vinegar, walnuts, whole wheat flour, and Worcestershire sauce.)

	Breakfast	Lunch	Dinner
Sunday	Orange Juice Scrambled Eggs (p. 231) Cinnamon Stack Biscuits (p. 249) or Cinnamon Toast (p. 252) Milk	Gazpacho (p. 152) Broiled Shrimp Buns (p. 165) Fresh Fruit Cup (p. 175) Milk	Chicken with Herb Sauce (p. 125) Brown or White Rice (p. 257) Broccoli with Buttered Crumbs (p. 192) Thirty-Minute Cocoa Cake (p. 264) Milk or Other Beverage
Monday	Fresh Fruit Cup (leftover) Prepared Cereal Cinnamon Biscuits (leftover) Milk	Chicken (leftover) Salad Sandwiches Vegetable Sticks Cocoa Cake (leftover) Milk	Cheesy 'Chilada Casserole (p. 112) Buttered Asparagus (p. 184) Sliced Bananas Milk or Other Beverage
Tuesday	Orange Juice Cooked Wheat Cereal with Dates Milk	Tuna Fish and Cheese Sandwiches (p. 217) Sliced Tomatoes Pears Milk	Five-Minute Pizzas (p. 162) Carrot Raisin Slaw (p. 215) Thirty-Minute Cocoa Cake (leftover) Milk or Other Beverage
Wednesday	Stewed Pears Oatmeal with Butter and Brown Sugar Milk	Peanut Butter Sandwiches with Mayonnaise and Lettuce (p. 161) Vegetable Sticks Nut-Stuffed Dates Milk	Clam Chowder (p. 157) Apple Grapefruit Salad, with French Dressing (p. 223) Broiled English Muffin Halves (leftover) Milk or Other Beverage
Thursday	Sliced Oranges Pancakes with Jam Milk	Deviled Eggs (p. 232) Lettuce and Tomato Sandwiches Banana Shakes (p. 172)	Cheese Rarebit (p. 238) on Whole Grain Toast Brussels Sprouts with Crumbs (p. 194) Milk or Other Beverage
Friday	Orange Juice Fried Eggs Whole Wheat Toast Bacon Milk	Cream Cheese Sandwiches with Nuts (p. 163) Broccoli Sticks Milk	Clam Chowder (leftover) Oatmeal Muffins (p. 250) Raw Vegetable Salad (p. 218), with Catalina Dressing (p. 223) Milk or Other Beverage
Saturday	Sautéed Apple Slices (p. 176) Oatmeal Muffins (leftover) with Jam Hot Chocolate (p. 172)	Cream of Mushroom Soup Pear Swiss Waldorf Salad (p. 207) Parmesan Toast (p. 252) Milk	Sausage Gravy (p. 115) on Baked Potatoes Broccoli Stir-Fry (p. 191) Grapefruit Halves Milk or Other Beverage

Shopping List March Third Week

	Product	Quantity	Variation for Your Family
Fresh Produce	Apples	4	
	Asparagus	1½ pounds	
	Bananas	5	
	Broccoli	2½ pounds	
	Brussels sprouts	¾ pound	
	Carrots	1¼ pounds	
	Celery	1 stalk	
	Cucumber	1	
	Grapefruit	6	
	Green peppers	2	
	Lemons	2	
	Lettuce, romaine	1 head	
	Mushrooms	½ pound	
	Onions, dry yellow	2	
	Onions, green	1 bunch	
	Oranges	5 (1¾ pounds)	
	Pears (or apples)	10	
	Potatoes	6 (2 pounds)	
	Tomatoes	5 large	
Canned Goods	Beans, pinto	1 can (1 pound) or ½ pound dried pinto beans	
	Clams, minced	2 cans (6½ ounces each)	
	Green chilies	1 can (4 ounces)	
	Soup, cream of mushroom	2 cans (10¾ ounces each)	
	Shrimp, broken deveined	1 can (4½ ounces)	
	Tomato juice	1 can (24 ounces)	
	Tomato sauce	1 can (15 ounces)	
	Tomatoes	1 can (1 pound)	
	Tuna fish, chunk-style	1 can (6½ ounces)	
Frozen Foods	Orange juice, frozen concentrate	3 cans (6 ounces each)	
Dairy Products	Butter or margarine	1¼ pounds	
	Cheese, Cheddar	1¼ pounds	
	Cheese, cream	1 package (8 ounces)	
	Cheese, Monterey Jack or Swiss or Mozzarella	¾ pound	
	Eggs	1½ dozen	
	Half-and-half	1½ quarts	
	Milk, low-fat	3½ gallons	
	Sour cream	1 carton (8 ounces)	
Bread and Cereal Products	Bread, whole wheat	2 loaves (1½ pounds each)	
	Buns, hamburger	4	
	Croutons	1 box	
	English muffins	1 package of 6	
	Tortillas, corn	1 package of 12	
Meat, Poultry, and Fish	Bacon	½ pound	
	Beef, ground	1 pound	
	Chicken breast halves	6	
	Pastrami	2 packages (2.5 ounces each)	
	Pork sausage	1 pound	
Miscellaneous	Dates, pitted	1 package (8 ounces)	
	Picante sauce	1 jar (12 ounces) or homemade	

(Check staple supplies for basil, bay leaves, brown sugar, catsup or chili sauce, cinnamon, confectioners' sugar, Dijon mustard, dried parsley, dry bread crumbs, dry mustard, garlic, garlic salt, ground cumin, jam, mayonnaise, oil, onion salt, oregano, paprika, Parmesan cheese, peanut butter, raisins, red wine vinegar, rice, rolled oats, rosemary, sage, soy sauce, Tabasco sauce, vanilla, walnuts, and Worcestershire sauce.)

	Breakfast	Lunch	Dinner
Sunday	Orange Juice Pick-Up (p. 171) French Toast with Cinnamon and Sugar (p. 256) Milk	Crab Salad in Avocados (p. 222) Butterscotch Cookies (p. 270) Milk	Stuffed Cornish Game Hens (p. 133) Brown Rice Pilaff (p. 257) Glazed Onions (p. 185) Spinach Apple Toss (p. 186) Caramel Custard (p. 287) Milk or Other Beverage
Monday	Orange Juice Whole Wheat Cereal Toast with Jam Milk	Chicken Vegetable Soup Parmesan Toast (p. 252) Custard (leftover) Milk or Other Beverage	Sweet and Sour Meatballs (p. 109), make one full recipe meatballs, save half Brown Rice Pilaff (leftover) Parsleyed Carrots (p. 186) Milk or Other Beverage
Tuesday	Sliced Bananas on Prepared Cereal Whole Wheat Toast Milk	Tomato and Cheese Sandwiches Grapes Milk	Salmon Tetrazzini (p. 141) Broccoli with Buttered Crumbs (p. 192) Molded Citrus Salad (p. 210) Milk or Other Beverage
Wednesday	Sliced Oranges Cooked Cornmeal Cereal (p. 256) Bacon Strips Milk	Peanut Butter and Grated Carrot Sandwiches (p. 161) Banana Halves Chocolate Milk (p. 172)	Meatballs (leftover) and Gravy on Colcannon (p.108) Molded Citrus Salad (leftover) Butterscotch Cookies (leftover) Milk or Other Beverage
Thursday	Orange Juice Whole Wheat Toast Jam Milk	Meatballs (leftover) Tomato, Lettuce, and Mayonnaise Sandwiches Milk	Salmon Tetrazzini (leftover) Cabbage Slaw (p. 214) Banana Bavarian Pudding (p. 280) Milk or Other Beverage
Friday	Grapes Swedish Pancakes (p. 255) Milk	Tuna Olive Sandwiches Vegetable Sticks Banana Halves Milk	Western Omelet (p. 233) on Toast Tomato Slices Dilly Beans (p. 183) Broiled Grapefruit (p. 175) Milk
Saturday	Swiss Oatmeal (p. 256) Cinnamon Toast (p. 252) Milk	Hot Dogs with Relish Sliced Tomatoes Milk	End-of-Week Vegetable Soup (p. 149) Butterscotch Cookies (leftover) Milk

Shopping List March Fourth Week

	Product	Quantity	Variation for Your Family
Fresh Produce	Apples, red	3	
	Avocados	2 large	
	Bananas	9	
	Beans, green	1 pound or 1 package (10 ounces) frozen	
	Broccoli	1 pound	
	Cabbage	1 small head	
	Carrots	1 pound	
	Fennel root or celery	1 stalk	
	Grapefruit	2 large	
	Grapes, green or purple	1 pound	
	Green peppers	1	
	Lemons	1	
	Lettuce, romaine	1 head	
	Mushrooms	$1/2$ pound	
	Onions, dry yellow	7 medium	
	Onions, green	1 bunch	
	Oranges	4	
	Potatoes	3 (1 pound)	
	Spinach	2 bunches or 1 cello bag (10 ounces)	
	Tomatoes	8 large	
Canned Goods	Grapefruit	1 can (1 pound)	
	Mandarin oranges	2 cans (11 ounces each)	
	Olives, chopped ripe	1 small can ($2^1/4$ ounces)	
	Pimiento	1 can or jar (2 ounces)	
	Pineapple chunks	1 can (8 ounces)	
	Salmon, pink or red	1 can ($15^1/2$ ounces)	
	Soup, chicken vegetable	2 cans ($10^1/2$ ounces each)	
	Tuna fish, chunk-style	1 can ($6^1/2$ ounces)	
	Water chestnuts	1 can (5 ounces)	
Frozen Foods	Orange juice, frozen concentrate	4 cans (6 ounces each)	
Dairy Products	Butter or margarine	1 pound plus 1 stick butter (no substitute)	
	Cheese, Cheddar	$1/2$ pound	
	Cheese, Swiss	12 ounces	
	Eggs	$1^1/2$ dozen	
	Half-and-half	1 pint	
	Milk, low-fat	$3^1/2$ gallons	
	Sour cream	1 carton (8 ounces)	
Bread and Cereal Products	Bread, whole wheat	2 large loaves	
	Buns, hot dog	8	
	Spaghetti	1 pound	
Meat, Poultry, and Fish	Bacon	1 pound	
	Beef, ground	1 pound	
	Cornish game hens, frozen	2	
	Crab meat	$3/4$ pound or 2 cans ($7^1/2$ ounces each)	
	Frankfurters	1 pound	
	Pork sausage, bulk	$1/2$ pound	

(Check staple supplies for beef bouillon cubes, brown sugar, celery salt, celery seed, cinnamon, cornstarch, Dijon mustard, dried dill weed, dried parsley, dry bread crumbs, dry mustard, evaporated milk, fennel seed, garlic, ground cloves, ground nutmeg, honey, jam, mayonnaise, oil, onion, paprika, Parmesan cheese, peanut butter, pickle relish, rice, rolled oats, sage, salt, soy sauce, uncooked whole wheat cereal, unflavored gelatin, unsweetened cocoa, vinegar, walnuts, and yellow cornmeal.)

	Breakfast	Lunch	Dinner
Sunday	Orange Juice French Toast (p. 256) with Syrup Small Sausage Patties (use ½ pound meat) Milk	Cottage Cheese and Pineapple Salad (p. 205) Vegetable Sticks Baking Powder Biscuits (p. 249) Milk	Orange-Glazed Pork Roast (p. 117) Pan-Roasted Potatoes (p. 182) Basil Carrots (p. 186) Frozen Wheat Bread Rolls (p. 246) Honey-Sauced Fresh Pineapple (p. 289) Milk or Other Beverage
Monday	Grapefruit Halves Cottage Cheese Toasted Biscuits (leftover) with Jam Milk	Egg Salad Sandwiches (p. 168), using leftover rolls Raw Vegetable Sticks Milk	Hot Pork (leftover) Sandwiches Stir-Fried Brussels Sprouts (p. 195) Fresh Pineapple (leftover) Milk or Other Beverage
Tuesday	Sliced Oranges Oatmeal with Raisins Whole Wheat Toast with Jam Milk	Pork Sandwiches (leftover) Stuffed Celery (p. 182) Applesauce Milk	Barbecued Chicken Thighs (p. 122) Baked Sweet Potatoes (p. 199) Dilly Beans (p. 183) Cran-Apple Salad Mold (p. 208) Milk or Other Beverage
Wednesday	Apple Puff Pancakes (p. 254) Small Sausage Patties (use ½ pound meat) Milk	Canned Corned Beef Sandwiches Pineapple and Cheddar Cheese Cubes Stuffed Celery (p. 182) Milk	Quick Chow Mein with (leftover) Pork (p. 124) Steamed Rice (p. 257) Sliced Oranges on Greens, with French Dressing (p. 223) Milk
Thursday	Sliced Bananas on Prepared Cereal Cinnamon Toast Milk	Peanut Butter Sandwiches (p. 161) Carrot Sticks Apple Halves Milk	Barbecued Chicken Thighs (leftover) Fried Rice (p. 257), using leftover rice Crisscross Salad (p. 212) Milk
Friday	Orange Juice Swiss Oatmeal (p. 256) Milk	Broiled Cheese Sandwiches (p. 163) Crisscross Salad (leftover) Milk	Shrimp Salad with Herbs on Tomatoes or Avocados (p. 221) Twin Mountain Muffins (p. 251) Baked Apple Tapioca (p. 282) Milk or Other Beverage
Saturday	Orange Juice Scrambled Eggs with (leftover) Corned Beef Toasted Muffins (leftover) with Jam Milk	Grilled Tuna Sandwiches (p. 217) Crisscross Salad (leftover) Milk	Asparagus Melt (p. 169) Fruit (Banana Orange) Shake (p. 172)

Shopping List April First Week

	Product	Quantity	Variation for Your Family
Fresh Produce	Apples, tart	8	
	Asparagus	1 pound or 1 package (10 ounces) frozen asparagus spears	
	Bananas	5	
	Beans, green	1 pound	
	Broccoli	1 pound	
	Brussels sprouts	³/₄ pound	
	Cabbage, green	1 small head	
	Carrots	1¹/₂ pounds	
	Celery	1 stalk	
	Grapefruit	2	
	Green peppers	1 small	
	Lemons	1	
	Lettuce, romaine	1 head	
	Limes	1	
	Onions, dry yellow	2	
	Onions, red	1	
	Oranges	8	
	Pineapple	1	
	Potatoes	6	
	Potatoes, sweet (or yams)	4 medium	
	Tomatoes (or avocados)	4 large	
Canned Goods	Applesauce	1 can (1 pound) or homemade (buy 4 additional apples)	
	Beans, kidney	1 can (8 ounces)	
	Corned beef	1 can (12 ounces)	
	Cranberry juice cocktail	1 bottle (32 ounces)	
	Mandarin oranges	1 can (11 ounces)	
	Pineapple slices	1 can (16 ounces)	
	Shrimp, small deveined	2 cans (4¹/₂ ounces each)	
	Tuna fish, chunk-style	1 can (6¹/₂ ounces)	
Frozen Foods	Bread dough, frozen whole wheat	1 loaf	
	Orange juice, frozen concentrate	3 cans (6 ounces each)	
Dairy Products	Butter or margarine	1 pound	
	Cheese, Cheddar	1³/₄ pounds	
	Cheese, cottage	1 carton (24 ounces)	
	Eggs	1¹/₂ dozen	
	Milk, low-fat	3¹/₂ gallons	
	Whipping cream	¹/₂ pint	
Bread and Cereal Products	Bread, French	1 loaf	
	Bread, whole wheat	2 loaves (1 pound each)	
	English muffins	1 package of 6	
Meat, Poultry, and Fish	Chicken thighs	8 (about 2¹/₄ pounds)	
	Pork roast, blade or "rib end"	5 pounds	
	Pork sausage, bulk	1 pound	

(Check staple supplies for active dry yeast, almonds, basil, beef bouillon cubes, cashews, catsup, celery seed, cinnamon, dried dill weed, dried parsley, dry mustard, evaporated milk, ground cloves, ground ginger, honey, Italian dressing, jam, maple-flavored syrup, mayonnaise, monosodium glutamate, oil, peanut butter, quick-cooking tapioca, raisins, rice, rolled oats, soy sauce, tarragon, unflavored gelatin, vinegar, and walnuts.)

Menus April Second Week

	Breakfast	Lunch	Dinner
Sunday	Fresh Fruit Cup (p. 175) Grilled Sweet Rolls (p. 246) Milk	Mushroom Omelet (p. 234) Stuffed Celery (p. 182) Toast with Jam Hot Chocolate (p. 172)	Chicken Divan with Rice (p. 127) Marinated Fresh Vegetables (p. 200) Applesauce (p. 176) Pumpkin Cookies (p. 273), double the recipe Milk
Monday	Orange Juice Swiss Oatmeal (p. 256) Milk	Peanut Butter and Raisin Sandwiches (p. 161) Marinated Vegetables (leftover) Pumpkin Cookies (leftover) Milk	Split Pea Soup with Sausage Balls (p. 152) Simple Carrot Slaw (p. 215) Easy French Bread (p. 244) Fresh Fruit Cup (leftover) Milk or Other Beverage
Tuesday	Grapefruit Halves Prepared Cereal Toast with Jam Milk	Luncheon Meat and Pickle Sandwiches Marinated Vegetables (leftover) Milk	Chicken Divan (leftover) Waldorf Salad (p. 206) Pumpkin Cookies (leftover) Milk or Other Beverage
Wednesday	Orange Slices Oatmeal with Butter and Brown Sugar Milk	Cream Cheese and Nut Sandwiches (p. 163) Carrot Sticks Milk	Super Salmon on Toast (p. 142) Buttered Broccoli (p. 192) Waldorf Salad (if any leftover) Pumpkin Cookies (leftover) Milk or Other Beverage
Thursday	Grapefruit Halves Puff Pancakes (p. 254) Milk	Ground Nut and Raisin Sandwiches (p. 162) Celery Sticks Milk	Split Pea Soup with Sausage Balls (leftover) Toast Applesauce (p. 176) Milk or Other Beverage
Friday	Orange Halves Prepared Cereal Mix Milk	Tuna Sandwiches with (leftover) Water Chestnuts (p. 217) Apple Halves Pumpkin Cookies (leftover) Milk	Ringtum Diddy on Toast (p. 239) Buttered Peas (p. 191) Pumpkin Cookies (leftover) Milk or Other Beverage
Saturday	Orange Juice French Toast with Cinnamon and Sugar Milk	Fried Egg Sandwiches (p. 167) Stuffed Celery (p. 182) Banana Shake (p. 172)	Lazy Susan Dinner (p. 143) Milk

Shopping List April Second Week

	Product	Quantity	Variation for Your Family
Fresh Produce	Apples	6, including 3 red	
	Bananas	5	
	Broccoli	2 pounds	
	Carrots	1 pound	
	Celery	1 stalk	
	Grapefruit	4	
	Green peppers	1	
	Lemons	1	
	Mushrooms	1/4 pound	
	Onions, dry yellow	2	
	Oranges	7	
	Potatoes	1 medium	
	Tomatoes	2 large	
	Zucchini	1 small to medium	
Canned Goods	Applesauce	2 cans (1 pound each) or homemade (buy 8 additional apples)	
	Cider or clear apple juice	1 bottle (32 ounces)	
	Pumpkin	1 can (1 pound)	
	Salmon	1 can (7³/₄ ounces) or 1/2 pound fresh	
	Soup, cream of chicken	1 can (10³/₄ ounces)	
	Tomatoes	1 can (1 pound) or fresh (buy 2 additional tomatoes)	
	Tuna fish, chunk-style	1 can (6¹/₂ ounces)	
	Water chestnuts	1 can (8 ounces)	
Frozen Foods	Orange juice, frozen concentrate	3 cans (6 ounces each)	
	Peas	1 package (10 ounces)	
Dairy Products	Butter or margarine	1 pound	
	Cheese, Cheddar	1 pound	
	Cream cheese	1 package (8 ounces)	
	Eggs	1 dozen	
	Milk, low-fat	3¹/₂ gallons	
	Sour cream (or plain yogurt)	1 container (8 ounces)	
Bread and Cereal Products	Bread, French	1 loaf	
	Bread, whole grain	2 loaves (1¹/₂ pounds each)	
	Sweet rolls, day-old	4 or homemade	
Meat, Poultry, and Fish	Beef, ground	1/2 pound	
	Chicken, broiler-fryer	1 (3 pounds)	
	Luncheon meat	2 packages (2.5 ounces each)	
	Pork sausage, bulk	1 pound	
Miscellaneous	Split peas, dried green	1 pound	

(Check staple supplies for active dry yeast, bay leaves, brown sugar, catsup, cayenne pepper, cider vinegar, cinnamon, coconut, confectioners' sugar, curry powder, dry mustard, ground cloves, ground ginger, ground nutmeg, jam, maple flavoring, marjoram, mayonnaise, paprika, peanut butter, pickles, prepared cereal, raisins, rice, rolled oats, shortening, Tabasco sauce, thyme, vanilla, and walnuts.)

	Breakfast	Lunch	Dinner
Sunday	Orange Juice Omelet (p. 234) Twin Mountain Muffins (p. 251) Milk	Shrimp and Cucumber Salad (p. 222) Twin Mountain Muffins (leftover) Milk	Maple-Glazed Baked Ham (p. 118) Baked Sweet Potatoes with Herb Butter (p. 199) Asparagus with Lemon Mayonnaise (p. 184) Frozen Wheat Bread Rolls (p. 246) Banana Bavarian Pudding (p. 280) Milk or Other Beverage
Monday	Applesauce (p. 176) Oatmeal Toasted Rolls (leftover) Milk	Ham (leftover) Salad Sandwiches in Pita Bread (p. 213) Stuffed Celery (p. 182) Orange Halves Milk	Chicken Vegetable Stir-Fry (p. 128) Steamed Rice (p. 257) Buttered Green Beans (p. 183) Banana Bavarian Pudding (leftover) Milk or Other Beverage
Tuesday	Sliced Oranges Prepared Cereal Milk	Sliced Ham Sandwiches Vegetable Sticks Apple Halves Milk	Lentil Soup, Gypsy Style (p. 154), using leftover ham Easy Bread Sticks (p. 245) Cabbage Pineapple Slaw (p. 214) Milk or Other Beverage
Wednesday	Orange Juice Cream of Wheat with Brown Sugar Milk	Cream of Tomato Soup (p.148) Chicken Vegetable Stir-Fry (leftover) Toast Milk	Broiled Ham (leftover) with Baby Limas and Cheese (p. 118) Corn Bread with Honey (p. 245) Baked Apples (p. 283) Milk or Other Beverage
Thursday	Grapefruit Halves Prepared Cereal Corn Bread (leftover) Milk	Tuna and Pickle Sandwiches Tomato Wedges Butterscotch Crunchies (p. 269)	Lentil Soup, Gypsy Style (leftover) Parmesan Toast (p. 252) Waldorf Salad (p. 206) Milk or Other Beverage
Friday	Swiss Oatmeal (p. 256) Toast Milk	Peanut Butter Sandwiches (p. 161) Vegetable Sticks Orange Halves Milk	Red Snapper with Pasta (p. 230) Broccoli with Buttered Crumbs (p. 192) French Bread (p. 244) Grapefruit and Apple Salad (p. 206) Milk or Other Beverage
Saturday	Orange Juice Prepared Cereal Milk	Broiled Cheese Sandwiches (p. 163) Cabbage Pineapple Slaw (p. 214) Milk	Ground Beef Fricassee on Toast (p. 107) Carrots Applesauce Butterscotch Crunchies (leftover) Milk or Other Beverages

Shopping List April Third Week

	Product	Quantity	Variation for Your Family
Fresh Produce	Apples	9 large	
	Asparagus	1¹/₃ pounds	
	Bananas	7	
	Broccoli	1 pound	
	Cabbage, green	1 medium to large head	
	Carrots	1 pound	
	Celery	1 stalk	
	Cucumbers, large	3	
	Gingerroot	1 piece (freeze leftover)	
	Grapefruit	4 large	
	Green beans	1 pound	
	Green peppers	1 large	
	Lemons	3	
	Lettuce, romaine	1 head	
	Onions, dry yellow	3	
	Onions, green	1 bunch	
	Oranges	9	
	Potatoes, sweet (or yams)	4 medium	
	Tomatoes	2 large	
Canned Goods	Applesauce	2 cans (1 pound each) or homemade	
	Pineapple, crushed	1 can (8 ounces)	
	Shrimp	1 can (4¹/₂ ounces) or 4 ounces frozen	
	Tomato juice	1 can (24 ounces)	
	Tomato sauce	1 can (15 ounces)	
	Tuna fish, chunk-style	1 can (6¹/₂ ounces)	
Frozen Foods	Bread dough, frozen whole wheat	1 loaf	
	Lima beans, small green	1 package (10 ounces)	
	Orange juice, frozen concentrate	3 cans (6 ounces each)	
Dairy Products	Butter or margarine	1 pound	
	Cheese, Cheddar	1 pound	
	Eggs	1 dozen	
	Milk, low-fat	3¹/₂ gallons	
	Sour cream	1 carton (8 ounces)	
	Whipping cream	¹/₂ pint	
Bread and Cereal Products	Bread, pocket	2 individual round loaves	
	Bread, whole wheat	2 loaves (1¹/₂ pounds each)	
	Pasta wheels (rotelle) or spaghetti	8 ounces	
Meat, Poultry, and Fish	Beef, ground	1 pound	
	Chicken breast halves	2	
	Fish, red snapper or other	1 pound	
	Ham, fully cooked boneless	4 pounds	
Miscellaneous	Butterscotch chips	2 packages (6 ounces each)	
	Lentils, dried	¹/₂ pound	

(Check staple supplies for basil, brown sugar, cashews, cinnamon, cornflakes, cornstarch, cream of wheat, dried dill weed, dry bread crumbs, dry mustard, garlic, gelatin, ground cloves, honey, maple-flavored syrup, marjoram, mayonnaise, mixed dried herbs, mustard pickles, nuts, oil, Parmesan cheese, peanut butter, pickles, prepared cereal, prepared mustard, raisins, rice, rolled oats, soy sauce, unflavored gelatin, walnuts, whole cloves, and yellow cornmeal.)

	Breakfast	Lunch	Dinner
Sunday	Orange Julius (p. 171) Swedish Pancakes (p. 255) Milk	Tossed Green Salad with Tomatoes Olive Nut Sandwiches (p. 163) Milk	Mushroom Quiche (p. 237) Brussels Sprouts with Cream (p. 194) Spinach Apple Toss (p. 186) Apricot Spice Cake (p. 264) Milk or Other Beverage
Monday	Sautéed Apple Slices (p. 176) Oatmeal Milk	Quiche Wedges (leftover) Tomato Slices on Greens Milk	Hamburger Vegetable Soup with Cheese (p. 150) Easy French Bread (p. 244) Apricot Spice Cake (leftover) Milk or Other Beverage
Tuesday	Orange Juice Oatmeal with Butter and Brown Sugar Milk	Tuna Salad Sandwiches (p. 217) Celery Sticks Apple Halves Milk	Oven-Fried Chicken (p. 121), double the recipe Pan-Roasted Potatoes (p. 182) Glazed Carrots (p. 187) Milk or Other Beverage
Wednesday	Orange Juice Pick-Up (p. 171) Whole Wheat Toast Milk	Chicken Salad Sandwiches (p. 217) Carrot Sticks Banana Halves Milk	Hamburger Vegetable Soup with Cheese (leftover) Bread and Butter Baked Apples (p. 283) Milk or Other Beverage
Thursday	Grapefruit Halves Prepared Cereal with Raisins Milk	Peanut Butter and Apple Sandwiches (p. 161) Celery Sticks Milk	Chicken Cashew (p. 126), using leftover chicken Buttered Broccoli (p. 192) Hasty Tasty Orange Bavarian (p. 208) Milk or Other Beverage
Friday	Grapefruit Halves Scrambled Eggs (p. 231) Toast with Jam Milk	Luncheon Meat Sandwiches Stuffed Celery (p. 182) Milk	Creamed Tuna Fish on Toast (p. 136) Buttered Peas (p. 191) Hasty Tasty Orange Bavarian (leftover) Milk or Other Beverage
Saturday	Orange Juice French Toast (p. 256) Maple-Flavored Syrup (p. 253) Pan-Fried Sausage Links (p. 115) Milk	Tomato Juice Apple Puff Pancakes (p. 254) Simple Carrot Slaw (p. 215) Milk	Lazy Susan Dinner (p. 143) Parmesan Toast (p. 252) Milk or Other Beverage

Shopping List April Fourth Week

	Product	Quantity	Variation for Your Family
Fresh Produce	Apples	10, including 2 red	
	Bananas	4	
	Broccoli	1 pound	
	Brussels sprouts	³/₄ pound small	
	Carrots	1 pound	
	Celery	1 stalk	
	Grapefruit	6	
	Green peppers	1	
	Lettuce, romaine	1 head	
	Mushrooms	¹/₂ pound	
	Onions, dry yellow	2	
	Onions, green	1 bunch	
	Potatoes	3 pounds	
	Spinach,	1 bunch (about ³/₄ pound)	
	Tomatoes	4 large	
Canned Goods	Apricot halves	1 can (17 ounces) or 2 cups thick puree	
	Chow mein noodles	1 can (3 ounces)	
	Olives, ripe, chopped or sliced	1 can (4¹/₂ ounces)	
	Pineapple, crushed	1 can (8 ounces)	
	Soup, cream of mushroom	1 can (10³/₄ ounces)	
	Tomato juice	1 can (24 ounces)	
	Tomatoes, whole	1 can (29 ounces)	
	Tuna fish, chunk-style	2 cans (6¹/₂ ounces each)	
Frozen Foods	Orange juice, frozen concentrate	4 cans (6 ounces each)	
	Peas	1 package (10 ounces)	
	Unbaked pastry shell	1 9-inch	
Dairy Products	Cheese, cream	1 package (3 ounces)	
	Cheese, Monterey Jack	¹/₂ pound	
	Cheese, Swiss	12 ounces	
	Eggs	1 dozen	
	Half-and-half	1 pint	
	Milk, low-fat	3¹/₂ gallons	
	Whipping cream	¹/₂ pint	
Bread and Cereal Products	Bread, French	1 loaf	
	Bread, whole grain	2 loaves (1 pound each)	
Meat, Poultry, and Fish	Bacon	5 strips	
	Beef, ground	1 pound	
	Chickens, broiler-fryer	2 (3 pounds each)	
	Pastrami or spiced beef luncheon meat	2 packages (2¹/₄ ounces each)	
	Pork sausage links	¹/₂ pound	

(Check staple supplies for active dry yeast, bay leaves, brown sugar, cashews, cinnamon, confectioners' sugar, ground cloves, ground nutmeg, honey, jam, maple-flavored syrup, mayonnaise, nuts, oil, Parmesan cheese, peanut butter, pickles, prepared cereal, raisins, rolled oats, unflavored gelatin, and vinegar.)

Menus May Second Week

	Breakfast	Lunch	Dinner
Sunday	Grapefruit Halves Toast with Jam Milk	Spinach Apple Toss (p. 186) Cheese Slices French Bread Milk	Baked Halibut (p. 139) Parsleyed New Potatoes (p. 178) Vegetables with Dill Dressing (p. 200) Strawberry Tarts (p. 289) Milk or Other Beverage
Monday	Swiss Oatmeal with Apples (p. 256) Cinnamon Toast (p. 252) Milk	Cheese Sandwiches Dill Pickles Vegetable Sticks Gingersnaps (p. 269) Milk	Chicken Crisp (p. 127) Cabbage Stir-Fry (p. 197) Sliced Oranges on Romaine, with French Dressing (p. 223) Milk or Other Beverage
Tuesday	Orange Juice Prepared Cereal Whole Wheat Toast Milk	Deviled Ham Sandwiches with Pickles Apple Halves Milk	Cream of Tomato Soup (p. 148) Crisscross Salad (p. 212) Frosty Fruit (leftover) Milk or Other Beverage
Wednesday	Orange Juice French Toast (p. 256) with Cinnamon and Sugar Milk	Peanut Butter and Celery Sandwiches (p. 161) Banana Halves Gingersnaps (leftover)	Baked Cod with Tomato-Caper Sauce (p. 138) Crisscross Salad (leftover) Easy French Bread (p. 244) Milk or Other Beverage
Thursday	Applesauce Pancakes (p. 253) Maple-Flavored Syrup Milk	Peanut Butter Sandwiches Crisscross Salad (if any leftover) Apple Halves Milk	Cheese Strata (p. 238) Orange-Glazed Brussels Sprouts (p. 194) Grapefruit Romaine Salad Gingersnaps (leftover) Milk or Other Beverage
Friday	Orange Juice Oatmeal with Cinnamon and Sugar Milk	Ground Nut and Raisin Sandwiches on French Bread (p. 162) Carrot Sticks Milk	Baked Cod with Tomato- Caper Sauce (leftover) Basil Carrots (p. 186) Cabbage Slaw (p. 214) Strawberry Shortcake (p. 249) Milk or Other Beverage
Saturday	Orange Juice Prepared Cereal with Sliced Bananas Milk	Grilled Deviled Ham Sandwiches Sliced Tomatoes Milk	Cheesy Egg Cups (p. 232) Buttered Peas (p. 191) Whole Wheat Toast Strawberry Shortcake (leftover) Milk

Shopping List May First Week

	Product	Quantity	Variation for Your Family
Fresh Produce	Apples	5	
	Asparagus	1½ pounds	
	Bananas	4	
	Broccoli	1¼ pound	
	Brussels sprouts	¾ pound	
	Cabbage, green	1 small head	
	Carrots	1 pound	
	Celery	1 stalk	
	Grapes, seedless	⅓ pound	
	Lemons	2	
	Lettuce, romaine	1 head	
	Mushrooms	½ pound	
	Onions, red	1	
	Oranges	2 large	
	Potatoes	4 (2 pounds)	
	Rhubarb	1 pound	
	Strawberries	1 quart	
	Tomatoes	5 (2 pounds)	
Canned Goods	Applesauce	1 can (1 pound)	
	Beef broth	1 can (10½ ounces)	
	Beans, kidney	1 can (8 ounces)	
	Chow mein noodles	1 can (3 ounces)	
	Deviled ham	1 can (4½ ounces)	
	Grapefruit	1 can (1 pound)	
	Pineapple tidbits	1 can (1 pound 4 ounces)	
	Soup, golden mushroom	1 can (10¾ ounces)	
	Tomato juice	1 can (24 ounces)	
	Tuna fish, chunk-style	1 can (6½ ounces)	
Frozen Foods	Orange juice, frozen concentrate	3 cans (6 ounces each)	
	Peas	1 package (10 ounces)	
Dairy Products	Butter or margarine	1 pound	
	Cheese, Cheddar	1½ pounds	
	Eggs	1 dozen	
	Milk, low-fat	3½ gallons	
	Sour cream	1 carton (16 ounces)	
Bread and Cereal Products	Bread, enriched white	1 loaf (1 pound)	
	Bread, French	1 loaf	
	Bread, whole wheat	2 loaves (1½ pounds each)	
Meat, Poultry, and Fish	Bacon	½ pound	
	Beef, cube steaks	4	
	Chicken, broiler-fryer	1 (3 pounds)	
	Cod, fresh or frozen fillets	1½ to 2 pounds	
Miscellaneous	Capers	1 bottle (2¼ ounces)	

(Check staple supplies for basil, beef bouillon cubes, cinnamon, Dijon mustard, dried red chili peppers, dried mixed herbs, dried parsley, dry bread crumbs, dry mustard, garlic, garlic salt, ground cloves, ground ginger, honey, maple-flavored syrup, mayonnaise, molasses, nuts, oil, onion powder, paprika, Parmesan cheese, peanut butter, pickles, prepared cereal, raisins, rolled oats, shortening, soft bread crumbs, soy sauce, Worcestershire sauce, and yellow cornmeal.)

	Breakfast	Lunch	Dinner
Sunday	Grapefruit Halves Toast with Jam Milk	Spinach Apple Toss (p. 186) Cheese Slices French Bread Milk	Baked Halibut (p. 139) Parsleyed New Potatoes (p. 178) Vegetables with Dill Dressing Strawberry Tarts (p. 289) Milk or Other Beverage
Monday	Orange Juice Cottage Cheese Whole Wheat Toast with Jam Milk	Luncheon Meat and Tomato Sandwiches Vegetable Sticks Apple Halves Milk	Greek Cabbage Casserole (p. 106) Glazed Carrots (p. 187) Strawberry Tarts (leftover) Milk or Other Beverage
Tuesday	Sliced Oranges Cream of Wheat Milk	Peanut Butter and Apple Sandwiches (p. 161) Carrot Sticks Chocolate Milk (p. 172)	Canned Corned Beef Slices Vegetables with Dill Dressing (leftover) Bread and Butter Stewed Rhubarb (p. 288) Milk or Other Beverage
Wednesday	Grapefruit Halves Prepared Cereal Toast with Jam Milk	Broiled Cheese and Tomato Sandwiches (p. 164) Apple Halves Milk	Greek Cabbage Casserole (leftover) Basil Carrots (p. 186) Apple Banana Bread (p. 243) Milk or Other Beverage
Thursday	Sautéed Apple Slices (p. 176) Cooked Wheat Cereal with Raisins Milk	Apple Banana Bread (leftover) with Cream Cheese Carrot Sticks Milk	Barbecued Chicken Thighs (p. 122) Potato Salad (p. 211) Sliced Tomatoes Ruby Grapefruit (p. 290) Milk or Other Beverage
Friday	Orange Juice Swiss Oatmeal (p. 256) Milk	Sliced Tomatoes Cottage Cheese Parmesan Toast (p. 252) Milk	Broccoli Cheese Soup (p. 148) Toasted French Bread Ruby Grapefruit (leftover) Milk or Other Beverage
Saturday	Sliced Oranges Whole Wheat Toast with Peanut Butter and Jam Milk	Broccoli Cheese Soup (leftover) French Bread Banana Pops (p. 289) Milk	Barbecued Chicken Thighs (leftover) Potato Salad (leftover) Banana Pops (leftover) Milk or Other Beverage

Shopping List May Second Week

	Product	Quantity	Variation for Your Family
Fresh Produce	Apples, red	6	
	Bananas	5	
	Broccoli	1/2 pound	
	Cabbage, green	1 large head	
	Carrots	2 1/2 pounds	
	Grapefruit	8	
	Lemons	3	
	Mushrooms	1/2 pound	
	Onions, dry yellow	3	
	Oranges	8	
	Potatoes	5 pounds, including 12 new potatoes	
	Rhubarb	1 pound	
	Spinach	2 bunches or 1 cello bag (10 ounces)	
	Strawberries	1 quart	
	Tomatoes	11 (4 pounds)	
	Zucchini	2 medium	
Canned Goods	Applesauce	1 can (1 pound)	
	Corned beef	1 can (12 ounces)	
	Tuna fish, chunk-style	1 can (6 1/2 ounces), packed in water	
Frozen Foods	Orange juice, frozen concentrate	2 cans (6 ounces each)	
	Raspberries	1 package (10 ounces)	
Dairy Products	Butter or margarine	1 pound	
	Cheese, Cheddar or other	1 1/2 pounds	
	Cheese, cottage	1 carton (16 ounces)	
	Cheese, cream	1 package (8 ounces)	
	Cream, heavy	1/2 pint	
	Eggs	1 1/2 dozen	
	Milk, low-fat	3 1/2 gallons	
	Sour cream	1 carton (8 ounces)	
Bread and Cereal Products	Bread, French	1 loaf	
	Bread, whole grain	2 loaves (1 pound each)	
	Crackers, wheat	small package	
	Tart shells	8 (from bakery)	
Meat, Poultry, and Fish	Bacon	4 slices	
	Beef, ground	1 pound	
	Chicken thighs	8 (2 3/4 pounds)	
	Halibut fillets	1 pound (4 small fillet pieces)	
	Luncheon meat	2 packages (2 1/4 ounces each) pastrami or corned beef	
Miscellaneous	Barbecue sauce	1 jar (8 ounces) or 1 cup homemade	
	Capers	1 jar	
	Milk chocolate	1 bar (8 ounces)	

(Check staple supplies for almond extract, basil, catsup, celery seed, chicken bouillon cubes, cinnamon, cornstarch, cream of wheat, Dijon mustard, dill weed, dried parsley, dry mustard, fennel seed, French dressing, gherkin sweet pickles, jam, marjoram, mayonnaise, mint leaves (fresh or dried), monosodium glutamate, oil, onion powder, paprika, Parmesan cheese, peanut butter, prepared cereal, raisins, rice, rolled oats, shortening, uncooked whole wheat cereal, unsweetened cocoa, vanilla, and vinegar.)

	Breakfast	Lunch	Dinner
Sunday	Apple Pancakes (p. 253) Maple-Flavored Syrup (p. 253) Pork Sausage Patties Milk	Grapefruit and Crab Salad (p. 206) Sliced Tomatoes Parmesan Toast (p. 252) Milk	Broiled Swordfish (or other fish) Steaks with Cumin (p. 138) Parsleyed New Potatoes (p. 178) Green Beans with Almonds (p. 183) Molded Custard Ring with Strawberries and Cream (p. 286) Milk or Other Beverage
Monday	Orange Juice Prepared Cereal Toast with Honey Milk	Peanut Butter and Grated Carrot Sandwiches (p.161) Apple Halves Celebration Cookies (p. 275) Milk	Quick and Easy Cassoulet (p. 128) Beet Greens (p. 196) French Rolls Molded Custard Ring with Strawberries and Cream (leftover) Milk or Other Beverage
Tuesday	Sliced Bananas Oatmeal with Cinnamon and Sugar Milk	Cheese Sandwiches Mustard Pickles Celery Sticks Orange Halves Milk	Chicken Asparagus Stir-Fry (p. 128) Tossed Greens with Oranges, with French Dressing (p. 223) Celebration Cookies (leftover) Milk or Other Beverage
Wednesday	Grapefruit Sections Prepared Cereal Milk	Tuna Salad Sandwiches (p. 217) Dill Pickles Strawberry Fruit Shake (p. 172)	Quick and Easy Cassoulet (leftover) Basil Carrots (p. 186) Chocolate Peanut Butter Pudding (p. 279) Milk or Other Beverage
Thursday	Orange Juice Pick-Up (p. 171) Toast with Peanut Butter and Honey Milk	Chicken Asparagus Stir-Fry (leftover) in Pita Bread Milk	Cheese Rarebit on Toast (p. 238) Dilly Beans (p. 183) Chopped Carrot and Celery Salad Celebration Cookies (leftover) Milk or Other Beverage
Friday	Sliced Oranges Scrambled Eggs (p. 231) Toast with Honey Milk	Hoagie Sandwiches (p. 164) Vegetable Sticks Black Cows (p. 172)	Spoonburgers (p. 168) Waldorf Salad (p. 206) Milk
Saturday	Orange Juice Swedish Pancakes (p. 255) Pork Sausage Patties Milk	Spoonburgers (leftover) Vegetable Sticks Chocolate Banana Shakes (p. 172)	Broccoli Light Soup (p. 149) Parmesan Toast (p. 252) Apple Crisp (p. 282) Milk

Shopping List May Third Week

	Product	Quantity	Variation for Your Family
Fresh Produce	Apples, red, tart	8 large	
	Asparagus	1½ pounds	
	Bananas	6	
	Beans, green	1 pound	
	Beet greens	2 bunches	
	Broccoli	1 pound	
	Carrots	1 pound	
	Celery	1 stalk	
	Gingerroot	1 piece	
	Grapefruit	6	
	Lemons	1	
	Lettuce, romaine	1 head	
	Onions, dry yellow	2 pounds	
	Oranges	10 (5 pounds)	
	Potatoes	1 medium	
	Potatoes, new	1½ pounds	
	Strawberries	1 quart	
	Tomatoes	2 large	
Canned Goods	Beans, great northern or other white beans	2 cans (1 pound each)	
	Crab	1 can (7½ ounces) or ½ pound fresh	
	Tomato sauce	2 cans (8 ounces each)	
	Tuna fish, chunk-style	1 can (6½ ounces), packed in water	
Frozen Foods	Orange juice, frozen concentrate	3 cans (6 ounces each)	
Dairy Products	Butter or margarine	1 pound	
	Cheese, Cheddar	1 pound	
	Cheese, Parmesan	1 container (3 ounces)	
	Cheese, Swiss	8 ounces	
	Eggs	1½ dozen	
	Milk, low-fat	3½ gallons	
	Sour cream	1 carton (8 ounces)	
	Whipping cream	½ pint	
Bread and Cereal Products	Bread, pita	2 round loaves (to cut in half)	
	Bread, whole grain	2 loaves (1½ pounds each)	
	Buns, hamburger	8	
	French rolls (for Hoagies)	8 (or hamburger or hot dog buns)	
Meat, Poultry, and Fish	Beef, ground	1 pound	
	Chicken breast halves	3	
	Pork sausage, bulk	1 pound	
	Salami or pastrami	6 ounces, sliced thin	
	Sausage, cooked smoked	½ pound	
	Swordfish (or other) steaks	1½ pounds	
Miscellaneous	Root beer	1 quart	

(Check staple supplies for almond extract, almonds, basil, brown sugar, cashews, catsup, cayenne pepper, chili powder, cinnamon, coriander, cornstarch, curry powder, dill pickles, dried dill weed, dried parsley, evaporated milk, French dressing, garlic, ground cumin, ground nutmeg, honey, leaf thyme, maple-flavored syrup, mayonnaise, mustard pickles, oil, Parmesan cheese, peanut butter, prepared cereal, prepared mustard, soy sauce, thyme, unflavored gelatin, unsweetened chocolate, vanilla, walnuts, white wine or other vinegar, and Worcestershire sauce.)

	Breakfast	Lunch	Dinner
Sunday	Orange Juice Cheesy Egg Cups (p. 232) Toast Milk	Tuna and Apple Salad (p. 217) Parmesan Toast (p. 252) Chocolate Chews (p. 270) Milk	Sesame Baked Chicken Breasts with Mushroom Sauce (p. 122) Asparagus with Lemon Wedges Butterhorns (p. 248), make ahead Frozen Strawberry Squares (p. 290) Milk or Other Beverage
Monday	Orange Halves Cream of Wheat with Raisins Toast Milk	Tuna Salad on (leftover) Butterhorns Vegetable Sticks Fresh Strawberries Milk	Hamburger Scramble (p. 110) Tasty Broccoli (p. 192) Frozen Strawberry Squares (leftover) Milk or Other Beverage
Tuesday	Sliced Oranges Cooked Cornmeal with Shredded Cheese Milk	Hamburger Scramble (leftover) in Buns Apple Halves Milk	Sesame Baked Chicken Breasts (leftover) Three Bean Salad (p. 212) Butterhorns (leftover) Chocolate Chews (leftover) Milk or Other Beverage
Wednesday	Orange Juice Prepared Cereal with Strawberries Milk	Cheese on Rye Three Bean Salad (leftover) Banana Halves Milk	Frankfurters in Buns Scalloped Spring Cabbage (p. 197) Chocolate Chews (leftover) Milk or Other Beverage
Thursday	Orange Juice Fried Cornmeal Mush (p. 256) Maple-Flavored Syrup (p. 253) Milk	Peanut Butter and Apple Sandwiches (p. 161) Vegetable Sticks Chocolate Chews (leftover) Milk	Cream of Zucchini Soup (p. 148) Three Bean Salad (leftover) Fresh Strawberries, with Sour Cream Fruit Topping (p. 175) Milk or Other Beverage
Friday	Apple Pancakes (p. 253) Maple-Flavored Syrup (p. 253) Canned Corned Beef Slices Milk	Cabbage Shrimp Slaw (p. 215) Parmesan Rye Toast (p. 252) Milk	Broiled Cheese and Tomato Sandwiches (p. 164) Sautéed Brussels Sprouts (p. 194) Ruby Grapefruit (p. 290) Milk or Other Beverage
Saturday	Ruby Grapefruit (leftover) Swiss Oatmeal (p. 256) Milk	Cream of Zucchini Soup (leftover) with Frankfurter Slices Carrot Sticks Parmesan Toast (p. 252) Milk	Lazy Susan Dinner (p. 143) Milk

Shopping List May Fourth Week

	Product	Quantity	Variation for Your Family
Fresh Produce	Apples	4	
	Asparagus	1½ pounds	
	Bananas	2	
	Broccoli	1 pound	
	Brussels sprouts	¾ pound	
	Cabbage, green	1 medium head	
	Carrots	½ pound	
	Celery	1 stalk	
	Grapefruit	4	
	Lemons	1	
	Lettuce, iceberg	1 small head	
	Mushrooms	¼ pound	
	Onions, dry yellow	4	
	Oranges	8	
	Strawberries	1 quart	
	Tomatoes	2 large	
	Zucchini	4 medium	
Canned Goods	Beans, cut green	1 can (1 pound)	
	Bean, garbanzo	1 can (1 pound)	
	Beans, red kidney	1 can (1 pound)	
	Chicken broth	1 can (10½ ounces)	
	Corned beef	1 can (12 ounces)	
	Mushrooms, button or sliced	1 can (4 ounces)	
	Shrimp, small deveined	1 can (4½ ounces)	
	Tomatoes	1 can (1 pound)	
	Tuna fish, chunk-style	2 cans (6½ ounces each), packed in water	
Frozen Foods	Orange juice, frozen concentrate	2 cans (6 ounces each)	
	Raspberries	1 package (10 ounces)	
	Strawberries	1 package (10 ounces)	
Dairy Products	Butter or margarine	1½ pounds	
	Cheese, Cheddar	1½ pounds	
	Cheese, Swiss	8 ounces	
	Eggs	1½ dozen	
	Milk, low-fat	3½ gallons	
	Sour cream	1 carton (8 ounces)	
	Whipping cream	1 pint	
Bread and Cereal Products	Bread, rye	1 loaf	
	Bread, whole grain	1 loaf (1½ pounds)	
	Buns, hamburger	4	
	Buns, hot dog	4	
Meat, Poultry, and Fish	Beef, ground	½ pound	
	Chicken breast halves	8	
	Frankfurters	1 pound	

(Check staple supplies for active dry yeast, brown sugar, cayenne pepper, chicken bouillon cubes, cinnamon, confectioners' sugar, cream of wheat, dried parsley, dry bread crumbs, ground allspice, ground nutmeg, maple-flavored syrup, mayonnaise, mixed dried herbs, nuts, oil, Parmesan cheese, peanut butter, prepared cereal, prepared mustard, raisins, rice, rolled oats, sesame seeds, shortening, soy sauce, unsweetened chocolate, vanilla, vinegar, and yellow cornmeal.)

	Breakfast	Lunch	Dinner

Sunday	Orange Julius (p. 171)
	Scrambled Eggs (p. 231)
	Baking Powder Biscuits
	  (p. 249)
	Milk
		Shrimp Salad with Herbs
		  in Tomato Cups (p. 221)
		Toasted Biscuits (leftover)
		Milk
			Oven-Fried Chicken (p. 121)
			Baked Potatoes
			Chicken Gravy (p. 121)
			Broccoli with Buttered
			  Crumbs (p. 192)
			Frozen Fruit Salad (p. 207)
			Milk

Monday	Orange Juice
	Cottage Cheese
	Whole Wheat Toast
	Milk
		Shrimp Salad Sandwiches
		  on Whole Wheat Bread
		  (using leftover shrimp
		  salad)
		Vegetable Sticks
		Milk
			Spoonburgers (p. 168)
			Stir-Fried Vegetables (p. 199)
			Raisin Nut Nibbles (p. 271)
			Milk or Beverage

Tuesday	Orange and Banana Slices
	Prepared Cereal
	Milk
		Corned Beef Sandwiches
		  with Mustard Pickles
		Vegetable Sticks
		Nectarines
		Milk
			Tuna Rice Skillet
			  (p. 135)
			Dilly Beans (p. 183)
			Frozen Fruit Salad (leftover)
			Milk or Beverage

Wednesday	Orange Juice
	Whole Wheat Toast with
	  Peanut Butter and Honey
	Milk
		Zucchini, Tomato, and
		  Cheese Sandwiches
		Stuffed Celery (p. 182)
		Raisin Nut Nibbles
		  (leftover)
		Milk
			Mixed Vegetables
			  with Poached Eggs (p. 235)
			Whole Wheat Toast
			Fresh Pineapple
			Milk or Beverage

Thursday	Fresh Pineapple (leftover)
	Oatmeal with Butter and
	  Brown Sugar
	Milk
		Tomato Juice
		Broiled Cheese
		  Sandwiches (p. 163)
		Nectarines
		Milk
			Tuna (leftover) Stuffed
			  Green Peppers (p. 110)
			Mixed Vegetables (leftover)
			Raisin Nut Nibbles (leftover)
			Milk or Beverage

Friday	Orange Juice
	Prepared Cereal
	Cinnamon Toast
	Milk
		Peanut Butter and
		  Pineapple Sandwiches
		  (p. 161)
		Vegetable Sticks
		Milk
			Cream of Zucchini Soup
			  (p. 148)
			Carrot Pineapple Slaw
			  (p. 215)
			Toasted French Bread
			Milk or Beverage

Saturday	Sautéed Nectarine Slices
	French Toast (p. 256) with
	  Cinnamon and Sugar
	Milk
		Cream of Zucchini Soup
		  (leftover)
		Tomato and Cottage
		  Cheese Salad
		Milk
			Hot Dogs
			Vegetable Sticks
			Chocolate Banana Shakes
			  (p. 172)

Shopping List June First Week

	Product	Quantity	Variation for Your Family
Fresh Produce	Bananas	9	
	Beans, green	1 pound	
	Broccoli	1 pound	
	Brussels sprouts	³/₄ pound	
	Cabbage,	1 medium head	
	Carrots	1 pound	
	Celery	1 stalk	
	Green peppers	7	
	Lemons	1	
	Lettuce, red	1 head	
	Mushrooms	¹/₄ pound	
	Nectarines	10	
	Onions, dry yellow	5 (about 1¹/₂ pounds)	
	Oranges	2	
	Parsley	1 bunch	
	Pineapple	1	
	Potatoes, baking	4	
	Tomatoes	8, including 4 large	
	Zucchini	6 medium to large	
Canned Goods	Corn, whole kernel	1 can (8 ounces)	
	Corned beef	1 can (12 ounces)	
	Olives, sliced ripe	1 can (2¹/₄ ounces)	
	Pineapple, crushed, in juice	1 can (20 ounces)	
	Shrimp, small deveined	2 cans (4¹/₂ ounces each)	
	Tomato juice	1 can (24 ounces)	
	Tomato sauce	1 can (8 ounces) *and* 1 can (16 ounces)	
	Tomatoes, stewed	1 can (8 ounces)	
	Tuna fish, chunk-style	2 cans (6¹/₂ ounces each)	
Frozen Foods	Orange juice, frozen concentrate	4 cans (6 ounces each)	
Dairy Products	Butter or margarine	1 pound	
	Cheese, Cheddar	1¹/₂ pounds	
	Cheese, cream	1 package (3 ounces)	
	Cheese, cottage	1 carton (16 ounces)	
	Eggs	1¹/₂ dozen	
	Half-and-half	1 pint	
	Milk, low-fat	3¹/₂ gallons	
	Whipping cream	¹/₂ pint	
Bread and Cereal Products	Bread, French	1 loaf	
	Bread, whole grain	2 loaves (1 pound each)	
	Buns, hamburger	8	
	Buns, hot dog	6	
Meat, Poultry, and Fish	Bacon	2 slices	
	Beef, ground	1 pound	
	Chicken, broiler-fryer	1 (3 pounds)	
	Frankfurters	1 pound	
Miscellaneous	Maraschino cherries	1 small bottle	
	Marshmallows	¹/₂ pound	

(Check staple supplies for basil, beef bouillon cubes, brown sugar, catsup, celery salt, chicken bouillon cubes, chili powder, cinnamon, curry powder, evaporated milk, ground nutmeg, honey, marjoram, mayonnaise, monosodium glutamate, mustard pickles, oil, oregano, paprika, peanut butter, peanuts, pickles, prepared cereal, raisins, rice, rolled oats, shortening, tarragon, unsweetened cocoa, vinegar, walnuts, and Worcestershire sauce.)

Menus June Second Week (Vegetarian Menus)

	Breakfast	Lunch	Dinner
Sunday	Orange Julius (p. 171) Cheesy Egg Cups (p. 232) Toast with Jam Milk	Lettuce, Tomato, and Swiss Cheese Salad, with French Dressing (p. 223) Garlic Bread Milk	Vegetarian Lasagne (p. 229) Garlic Bread Fresh Cherry Cobbler (p. 288) Milk
Monday	Orange Juice Toast with Cottage Cheese and Jam Milk	Peanut Butter Sandwiches Carrot Sticks Banana Halves Milk	Mushroom Patties (p. 185) Broccoli with Cheese Sauce (p. 193) Fresh Cherry Cobbler (leftover) Milk or Other Beverage
Tuesday	Cantaloupe Prepared Cereal Milk	Carrot Raisin Sandwiches (p. 164) Cheddar Cheese Sticks Milk	Vegetable Lasagne (leftover) Sliced Orange Salad with Cottage Cheese Milk or Other Beverage
Wednesday	Sliced Oranges Swiss Oatmeal (p. 256) Milk	Peanut Butter and Grated Carrot Sandwiches (p. 161) Nectarines Milk	Mushroom Patties (leftover) Scalloped Spring Cabbage (p. 197) Sliced Tomatoes Milk
Thursday	Orange Juice Pick-Up (p. 171) Prepared Cereal with Honey Milk	Ground Nut and Raisin Sandwiches (p. 162) Vegetable Sticks Milk	Meatless Chili on Rice (p. 154) Stir-Fried Vegetables (p. 199) Cantaloupe Milk
Friday	Orange Juice Oatmeal with Raisins Hot Chocolate (p. 172)	Meatless Chili (leftover) Vegetable Sticks Whole Wheat Bread Milk	Lentil Salad in Tomatoes (p. 212) Broiled Cheese on Whole Wheat Bread Applesauce Milk
Saturday	Orange Juice Cottage Cheese Pancakes (p. 255) Maple-Flavored Syrup (p. 253) Milk	Lentil Salad (leftover) Cornmeal Muffins (p. 250) Apple Halves Milk	Meatless Chili (leftover) Cabbage Apple Slaw (p. 215) Cornmeal Muffins (leftover) Milk

	Product	Quantity	Variation for Your Family
Fresh Produce	Apples	6 large	
	Bananas	3	
	Broccoli	1 pound	
	Cabbage, green	1 head	
	Cantaloupe	2	
	Carrots	2 pounds	
	Celery	1 stalk	
	Green peppers	1	
	Lemons	1	
	Lettuce, romaine	1 head	
	Mushrooms	1¼ pounds	
	Nectarines	4	
	Onions, dry yellow	3 large	
	Onions, green	1 bunch	
	Oranges	10	
	Parsley	1 bunch	
	Spinach	1 pound (2 bunches)	
	Sweet cherries	1 pound (3 cups) or 1 can (29 ounces)	
	Tomatoes	8 large	
Canned Goods	Applesauce	1 can (1 pound)	
	Olives, sliced ripe	1 can (2¼ ounces)	
	Tomato paste	1 can (6 ounces)	
	Tomato sauce	1 can (15 ounces)	
	Tomatoes, whole	1 can (29 ounces)	
Frozen Foods	Orange juice, frozen concentrate	3 cans (6 ounces each)	
Dairy Products	Butter or margarine	1 pound	
	Cheese, Cheddar	2 pounds	
	Cheese, cottage	2 cartons (16 ounces each)	
	Cheese, Monterey Jack	½ pound	
	Cheese, Swiss	¼ pound	
	Eggs	1½ dozen	
	Milk, low-fat	3½ gallons	
Bread and Cereal Products	Bread, French	2 loaves	
	Bread, whole grain	1 loaf (1½ pounds)	
	Noodles, lasagne	6 ounces (10 noodles)	
Miscellaneous	Beans, dried pinto or kidney	1 pound	
	Lentils, dried	½ pound	

(Check staple supplies for basil, bay leaves, celery seed, chili powder, cinnamon, curry powder, dried red chili peppers, dry mustard, French dressing, garlic, ground cumin, honey, jam, maple-flavored syrup, marjoram, mayonnaise, monosodium glutamate, oil, onion powder, oregano, paprika, peanut butter, prepared cereal, raisins, rice, rolled oats, shortening, soft bread crumbs, sweet pickles or relish, Tabasco sauce, unsweetened cocoa, vinegar, walnuts, and yellow cornmeal.)

	Breakfast	Lunch	Dinner
Sunday	French Toast with Cinnamon and Sugar (p. 256) Banana Shakes (p. 172)	Tuna Bunwiches (p. 166) Carrot Peanut Slaw (p. 216) Milk	Oriental Chicken (p. 124) Broccoli with Orange Sauce (p. 192) Glazed Carrots (p. 187) Apple Nut Pudding (p. 281) Milk or Other Beverage
Monday	Orange Juice Cooked Cornmeal with Butter and Brown Sugar Milk	Swiss Cheese on Rye Pickles Stuffed Celery (p. 182) Milk	Tuna Bunwiches (leftover) Cabbage Pineapple Slaw (p. 214) Apple Nut Pudding (leftover) Milk or Other Beverage
Tuesday	Sliced Oranges Swiss Oatmeal (p. 256) Milk	Tuna Bunwiches (leftover) Waldorf Salad (p. 206) Milk	Herb-Broiled Fish Fillets (p. 137) Parsleyed Carrots (p. 186) Tomato Slices on Romaine, with French Dressing (p. 223) Milk or Other Beverage
Wednesday	Orange Juice Fried Cornmeal Mush (p. 256) Maple-Flavored Syrup (p. 253) Milk	Peanut Butter and Orange Sandwiches (p. 161) Vegetable Sticks Milk	Skillet Macaroni and Cheese (p. 228) Broccoli with Lemon Juice Rye Toast with Jam Milk or Other Beverage
Thursday	Sliced Bananas Prepared Cereal Honey Milk	Deviled Ham and Cheese on Rye Vegetable Sticks Oranges Milk	Haystacks (p. 111) Avocado Grapefruit Salad (p. 206) Snickerdoodles (p. 274) Milk or Other Beverage
Friday	Orange Juice Cooked Cereal with Raisins Milk	Haystacks (leftover) Vegetable Sticks Milk	Skillet Macaroni and Cheese (leftover) Minted Peas (p. 191) Cantaloupe Milk or Other Beverage
Saturday	Orange Juice Apple Pancakes (p. 253) Maple-Flavored Syrup (p. 253) Milk	Haystacks (leftover) Sliced Oranges Snickerdoodles (leftover) Milk	Scrambled Eggs (p. 231) Sautéed Spinach with Bacon (p. 186) Twin Mountain Muffins (p. 251) Honey Milk or Other Beverage

Shopping List June Third Week

	Product	Quantity	Variation for Your Family
Fresh Produce	Apples	4	
	Avocados	1 large or 2 small	
	Bananas	6	
	Broccoli	1 pound	
	Cabbage	1 medium head	
	Cantaloupe	1	
	Carrots	1½ pounds	
	Celery	1 stalk	
	Grapefruit	4	
	Green peppers	2	
	Lemons	2	
	Lettuce, romaine	1 head	
	Mushrooms	¼ pound	
	Onions, dry yellow	3 medium	
	Onions, green	1 bunch	
	Oranges	8	
	Spinach	2 bunches	
	Tomatoes	4 large	
Canned Goods	Deviled ham	1 can (4½ ounces)	
	Olives, sliced ripe	1 can (2¼ ounces)	
	Pimiento	1 jar (2 ounces)	
	Tomato paste	1 can (6 ounces)	
	Tomato sauce	1 can (8 ounces)	
	Tuna fish, chunk-style	1 can (6½ ounces)	
Frozen Foods	Orange juice, frozen concentrate	4 cans (6 ounces each)	
	Peas	1 package (10 ounces)	
Dairy Products	Butter or margarine	1 pound	
	Cheese, Cheddar	1 pound	
	Cheese, cream	1 package (3 ounces)	
	Cheese, Swiss	½ pound	
	Eggs	1½ dozen	
	Milk, low-fat	3½ gallons	
	Sour cream	1 carton (8 ounces)	
Bread and Cereal Products	Bread, French	1 loaf	
	Bread, rye	1 loaf	
	Bread, whole grain	1 loaf (1 pound)	
	Buns, hamburger	8	
	Macaroni, uncooked	7 ounces (1¾ cups)	
Meat, Poultry, and Fish	Bacon	1 package (12 ounces)	
	Beef, ground	1 pound	
	Chicken breast halves	4	
	Fish fillets	1 pound (haddock, cod, or halibut)	
Miscellaneous	Corn chips	1 bag (11½ ounces)	
	Olives, stuffed	1 small jar	

(Check staple supplies for basil, brown sugar, chili powder, cinnamon, Dijon mustard, dried parsley, dry mustard, evaporated milk, French dressing, garlic, garlic salt, ground cumin, ground ginger, ground nutmeg, honey, jam, maple-flavored syrup, mayonnaise, mint leaves (dried or fresh), oregano, Parmesan cheese, peanut butter, peanuts, pickles, raisins, rice, rosemary, rum or almond extract, soy sauce, Tabasco sauce, vanilla, walnuts, and yellow cornmeal.)

	Breakfast	Lunch	Dinner
Sunday	Cantaloupe Prepared Cereal Cinnamon Toast (p. 252) Milk	Spinach Salad with Mandarin Oranges (p. 219) Cheese Muffins (p. 251) Milk	Vegetables in Puff Pancake (p. 201) Pan-Fried Sausage Links (p. 115) Banana Bavarian Pudding (p. 280) Apple Oatmeal Cookies (p. 272) Milk or Other Beverage
Monday	Sliced Oranges Prepared Cereal Toasted Cheese Muffins (leftover), with Jam Milk	Egg Salad Sandwiches (p. 168) Vegetable Sticks Apple Oatmeal Cookies (leftover) Milk	Barbecued Hamburgers (p. 169) Cabbage Slaw (p. 214) Chocolate Pudding (p. 279) Milk or Other Beverage
Tuesday	Orange Juice Whole Grain Toast with Peanut Butter and Jam Milk	Barbecued Hamburgers (leftover) Vegetable Sticks Banana Shakes (p. 172)	Creamed Asparagus on Toast with Shredded Cheese (p. 184) Butter-Braised Cabbage (p. 197) Milk or Other Beverage
Wednesday	Cantaloupe Wedges Toast with Jam Milk	Peanut Butter and Orange Slice Sandwiches (p. 161) Apple Oatmeal Cookies (leftover) Milk	Barbecued Hamburgers (leftover) Scalloped Spring Cabbage (p. 197) Milk or Other Beverage
Thursday	Orange Juice Prepared Cereal Honey Milk	Bacon, Lettuce, and Tomato Sandwiches Apple Halves Chocolate Milk (p. 172)	Tuna Loaf (p. 135) Creamed New Potatoes and Peas (p. 178) Cantaloupe Milk or Other Beverage
Friday	Applesauce Broiled Cheese Sandwiches (p. 163) Milk	Luncheon Meat and Cheese Sandwiches Pickles Vegetable Sticks Milk	Corned Beef Hash (p. 106) Tomato Slices Milk or Other Beverage
Saturday	Orange Juice Pancakes (p. 253) Maple-Flavored Syrup (p. 253) Milk	Cheesy Egg Cups (p. 232) Stewed Tomatoes (p. 188) Toast with Jam Milk	Tuna Loaf (leftover) Tomato Sauce (canned) Carrot Raisin Slaw (p. 216) Bread and Butter Sliced Bananas, with Sour Cream Fruit Topping (p. 175) Milk or Other Beverage

Shopping List June Fourth Week

	Product	Quantity	Variation for Your Family
Fresh Produce	Apples	5	
	Asparagus	1½ pounds	
	Avocados	1 medium	
	Bananas	8	
	Cabbage	1 head	
	Cantaloupe	3	
	Carrots	1 pound	
	Cucumbers	1 small	
	Lemons	1	
	Mushrooms	1¼ pounds	
	Onions, dry yellow	2	
	Onions, green	1 bunch	
	Oranges	7	
	Potatoes	3 pounds, including 1½ pounds new potatoes, if available and reasonable	
	Spinach	1 bunch	
	Tomatoes	8, including ½ pound cherry tomatoes, if available and reasonable	
	Zucchini	1 medium	
Canned Goods	Applesauce	1 can (1 pound)	
	Corned beef	1 can (12 ounces)	
	Mandarin oranges	1 can (11 ounces)	
	Tomato sauce	1 can (8 ounces)	
	Tuna fish, chunk-style	2 cans (6½ ounces each)	
Frozen Foods	Orange juice, frozen concentrate	4 cans (6 ounces each)	
	Peas	1 package (10 ounces)	
Dairy Products	Butter or margarine	1 pound	
	Cheese, Cheddar	2 pounds	
	Cheese, Gouda, Gruyere or Monterey Jack	½ pound	
	Eggs	1½ dozen	
	Half-and-half	1 pint	
	Milk, low-fat	3½ gallons	
	Sour cream	1 carton (8 ounces)	
	Whipping cream	½ pint	
Bread and Cereal Products	Bread, whole grain	2 loaves (1½ pounds each)	
	Buns, hamburger	8	
Meat, Poultry, and Fish	Bacon	½ pound	
	Beef, ground	1½ pounds	
	Pastrami	2 packages (2¼ ounces each)	
	Pork sausage links	½ pound	

(Check staple supplies for basil, bouillon cubes, brown sugar, catsup, cinnamon, cornstarch, dill weed, dried parsley, dry bread crumbs, dry mustard, evaporated milk, ground nutmeg, honey, jam, maple-flavored syrup, mayonnaise, oil, peanut butter, prepared cereal, prepared mustard, raisins, rolled oats, soft bread crumbs, summer savory or savory, sweet pickles or relish, Tabasco sauce, thyme, unflavored gelatin, unsweetened chocolate, unsweetened cocoa, vanilla, vinegar, and walnuts.)

	Breakfast	Lunch	Dinner
Sunday	Orange Juice Streusel Coffee Cake (p. 266) Milk	White Gazpacho (p. 153) Parmesan Toast made with French Bread (p. 252) Milk	Jellied Salmon Loaf (p. 141) Broccoli with Buttered Crumbs (p. 192) Cabbage Slaw (p. 214) Frozen Wheat Bread Rolls (p. 246) Peach Cobbler (p. 288) Milk or Other Beverage
Monday	Sliced Fresh Peaches Oatmeal with Butter and Brown Sugar Milk	Pimiento Cheese Spread on (leftover) Rolls (p. 163) Vegetable Soup (canned) Coconut Date Cookies (p. 276) Milk	Zucchini Corn Chowder (p. 156) Tomato, Cucumber, and Cottage Cheese Salad Peach Cobbler (leftover) Milk or Other Beverage
Tuesday	Orange Juice Apple Pancakes (p. 253) Maple-Flavored Syrup (p. 253) Milk	Zucchini Corn Chowder (leftover) Broiled Cheese on Toast Milk	Jellied Salmon Loaf (leftover) Dilly Beans (p. 183) Cornmeal Muffins (p. 250) Applesauce (p. 176) Milk or Other Beverage
Wednesday	Orange Juice Prepared Cereal with Honey Milk	Peanut Butter and Bacon Sandwiches (p. 161) Carrot and Celery Sticks Sliced Fresh Peaches Milk	Chicken Oriental Salad (p. 214) Parsleyed Carrots (p. 186) Coconut Date Cookies (leftover) Milk or Other Beverage
Thursday	Orange Juice Scrambled Eggs with Bacon (p. 231) Whole Wheat Toast Milk	Cream Cheese and Stuffed Olive Sandwiches (p. 163) Carrot Sticks Applesauce (leftover) Milk	Chicken Oriental Salad (leftover) Sliced Tomatoes Whole Wheat Bread with Butter Milk or Beverage
Friday	Orange Juice Cottage Cheese Cinnamon Toast (p. 252) Milk	Tuna Apple Sandwiches (p. 217) Pickles and Vegetable Sticks Coconut Date Cookies (leftover) Milk	Barbecued Frankfurters (p. 120) Steamed Rice (p. 257) Stir-Fried Vegetables (p. 199) Coconut Date Cookies (leftover) Milk or Other Beverage
Saturday	Orange Juice Swiss Oatmeal (p. 256) Milk	Fried Egg Sandwiches (p. 167) with Frankfurter Slices Celery Sticks Fresh Peach Shake (p. 172)	Baked Potatoes with Mushroom Topping (p. 180) Simple Carrot Slaw (p. 215) Coconut Date Cookies (leftover) Milk or Other Beverage

Shopping List July First Week

	Product	Quantity	Variation for Your Family
Fresh Produce	Apples	8	
	Beans, green	1 pound	
	Broccoli	1 pound	
	Cabbage, green	1 large head	
	Carrots	2 pounds	
	Celery	1 stalk	
	Corn	3 ears	
	Cucumbers	2	
	Green peppers	2 medium	
	Lemons	2	
	Lettuce, leaf	1 head	
	Mushrooms	¹/₂ pound	
	Onions, dry yellow	2	
	Onions, green	1 bunch	
	Oranges	1	
	Parsley	1 bunch	
	Peaches	4 pounds	
	Potatoes, baking	4 medium large	
	Tomatoes	8 large	
	Zucchini	1 pound	
Canned Goods	Pimientos	1 jar or can (2 ounces)	
	Salmon, pink or red	1 can (15 ounces)	
	Soup, vegetable	2 cans (10¹/₂ ounces each)	
	Tuna fish, chunk-style	1 can (6¹/₂ ounces)	
Frozen Foods	Bread dough, frozen whole wheat	1 loaf	
	Orange juice, frozen concentrate	4 cans (6 ounces each)	
Dairy Products	Butter or margarine	1 pound	
	Cheese, Cheddar	1 pound	
	Cheese, cottage	1 carton (1 pound)	
	Cheese, cream	1 package (8 ounces)	
	Eggs	2 dozen	
	Milk, low-fat	3¹/₂ gallons	
	Sour cream	1 carton (8 ounces)	
	Yogurt, plain	1 carton (8 ounces)	
Bread and Cereal Products	Bread, French	1 loaf	
	Bread, whole wheat	1 loaf (1¹/₂ pounds)	
Meat, Poultry, and Fish	Bacon	1 pound	
	Chicken breast halves	2 or 2 cans chicken (5 ounces each)	
	Frankfurters	1 pound	
Miscellaneous	Barbecue sauce	1 bottle (12 ounces) or homemade	
	Coconut, flaked	1 package (6 ounces)	
	Dates, pitted	8 ounces	
	Olives, stuffed	1 medium jar	
	Ramen oriental noodles, chicken flavor	1 package (3 ounces)	

(Check staple supplies for almonds, basil, brown sugar, catsup, chicken bouillon cubes, cinnamon, coconut, dill weed, dry bread crumbs, dry mustard, evaporated milk, garlic, honey, maple-flavored syrup, mayonnaise, monosodium glutamate, nuts, oil, paprika, Parmesan cheese, peanut butter, prepared cereal, rice, rolled oats, savory, sesame seeds, shortening, tarragon, unflavored gelatin, white vinegar, and yellow cornmeal.)

	Breakfast	Lunch	Dinner
Sunday	Cantaloupe Cheesy Egg Cups (p. 232) Toast with Jam Milk	Orange and Cottage Cheese Salad Celery and Carrot Sticks Apple Peanut Butter Cookies (p. 274) Milk	Oven-Fried Chicken with Parmesan (p. 121), double the recipe Potato Salad (p. 211) Sautéed Brussels Sprouts (p. 194) Lemon Torte (p. 284) Milk or Other Beverage
Monday	Orange Juice Prepared Cereal with Raisins Milk	Peanut Butter and Fresh Plum Sandwiches (p. 161) Vegetable Sticks Milk	Pork 'N' Cabbage (p. 119) Sliced Tomatoes Corn on the Cob Lemon Torte (leftover) Milk or Other Beverage
Tuesday	Orange Juice French Toast (p. 256) Maple-Flavored Syrup (p. 253) Milk	Pork 'N' Cabbage (leftover) in Pocket Bread Fresh Plums Milk	Oven-Fried Chicken with Parmesan (leftover) Potato Salad (leftover) Parsleyed Carrots and Zucchini (p. 186) Apple Peanut Butter Cookies (leftover) Milk or Other Beverage
Wednesday	Orange Juice Prepared Cereal Toast with Honey Milk	Olive Nut Sandwiches (p. 163) Vegetable Sticks Apple Peanut Butter Cookies (leftover) Milk	Salmon Fondue (p. 143) Raw Vegetable Salad with Catalina Dressing (p. 218) Chilled Melon with Lime Wedges Milk or Other Beverage
Thursday	Swiss Oatmeal with Chopped Fresh Plums Added (p. 256) Toast Milk	Broiled Cheese Sandwiches (p. 163) Sliced Tomatoes Raw Vegetable Salad (leftover) Milk	Salmon Fondue (leftover) Buttered Asparagus Sliced Orange Salad, with French Dressing (p. 223) Milk or Other Beverage
Friday	Orange Juice Prepared Cereal with Cinnamon and Sugar Milk	Tuna Salad Sandwiches (p. 217) Carrot Raisin Slaw (p. 216) Fresh Plums Milk	Pork Sausage Patties Baked Stuffed Zucchini (p. 189) Apple Peanut Butter Cookies (leftover) Milk or Other Beverage
Saturday	Orange Juice Cottage Cheese Pancakes (p. 255) Maple-Flavored Syrup (p. 253) Milk	Canned Corned Beef Stir-Fried Vegetables (p. 199) French Bread Milk	Bacon, Lettuce, and Tomato Sandwiches Chocolate Banana Shakes (p. 172)

	Product	Quantity	Variation for Your Family
Fresh Produce	Apples	2	
	Asparagus	1 pound	
	Bananas	2	
	Brussels sprouts	³/₄ pound	
	Cabbage	1 head (2 pounds)	
	Cantaloupe (or other melon)	2	
	Carrots	1¹/₂ pounds	
	Celery	1 stalk	
	Corn	4 ears	
	Green peppers	1	
	Lemons	2	
	Lettuce, iceberg	1 head	
	Limes	1	
	Mushrooms	¹/₄ pound	
	Onions, dry yellow	1 large	
	Oranges	9 or 10 (3 pounds)	
	Plums	3 pounds	
	Potatoes	6 medium	
	Tomatoes	8 large	
	Zucchini	7 medium	
Canned Goods	Corned beef	1 can (12 ounces)	
	Olives, sliced	1 can (4¹/₄ ounces)	
	Pork luncheon meat	1 can (12 ounces)	
	Salmon, red or pink	1 can (16 ounces)	
	Tuna fish, chunk-style	1 can (6¹/₂ ounces)	
Frozen Foods	Orange juice, frozen concentrate	4 cans (6 ounces each)	
Dairy Products	Butter or margarine	1 pound plus 1 stick butter	
	Cheese, Cheddar	1 pound	
	Cheese, cottage	1 carton (16 ounces)	
	Eggs	2 dozen	
	Milk, low-fat	3¹/₂ gallons	
	Whipping cream	1 pint	
Bread and Cereal	Bread, French	1 loaf	
	Bread, pocket	2 round loaves (freeze remaining loaves)	
Products	Bread, whole grain	2 loaves (1¹/₂ pounds); 1 loaf (1 pound)	
Meat, Poultry, and Fish	Bacon	¹/₂ pound	
	Chickens, broiler-fryer	2 (3 pounds each)	
	Pork sausage, bulk	1 pound	
Miscellaneous	Paper cupcake liners	1 package	

(Check staple supplies for brown sugar, cinnamon, cream of tartar, Dijon mustard, French dressing, honey, jam, maple flavoring, mayonnaise, nuts, oil, paprika, peanut butter, pecans, peppermint extract, pickles, prepared cereal, prepared mustard, raisins, rolled oats, shortening, soy sauce, unsweetened chocolate, and vinegar.)

	Breakfast	Lunch	Dinner

Sunday	Orange Juice
	Mushroom Omelet (p. 234)
	Toast
	Milk
		Tuna Bunwiches (p. 166)
		Raw Vegetable Sticks
		Chocolate Milk (p. 172)
			Fish Zucchini Bake (p. 136)
			Broiled Tomatoes with
			  Crumbs (p. 188)
			Grape Pecan Salad (p. 207)
			Thirty-Minute Cocoa Cake
			  (p. 264)
			Milk or Other Beverage

Monday	Orange Juice
	Toast with Peanut Butter
	  and Honey
	Milk
		Pastrami and Zucchini
		  Sandwiches
		Plums
		Milk
			Greek Cabbage Casserole
			  (p. 106)
			Sliced Tomatoes
			Thirty-Minute Cocoa Cake
			  (leftover)
			Milk or Other Beverage

Tuesday	Orange Juice
	Prepared Cereal
	Whole Wheat Toast
	Milk
		Ground Nut and Raisin
		  Sandwiches (p. 162)
		Raw Zucchini Sticks
		Milk
			Tuna Bunwiches (leftover)
			Stir-Fried Brussels Sprouts
			  (p. 195)
			Pineapple Shredded Cheese
			  Salad (p. 210)
			Milk or Other Beverage

Wednesday	Orange Juice
	Prepared Cereal with
	  Coconut
	Milk
		Chicken Salad Sandwiches
		  (p. 217)
		Vegetable Sticks
		Milk
			Greek Cabbage Casserole
			  (leftover)
			Basil Carrots (p. 186)
			Sour Cream Fruit Salad
			  (p. 209)
			Milk or Other Beverage

Thursday	Orange Juice
	French Toast with
	  Cinnamon and Sugar
	Milk
		Cream Cheese, Stuffed
		  Olive, and Raw
		  Vegetable Sandwiches
		  (p. 163)
		Sour Cream Fruit Salad
		  (leftover)
		Milk
			Tomato Cottage Cheese
			  Salad
			Cornmeal Muffins (p. 250)
			Thirty-Minute Cocoa Cake
			  (leftover)
			Milk or Other Beverage

Friday	Orange Juice
	Cottage Cheese
	Toasted Cornmeal Muffins
	  (leftover)
	Milk
		Peanut Butter,
		  Mayonnaise, and Lettuce
		  Sandwiches (p. 161)
		Vegetable Sticks
		Applesauce (p. 176)
		  (double recipe)
		Milk
			Pork Pineapple Bake (p. 119)
			Simple Carrot Slaw (p. 215)
			Thirty-Minute Cocoa Cake
			  (leftover)
			Milk or Other Beverage

Saturday	Stewed Fresh Plums
	  (p. 177)
	Prepared Cereal
	Toast with Jam
	Milk
		Tomato Juice
		Apple Puff Pancakes
		  (p.254)
		Cheese Sticks
		Milk
			Fried Egg and Corned Beef
			  Sandwiches (p. 167)
			Sliced Tomatoes
			Applesauce (leftover)
			Chocolate Milk or Other
			  Beverage

Shopping List July Third Week

	Product	Quantity	Variation for Your Family
Fresh Produce	Apples, tart	10	
	Brussels sprouts	³/₄ pound	
	Cabbage	1 large head	
	Carrots	2 pounds	
	Celery	1 stalk	
	Grapes, green seedless	1 pound	
	Green peppers	1	
	Lemons	1	
	Lettuce, iceberg	1 small head	
	Mushrooms	¹/₂ pound	
	Onions, dry yellow	2	
	Plums	2¹/₂ pounds	
	Tomatoes	10 large	
	Zucchini	1 pound	
Canned Goods	Chicken, chunk-style	1 can (5 ounces)	
	Mandarin oranges	1 can (11 ounces)	
	Pineapple slices	1 can (8 ounces)	
	Pineapple tidbits or chunks	1 can (1 pound 4 ounces)	
	Pork luncheon meat	1 can (12 ounces)	
	Tomato juice	1 can (24 ounces)	
	Tomato sauce	1 can (8 ounces)	
	Tuna fish, chunk-style	1 can (6¹/₂ ounces)	
Frozen Foods	Orange juice, frozen concentrate	4 cans (6 ounces each)	
Dairy Products	Butter or margarine	1¹/₂ pounds	
	Cheese, Cheddar	1¹/₄ pounds	
	Cheese, cottage	1 carton (16 ounces)	
	Cheese, cream	1 package (3 ounces) *and* 1 package (8 ounces)	
	Eggs	2 dozen	
	Milk, low-fat	3¹/₂ gallons	
	Sour cream	1 carton (8 ounces)	
Bread and Cereal Products	Bread, French	1 loaf	
	Bread, whole wheat	2 loaves (1¹/₂ pounds each)	
	Buns, hamburger	8	
Meat, Poultry, and Fish	Beef, ground	³/₄ pound	
	Corned beef, smoked, pressed	2 packages (2¹/₄ ounces each)	
	Fish fillets (fresh or frozen)	1 pound (haddock, cod, perch, or sole)	
	Pastrami	2 packages (2¹/₄ ounces each)	
Miscellaneous	Marshmallows	1 package (12 ounces)	
	Olives, stuffed	1 small bottle	

(Check staple supplies for basil, bouillon cubes, cinnamon, coconut, confectioners' sugar, dill pickles, dried dill weed, dried mixed herbs, dried parsley, dry bread crumbs, fennel seed, ground cloves, honey, jam, mayonnaise or salad dressing, mint leaves (dried), nuts, oil, Parmesan cheese, peanut butter, pecans, prepared cereal, raisins, rice, shortening, soy sauce, sweet pickles or relish, unsweetened cocoa, vanilla, and yellow cornmeal.)

	Breakfast	Lunch	Dinner
Sunday	Orange Juice Pick-Up (p. 171) Whole Wheat Toast with Peanut Butter and Honey Milk	Swiss Fondue (p. 239) French Bread Tomato Wedges Milk	Baked Lamb Chop Dinner (p. 114) Buttered Broccoli (p. 192) Fresh Peach Shortcake (p. 249) Milk or Other Beverage
Monday	Chilled Melon with Lime Wedges Prepared Cereal Milk	Cream Cheese and Raw Vegetable Sandwiches (p. 163) Fresh Plums Milk	Tomato Soup (canned) Fresh Peach and Cottage Cheese Salad (p. 205) Pigs in Blankets (p. 116) Milk or Other Beverage
Tuesday	Orange Juice Poached Eggs on Toast (p. 235) Milk	Carrot, Raisin, and Peanut Slaw (p. 216) Whole Wheat Bread Milk	Lamb Chops and Potatoes (leftover) Orange-Glazed Brussels Sprouts (p. 194) Fresh Peach Shortcake (leftover) Milk or Other Beverage
Wednesday	Orange Juice Prepared Cereal Toast with Jam Milk	Peanut Butter and Apple Sandwiches (p. 161) Vegetable Sticks Milk	Cottage Cheese and Melon Salad with Poppy Seed Dressing (p. 224) Buttered Peas (p. 191) Cheese Muffins (p. 251) Milk or Other Beverage
Thursday	Orange Juice Prepared Cereal Toasted Cheese Muffins (leftover) Milk	Pork Luncheon Meat, Cheese, and Pickle Sandwiches Carrot Sticks Fresh Plums Milk	Broiled Shrimp Buns (p. 165) Stuffed Celery (p. 182) Sliced Peaches Milk or Other Beverage
Friday	Orange Juice French Toast with Softened Cream Cheese and Jam Milk	Tuna Apple Sandwiches (p. 217) Vegetable Sticks Milk	Luncheon Meat Salad (p. 221) Baking Powder Biscuits (p. 249), with Jam Baked Custard (p. 286) Milk or Other Beverage
Saturday	Orange Juice Waffles (p. 255) Maple-Flavored Syrup (p. 253) Milk	Luncheon Meat Salad (leftover) Toasted Biscuits (leftover) Sliced Peaches Milk	Fresh Mushroom Soup (p. 147) with Croutons Broccoli Melt (p. 169) Milk or Other Beverage

Shopping List. July Fourth Week

	Product	Quantity	Variation for Your Family
Fresh Produce	Apples	2	
	Broccoli	1³/₄ pounds	
	Brussels sprouts	³/₄ pound	
	Cantaloupe (or other melon)	2 small or 1 large	
	Carrots	1¹/₂ pounds	
	Celery	1 stalk	
	Green peppers	1	
	Lettuce, romaine	1 head	
	Limes	1	
	Mushrooms	1¹/₄ pounds	
	Onions, dry yellow	2	
	Onions, green	1 bunch	
	Parsley	1 bunch	
	Peaches	12 (about 5 pounds)	
	Peas	1¹/₂ pounds fresh or 1 package (10 ounces) frozen	
	Plums	8	
	Potatoes	8 large or 16 small	
	Tomatoes	6 large	
Canned Goods	Chicken broth (bouillon)	4 cans (10³/₄ ounces each)	
	Dried onion rings	1 can (3 ounces)	
	Pork luncheon meat	1 can (12 ounces)	
	Shrimp, small deveined	2 cans (4¹/₂ ounces each)	
	Soup, tomato	2 cans (10³/₄ ounces each)	
	Tuna fish, chunk-style	1 can (6¹/₂ ounces)	
Frozen Foods	Orange juice, frozen concentrate	4 cans (6 ounces each)	
Dairy Products	Butter or margarine	1 pound	
	Cheese, Cheddar	1¹/₄ pounds	
	Cheese, cottage	1 carton (16 ounces)	
	Cheese, cream	1 package (8 ounces)	
	Cheese, Swiss	³/₄ pound (12 ounces)	
	Eggs	1¹/₂ dozen	
	Milk, low-fat	3¹/₂ gallons	
	Whipping cream	¹/₂ pint	
Bread and Cereal Products	Biscuits, refrigerated	1 tube (7¹/₂ ounces)	
	Bread, French	2 loaves	
	Bread, whole grain	2 loaves (1¹/₂ pounds)	
	Buns, hamburger	4	
	Croutons	1 box	
	Rolls, refrigerated crescent	1 package (8 ounces)	
Meat, Poultry, and Fish	Lamb shoulder chops	8	
	Pork sausage links	³/₄ pound (about 12 links)	

(Check staple supplies for basil, chili sauce, confectioners' sugar, cornstarch, dill pickles, dry mustard, French dressing, garlic, ground nutmeg, honey, jam, maple-flavored syrup, mayonnaise or salad dressing, oil, Parmesan cheese, peanut butter, peanuts, poppy seeds, prepared cereal, raisins, tarragon, unsweetened chocolate, unsweetened cocoa, vanilla, vinegar, and Worcestershire sauce.)

	Breakfast	Lunch	Dinner
Sunday	Stewed Fresh Plums (p. 177) Whole Wheat Pancakes (p. 254) Maple-Flavored Syrup (p. 253) Milk	Cottage Cheese and Pineapple Salad (p. 205) Vegetable Sticks Thin Butter Toast (p. 252) Milk	Crab Salad in Avocados (p. 222) Buttered Broccoli (p. 192) Molded Citrus Salad (p. 210) Gingerbread with Lemon Sauce (p. 243) Milk or Other Beverage
Monday	Sliced Fresh Peaches Prepared Cereal Milk	Tuna Salad Sandwiches (p. 217) Vegetable Sticks Refrigerated Peanut Butter Cookies (p. 274) Milk	Broccoli Cheese Soup (p. 148) with Croutons Molded Citrus Salad (leftover) Gingerbread with Lemon Sauce (leftover) Milk or Other Beverage
Tuesday	Orange Juice Prepared Cereal Milk	Peanut Butter and Banana Sandwiches (p. 161) Celery Sticks Plums Milk	Pork Chop Skillet (p. 116) Garden Scramble (p. 201) Milk or Other Beverage
Wednesday	Orange Juice Cottage Cheese Toast with Jam Milk	Carrot Raisin Sandwiches (p. 164) Apple Halves Peanut Butter Cookies (leftover) Milk	Broccoli Cheese Soup (leftover) Raw Vegetable Salad (p. 218) Chocolate Pudding (p. 279) Milk or Other Beverage
Thursday	Sliced Fresh Peaches Prepared Cereal Milk	Pork Luncheon Meat and Cheese Sandwiches Garden Scramble (leftover) Milk	Tuna Pasta Salad (p. 227), double the recipe Ambrosia (p. 176) Refrigerated Peanut Butter Cookies (leftover) Milk or Other Beverage
Friday	Orange Juice French Toast with Syrup Pork Luncheon Meat (leftover) Milk	Deviled Ham Sandwiches Vegetable Sticks Plums Milk	Tuna Pasta Salad (leftover) Cauliflower with Parmesan Crumbs (p. 195) Baked Custard (p. 286) Milk or Other Beverage
Saturday	Orange Juice Swiss Oatmeal (p. 256) Toast with Honey Milk	Fried Egg Sandwiches (p. 167) with Tomato Slices Vegetable Sticks Milk	Lazy Susan Dinner (p. 143) Milk or Other Beverage

Shopping List August First Week

	Product	Quantity	Variation for Your Family
Fresh Produce	Apples	3	
	Avocados	4	
	Bananas	2	
	Broccoli	2 pounds	
	Carrots	1 pound	
	Cauliflower	1 head	
	Lemons	1	
	Lettuce, leaf	1 head	
	Mushrooms	¹/₂ pound	
	Onions, dry yellow	2 large	
	Onions, green	1 bunch	
	Oranges	4	
	Parsley	1 bunch	
	Peaches	8	
	Peppers, red or green	2	
	Plums	2 pounds	
	Tomatoes	6 large	
	Zucchini	2 medium	
Canned Goods	Chicken broth	1 can (10³/₄ ounces)	
	Deviled ham	1 can (4¹/₂ ounces)	
	Grapefruit sections	1 can (1 pound)	
	Mandarin oranges	2 cans (11 ounces each)	
	Pineapple slices	1 can (8 ounces)	
	Pork luncheon meat	1 can (12 ounces)	
	Tomatoes	1 can (1 pound)	
	Tuna fish, chunk-style	3 cans (6¹/₂ ounces each)	
Frozen Foods	Orange juice, frozen concentrate	4 cans (6 ounces each)	
Dairy Products	Butter or margarine	1 pound	
	Cheese, Cheddar	1¹/₂ pounds	
	Cheese, cottage	1 carton (1 pound)	
	Cheese, cream	1 package (8 ounces)	
	Eggs	1¹/₂ dozen	
	Milk, low-fat	4 gallons	
Bread and Cereal Products	Bread, French	2 loaves	
	Bread, whole wheat	1 loaf (1¹/₂ pounds)	
	Noodles, narrow	8 ounces	
	Vermicelli or spaghetti	8 ounces	
Meat, Poultry, and Fish	Crab, regular or imitation	³/₄ pound or 2 cans (7¹/₂ ounces each)	
	Pork chops, thin	4	
Miscellaneous	Cashews	4 ounces	
	Coconut	1 package (3¹/₂ ounces)	

(Check staple supplies for basil, bouillon cubes, brown sugar, catsup, cayenne pepper, celery salt, cinnamon, cornstarch, dry bread crumbs, garlic, ground ginger, ground nutmeg, honey, jam, maple-flavored syrup, mayonnaise or salad dressing, molasses, oil, Parmesan cheese, peanut butter (chunky), pickles, prepared cereal, raisins, rolled oats, sesame seeds, soy sauce, unflavored gelatin, unsweetened chocolate, vanilla, vinegar, and whole wheat flour.)

	Breakfast	Lunch	Dinner
Sunday	Orange Juice Toasted English Muffins Jam Milk	Grilled Tuna Sandwiches (p. 217) Vegetable Sticks Chocolate Milk (p. 172)	Lamb Shish Kabobs (p. 114) Rice Pilaff (p. 258) Stir-Fried Vegetables (p. 199) Peach Cobbler (p. 288) Milk or Other Beverage
Monday	Orange Juice Toast with Cottage Cheese and Jam Milk	English Muffin Halves Broiled with Cheese Sliced Peaches Milk	Cream of Tomato Soup (p. 148) Cottage Cheese with Red and/or Green Peppers Peach Cobbler (leftover) Milk or Other Beverage
Tuesday	Sliced Fresh Peaches Prepared Cereal Milk	Peanut Butter and Bacon Sandwiches (p. 161) Vegetable Sticks Fresh Plums Milk	Lamb Shish Kabobs (leftover) Rice Pilaff (leftover) Spiced Red Cabbage (p. 198) Milk or Other Beverage
Wednesday	Orange Juice Prepared Cereal Toast with Honey Milk	Corned Beef Sandwiches Mustard Pickles Vegetable Sticks Milk	Baked Potatoes with Seafood Sauce (p. 179) Caesar Salad (p. 218) Apple Crisp (p. 282) Milk or Other Beverage
Thursday	Orange Juice French Toast with Cinnamon and Sugar (p. 256) Milk	Pastrami, Cheese, and Tomato Sandwiches Vegetable Sticks Chocolate Milk	Scrambled Eggs (p. 231) with (leftover) Corned Beef Sunshine Cabbage Salad (p. 215) Toast with Jam Milk or Other Beverage
Friday	Orange Juice Toast with Peanut Butter and Honey Milk	Ground Nut and Raisin Sandwiches (p. 162) Vegetable Sticks Milk	Barbecued Chicken Thighs (p. 122) Skillet Cabbage Salad (p. 215), using red and green cabbage Apple Crisp (if any leftover) Milk or Other Beverage
Saturday	Orange Juice Puff Pancakes with Fresh Peach Slices (p. 254) Milk	Quick Chili (p. 155) Sunshine Cabbage Salad (leftover) French Bread with Cheese Fresh Plums Milk	Lazy Susan Dinner (p. 143) Milk or Other Beverage

Shopping List August Second Week

	Product	Quantity	Variation for Your Family
Fresh Produce	Apples	8	
	Cabbage, green	2 large heads	
	Cabbage, red	1 small head	
	Carrots	½ pound	
	Celery	1 stalk	
	Lemons	2	
	Lettuce, iceberg	1 head	
	Lettuce, romaine	1 head	
	Melon	1 medium	
	Mushrooms	¼ pound	
	Onions, dry yellow	4 large	
	Parsley	1 bunch	
	Peaches	3 pounds	
	Peppers, red or green	1	
	Plums	3 pounds	
	Potatoes, baking	5	
	Tomatoes	4 or 5 large	
Canned Goods	Beef bouillon, condensed	2 cans (11 ounces each)	
	Beans, kidney	1 can (16 ounces)	
	Corned beef	1 can (12 ounces)	
	Pineapple tidbits	1 can (8 ounces)	
	Tuna fish, chunk-style	1 can (6½ ounces)	
Frozen Foods	Orange juice, frozen concentrate	6 cans (6 ounces each)	
Dairy Products	Butter or margarine	1 pound	
	Cheese, blue	1 package (2 ounces)	
	Cheese, Cheddar	1 pound	
	Cheese, cottage	1 carton (16 ounces)	
	Eggs	1½ dozen	
	Milk, low-fat	3½ gallons	
Bread and Cereal Products	Bread, French	1 loaf	
	Bread, whole wheat	1 loaf (1½ pounds)	
	Croutons	1 small package, unseasoned	
	English muffins	1 package (6 count)	
Meat, Poultry, and Fish	Bacon	1 pound	
	Beef, ground	½ to 1 pound	
	Chicken thighs	8 (2½ pounds)	
	Crabmeat	1 can (7½ ounces)	
	Lamb, boneless shoulder or leg	2 to 3 pounds	
	Pastrami	2 packages (2¼ ounces each)	
Miscellaneous	Barbecue sauce	1 jar (12 or 16 ounces) or homemade	

(Check staple supplies for basil, beef bouillon cubes, brown sugar, chervil, chicken bouillon cubes, chili powder, cinnamon, dry mustard, garlic, ground ginger, honey, jam, marjoram, mayonnaise, molasses, oil, Parmesan cheese, peanut butter, pickles, prepared cereal, raisins, rice, rolled oats, soy sauce, unsweetened cocoa, vanilla, vinegar, walnuts, and Worcestershire sauce.)

	Breakfast	Lunch	Dinner
Sunday	Orange Juice Toast with Jam Milk	Tuna Bunwiches (p. 166) Spinach Apple Toss (p. 186) Milk	Kung Po Chicken (p. 125), double the recipe Steamed Rice (p. 257) Broccoli Stir-Fry (p. 191) Lemon Surprise Pudding (p. 280) Milk or Other Beverage
Monday	Orange Juice Prepared Cereal with Honey Milk	Tomato Soup (canned) Spinach Apple Toss (leftover) Whole Wheat Toast Gingersnaps (p. 269) Milk	Zucchini Egg Scramble with Cheese Sauce (p. 236) Broiled Tomato Halves (p. 188) Whole Wheat Toast Milk or Other Beverage
Tuesday	Orange Juice Swiss Oatmeal (p. 256) Milk	Tuna Bunwiches (leftover) Carrot Sticks Chocolate Milk (p. 172)	Kung Po Chicken (leftover) Fried Rice (p. 257) Green Beans with Almonds (p. 183) Sliced Oranges on Greens with Poppy Seed Dressing (p. 224) Milk or Other Beverage
Wednesday	Orange Juice Prepared Cereal Toast with Honey Milk	Luncheon Meat Sandwiches Raw Zucchini Sticks Sliced Peaches Milk	Frankfurters with Hot Potato Salad (p. 211) Sautéed Brussels Sprouts (p. 194) Milk or Other Beverage
Thursday	Orange Juice Toast with Cream Cheese and Jam Milk	Frankfurters and Potato Salad (leftover) Sliced Tomatoes Gingersnaps (leftover) Milk	Super Salmon on Noodles (p. 142), double the recipe Buttered Peas Fresh Melon with Lime Wedges Milk or Other Beverage
Friday	Orange Juice Prepared Cereal Milk	Peanut Butter and Raisin Sandwiches (p. 161) Carrot Sticks Gingersnaps (leftover) Milk	Super Salmon on Toast (leftover) Carrot Peanut Slaw (p. 216), double the recipe Banana Cream Pudding (p. 279) Milk or Other Beverage
Saturday	Orange Juice French Toast (p. 256) Maple-Flavored Syrup (p. 253) Milk	Vegetable Beef Soup (canned) Carrot Peanut Slaw (leftover) Whole Wheat Toast Plums Milk	Hamburgers (p. 129) with Cheese, Lettuce, and Tomatoes Chocolate Banana Shakes (p. 172)

Shopping List August Third Week

	Product	Quantity	Variation for Your Family
Fresh Produce	Apples, tart	1	
	Bananas	5	
	Beans, green	1 pound	
	Broccoli	1 pound	
	Brussels sprouts	3/4 pound	
	Carrots	1 pound	
	Celery	1 stalk	
	Gingerroot	1 piece	
	Green peppers	1	
	Lemons	4	
	Lettuce, red	1 head	
	Limes	2	
	Melon	1 medium or small	
	Onions, dry yellow	3 large	
	Onions, green	1 bunch	
	Oranges	4	
	Peaches	4	
	Peas, in the pod	1 1/2 pounds or 1 package (10 ounces) frozen	
	Plums	1 pound	
	Potatoes, baking	6 medium to large	
	Spinach	2 bunches or 1 bag (10 ounces)	
	Tomatoes	6 large	
	Zucchini	2 medium	
Canned Goods	Pineapple juice	1 can (6 ounces)	
	Salmon, red or pink	1 can (1 pound)	
	Soup, tomato	2 cans (10 3/4 ounces each) or homemade	
	Soup, vegetable beef	1 can (10 1/2 ounces)	
	Tuna fish, chunk-style	1 can (6 1/2 ounces)	
	Water chestnuts	1 can (4 ounces)	
Frozen Foods	Orange juice, frozen concentrate	5 cans (6 ounces each)	
Dairy Products	Butter or margarine	1 pound	
	Cheese, Cheddar	1 pound	
	Cheese, cream	1 package (8 ounces)	
	Eggs	2 dozen	
	Milk, low-fat	3 1/2 gallons	
Bread and Cereal Products	Bread, French	1 loaf	
	Bread, whole wheat	2 loaves (1 1/2 pounds each)	
	Buns, hamburger	1 dozen	
	Noodles	8 ounces	
Meat, Poultry, and Fish	Bacon	1 pound	
	Beef, ground	1 pound	
	Beef, smoked, pressed, sliced	2 packages (2 1/4 ounces each)	
	Chicken breast halves	4	
	Frankfurters, dinner-size	1 pound	
Miscellaneous	Olives, stuffed	1 tall thin jar	

(Check staple supplies for almonds, basil, butter, cinnamon, coriander, cornstarch, dried red chili peppers, dry mustard, French dressing, garlic, ground cloves, ground ginger, honey, jam, maple-flavored syrup, mayonnaise, molasses, noodles, oil, Parmesan cheese, peanuts, prepared cereal, raisins, rice, rolled oats, soy sauce, sweet pickles or relish, Tabasco sauce, unsweetened cocoa, vanilla, vinegar, and walnuts.)

	Breakfast	Lunch	Dinner
Sunday	Orange Juice Waffles (p. 255) Maple-Flavored Syrup (p. 253) Milk	Bacon, Lettuce, and Tomato Sandwiches Milk	Salmon Dinner Salad (p. 216), make ahead Frozen Wheat Bread Rolls (p. 246) Molded Custard Ring with Fresh Peaches (p. 286) Milk or Other Beverage
Monday	Orange Juice Cream of Wheat with Butter and Brown Sugar Milk	Salmon Salad (leftover) in Pocket Bread Tomato Wedges Ginger Cakes (p. 266) Milk	Quick and Easy Cassoulet (p. 128) Parsleyed Carrots (p. 186) Molded Custard Ring (leftover) with Fresh Peaches Milk or Other Beverage
Tuesday	Orange Juice Toast with Cottage Cheese and Jam Milk	Deviled Pork Sandwiches (p. 165) Stuffed Celery (p. 182) Nectarines Milk	Corned Beef Potato Salad (p. 210) Sliced Tomatoes Cornmeal Muffins with Honey (p. 250) Milk or Other Beverage
Wednesday	Orange Juice Prepared Cereal with Raisins Milk	Deviled Pork (leftover) Sandwiches on Rye Bread Vegetable Sticks Nectarines Milk	Quick and Easy Cassoulet (leftover) Cabbage Pineapple Slaw (p. 214) Ginger Cakes (leftover) Milk or Other Beverage
Thursday	Sliced Peaches Prepared Cereal Toast Milk	Corned Beef Potato Salad (leftover) Tomato Wedges Toasted Corn Muffins (leftover) with Honey Milk	Chicken Oriental Salad (p. 214) Orange-Glazed Brussels Sprouts (p. 194) Peach Crisp (p. 282) Milk or Other Beverage
Friday	Orange Juice Scrambled Eggs (p. 231) with (leftover) Corned Beef Milk	Deviled Pork (leftover) Sandwiches Vegetable Sticks Banana Halves Milk	Mexicali Salad (p. 218) Green Beans and Onions (p. 183) Melon Wedges Milk or Other Beverage
Saturday	Orange Juice French Toast (p. 256) with Jam Milk	Pineapple and Cottage Cheese Salad Raw Vegetables Toast Milk	Grilled Tuna Sandwiches (p. 217) Cabbage Tomato Slaw (p. 214) Milk or Other Beverage

Shopping List August Fourth Week

	Product	Quantity	Variation for Your Family
Fresh Produce	Bananas	2	
	Beans, green	1 pound	
	Broccoli	1 pound	
	Brussels sprouts	³/₄ pound	
	Cabbage	1 large head	
	Carrots	1 pound	
	Cauliflower	1 small head	
	Celery	1 stalk	
	Lemons	1	
	Lettuce, iceberg	2 medium heads	
	Melon	1	
	Nectarines	1 pound	
	Onions, dry yellow	3	
	Onions, green	2 bunches	
	Peaches	4 pounds	
	Potatoes	1¹/₂ pounds	
	Tomatoes	12 large	
Canned Goods	Beans, great northern white	2 cans (15 ounces each)	
	Chili beans without meat	1 can (16 ounces)	
	Corned beef	1 can (12 ounces)	
	Pineapple, crushed	1 can (8 ounces)	
	Pineapple slices	1 can (8 ounces)	
	Pork luncheon meat	1 can (12 ounces)	
	Salmon, red or pink	1 can (1 pound)	
	Tomato sauce	1 can (8 ounces)	
	Tuna fish, chunk-style	1 can (6¹/₂ ounces)	
Frozen Foods	Bread dough, frozen whole wheat	1 loaf	
	Orange juice, frozen concentrate	5 cans (6 ounces each)	
	Peas	1 package (10 ounces)	
Dairy Products	Butter or margarine	1 pound	
	Cheese, Cheddar	1 pound	
	Cheese, cottage	1 carton (24 ounces)	
	Eggs	1¹/₂ dozen	
	Milk, low-fat	3¹/₂ gallons	
	Sour cream	1 carton (8 ounces)	
	Whipping cream	¹/₂ pint	
	Yogurt, plain	1 carton (8 ounces)	
Bread and Cereal Products	Bread, French	1 loaf	
	Bread, pocket	2 round flat loaves (freeze any remaining)	
	Bread, rye	1 loaf	
	Bread, whole wheat	1 loaf (1 pound)	
Meat, Poultry, and Fish	Bacon	¹/₂ pound	
	Chicken breast halves	4	
	Sausage, fully cooked, smoked	¹/₂ pound	
Miscellaneous	Corn chips	1 package (11¹/₂ ounces)	
	Horseradish, fresh	1 small jar	
	Ramen oriental noodles, chicken flavor	1 package (3 ounces)	

(Check staple supplies for almond extract, almonds, brown sugar, catsup, celery salt, cinnamon, confectioners' sugar, cream of wheat, curry powder, Dijon mustard, dill pickles, dried parsley, garlic, garlic powder, garlic salt, ground cloves, ground ginger, honey, horseradish, jam, maple-flavored syrup, mayonnaise or salad dressing, molasses, monosodium glutamate, oil, onion salt, peanut butter, peanuts, pickle relish, prepared cereal, raisins, rolled oats, sesame seeds, shortening, thyme, unflavored gelatin, vanilla, vinegar, walnuts, whole cloves, and yellow cornmeal.)

Menus September First Week

	Breakfast	Lunch	Dinner
Sunday	Orange Juice Waffles (p. 255) Maple-Flavored Syrup (p. 253) Bacon Milk	Chicken Pineapple Salad (p. 213) Stuffed Celery (p. 182) Three-Grain Peanut Butter Bread (p. 246) Milk	Lamb Stew (p. 158) Easy French Bread (p. 244) Ice Cream with Fresh Peaches Milk or Other Beverage
Monday	Orange Juice Prepared Cereal with Coconut Milk	Cheese Sandwiches on (leftover) Three-Grain Bread Raw Vegetables Fresh Peaches Milk	Chicken Pineapple Salad (leftover) Zucchini Italiano (p. 189) Ice Cream Milk or Other Beverage
Tuesday	Orange Juice Toast with Peanut Butter and Jam Milk	Egg Salad Sandwiches on Rye Bread (p. 168) Vegetable Sticks Ice Cream with Peaches Milk	Lamb Pie (p. 158), using leftover stew Cabbage Raisin Slaw (p. 215) Three-Grain Peanut Butter Bread (leftover) Milk or Other Beverage
Wednesday	Orange Juice Cooked Oatmeal with Raisins Toast Milk	Tuna Salad Sandwiches (p. 217) Vegetable Sticks Grapes Chocolate Milk (p. 172)	Pork 'N' Cabbage (p. 119) Parsleyed Carrots (p. 186) Cornmeal Muffins (p. 250) Autumn Pears (p. 288) Milk or Other Beverage
Thursday	Sliced Bananas Prepared Cereal Toasted Cornmeal Muffins (leftover) Milk	Pork 'N' Cabbage (if any leftover) Peanut Butter and Bacon Sandwiches (p. 161) Oranges Milk	Fish Sticks Oven-Fried Potatoes (p. 181) Buttered Broccoli (p. 192) Cornmeal Muffins (leftover) Honey Butter (p. 253) Milk or Other Beverage
Friday	Sliced Fresh Peaches Pigs in Blankets (p. 116) Milk	Corned Beef and Cheese Sandwiches on Rye Vegetable Sticks Ice Cream Milk	Barbecued Chicken Thighs (p. 122) Steamed Brown Rice (p. 257) Green Beans and Onions (p. 183) Ambrosia (p. 176) Milk or Other Beverage
Saturday	Orange Juice Prepared Cereal Toast Milk	Cream of Tomato Soup (p. 148) Pigs in Blankets (leftover) Stuffed Celery (p. 182) Ambrosia (leftover) Milk	Barbecued Chicken Thighs (leftover) Fried (leftover) Brown Rice Broccoli with Orange Sauce (p. 192) Milk or Other Beverage

Shopping List September First Week

	Product	Quantity	Variation for Your Family
Fresh Produce	Bananas	2	
	Brussels sprouts	3/4 pound	
	Beans, green	1 pound	
	Cabbage	1 large head	
	Carrots	2 pounds	
	Celery	1 stalk	
	Grapes, seedless	1/2 pound	
	Lemons	1	
	Lettuce, leaf	1 head	
	Onions, dry yellow	6 medium	
	Onions, green	1 bunch	
	Oranges	4	
	Peaches	3 pounds	
	Pears	4	
	Potatoes	8	
	Tomatoes	5	
	Zucchini	1 pound (1 1/2 inches in diameter)	
Canned Goods	Beef broth (bouillon)	1 can (10 1/2 ounces)	
	Pineapple slices	1 can (8 ounces)	
	Pork luncheon meat	1 can (12 ounces)	
	Tuna fish, chunk-style	1 can (6 1/2 ounces)	
Frozen Foods	Ice cream, vanilla	1/2 gallon	
	Orange juice, frozen concentrate	5 cans (6 ounces each)	
Dairy Products	Butter or margarine	1 pound	
	Cheese, Cheddar or Monterey Jack	1/2 pound	
	Eggs	1 1/2 dozen	
	Milk, low-fat	4 gallons	
Bread and Cereal Products	Biscuits, refrigerated	1 can (7.5 ounces)	
	Bread, French	1 loaf	
	Bread, rye	1 loaf	
	Bread, whole wheat	1 loaf (1 pound)	
	Rolls, refrigerated crescent	1 can (8 ounces)	
Meat, Poultry, and Fish	Bacon	1 pound	
	Chicken breast halves	2 (freeze extra breasts for later use)	
	Chicken thighs	8	
	Fish sticks, frozen	1 pound	
	Lunch meat (corned beef, smoked, pressed, sliced)	2 packages (2 1/4 ounces each)	
	Lamb stew meat	1 1/2 pounds	
	Pork sausage links	12 (3/4 pound)	
Miscellaneous	Barbecue sauce	1 cup	
	Olives, stuffed	1 tall thin jar	

(Check staple supplies for active dry yeast, brown sugar, chicken bouillon cubes, coconut, dill pickles, garlic, honey, jam, light corn syrup, maple-flavored syrup, mayonnaise or salad dressing, nonfat dry milk, oregano, peanut butter, pecans, prepared cereal, raisins, rice, rolled oats, unsweetened cocoa, and yellow cornmeal.)

	Breakfast	Lunch	Dinner

Sunday	Orange Juice
	Scrambled Eggs with
	  Cheese (p. 231)
	Toast with Jam
	Milk
		Broiled Shrimp Buns
		  (p. 165)
		Spinach and Bacon Salad
		  (p. 219)
		Applesauce
		Milk
			Oriental Chicken (p. 124)
			Baked Sweet Potatoes (p. 199)
			Gingered Vegetables (p. 200)
			Frozen Strawberry Squares
			  (p. 290)
			Milk or Other Beverage

Monday	Orange Juice
	Prepared Cereal with
	  Honey
	Toast
		Peanut Butter Sandwiches
		Stuffed Celery (p. 182)
		Banana Halves
		Milk
		Milk
			Hamburger Scramble (p. 110)
			Frozen Strawberry Squares
			  (leftover)
			Milk or Other Beverage

Tuesday	Orange Juice
	French Toast (p. 256)
	Maple-Flavored Syrup
	  (p. 253)
	Milk
		Bacon, Lettuce, and
		  Tomato Sandwiches
		Banana Shakes (p. 172)
			Macaroni and Cheese (p. 229)
			Cabbage Stir-Fry (p. 197)
			Whole Wheat Bread
			Frozen Strawberry Squares
			  (leftover)
			Milk or Other Beverage

Wednesday	Orange Juice
	Oatmeal with Butter and
	  Brown Sugar
	Toast
	Milk
		Macaroni and Cheese
		  (leftover)
		Vegetable Sticks
		Milk
			Creamed Tuna Fish on Toast
			  (p. 136)
			Cabbage Slaw (p. 214)
			Fresh Fruit Cup (p. 175)
			Milk or Other Beverage

Thursday	Orange Juice
	Prepared Cereal with
	  Honey
	Toast
	Milk
		Pineapple and Cream
		  Cheese Sandwiches
		  (p. 163)
		Vegetable Sticks
		Milk
			Chicken Cider Stew (p. 160)
			Broccoli with Buttered
			  Crumbs (p. 192)
			Rye Bread
			Fresh Fruit Cup (leftover)
			Milk or Other Beverage

Friday	Orange Juice
	Toast with Peanut Butter
	  and Honey
	Milk
		Swiss Cheese Sandwiches
		  on Rye
		Pickles
		Fresh Peaches
		Milk
			Herb-Broiled Fish Fillets
			  (p. 137)
			Baked Hubbard Squash
			  (p. 189)
			Spinach and Tomato Salad
			  with French Dressing
			  (p. 223)
			Whole Wheat Muffins
			  (p. 251)
			Milk or Other Beverage

Saturday	Orange Juice
	Nut Waffles (p. 255)
	Milk
		Chicken Stew (leftover)
		Cabbage Slaw
		Whole Wheat Muffins
		  (leftover), Toasted
		Milk
			Cheese and Tomato Omelet
			  (p. 234)
			Saucy Brussels Sprouts
			  (p. 194)
			Toasted Muffins (leftover)
			Sliced Peaches
			Milk or Other Beverage

Shopping List September Second Week

	Product	Quantity	Variation for Your Family
Fresh Produce	Apples	2	
	Bananas	6	
	Broccoli	1 pound	
	Brussels sprouts	3/4 pound	
	Cabbage	1 head (1½ pounds)	
	Carrots	2 pounds (1-inch in diameter)	
	Celery	1 stalk	
	Gingerroot	1 piece	
	Grapefruit	2	
	Lemons	1	
	Lettuce, leaf	1 small head	
	Mushrooms	½ pound	
	Onions, dry yellow	2 medium	
	Onions, green	1 bunch	
	Parsley	1 bunch	
	Peaches	2½ pounds	
	Potatoes, sweet (or yams)	6 medium	
	Spinach	1 pound	
	Squash, hubbard	1½ pounds	
	Sugar peas	⅛ pound	
	Tomatoes	10 large (4 or 5 pounds)	
Canned Goods	Apple juice	1 can (6 ounces) or 1 cup apple cider	
	Applesauce	1 can (1 pound)	
	Pineapple, crushed	1 can (8 ounces)	
	Shrimp, small deveined	1 can (4½ ounces)	
	Tomatoes	1 can (8 ounces)	
	Tuna fish, chunk-style	1 can (6½ ounces)	
Frozen Foods	Orange juice, frozen concentrate	6 cans (6 ounces each)	
	Strawberries	1 package (10 ounces)	
Dairy Products	Butter or margarine	1 pound	
	Cheese, Cheddar	2 pounds	
	Cheese, cream	1 package (8 ounces)	
	Cheese, Swiss	½ pound	
	Eggs	2 dozen	
	Milk, low-fat	3½ gallons	
	Whipping cream	½ pint	
Bread and Cereal Products	Bread, French	1 loaf	
	Bread, rye	1 loaf	
	Bread, whole wheat	1 loaf (1 pound)	
	Buns, hamburger	4	
	Macaroni, elbow	6 ounces	
Meat, Poultry, and Fish	Bacon	1 pound	
	Beef, lean ground	½ pound	
	Chicken breasts	4 halves	
	Chicken thighs	8 (2½ pounds)	
	Fish fillets, fresh or frozen	1 pound (haddock, cod, perch, or sole)	

(Check staple supplies for basil, brown sugar, catsup, Dijon mustard, dried red chili peppers, dry bread crumbs, evaporated milk, French dressing, gherkin sweet pickles, ground ginger, honey, jam, maple-flavored syrup, mayonnaise, mixed dried herbs, oil, paprika, peanut butter, peanuts, pecans, prepared cereal, rice, rolled oats, savory, soy sauce, walnuts, white wine or other vinegar, and whole wheat flour.)

	Breakfast	Lunch	Dinner

Sunday	Orange Juice
	Puff Pancakes (p. 254) with
	  Sautéed Fresh Peaches
	Milk
		Frozen Shrimp Cocktail
		  (p. 140)
		Cabbage Slaw (p. 214)
		French Bread
		Milk
			Meat Loaf (p. 113)
			Baked Sweet Potato Chips
			  (p. 199)
			Brussels Sprouts with Cream
			  (p. 194)
			Lemon Torte (p. 284)
			Milk or Other Beverage

Monday	Orange Juice
	Prepared Cereal with
	  Honey
	Milk
		Meat Loaf (leftover)
		  Sandwiches
		Celery Sticks
		Grapes
		Milk
			Barbecued Chicken Thighs
			  (p. 122)
			Steamed Rice (p. 257)
			Buttered Broccoli (p. 192)
			Chocolate Chip Oatmeal
			  Cookies (p. 272)
			Milk or Other Beverage

Tuesday	Orange Juice
	French Toast (p. 256) with
	  Cinnamon and Sugar
	Milk
		Barbecued Chicken Thighs
		  (leftover)
		Stuffed Celery (p. 182)
		Whole Wheat Bread
		Grapes
		Milk
			Scalloped Potatoes (p. 181)
			  with (leftover) Meat Loaf
			Stewed Tomatoes (p. 188)
			Simple Carrot Slaw (p. 215)
			Chocolate Chip Oatmeal
			  Cookies (leftover)
			Milk or Other Beverage

Wednesday	Orange Juice
	Swiss Oatmeal (p. 256)
	Milk
		Pineapple and Cottage
		  Cheese Salad (p. 205)
		Vegetable Sticks
		Chocolate Chip Oatmeal
		  Cookies (leftover)
		Milk
			Tuna Burgers (p. 166),
			  double the recipe
			Crisscross Salad (p. 212)
			Sliced Peaches
			Milk or Other Beverage

Thursday	Orange Juice
	Prepared Cereal with
	  Raisins
	Milk
		Tuna Burgers (leftover)
		Vegetable Sticks
		Chocolate Chip Oatmeal
		  Cookies (leftover)
		Milk
			Broiled Cheese Sandwiches
			Crisscross Salad (leftover)
			Apple Crisp (p. 282)
			Milk or Other Beverage

Friday	Orange Juice
	Cottage Cheese
	Toast with Jam
	Milk
		Peanut Butter and Apple
		  Sandwiches (p. 161)
		Crisscross Salad (if any
		  leftover)
		Milk
			Super Salmon on Toast
			  (p. 142)
			Sautéed Brussels Sprouts
			  (p. 194)
			Apple Crisp (if any leftover)
			Milk or Other Beverage

Saturday	Orange Juice
	Apple Pancakes (p. 253)
	  with Brown Sugar
	Milk
		Tomato Juice
		Fried Egg and Pastrami
		  Sandwiches
		Vegetable Sticks
		Banana Halves
		Milk
			Lazy Susan Dinner (p. 143)
			Chocolate Chip Oatmeal
			  Cookies (leftover)
			Milk or Other Beverage

	Product	Quantity	Variation for Your Family
Fresh Produce	Apples, tart	5	
	Bananas	2	
	Broccoli	2 pounds	
	Brussels sprouts	1 1/2 pounds small	
	Cabbage, green	1 head	
	Carrots	1 pound	
	Celery	1 stalk	
	Grapes, red or green	1 pound	
	Lemons	2	
	Onions, dry yellow	2	
	Onions, red	1 small	
	Peaches	3 pounds	
	Potatoes	1 1/3 pounds	
	Potatoes, sweet, (or yams)	2 medium	
	Tomatoes	7 large	
Canned Goods	Beans, red kidney	1 can (8 ounces)	
	Pineapple slices	1 can (8 ounces)	
	Salmon, red or pink	1 can (7 3/4 ounces)	
	Shrimp, small deveined	1 can (4 1/2 ounces)	
	Tomato juice	1 can (46 ounces)	
	Tuna fish, chunk-style	2 cans (6 1/2 ounces each)	
	Water chestnuts	1 can (8 ounces)	
Frozen Foods	Orange juice, frozen concentrate	6 cans (6 ounces each) or 3 cans (12 ounces each)	
Dairy Products	Butter or margarine	1 pound	
	Cheese, Cheddar	1 pound	
	Cheese, cottage	1 carton (1 pound)	
	Cheese, cream	1 package (3 ounces)	
	Eggs	2 dozen	
	Milk, low-fat	3 1/2 gallons	
	Whipping cream	1 pint	
Bread and Cereal Products	Bread, French	1 loaf	
	Bread, whole wheat	1 loaf (1 1/2 pounds)	
	Buns, hamburger	8	
Meat, Poultry, and Fish	Beef, ground	1 1/2 pounds	
	Chicken thighs	8	
	Pastrami	1 package (2 1/4 ounces)	
Miscellaneous	Chili sauce	1 jar	
	Chocolate chips	1 package (6 ounces)	
	Horseradish, fresh	1 small jar	

(Check staple supplies for basil, brown sugar, catsup, cinnamon, cream of tartar, Dijon mustard, dry bread crumbs, dry mustard, garlic salt, ground nutmeg, honey, horseradish, jam, mayonnaise or salad dressing, nuts, oil, paprika, peanut butter, prepared cereal, raisins, rice, rolled oats, sage, shortening, sweet pickles or relish, Tabasco sauce, unsweetened cocoa, vanilla, walnuts, and Worcestershire sauce.)

Menus September Fourth Week (Vegetarian Menus)

	Breakfast	Lunch	Dinner
Sunday	Orange Juice French Toast (p. 256) Maple-Flavored Syrup (p. 253) Milk	Fresh Mushroom Soup (p. 147) Spinach Orange Salad (p. 220) Thin Butter Toast (p. 252) Milk	Egg Casserole (p. 233) Orange-Glazed Brussels Sprouts (p. 194) Sliced Tomatoes Toasted English Muffins Fresh Apple Cake (p. 268) Milk or Other Beverage
Monday	Orange Juice Oatmeal Broiled English Muffin Halves (leftover) Milk	Peanut Butter and Date Sandwiches on Whole Wheat (p. 161) Carrot Sticks Apple Cake (leftover) Milk	Meatless Chili (p. 154) Steamed Rice (p. 257) Buttered Broccoli (p. 192) Peaches with Sour Cream Fruit Topping (p. 175) Milk or Other Beverage
Tuesday	Orange Juice Prepared Cereal with Sliced Bananas Milk	Cream Cheese and Chopped Date Sandwiches (p. 163) Vegetable Sticks Milk	Chili-Stuffed Green Peppers (p. 110), using leftover chili Raw Vegetable Salad (p. 218) Corn Bread (p. 245) Sliced Peaches Milk or Other Beverage
Wednesday	Orange Juice Corn Bread (leftover) Honey Butter Milk	Chili on Rice (using leftovers) Simple Carrot Slaw (p. 215) Milk	Broiled Cheese Sandwiches (p. 163) Vegetable with Dill Dressing Melon Milk or Other Beverage
Thursday	Orange Juice Prepared Cereal with Cinnamon and Sugar Milk	Egg Salad Sandwiches (p. 168) Vegetable Sticks Apple Cake (leftover) Milk	Mushroom Quiche (p. 237) Cabbage Pineapple Slaw (p. 214) Milk or Other Beverage
Friday	Orange Juice Swiss Oatmeal (p. 256) Toast Milk	Peanut Butter and Pineapple Sandwiches (p. 161) Carrot Sticks Milk	Broccoli Cheese Soup (p. 148) Waldorf Salad (p. 206) Whole Wheat Bread Banana Pops (p. 289)
Saturday	Orange Juice Cooked Wheat Cereal with Dates Milk	Broccoli Cheese Soup (leftover) Waldorf Salad (leftover) Whole Wheat Toast Banana Pops (leftover) Milk	Ringtum Diddy on Toast (p. 239) Green Beans with Toasted Sesame Chocolate Velvet (p. 291) with Bananas Milk or Other Beverage

Shopping List September Fourth Week

	Product	Quantity	Variation for Your Family
Fresh Produce	Apples, tart	6 medium	
	Bananas	6	
	Beans, green	1 pound	
	Broccoli	1½ pounds	
	Brussels sprouts	¾ pound	
	Cabbage, green	1 small head	
	Carrots	1 pound	
	Celery	1 stalk	
	Green peppers	6	
	Lemons	3	
	Melons	1	
	Mushrooms	¾ pound	
	Onions, dry yellow	8 (about 4 pounds)	
	Onions, green	1 bunch	
	Oranges	2	
	Parsley	1 bunch	
	Peaches	3 pounds	
	Spinach	1 pound (or 10-ounce cello bag)	
	Tomatoes	4	
	Zucchini	½ pound	
Canned Goods	Chicken broth, condensed	2 cans (10¾ ounces each)	
	Pineapple, crushed	1 can (8 ounces)	
	Soup, cream of celery or chicken	1 can (10½ ounces)	
	Tomatoes, stewed	1 can (8 ounces)	
	Tomatoes, whole	1 can (29 ounces) *and* 1 can (1 pound)	
Frozen Foods	Frozen whipped topping	1 carton (8 ounces)	
	Orange juice, frozen concentrate	7 cans (6 ounces each)	
Dairy Products	Butter or margarine	1 pound	
	Cheese, Cheddar	2 pounds	
	Cheese, cream	1 package (8 ounces)	
	Cheese, Swiss	4 ounces	
	Eggs	1½ dozen	
	Half-and-half	1 pint	
	Milk, low-fat	4 gallons	
	Sour cream	1 carton (16 ounces)	
Bread and Cereal Products	Bread, French	1 large loaf	
	Bread, whole wheat	2 loaves (1 pound)	
	English muffins	1 package (6 muffins)	
Miscellaneous	Beans, dry small red or pinto	1 pound	
	Chocolate, German sweet	4 ounces	
	Dates, pitted	1 package (8 ounces)	
	Milk chocolate	1 bar (8 ounces)	
	Pastry mix	1 package	
	Wooden skewers	8	

(Check staple supplies for bay leaves, celery seeds, chili powder, cinnamon, curry powder, Dijon mustard, dill weed, dried red chili peppers, dried parsley, dry mustard, garlic, ground allspice, ground cloves, ground cumin seed, ground nutmeg, honey, maple-flavored syrup, marjoram, mayonnaise, nuts, oil, onion powder, paprika, Parmesan cheese, peanut butter, peanuts, rice, rolled oats, sesame seeds, Tabasco sauce, tarragon, vanilla, vinegar, and yellow cornmeal.)

	Breakfast	Lunch	Dinner
Sunday	Broiled Grapefruit (p. 175) Puff Pancakes (p. 254) Maple-Flavored Syrup (p. 253) Milk	Cheese Rarebit on Toast (p. 238) Cabbage Tomato Slaw (p. 214) Milk	Stuffed Whole Salmon (p. 138) New Potatoes with Sesame Seeds (p. 178) Broccoli Stir-Fry (p. 191) Molded Grape Salad (p. 209) Pumpkin Cookies (p. 273) (double recipe) Milk or Other Beverage
Monday	Orange Juice Toast with Peanut Butter and Jam Banana Shake (p. 172)	Peanut Butter Sandwiches (p. 161) Vegetable Sticks Molded Grape Salad (leftover) Milk	Spaghetti Squash, Italian Style (p. 111) Sautéed Brussels Sprouts (p. 194) Tossed Green Salad Pumpkin Cookies (leftover) Milk or Other Beverage
Tuesday	Orange Juice Oatmeal with Sliced Bananas Milk	Tuna Salad Sandwiches (p. 217) Carrot Sticks Grapes Milk	Baked Potato with Seafood Sauce (p. 179), using leftover Salmon Buttered Peas (p. 190) Pumpkin Cookies (leftover) Milk or Other Beverage
Wednesday	Orange Juice Prepared Cereal with Raisins Milk	Peanut Butter and Grated Carrot Sandwiches (p. 161) Banana Halves Milk	Spaghetti Squash, Italian Style (leftover) Pear Swiss Waldorf Salad (p. 207) Easy French Bread (p. 244) Milk or Other Beverage
Thursday	Orange Juice Mix of Prepared Cereals with Cinnamon and Sugar Milk	Egg Salad Sandwiches (p. 168) Vegetable Sticks Chocolate Milk (p. 172)	Chicken Oriental Salad (p. 214) Green Beans with Almonds (p. 183) Hawaiian Fruit Cup (p. 176) Milk or Other Beverage
Friday	Grapefruit Halves French Toast (p. 256) Maple-Flavored Syrup (p. 253) Milk	Swiss Cheese on Rye Sandwiches Vegetable Sticks Hawaiian Fruit Cup (leftover) Milk	Chicken Oriental Salad (leftover) Tomato Slices Easy French Bread (leftover) Milk or Other Beverage
Saturday	Grapefruit Halves Cream of Wheat with Butter and Brown Sugar Milk	Broiled Cheese Sandwiches (p. 163) Vegetable Sticks Milk	Hamburgers (p. 129) Glazed Carrots (p. 187) Pumpkin Cookies (leftover) Strawberry Shake (p. 172)

Shopping List October First Week

	Product	Quantity	Variation for Your Family
Fresh Produce	Bananas	11	
	Beans, green	1 pound	
	Broccoli	1 pound	
	Brussels sprouts	³/₄ pound	
	Cabbage	1 medium head	
	Carrots	1¹/₂ pounds	
	Celery	1 stalk	
	Gingerroot	1 piece	
	Grapefruit	6	
	Grapes, Tokay	1 pound	
	Green peppers	1	
	Lemons	3	
	Lettuce, romaine	1 head	
	Mushrooms	¹/₄ pound	
	Onions, dry yellow	1 medium	
	Onions, green	1 bunch	
	Potatoes, russets	4 pounds	
	Pears	2	
	Squash, spaghetti	1 large	
	Tomatoes	5 large	
Canned Goods	Chicken broth, condensed	1 can (10³/₄ ounces)	
	Mandarin oranges	1 can (11 ounces)	
	Pineapple tidbits or chunks	1 can (20 ounces)	
	Pumpkin	1 can (1 pound)	
	Tomatoes	1 can (29 ounces)	
	Tomato paste	1 can (6 ounces)	
	Tuna fish, chunk-style	1 can (6¹/₂ ounces)	
Frozen Foods	Grape juice, frozen concentrate	1 can (6 ounces)	
	Orange juice, frozen concentrate	3 cans (6 ounces each)	
	Peas	1 package (10 ounces)	
	Strawberries	1 package (10 ounces)	
Dairy Products	Butter or margarine	1 pound	
	Cheese, Cheddar	1 pound	
	Cheese, Swiss	8 ounces	
	Eggs	1 dozen	
	Milk, low-fat	3¹/₂ gallons	
Bread and Cereal Products	Bread, French	1 loaf	
	Bread, rye	1 loaf	
	Bread, whole wheat	1 loaf (1¹/₂ pounds)	
	Buns, hamburger	4	
	Stuffing mix, seasoned	1 box (5 ounces)	
Meat, Poultry, and Fish	Beef, ground	2 pounds	
	Chicken breast halves	2	
	Pork sausage	¹/₂ pound seasoned bulk	
	Whole fish	Approximately 4 pounds	
Miscellaneous	Ramen oriental noodles, chicken flavor	1 package (3 ounces)	

(Check staple supplies for active dry yeast, beef bouillon cubes, brown sugar, cinnamon, coconut, confectioners' sugar, cream of wheat, dried parsley, dry mustard, evaporated milk, French dressing, garlic, ginger, lemon extract, maple flavoring, maple-flavored syrup, mayonnaise or salad dressing, nutmeg, oil, oregano, peanut butter, pickles, prepared cereal, prepared mustard, raisins, rolled oats, sesame seeds, shortening, slivered almonds, soy sauce, Tabasco sauce, unflavored gelatin, unsweetened cocoa, vinegar, walnuts, and Worcestershire sauce.)

	Breakfast	Lunch	Dinner

Sunday	Orange Juice
	Pancakes (p. 253)
	Maple-Flavored Syrup
	  (p. 253)
	Milk
		Cream of Tomato Soup
		  (p. 148)
		Grape Pecan Salad (p. 207)
		Vegetable Sticks
		Thin Butter Toast (p. 252)
		Milk
			Roast Leg of Lamb (p. 115)
			Pan-Roasted Potatoes (p. 182)
			Minted Peas (p. 191)
			Oatmeal Cake (p. 265)
			Milk or Other Beverage

Monday	Grapefruit Halves
	Cream of Wheat
	Toast
	Milk
		Carrot Pineapple Slaw
		  (p. 215)
		Cheese Slices
		Banana Nut Bread (p. 244)
		Grapes
		Milk
			Hot Lamb (leftover)
			  Sandwiches
			Sliced Tomatoes
			Oatmeal Cake (leftover)
			Milk or Other Beverage

Tuesday	Grapefruit Halves
	Prepared Cereal
	Milk
		Cream Cheese and
		  Chopped Raw Vegetable
		  Sandwiches (p. 163)
		Chocolate Milk (p. 172)
			Ratatouille (p. 202)
			Swiss Cheese with French
			  Bread
			Fresh Pear Cobbler (p. 288)
			Milk or Other Beverage

Wednesday	Orange Juice
	Cooked Cornmeal with
	  Raisins
	Milk
		Broiled Cheese
		  Sandwiches (p. 163)
		Ratatouille (leftover)
		Oatmeal Cake (leftover)
		Milk
			Lemon Clam Spaghetti
			  (p. 227)
			Caesar Salad (p. 218)
			French Bread
			Pear Cobbler (leftover)
			Milk or Other Beverage

Thursday	Orange Juice
	Prepared Cereal
	Milk
		Tuna and Carrot
		  Sandwiches (p. 217)
		Pears
		Milk
			Squash Bisque (p. 149)
			Cabbage Shrimp Slaw
			  (p. 214)
			Oatmeal Muffins (p. 250)
			Milk or Other Beverage

Friday	Orange Juice
	Cooked Wheat Cereal
	Toasted Oatmeal Muffins
	  (leftover)
	Milk
		Squash Bisque (leftover)
		Cheese Sandwiches
		Vegetable Sticks
		Milk
			Lemon Clam Spaghetti
			  (leftover)
			Buttered Broccoli (p. 192)
			Applesauce (p. 176),
			  canned or homemade
			Milk or Other Beverage

Saturday	Grapefruit Sections
	French Toast (p. 256)
	Maple-Flavored Syrup
	  (p. 253)
		Egg Salad Sandwiches
		  (p. 168)
		Cabbage Stir-Fry (p. 197)
		Banana Pineapple Shake
		  (p. 172)
			Cheese Soufflé (p. 237)
			Pear Swiss Waldorf Salad
			  (p. 207), using cabbage in
			  place of celery
			Milk or Other Beverage

	Product	Quantity	Variation for Your Family
Fresh Produce	Apples, tart	4 or 1 can (1 pound) applesauce	
	Bananas	8	
	Broccoli	1 pound	
	Cabbage	1 small head	
	Carrots	1 pound	
	Eggplant	2 small	
	Grapes, green seedless	1³/₄ pounds	
	Grapefruit	6	
	Green peppers	2	
	Lemons	4	
	Lettuce, iceberg	1 head	
	Lettuce, romaine	1 head	
	Onions, dry yellow	4 large	
	Parsley	1 bunch	
	Pears	7	
	Potatoes	10	
	Squash, acorn	2	
	Tomatoes	8 large	
	Zucchini squash	4 small	
Canned Goods	Clams	2 cans (6¹/₂ ounces each)	
	Pineapple, crushed	1 can (8 ounces)	
	Shrimp, small deveined	1 can (4¹/₂ ounces)	
	Tomato juice	1 can (24 ounces)	
	Tuna fish, chunk-style	1 can (6¹/₂ ounces)	
Frozen Foods	Orange juice, frozen concentrate	3 cans (6 ounces each)	
	Peas	1 package (10 ounces)	
Dairy Products	Butter or margarine	1¹/₂ pounds	
	Cheese, blue	2 ounces (remainder will keep refrigerated)	
	Cheese, Cheddar	2 pounds	
	Cheese, cream	1 package (3 ounces), *and* 1 package (8 ounces)	
	Cheese, Swiss	³/₄ pound	
	Eggs	2 dozen	
	Half-and-half	1 pint (use remainder over cereal)	
	Milk, low-fat	4 gallons	
Bread and Cereal Products	Bread, French	1 loaf	
	Bread, whole wheat	2 loaves (1 pound each)	
	Croutons, plain	1 small package	
	Spaghetti	1 pound	
Meat, Poultry, and Fish	Leg of lamb	1 5-pound roast	
Miscellaneous	Coconut	1 package (3¹/₂ ounces)	
	Pecans	4 ounces	

(Check staple supplies for basil, bay leaf, brown sugar, cayenne pepper, chicken bouillon cubes, cinnamon, cream of wheat, dried red chili peppers, evaporated milk, garlic, ground cloves, ground nutmeg, maple-flavored syrup, mayonnaise, nuts, oil, Parmesan cheese, peanut butter, pecans, pickles, prepared cereal, prepared mustard, raisins, rice, rolled oats, rosemary, shortening, soy sauce, Tabasco sauce, thyme, uncooked whole wheat cereal, unsweetened cocoa, vanilla, walnuts, Worcestershire sauce, and yellow cornmeal.)

	Breakfast	Lunch	Dinner
Sunday	Sliced Oranges Mushroom Omelet (p. 234) Cinnamon Toast (p. 252) Milk	Cheese Rarebit on Toast (p. 238) Celery Sticks Grapefruit Halves Milk	Salmon in Parchment (p. 142) Creamed New Potatoes and Peas (p. 178) Gingered Vegetables (p. 200) Upside Down Pumpkin Cake (p. 263) Milk or Other Beverage
Monday	Grapefruit Halves Cooked Whole Wheat Cereal with Dates Milk	Salmon (leftover) Sandwiches Celery Sticks Apple Oatmeal Cookies (p. 272) Milk	Oven-Fried Chicken (p. 121) Baked Potatoes Sweet 'N' Sour Carrots (p. 188) Upside Down Pumpkin Cake (leftover) Milk or Other Beverage
Tuesday	Sliced Bananas Prepared Cereal Toast Milk	Peanut Butter and Sliced Orange Sandwiches (p. 161) Stuffed Celery (p. 182) Milk	Minestrone (p. 151) Waldorf Salad (p. 206) Apple Oatmeal Cookies (leftover) Milk or Other Beverage
Wednesday	Orange Juice Cottage Cheese Toast with Jam Milk	Cheese and Tomato Sandwiches Nut-Stuffed Dates Milk	Pizza-by-the-Yard (p. 162) Cider Fruit Salad Mold (p. 208), double the recipe Milk or Other Beverage
Thursday	Grapefruit Halves Oatmeal with Butter and Brown Sugar Milk	Peanut Butter and Ripe Olive Sandwiches (p. 161) Celery Sticks Banana Halves Milk	Minestrone (leftover) Romaine and Tomato Salad French Bread Milk or Other Beverage
Friday	Orange Juice Poached Eggs on Toast (p. 235) Milk	Ground Nut and Raisin Sandwiches (p. 162) Stuffed Celery (p. 182) Milk	Sweet and Sour Pork (p. 117) Steamed Rice (p. 257) Cabbage and Peanut Slaw (p. 214) Sliced Bananas, with Sour Cream Fruit Topping (p. 175) Milk or Other Beverage
Saturday	Grapefruit Halves Puff Pancakes (p. 254) Maple-Flavored Syrup (p. 253) Milk	Pizza-by-the-Yard (leftover) Raw Vegetable Sticks Apple Oatmeal Cookies (leftover) Milk	Cream of Asparagus Soup (canned) Cottage Cheese with (leftover) Cider Fruit Salad Mold Whole Wheat Toast Milk

Shopping List October Third Week

	Product	Quantity	Variation for Your Family
Fresh Produce	Apples, red	6	
	Bananas	5	
	Cabbage	1 small head	
	Carrots	2¾ pounds	
	Celery	1 stalk	
	Gingerroot	1 piece	
	Grapefruit	9	
	Grapes, Tokay	¼ pound	
	Lemons	1	
	Lettuce, romaine	1 head	
	Mushrooms	¾ pound	
	Onions	2 large	
	Oranges	8	
	Parsley	1 bunch	
	Potatoes	3½ pounds, including 8 new potatoes and 4 baking potatoes	
	Potatoes, sweet (or yams)	4 medium	
	Sugar peas	2 ounces	
	Tomatoes	6 large	
	Zucchini squash	1¼ pounds small or medium	
Canned Goods	Beans, green	1 can (8 ounces)	
	Beans, garbanzo	1 can (1 pound)	
	Cider or clear apple juice	1 quart	
	Corn, whole kernel	1 can (12 ounces)	
	Olives, chopped ripe	1 can (4½ ounces)	
	Pumpkin	1 can (1 pound)	
	Soup, cream of asparagus	2 cans (10¾ ounces each)	
	Tomato paste	1 can (6 ounces)	
	Tomato sauce	2 cans (8 ounces each)	
	Tomatoes	1 can (1 pound)	
	Water chestnuts	1 can (8 ounces)	
Frozen Foods	Orange juice, frozen concentrate	2 cans (6 ounces each)	
	Peas	1 package (10 ounces)	
Dairy Products	Butter or margarine	1 pound	
	Cheese, Cheddar	1¾ pounds	
	Cheese, cottage	1 carton (16 ounces)	
	Cheese, cream	1 package (3 ounces)	
	Eggs	2 dozen	
	Half-and-half	1 pint	
	Milk, low-fat	3½ gallons	
	Sour cream	1 carton (16 ounces)	
	Whipping cream	½ pint	
Bread and Cereal Products	Bread, French	1 loaf (1 pound)	
	Bread, whole wheat	2 loaves (1½ pounds each)	
	Noodles, wide (or any pasta)	⅔ cup	
Meat, Poultry, and Fish	Beef, lean ground	1 pound	
	Chicken, broiler-fryer	1 (3 pounds)	
	Pork chops	2	
	Pork sausage, mild	¾ pound	
	Salmon, fresh or frozen	2 pounds (6 fillets)	
Miscellaneous	Almonds, sliced	4 ounces	
	Dates, pitted	1 package (8 ounces)	
	Parchment paper (from bakery)	6 pieces (8x8 inches each)	

(Check staple supplies for basil, beef bouillon cubes, brown sugar, catsup, cider vinegar, cinnamon, cornstarch, dill weed, dried parsley, dry mustard, garlic, garlic salt, ground allspice, ground cloves, ground ginger, ground nutmeg, honey, jam, maple-flavored syrup, oil, oregano, paprika, Parmesan cheese, peanut butter, peanuts, raisins, rice, rolled oats, soy sauce, thyme, uncooked whole wheat cereal, unflavored gelatin, unsweetened cocoa, vanilla, vinegar, walnuts, and Worcestershire sauce.)

	Breakfast	Lunch	Dinner

Sunday	Grapefruit Halves
	Grilled Sweet Rolls (p. 246)
	Milk
		Pear and Cottage Cheese
		  Salad
		Cranberry Muffins (p. 251)
		  or Toast
		Milk
			Oven-Fried Chicken (p. 121)
			Mashed Winter Squash
			  (p. 190)
			Buttered Peas (p. 191)
			Pumpkin Spice Cake (p. 263)
			Milk or Other Beverage

Monday	Orange Juice
	Cottage Cheese
	Cranberry Muffins
	  (leftover)
	Milk
		Oven-Fried Chicken
		  (leftover)
		Raw Vegetables
		Cut-Out Sugar Cookies
		  (p. 275)
		Milk
			Creamed Tuna on Toast
			  (p. 136)
			Buttered Carrots
			Cranberry Sherbet (p. 293)
			Milk or Other Beverage

Tuesday	Orange Juice
	Prepared Cereal with
	  Cinnamon and Sugar
	Milk
		Peanut Butter and
		Banana Sandwiches
		  (p. 161)
		Cabbage Slaw (p. 214)
		Milk
			Sausage Strata (p. 238)
			Baked Tomato Halves
			  (p. 188)
			Dilly Beans (p. 183)
			Pumpkin Spice Cake
			  (leftover)
			Milk or Other Beverage

Wednesday	Orange Juice
	Toast with Peanut Butter
	  and Jam
	Milk
		Pastrami on Rye with
		  Mustard
		Vegetable Sticks
		Milk
			Sausage Strata (leftover)
			Glazed Carrots (p. 187)
			Baked Apple Tapioca (p. 282)
			Milk or Other Beverage

Thursday	Sliced Oranges
	Oatmeal
	Toast with Jam
	Milk
		Ground Nut and Raisin
		  Sandwiches (p. 162)
		Vegetable Sticks
		Milk
			Stir-Fried Vegetables (p. 199)
			Cheese Toast (p. 253)
			Pear Slices on Greens, with
			  French Dressing (p. 223)
			Milk or Other Beverage

Friday	Orange Juice
	Oatmeal with Honey
	Milk
		Cheese Toast (leftover)
		Tomato Wedges
		Fresh Pear Halves
		Milk
			Baked Cod with Tomato-
			  Caper Sauce (p. 138),
			  half the recipe
			Baked Sweet Potatoes (p. 199)
			Sautéed Brussels Sprouts
			  (p. 194)
			Baked Apple Tapioca
			  (leftover)
			Milk or Other Beverage

Saturday	Sliced Bananas
	Toast with Peanut Butter
	  and Honey
	Milk
		Tomato Soup (canned)
		Broiled Cheese
		  Sandwiches (p. 163)
		Peanut Butter Stuffed
		  Celery
		Milk
			Deviled Ham Reubens
			  (p. 167)
			Cabbage and Green Pepper
			  Slaw (p. 214)
			Chocolate Banana Shake
			  (p. 172)

Shopping List October Fourth Week

	Product	Quantity	Variation for Your Family
Fresh Produce	Apples, tart	4	
	Bananas	4	
	Brussels sprouts	³/₄ pound	
	Cabbage	1 medium head	
	Carrots	2¹/₂ pounds	
	Celery	1 stalk	
	Cranberries	1 package (12 ounces)	
	Grapefruit	2	
	Green peppers	1	
	Lemons	2	
	Lettuce, romaine	1 head	
	Mushrooms	¹/₄ pound	
	Onions, dry yellow	1	
	Oranges	4	
	Pears	6	
	Potatoes, sweet (or yams)	4 medium	
	Squash, hubbard or other winter	1¹/₂ pounds	
	Tomatoes	7	
Canned Goods	Deviled ham	1 can (6¹/₂ ounces)	
	Pumpkin, solid pack	1 can (1 pound) (freeze remaining)	
	Soup, tomato	2 cans (10¹/₂ ounces each)	
	Tuna fish, chunk-style	1 can (6¹/₂ ounces)	
Frozen Foods	Orange juice, frozen concentrate	3 cans (6 ounces each)	
	Peas	1 package (10 ounces)	
Dairy Products	Butter or margarine	1 pound	
	Cheese, Cheddar	1¹/₂ pounds	
	Cheese, cottage	1 carton (16 ounces)	
	Cheese, Monterey Jack	8 ounces	
	Eggs	1 dozen	
	Milk, low-fat	3¹/₂ gallons	
Bread and Cereal Products	Bread, enriched white	1 loaf (1 pound)	
	Bread, rye	1 loaf (1¹/₂ pounds)	
	Bread, whole wheat	1 loaf (1¹/₂ pounds)	
	Sweet rolls, day-old	4	
Meat, Poultry, and Fish	Bacon	2 slices (optional)	
	Chicken, broiler-fryer	1 (3 pounds)	
	Fish fillets, fresh or frozen	1 pound (haddock, cod, or perch)	
	Pastrami	2 packages (2¹/₄ ounces each)	
	Pork sausage links	1 pound	
Miscellaneous	Capers	1 small jar	

(Check staple supplies for almond extract, basil, brown sugar, cinnamon, confectioners' sugar, dill weed, dried parsley, dry mustard, French dressing, garlic, ground cloves, ground nutmeg, honey, jam, mayonnaise, nuts, oil, paprika, Parmesan cheese, peanut butter, prepared cereal, prepared mustard, quick-cooking tapioca, raisins, rolled oats, shortening, unflavored gelatin, unsweetened cocoa, vanilla, and vinegar.)

	Breakfast	Lunch	Dinner
Sunday	Sliced Bananas Waffles with Brown Sugar (p. 255) Bacon Milk	Fresh Mushroom Soup (p. 147) Tomato and Avocado Salad with Catalina Dressing (p. 223) Thin Butter Toast (p. 252) Milk	Sesame Baked Chicken Breasts (p. 122) Fluffy Sweet Potatoes with Orange (p. 198) Cauliflower with Crumbs (p. 195) Apple Crisp (p. 282) Milk or Other Beverage
Monday	Grapefruit Halves Prepared Cereal Toast Milk	Crab Salad Sandwiches (p.222) on French Bread Carrot Sticks Apple Crisp (leftover) Milk	Salmon Tetrazzini (p. 141) Green Beans with Green Onions (p. 183) Grapefruit and Pomegranate Salad, with French Dressing (p. 223) Pumpkin Bars (p. 273) Milk or Other Beverage
Tuesday	Orange Juice Swiss Oatmeal (p. 256) Milk	Olive Nut Sandwiches (p. 163) Vegetable Sticks Pears Milk	Sesame Baked Chicken Breasts (leftover) Fluffy Sweet Potatoes with Orange (leftover) Pumpkin Bars (leftover) Milk or Other Beverage
Wednesday	Orange Juice French Toast with Cinnamon and Sugar Milk	Chicken Salad Sandwiches (p. 217) Stuffed Celery (p. 182) Grapes Milk	Salmon Tetrazzini (leftover) Buttered Peas (p. 190) Pumpkin Bars (leftover) Milk or Other Beverage
Thursday	Orange Juice Cooked Cornmeal with Raisins (p. 256) Milk	Pimiento Cheese Sandwiches (p. 163) Celery Sticks Grapes Milk	Pork Pineapple Bake (p. 119) Sautéed Spinach with Bacon (p. 186) Whole Wheat Bread Milk or Other Beverage
Friday	Grapefruit Halves Fried Cornmeal Mush (p. 256) Maple-Flavored Syrup (p. 253) Bacon (if any leftover) Milk	Peanut Butter and Green Pepper Sandwiches (p. 161) Vegetable Sticks Milk	Creole Beans and Rice (p. 259) Carrot Raisin Slaw (p. 216) Whole Wheat Bread Milk or Other Beverage
Saturday	Orange Juice Oatmeal with Butter and Brown Sugar Milk	Creole Beans and Rice (leftover) Celery Sticks Banana Shakes (p. 172)	Cheesy Egg Cups (p. 232) Stir-Fried Celery (p. 183) Pumpkin Bars (leftover) Milk or Other Beverage

Shopping List November First Week

	Product	Quantity	Variation for Your Family
Fresh Produce	Apples, cooking	4	
	Avocados	2 medium to large	
	Bananas	5	
	Beans, green	1 pound	
	Carrots	1 pound	
	Cauliflower	1 head, 5 inches in diameter	
	Celery	1 small stalk	
	Grapefruit	6	
	Grapes	$^1/_2$ pound	
	Green peppers	1	
	Lemons	2	
	Lettuce, romaine	1 head	
	Mushrooms	$1^1/_2$ pounds	
	Onions, dry yellow	2 medium	
	Onions, green	1 bunch	
	Oranges	1	
	Parsley	1 bunch	
	Pears	4	
	Pomegranates	1	
	Potatoes, sweet (or yams)	$2^1/_2$ pounds	
	Spinach	2 bunches ($^3/_4$ pound)	
	Tomatoes	2 large	
Canned Goods	Beans, chili-style	1 can ($15^1/_2$ ounces)	
	Chicken, chunk-style	1 can (5 ounces)	
	Chicken broth, condensed	3 cans ($10^3/_4$ ounces each)	
	Mushrooms, sliced	1 can (4 ounces)	
	Olives, sliced ripe	1 can ($2^1/_4$ ounces)	
	Pimientos	1 jar (2 ounces)	
	Pineapple slices	1 can (8 ounces)	
	Pork luncheon meat	1 can (12 ounces)	
	Pumpkin	1 can (16 ounces)	
	Salmon	1 can ($15^1/_2$ ounces)	
Frozen Foods	Orange juice, frozen concentrate	4 cans (6 ounces each)	
	Peas	1 package (10 ounces)	
Dairy Products	Butter or margarine	$1^1/_2$ pounds	
	Cheese, Cheddar	$^3/_4$ pound	
	Cheese, cream	1 package (3 ounces)	
	Eggs	1 dozen	
	Half-and-half	1 pint (use any leftover on cereal)	
	Milk, low-fat	4 gallons	
	Whipping cream	$^1/_2$ pint	
Bread and Cereal Products	Bread, French	1 loaf (1 pound)	
	Bread, whole wheat	1 loaf ($1^1/_2$ pounds)	
	Spaghetti	1 pound	
Meat, Poultry, and Fish	Bacon	1 package (12 ounces)	
	Chicken breast halves	8 large	
	Crab, regular or imitation	$^1/_2$ pound or 1 can ($7^1/_2$ ounces)	
Miscellaneous	Sesame seeds, polished or unpolished	$^1/_4$ cup	

(Check staple supplies for basil, brown sugar, catsup, chicken bouillon cubes, chili powder, cinnamon, confectioners' sugar, curry powder, Dijon mustard, dill pickles, dried parsley, dry bread crumbs, evaporated milk, French dressing, garlic, garlic salt, ground nutmeg, maple-flavored syrup, mayonnaise, oil, paprika, Parmesan cheese, peanut butter, prepared cereal, raisins, rice, rolled oats, soy sauce, vanilla, vinegar, walnuts, whole cloves, and yellow cornmeal.)

	Breakfast	Lunch	Dinner
Sunday	Orange Juice Waffles (p. 255) Maple-Flavored Syrup (p. 253) Bacon Milk	Grilled Tuna Sandwiches (p. 217) Apple Pomegranate Salad (p. 205) Milk	Pork Chop Skillet (p. 116) Sautéed Brussels Sprouts (p. 194) Apple Nut Pudding (p. 281) Milk or Other Beverage
Monday	Slice Bananas Cooked Wheat Cereal with Raisins Milk	Deviled Pork Sandwich Filling on Whole Wheat (p. 165) Celery Sticks Tangerines Milk	Easy Baked Tarragon Chicken (p. 121) Fluffy Sweet Potatoes with Orange (p. 198), half the recipe Cabbage Slaw (p. 214) Apple Nut Pudding (leftover) Milk or Other Beverage
Tuesday	Tangerines Oatmeal with Butter and Brown Sugar Milk	Chicken Sandwiches (leftover chicken) Stuffed Celery (p. 182) Banana Halves Milk	Herb-Broiled Fish Fillets (p. 137) Oven-Fried Potatoes (p. 181) Three Bean Salad (p. 212) Milk or Other Beverage
Wednesday	Orange Juice French Toast (p. 256) Jam Milk	Deviled Pork Sandwich Filling (leftover) on French Bread Vegetable Sticks Apple Halves Milk	Creamy Cauliflower Soup (p. 147) Three Bean Salad (leftover) Parmesan Toast (p. 252) Milk or Other Beverage
Thursday	Sliced Bananas Prepared Cereal Milk	Broiled Cheese Sandwiches (p. 163) Creamy Cauliflower Soup (leftover) Milk	Greek Cabbage Casserole (p. 106) Parsleyed Carrots (p. 186) Hawaiian Fruit Cup (p. 176) Milk or Other Beverage
Friday	Orange Juice Swiss Oatmeal (p. 256) Toast with Honey Milk	Deviled Pork Sandwich Filling (leftover) Three Bean Salad (if any leftover) Hawaiian Fruit Cup (leftover) Milk	Omelet with Cheese (p. 234) Broccoli with Orange Sauce (p. 192) Whole Wheat Toast Bananas, with Sour Cream Fruit Topping (p. 175) Milk or Other Beverage
Saturday	Grapefruit Halves Apple Pancakes (p. 253) Maple-Flavored Syrup (p. 253) Milk	Bacon, Lettuce, and Tomato Sandwiches Any vegetables Chocolate Milk (p. 172)	Greek Cabbage Casserole (leftover) End-of-the-Week Fruit Salad (p. 205) Milk or Other Beverage

Shopping List November Second Week

	Product	Quantity	Variation for Your Family
Fresh Produce	Apples, red tart	7	
	Bananas	7	
	Broccoli	1 pound	
	Brussels sprouts	³/₄ pound small	
	Cabbage	1 head	
	Carrots	1 pound	
	Cauliflower	1 medium head	
	Celery	1 stalk	
	Grapefruit	2	
	Lemons	4	
	Lettuce, romaine	1 small head	
	Mushrooms	¹/₄ pound	
	Onions, dry yellow	2	
	Parsley	1 bunch	
	Pomegranates	1	
	Potatoes, russets	3	
	Potatoes, sweet (or yams)	1¹/₄ pounds	
	Tangerines	4	
	Tomatoes	1 large	
Canned Goods	Beans, cut green	1 can (16 ounces)	
	Beans, garbanzo	1 can (16 ounces)	
	Beans, red kidney	1 can (16 ounces)	
	Chicken broth	1 can (10³/₄ ounces)	
	Mandarin oranges	1 can (11 ounces)	
	Pineapple chunks	1 can (20 ounces)	
	Pork luncheon meat	1 can (12 ounces)	
	Tomatoes	1 can (1 pound)	
	Tuna fish, chunk-style	1 can (6¹/₂ ounces)	
Frozen Foods	Orange juice, frozen concentrate	2 cans (6 ounces each)	
Dairy Products	Butter or margarine	1¹/₂ pounds	
	Cheese, Cheddar	1¹/₄ pounds	
	Eggs	1¹/₂ dozen	
	Half-and-half	1 pint	
	Milk, low-fat	3¹/₂ gallons	
	Sour cream	1 carton (8 ounces)	
	Whipping cream	¹/₂ pint	
Bread and Cereal Products	Bread, French	1 loaf	
	Bread, whole wheat	2 loaves (1¹/₂ pounds each)	
	Noodles, fine	8 ounces	
Meat, Poultry, and Fish	Bacon	1 pound	
	Beef, ground	1 pound	
	Chicken, broiler-fryer	1 (3 pounds)	
	Haddock, fresh or frozen fillets	1 pound	
	Pork chops, well-trimmed	4	
Miscellaneous	Capers	1 small jar	
	Coconut, flaked	1 package or can (3¹/₂ ounces)	
	Mint, fresh or dried	Few sprigs	

(Check staple supplies for basil, brown sugar, chicken bouillon cubes, cinnamon, cornstarch, dill weed, dried parsley, dry bread crumbs, fennel seed, gherkin sweet pickles, ground allspice, ground nutmeg, honey, jam, maple-flavored syrup, mayonnaise, oil, Parmesan cheese, peanut butter, prepared cereal, prepared mustard, raisins, rice, rolled oats, tarragon, uncooked whole wheat cereal, unsweetened cocoa, vanilla, vinegar, walnuts, and Worcestershire sauce.)

	Breakfast	Lunch	Dinner
Sunday	Grapefruit Halves Puff Pancakes (p. 254) Maple-Flavored Syrup (p. 253) Milk	Fruit and Cottage Cheese Salad (p. 205) Vegetable Sticks Cinnamon Toast (p. 252) Milk	Chicken and Rice Casserole (p. 129) Dilly Beans (p. 183) Raw Cranberry Salad (p. 209) Traditional Pumpkin Pie (p. 285) Milk or Other Beverage
Monday	Orange Juice Toast with Peanut Butter and Jam Milk	Tuna Bunwiches (p. 166) Sliced Tomatoes Grapes Milk	Egg Casserole (p. 233) Whole Wheat Toast Buttered Peas Carrot Raisin Slaw (p. 216) Milk or Other Beverage
Tuesday	Tangerines Prepared Cereal with Raisins Milk	Cream Cheese and Stuffed Olive Sandwiches (p. 163) Vegetable Sticks Banana Halves Milk	Chicken and Rice Casserole (leftover) Stir-Fried Celery and Carrots (p. 183) Instant Strawberry Ice Cream (p. 292) Milk or Other Beverage
Wednesday	Orange Juice Cream of Wheat Toast with Jam Milk	Tuna Bunwiches (leftover) Vegetable Sticks Milk	Barbecued Pork Luncheon Meat (p. 120) Steamed Rice (p. 257) Buttered Broccoli (p. 192) Milk or Other Beverage
Thursday	Orange Juice Oatmeal with Butter and Brown Sugar Milk	Luncheon Meat (leftover) Sandwiches Sliced Tomatoes Milk	Skillet Macaroni and Cheese (p. 228) Sautéed Brussels Sprouts (p. 194) Milk or Other Beverage
Friday	Sliced Oranges Prepared Cereal with Honey Milk	Peanut Butter and Jelly Sandwiches (p. 161) Vegetable Sticks Tangerines Milk	Chili Wheat (p. 155) Cabbage Slaw (p. 214) Corn Bread (p. 245) Milk or Other Beverage
Saturday	Orange Juice Corn Bread (leftover) Honey Milk	Chili Wheat (leftover) Stuffed Celery (p. 182) Potato Rolls or Toasted Buns Milk	Lazy Susan Dinner (p. 143) Milk or Other Beverage

Shopping List November Third Week

	Product	Quantity	Variation for Your Family
Fresh Produce	Bananas	3	
	Beans, green	1 pound	
	Broccoli	1 pound	
	Brussels sprouts	³/₄ pound	
	Cabbage	1 small head	
	Carrots	1 pound	
	Celery	1 stalk	
	Cranberries	1 package (12 ounces)	
	Grapefruit	2	
	Grapes	1¹/₄ pounds	
	Green peppers	2	
	Lemons	1	
	Lettuce, romaine	1 head	
	Mushrooms	¹/₂ pound	
	Onions, dry yellow	3	
	Onions, green	1 bunch	
	Oranges	6	
	Tangerines	8	
	Tomatoes	2 large	
Canned Goods	Peaches, sliced cling	1 can (1 pound)	
	Pimientos	1 can or jar (2 ounces) freeze any leftover	
	Pork luncheon meat	1 can (12 ounces)	
	Pumpkin	1 can (1 pound)	
	Soup, cream of celery or chicken	1 can (10¹/₂ ounces)	
	Tomato sauce	2 cans (8 ounces each)	
	Tomatoes	2 cans (29 ounces each)	
	Tuna fish, chunk-style	1 can (6¹/₂ ounces)	
Frozen Foods	Orange juice, frozen concentrate	4 cans (6 ounces each)	
	Peas	1 carton (10 ounces)	
	Strawberries	1 package (10 ounces)	
	Unbaked pastry shell	1 9-inch	
Dairy Products	Butter or margarine	1 pound	
	Cheese, Cheddar	1 pound	
	Cheese, cottage	1 carton (1 pound)	
	Cheese, cream	1 package (8 ounces)	
	Eggs	1¹/₂ dozen	
	Milk, low-fat	3¹/₂ gallons	
	Sour cream	1 carton (8 ounces)	
	Whipping cream	1 pint	
Bread and Cereal Products	Bread, whole wheat	1 loaf (1¹/₂ pounds)	
	Macaroni, elbow	7 ounces	
	Potato rolls or hamburger buns	12	
	Whole wheat kernels	1¹/₂ cups	
Meat, Poultry, and Fish	Beef, ground	1 pound	
	Chicken, broiler-fryer	1 (3 pounds)	
Miscellaneous	Gelatin, lemon flavor	1 package (3 ounces)	
	Chili seasoning mix	1 package (1³/₄ ounces)	
	Olives, stuffed	1 small jar	
	Pecans	4 ounces	

(Check staple supplies for brown sugar, chicken bouillon cubes, chili powder, cider vinegar, cinnamon, cream of wheat, dill weed, dried parsley, dry mustard, evaporated milk, garlic salt, ground cloves, ground ginger, honey, jam, maple-flavored syrup, mayonnaise, oregano, peanut butter, pecans, prepared cereal, prepared mustard, raisins, rice, rolled oats, shortening, soy sauce, sweet pickles or relish, turmeric, unflavored gelatin, Worcestershire sauce, and yellow cornmeal.)

	Breakfast	Lunch	Dinner
Sunday	Orange Julius (p. 171) Favorite Waffles (p. 255) Frozen Strawberries Milk	Pineapple and Cottage Cheese Salad (p. 205) Cinnamon Toast (p. 252) Milk	Roast Turkey (p. 130) Giblet Stuffing (p. 132) Fluffy Sweet Potatoes with Orange (p. 198), half the recipe Brussels Sprouts with Cream (p. 194) Grape Pecan Salad (p. 207) Freeze-Ahead Butterhorns (p. 248) Cranberry Pudding with Hot Butter Sauce (p. 281) Milk or Other Beverage
Monday	Sliced Bananas Prepared Cereal Cinnamon Toast (p. 252) Milk	Canned Corned Beef on Rye Celery Sticks Pickles Milk	Turkey Stack Sandwiches (p. 170), using leftover turkey Ruby Gapefruit (p. 290) Milk or Other Beverage
Tuesday	Applesauce Broiled Cheese Sandwiches (p. 163) Milk	Peanut Butter and Bacon Sandwiches (p. 161) Carrot Sticks Milk	Turkey Dressing Casserole (p. 134), using leftover turkey Turnip Carrot Puree (p. 187) Ruby Grapefruit (leftover) Milk or Other Beverage
Wednesday	Orange Juice Cooked Cornmeal with Honey (p. 256) Milk	Turkey (leftover) Sandwiches Stuffed Celery (p. 182) Milk	Scrambled Eggs (p. 231) with Swiss Cheese Broccoli with Orange Sauce (p.192) Waldorf Salad (p. 206) Cranberry Muffins (p. 251) Milk
Thursday	Orange Juice French Toast (p. 256) with Jam Cottage Cheese Milk	Tuna Salad Sandwiches (p. 217) Carrot Sticks Apple Halves Milk	Skier's Stew (p. 160) French Bread Milk or Other Beverage
Friday	Grapefruit Halves Oatmeal with Raisins Toast Milk	Peanut Butter and Jelly Sandwiches (p. 161) Stuffed Celery (p. 182) Milk	Fish Sticks (follow package directions) with Lemon Wedges Oven-Fried Potatoes (p. 181) Sweet 'N' Sour Carrots (p. 188) Fresh Fruit Cup (p. 175) Milk
Saturday	Orange Juice Whole Wheat Muffins (p. 251) Corned Beef (leftover) Butter and Jam Milk	Poached Eggs on Toast (p. 235) Sliced Tomatoes Celery Sticks Toast with Honey Milk	Skier's Stew (leftover) French Bread Fresh Fruit Cup (leftover) Milk or Other Beverage

Shopping List November Fourth Week

	Product	Quantity	Variation for Your Family
Fresh Produce	Apples, red tart	6	
	Bananas	3	
	Broccoli	1 pound	
	Brussels sprouts	³/₄ pound	
	Carrots	3 pounds	
	Celery	1 stalk	
	Cranberries	1 package (12 ounces)	
	Grapefruit	7 large	
	Grapes, green seedless	1 pound	
	Lemons	2	
	Lettuce, leaf	1 head	
	Onions, dry yellow	1	
	Oranges	3	
	Potatoes	3 pounds medium	
	Potatoes, sweet (or yams)	1¹/₄ pounds	
	Tomatoes	2 large	
	Turnips	¹/₂ pound	
Canned Goods	Applesauce	1 can (1 pound) or homemade (buy 4 extra apples)	
	Corned beef	1 can (12 ounces)	
	Pineapple slices	1 can (8 ounces)	
	Soup, cream of celery	1 can (10³/₄ ounces)	
	Soup, cream of mushroom	1 can (10³/₄ ounces)	
	Tomato sauce	1 can (8 ounces)	
	Tuna fish, chunk-style	1 can (6¹/₂ ounces)	
Frozen Foods	Fish sticks	1 package (1 pound)	
	Orange juice, frozen concentrate	3 cans (6 ounces each)	
	Raspberries	1 package (10 ounces)	
	Strawberries	1 package (10 ounces)	
Dairy Products	Butter or margarine	1¹/₂ pounds plus 1 stick butter (no substitute)	
	Buttermilk	¹/₂ pint	
	Cheese, Cheddar	4 ounces	
	Cheese, cottage	1 carton (16 ounces)	
	Cheese, cream	1 package (3 ounces)	
	Cheese, Swiss	1 pound	
	Eggs	1¹/₂ dozen	
	Milk, low-fat	4 gallons	
	Whipping cream	¹/₂ pint	
Bread and Cereal Products	Bread, French	1 loaf (1¹/₂ pounds)	
	Bread, rye	1 loaf (1 pound)	
	Bread, whole wheat	2 loaves (1¹/₂ pounds each)	
	Croutons (for stuffing)	1 package (9 ounces)	
Meat, Poultry, and Fish	Bacon	1 pound	
	Beef, stew meat	2 pounds	
	Turkey, hen or tom	1 (10 to 12 pounds)	
Miscellaneous	Dried onion soup	1 package (1¹/₂ ounces)	
	Pecans	4 ounces	
	Thousand Island dressing	¹/₂ pint	

(Check staple supplies for active dry yeast, bay leaves, brown sugar, catsup, cinnamon, curry powder, dried parsley, dry bread crumbs, evaporated milk, honey, jam, mayonnaise, oil, peanut butter, pecans, poultry seasoning, prepared cereal, raisins, rolled oats, sage, sweet pickles or relish, vanilla, vinegar, walnuts, whole wheat flour, and yellow cornmeal.)

	Breakfast	Lunch	Dinner

Sunday	Orange Juice
	Prepared Cereal
	Toast with Jam
	Milk
		Cheesy Potato Soup (p. 153)
		Avocado, Grapefruit, and
		    Apple Salad (p. 206)
		Whole Grain Toast
		Milk
			Pot Roast of Beef with
			    Vegetables (p. 103)
			Tomato Aspic Salad (p. 211)
			Banana Bavarian Pudding
			    (p. 280)
			Pepper Cookies (p. 271)
			Milk or Other Beverage

Monday	Orange Juice
	Broiled Cheese on Toast
	Milk
		Peanut Butter and Grated
		    Carrot Sandwiches
		    (p. 161)
		Apple Halves
		Pepper Cookies (leftover)
		Milk
			Broiled Shrimp Buns (p. 165)
			Tomato Aspic Salad (leftover)
			Milk or Other Beverage

Tuesday	Sliced Bananas
	Prepared Cereal
	Toast with Honey
	Milk
		Tuna Salad Sandwiches
		    (p. 217)
		Oranges
		Pepper Cookies (leftover)
		Milk
			Beef Pot Pie (p. 105), using
			    leftover roast
			Crisscross Salad (p. 212)
			Milk or Other Beverage

Wednesday	Orange Juice
	French Toast with
	    Cinnamon and Sugar
	    (p. 256)
	Milk
		Broiled Cheese and
		    Tomato Sandwiches
		    (p. 164)
		Mixed Vegetable Sticks
		Chocolate Milk (p. 172)
			Chicken Oriental Salad
			    (p. 214)
			Broccoli with Lemon Sauce
			    (p. 192)
			Fresh Fruit Cup (p. 175)
			Pepper Cookies (leftover)
			Milk or Other Beverage

Thursday	Fresh Fruit Cup (leftover)
	Prepared Cereal
	Whole Wheat Toast
	Milk
		Corned Beef and Cheese
		    Sandwiches on Whole
		    Wheat
		Vegetable Sticks
		Tangerines
		Milk
			Tuna Rice Skillet (p. 135)
			Crisscross Salad (leftover)
			Milk or Other Beverage

Friday	Orange Juice
	Puff Pancakes (p. 254)
	Maple-Flavored Syrup
	    (p. 253)
	Corned Beef Slices
	    (leftover)
	Milk
		Tomato Juice
		Peanut Butter and Honey
		    Sandwiches (p. 161)
		Stuffed Celery (p. 182)
		Apple Halves
		Milk
			Quick and Easy Cassoulet
			    (p. 128)
			Glazed Carrots (p. 187)
			Cider Fruit Salad Mold
			    (p. 208), double the recipe
			Milk or Other Beverage

Saturday	Orange Juice Prepared Cereal Toast with Honey Milk	Quick and Easy Cassoulet (leftover) Carrot Sticks Cider Salad Mold (leftover) Milk	Tuna Rice Skillet (leftover) Cabbage Slaw (p. 214) Milk or Other Beverage

Shopping List December First Week

	Product	Quantity	Variation for Your Family
Fresh Produce	Apples, red	7 large	
	Avocados	2 large	
	Bananas	6	
	Broccoli	2 pounds	
	Cabbage	1 medium head	
	Carrots	2 pounds	
	Celery	1 stalk	
	Grapefruit	3 large	
	Green peppers	1	
	Lemons	4	
	Lettuce, romaine	1 head	
	Onions, dry yellow	6 large	
	Onions, green	1 bunch	
	Onions, red	1	
	Oranges	6	
	Potatoes	8 medium baking	
	Tangerines	4	
	Tomatoes	2 large	
Canned Goods	Apple cider or clear apple juice	1 quart	
	Beans, great northern white	2 cans (1 pound each) or other white or kidney bean	
	Beans, red kidney	1 can (8 ounces)	
	Corned beef	1 can (12 ounces)	
	Olives, sliced ripe	1 can (2¼ ounces)	
	Shrimp, small deveined	1 can (4½ ounces)	
	Tomato juice	1 can (46 fluid ounces)	
	Tomato sauce	4 cans (8 ounces each)	
	Tuna fish, chunk-style	3 cans (6½ ounces each)	
Frozen Foods	Orange juice, frozen concentrate	4 cans (6 ounces each)	
Dairy Products	Butter or margarine	1 pound	
	Cheese, Cheddar	2 pounds	
	Cheese, cream	1 package (8 ounces)	
	Eggs	1 dozen	
	Milk, low-fat	3½ gallons	
	Whipping cream	½ pint	
Bread and Cereal Products	Bread, whole grain	2 loaves (1½ pounds each)	
	Buns, hamburger	4	
Meat, Poultry, and Fish	Beef, boneless pot roast	4 to 5 pounds (chuck, round, shoulder, etc.)	
	Chicken breast halves	4	
	Sausage, fully cooked, smoked	½ pound	
Miscellaneous	Brown gravy mix	2 packages (.87 ounces each)	
	Ramen oriental noodles, chicken flavor	1 package (3 ounces)	

(Check staple supplies for basil, brown sugar, cinnamon, dark corn syrup, dried parsley, French dressing, garlic, ground cloves, ground ginger, honey, Italian dressing, jam, maple-flavored syrup, marjoram, mayonnaise, monosodium glutamate, oil, paprika, peanut butter, prepared cereal, prepared mustard, rice, seasoned salt, sesame seeds, shortening, slivered almonds, sweet pickles or relish, thyme, unflavored gelatin, unsweetened cocoa, and vinegar.)

	Breakfast	Lunch	Dinner
Sunday	Fresh Fruit Cup (p. 175) Cheesy Egg Cups (p. 232) Toast with Jam Hot Chocolate with Marshmallows (p. 172)	Tuna Pasta Salad (p. 227) Broiled Grapefruit (p. 175) Milk	Easy Baked Tarragon Chicken (p. 121), double the recipe Sweet Potato Balls (p. 198) Broccoli Onion Casserole (p. 193) Rice in Cream with Raspberry Sauce (p. 292) Milk or Other Beverage
Monday	Sliced Bananas Prepared Cereal with Raisins Oatmeal Muffins (p. 250) Milk	Pimiento Cheese Spread Sandwiches (p. 163) Raw Broccoli Sticks Rice in Cream (leftover) Milk	Split Pea Soup with Sausage Balls (p. 152) Sliced Orange Salad Oatmeal Muffins (leftover) Apple Nut Pudding (p. 281) Milk or Other Beverage
Tuesday	Tangerines Oatmeal with Butter and Brown Sugar Milk	Tuna Avocado Sandwiches (p. 217) Carrot Sticks Apple Nut Pudding (leftover) Milk	Hot Chicken Salad (p. 123), using leftover chicken Broccoli Onion Casserole (leftover) Whole Wheat Bread Milk or Other Beverage
Wednesday	Orange Juice French Toast (p. 256) with Honey Butter (p. 253) Milk	Chicken (leftover) Sandwiches Carrot Sticks Banana Halves Milk	Split Pea Soup with Sausage Balls (leftover) Waldorf Salad (p. 206) Whole Grain Toast with Jam Milk or Other Beverage
Thursday	Grapefruit Halves Toast with Cream Cheese and Jam Milk	Split Pea Soup (leftover) Whole Grain Toast Applesauce Milk	Super Salmon on Noodles (p. 142) Spinach Orange Salad (p. 220) Whole Wheat Bread Honey Butter (p. 253) Milk or Other Beverage
Friday	Sliced Oranges Prepared Cereal with Honey Milk	Peanut Butter and Raisin Sandwiches (p. 161) Broccoli Sticks Banana Halves Milk	Mexicali Salad (p. 218) French Bread Apricot Soufflé (p. 287) Milk or Other Beverage
Saturday	Orange Juice Apple Pancakes (p. 253) Maple-Flavored Syrup (p. 253) Hot Chocolate with Marshmallows (p. 172)	Mexicali Salad (leftover) Sliced Tomatoes Apricot Soufflé (leftover) Milk	Lazy Susan Supper (p. 143) Milk or Other Beverage

	Product	Quantity	Variation for Your Family
Fresh Produce	Apples	6 large, including 3 red	
	Avocados	1 large or 2 small	
	Bananas	7	
	Broccoli	1½ pounds	
	Carrots	½ pound	
	Celery	1 stalk	
	Grapefruit	4 large	
	Lemons	5	
	Lettuce, iceberg	1 head	
	Mushrooms	4 ounces	
	Onions, dry yellow	5 medium	
	Onions, green	1 bunch	
	Oranges	12	
	Parsley	1 bunch	
	Potatoes	1 large	
	Potatoes, sweet (or yams)	1 pound	
	Spinach	1 bunch	
	Tangerines	4	
	Tomatoes	4 large	
	Zucchini	1 small	
Canned Goods	Applesauce	1 can (1 pound) or homemade (buy 4 additional apples)	
	Apricot halves	1 can (29 ounces)	
	Beans, chili (without meat)	1 can (1 pound)	
	Pimientos	1 can or jar (2 ounces)	
	Salmon, red or pink	1 can (7½ ounces)	
	Tuna fish, chunk-style	2 cans (6½ ounces each)	
	Water chestnuts	1 can (8 ounces)	
Frozen Foods	Orange juice, frozen concentrate	2 cans (6 ounces each)	
	Raspberries	1 package (10 ounces)	
Dairy Products	Butter or margarine	1¼ pounds	
	Cheese, Cheddar	2 pounds	
	Cheese, cream	1 package (8 ounces)	
	Eggs	1½ dozen	
	Milk, low-fat	3½ gallons	
	Whipping cream	2 pints	
Bread and Cereal Products	Bread, French	1 loaf	
	Bread, whole grain	2 long loaves	
	Noodles	8 ounces	
	Vermicelli or spaghetti	4 ounces	
Meat, Poultry, and Fish	Chickens, broiler-fryer	2 (3 pounds each)	
	Pork sausage, seasoned	1 pound	
Miscellaneous	Corn chips	1 package (11 ounces)	
	Marshmallows	1 bag (10 ounces)	
	Split peas, dried green	1 pound	

(Check staple supplies for almond extract, basil, brown sugar, catsup, chili powder, cinnamon, cornflakes, cornstarch, Dijon mustard, dried parsley, dry bread crumbs, evaporated milk, garlic, garlic salt, ground nutmeg, honey, jam, maple-flavored syrup, marjoram, mayonnaise, oil, onion salt, paprika, peanut butter, poppy seeds, prepared cereal, raisins, red wine vinegar, rice, rolled oats, slivered almonds, Tabasco sauce, tarragon, thyme, vanilla, walnuts, and whole wheat flour.)

	Breakfast	Lunch	Dinner
Sunday	Sliced Bananas Swiss Oatmeal (p. 256) Milk	Crab Salad Sandwiches (p. 222) on French Bread Avocado Grapefruit Salad (p. 206) Carrot Sticks Milk	Standing Rib Roast of Beef with Yorkshire Pudding (p. 103) Sautéed Brussels Sprouts (p. 194) Cran-Apple Salad Mold (p. 208), double recipe Chocolate Yule Log (p. 291) Milk or Other Beverage
Monday	Orange Juice Cooked Oatmeal with Raisins Milk	Peanut Butter and Apple Sandwiches (p. 161) Vegetable Sticks Chocolate Yule Log (leftover) Milk	French Dip Sandwiches (p. 166), using leftover beef Butter-Braised Cabbage (p. 197) Cran-Apple Salad Mold (leftover) Milk or Other Beverage
Tuesday	Bananas Broiled Cheese on Toast Hot Chocolate (p. 172)	Sliced Beef (leftover) Sandwiches Vegetable Sticks Oranges Milk	Chicken Oriental Salad (p. 214) Fluffy Sweet Potatoes with Orange (p. 198), make one-half recipe Whole Grain Bread with Butter Milk or Other Beverage
Wednesday	Sliced Oranges Cooked Whole Wheat Cereal Milk	Cream Cheese and Raw Vegetable Sandwiches (p. 163) Sliced Bananas, with Sour Cream Fruit Topping (p. 175) Milk	Irish-Italian Spaghetti (p. 231) Fresh Spinach Tossed with French Dressing (p. 223) Garlic French Bread (p. 245) Milk or Other Beverage
Thursday	Orange Juice French Toast with Jam Milk	Spaghetti (leftover) Waldorf Salad (p. 206) Garlic Bread (leftover) Milk	Clam Chowder (p. 157) Carrot Raisin Slaw (p. 216) Garlic French Bread (leftover) Milk or Other Beverage
Friday	Orange Juice Cottage Cheese Oatmeal Muffins (p. 250) Milk	Tuna and Apple Sandwiches (p. 217) Carrot Sticks Chocolate Milk	Sausage-Stuffed Acorn Squash (p. 118) Buttered Broccoli (p. 192) Oatmeal Muffins (leftover) Applesauce Milk or Other Beverage
Saturday	Orange Juice Cheese Omelet (p. 234) Toast with Honey Butter Hot Chocolate (p. 172)	Pineapple and Cottage Cheese Salad (p. 205) Peanut Butter Sandwiches Carrot Sticks Milk	Clam Chowder (leftover) Spinach Apple Toss (p. 186) Whole Grain Toast Milk or Other Beverage

Shopping List December Third Week

	Product	Quantity	Variation for Your Family
Fresh Produce	Apples, red	7	
	Avocados	2 large	
	Bananas	6	
	Broccoli	1 pound	
	Brussels sprouts	¾ pound small	
	Cabbage	1 head	
	Carrots	1 pound	
	Celery	1 stalk	
	Grapefruit	2 large	
	Green peppers	1	
	Lemons	1	
	Lettuce, romaine	1 head	
	Mushrooms	¼ pound	
	Onions, dry yellow	1	
	Onions, green	1 bunch	
	Oranges	9	
	Potatoes	2 medium	
	Spinach	3 bunches	
	Squash, acorn	2 medium	
	Sweet potatoes (yams)	1¼ pounds	
Canned Goods	Applesauce	1 can (1 pound)	
	Clams, chopped	2 cans (6½ ounces each)	
	Crab	1 can (7½ ounces)	
	Cranberry juice cocktail	1 bottle (32 ounces)	
	Mandarin oranges	1 can (11 ounces)	
	Pineapple slices	1 can (8 ounces)	
	Soup, cream of mushroom	1 can (10¾ ounces)	
	Soup, cream of tomato	1 can (10¾ ounces)	
	Tuna fish, chunk-style	1 can (6½ ounces)	
Frozen Foods	Orange juice, frozen concentrate	6 cans (6 ounces each)	
Dairy Products	Butter or margarine	1 pound	
	Cheese, Cheddar	4 ounces	
	Cheese, cottage	1 carton (16 ounces)	
	Cheese, cream	1 package (3 ounces)	
	Eggs	1½ dozen	
	Half-and-half	1 quart	
	Milk, low-fat	3½ gallons	
	Sour cream	1 carton (16 ounces)	
	Whipping cream	½ pint	
Bread and Cereal Products	Bread, French	2 loaves	
	Bread, whole grain	2 long loaves	
	Buns, hoagie	4 (for French dip sandwiches)	
	Spaghetti	8 ounces	
Meat, Poultry, and Fish	Bacon	4 strips	
	Beef, lean ground	1 pound	
	Beef, standing rib roast	4 pounds	
	Chicken breast halves	2	
	Pork sausage, bulk	1 package (12 ounces)	
Miscellaneous	Beef juice (au jus) mix	2 packages (.87 ounces each)	
	Marshmallows	12 large	
	Ramen oriental noodles, chicken flavor	1 package (3 ounces)	

(Check staple supplies for brown sugar, catsup, chili powder, cinnamon, confectioners' sugar, French dressing, garlic, honey, jam, mayonnaise, monosodium glutamate, oil, Parmesan cheese, peanut butter, peanuts, raisins, rolled oats, sesame seeds, slivered almonds, Tabasco sauce, uncooked whole wheat cereal, unsweetened chocolate, vanilla, vinegar, and walnuts.)

	Breakfast	Lunch	Dinner
Sunday	Ruby Grapefruit (p. 290) Mushroom Quiche (p. 237) Cinnamon Toast (p. 252) French Chocolate (p. 170)	Cream of Tomato Soup (p. 148) Broiled Cheese Sandwiches (p. 163) Vegetable Sticks Milk	Baked Halibut (p. 139), bake 1 pound extra halibut Tartar Sauce (p. 137) Stuffed Baked Potatoes (p. 179) Gingered Vegetables (p. 200) Frozen Strawberry Squares (p. 290) Milk or Other Beverage
Monday	Orange Juice Prepared Cereal with Raisins Milk	Tuna Bunwiches (p. 166) Carrot Sticks Apple Halves Milk	Porcupine Meatballs (p. 109) Baked Hubbard Squash (p. 189) Cabbage Slaw (p. 214) Ruby Grapefruit (leftover) Milk or Other Beverage
Tuesday	Orange Juice French Toast (p. 256) Maple-Flavored Syrup (p. 253) Milk	Peanut Butter and Banana Sandwiches (p. 161) Cottage Cheese Vegetable Sticks Milk	Halibut au Gratin (p. 139), make one-half recipe using leftover halibut Parsleyed Potatoes (p. 178) Green Beans with Almonds (p. 183) Frozen Strawberry Squares (leftover) Milk or Other Beverage
Wednesday	Orange Juice Prepared Cereal Toast with Honey Milk	Tuna Bunwiches (leftover) Cabbage Peanut Slaw (p. 214) Apple Halves Milk	Porcupine Meatballs (leftover) Glazed Carrots (p. 187) Hard Rolls with Butter Lemon Surprise Pudding (p. 280) Milk or Other Beverage
Thursday	Grapefruit Halves Oatmeal with Butter and Brown Sugar Milk	Luncheon Meat and Swiss Cheese Sandwiches Peanut Butter Stuffed Celery Banana Halves Milk	Oven-Fried Chicken (p. 121), double the recipe Barley Pilaff (p. 258) Broccoli with Orange Sauce (p. 192) Lemon Surprise Pudding (leftover) Milk
Friday	Sliced Oranges Toast with Peanut Butter and Honey Milk	Cream Cheese and Jelly Sandwiches (p. 163) Raw Vegetables Applesauce Milk	Creamed Tuna on Toast (p. 136) Orange-Glazed Brussels Sprouts (p. 194) Extra Toast, with Honey Butter (p. 253) Milk or Other Beverage
Saturday	Orange Juice Cottage Cheese Whole Wheat Toast with Jam Milk	Fried Egg Sandwiches (p. 167) Vegetable Sticks Peanut Butter Pudding (p. 279) Milk	Cold Fried Chicken (leftover) Barley Pilaff (leftover) Sweet 'N' Sour Carrots (p. 188) Broiled Grapefruit (p. 175) Milk or Other Beverage

Shopping List December Fourth Week

	Product	Quantity	Variation for Your Family
Fresh Produce	Apples	5	
	Bananas	4	
	Beans, green	1 pound	
	Broccoli	1 pound	
	Brussels sprouts	3/4 pound	
	Cabbage	1 head	
	Carrots	3 1/2 pounds	
	Celery	1 stalk	
	Gingerroot	1 piece	
	Grapefruit	8 large	
	Grapes, Tokay	1/4 pound	
	Green peppers	1	
	Lemons	7	
	Mushrooms	3/4 pound	
	Onions, dry yellow	2	
	Onions, green	1 bunch	
	Oranges	6	
	Parsley	1 bunch	
	Potatoes, russets	2 1/2 pounds	
	Squash, hubbard or banana	1 1/2 pounds	
	Sugar peas	1/8 pound	
Canned Goods	Applesauce	1 can (1 pound)	
	Olives, sliced ripe	1 can (4.5 ounces)	
	Tomato juice	1 can (46 fluid ounces)	
	Tomato paste	1 can (6 ounces)	
	Tuna fish, chunk-style	1 can (6 1/2 ounces)	
Frozen Foods	Orange juice, frozen concentrate	3 cans (6 ounces each)	
	Raspberries	1 package (10 ounces)	
	Strawberries	1 can (10 ounces)	
	Unbaked pastry shell	1 9-inch	
Dairy Products	Butter or margarine	1 pound	
	Cheese, Cheddar	1 3/4 pounds	
	Cheese, cottage	1 carton (16 ounces)	
	Cheese, cream	1 package (8 ounces)	
	Cheese, Swiss	8 ounces	
	Eggs	2 dozen	
	Half-and-half	1 pint	
	Milk, low-fat	4 gallons	
	Whipping cream	1/2 pint	
Bread and Cereal Products	Barley, pearl	1 1/2 cups	
	Bread, French	1 small loaf	
	Bread, whole grain	2 long loaves	
	Hard rolls	4	
	Potato rolls or hamburger buns	8	
Meat, Poultry, and Fish	Beef, lean ground	1 1/2 pounds	
	Chickens, broiler-fryer	2 (3 pounds each)	
	Halibut fillets	2 pounds	
	Pastrami	2 packages (2 1/4 ounces each)	
Miscellaneous	Capers	1 small jar	
	Olives, stuffed green	1 small jar	

(Check staple supplies for almonds, basil, bay leaves, brown sugar, buttermilk, catsup or chili sauce, celery salt, chicken bouillon cubes, cinnamon, cornstarch, dry bread crumbs, garlic, gherkin sweet pickles, ground ginger, honey, jam, maple-flavored syrup, mayonnaise, paprika, Parmesan cheese, peanut butter, peanuts, pecans, poppy seeds, prepared cereal, prepared mustard, raisins, rice, rolled oats, sweet pickles or relish, unsweetened chocolate, vanilla, whole cloves, and Worcestershire sauce.)

BEEF, LAMB, PORK, POULTRY, AND FISH

Beef

Pot Roast of Beef with Vegetables

¹/₂ cup all-purpose flour
1 teaspoon salt
¹/₂ teaspoon paprika
¹/₄ teaspoon pepper
4- to 5-pound beef pot roast
2 tablespoons shortening
1 cup water
5 small onions or 2 to 3 large
    onions, quartered
5 carrots, quartered
5 small potatoes, pared, or 2
    large potatoes, quartered
¹/₂ teaspoon salt
Pepper

Mix flour, 1 teaspoon salt, paprika, and pepper; rub flour mixture into both sides of pot roast. Brown meat well in hot shortening in large heavy Dutch oven or skillet. Add water. Cover tightly and simmer about 3 hours or until meat is nearly tender. Add vegetables, sprinkle with remaining salt and pepper to taste. Continue simmering until meat and vegetables are tender, about 45 minutes. Serve meat and vegetables immediately with juices from roast as desired. Makes 4 servings, plus enough meat for two other meals.

See menus for January, 3rd week; December, 1st week.

Roast Beef and Yorkshire Pudding

4 pounds rib roast
2 tablespoons vegetable oil
³/₄ cup all-purpose flour,
    stirred and measured
¹/₂ teaspoon salt
³/₄ cup milk
1 tablespoon water
2 eggs

Place beef, fat side up, in roasting pan, and coat with oil. For rare beef, roast at 450 degrees for 1¹/₄ hours (130 to 140 degrees F. internal temperature). Baste meat frequently.

Meanwhile, to prepare batter for Yorkshire Pudding, sift flour and salt into medium mixing bowl. Make a well in center and add milk and water gradually, beating with wooden spoon. In separate bowl, beat eggs until fluffy; add to flour mixture and beat until bubbles rise to surface. Refrigerate for 30 minutes. When meat is cooked, remove roast from pan and place on warm platter; cover with foil; allow to stand 25 minutes before carving.

Immediately bake Yorkshire Pudding. To do so, skim all but about 3 tablespoons fat from hot pan, leaving meat juices in pan. Beat batter once more and pour quickly into hot cooking pan. Bake, without opening oven door, at 450 degrees F. for 10 minutes; reduce heat to 350 degrees F. and bake for 15 minutes longer, until pudding rises and is golden brown. Serve immediately with slices of juicy roast beef. Makes 8 servings.

See menus for December, 3rd week.

Sauerbraten

2 cups red wine vinegar or
  apple-cider vinegar
2 cups water
1 teaspoon salt
¼ teaspoon pepper
½ cup chopped onion (1
  small onion)
2 tablespoons fresh celery
  leaves, chopped
2 teaspoons whole mixed
  pickling spice
5-pound pot roast
  (shoulder, chuck, rump,
  or round)
½ cup sugar
18 (more or less) old-fashioned
  gingersnaps, crushed

Combine vinegar, water, salt, pepper, onion, celery leaves, and pickling spice to make marinade. In large bowl or crock, place meat; pour marinade over meat, making sure it is covered with liquid. Cover; let stand in refrigerator overnight. Add sugar. In heavy kettle or Dutch oven, bake meat and marinade, covered, at 275 degrees F. for 4 hours or until tender. Or simmer meat and marinade, covered, on top of range for 3 hours. Remove meat to platter; keep hot. Strain liquid to remove spices. Return liquid to cooking pan; stir in enough gingersnap crumbs to thicken gravy; simmer until thick. Serve with Potato Pancakes (p. 182). Makes 8 servings.

See menus for February, 3rd week.

Beef Rouladin

2 tablespoons chopped onion
1 teaspoon dried parsley
¼ teaspoon salt
4 slices bacon, diced
⅓ cup soft bread crumbs
2 teaspoons Worcestershire
  sauce
2 cups (8 ounces) fresh
  mushrooms, divided
4 beef cube steaks
2 tablespoons vegetable oil
1¼ cups beef broth or
  bouillon (2 bouillon cubes
  in 1¼ cups water)
1 tablespoon lemon juice
1 can (10¾ ounces) golden
  mushroom soup
½ cup dairy sour cream
¼ cup stuffed green olives,
  sliced (optional)

Combine onion, parsley, salt, bacon, crumbs, Worcestershire sauce, and 1 cup chopped fresh mushrooms. Place equal portions of stuffing on each cube steak. Roll up steaks; fasten securely with wooden toothpicks or tie with string; dredge in flour. Brown well on all sides in hot oil. Place rolls snugly in casserole containing bouillon and lemon juice. Pour golden mushroom soup over top. Bake, covered, at 325 degrees F. for 1 hour or until tender, arranging 1 cup sliced mushrooms over top of meat rolls for last 10 minutes of cooking. To serve, top with sour cream and garnish with sliced stuffed olives, if desired. Makes 4 servings.

Note: Rouladin may be cooked in pressure cooker at 15 pounds pressure for 20 minutes, then unplugged to let pressure drop of its own accord.

See menus for May, 1st week.

Teriyaki Steak

³/₄ cup soy sauce
¹/₂ cup water
¹/₄ cup vegetable or olive oil
1 teaspoon sugar
¹/₂ teaspoon grated
  gingerroot
4-pound sirloin tip roast of
  beef, 2 inches thick

To make teriyaki sauce, combine soy sauce, water, oil, sugar, and gingerroot. Place roast in shallow dish or heavy plastic bag; pour marinade over and around meat, making sure all sides are coated; cover and refrigerate. Marinate meat for several hours or over night, turning meat often so all surfaces are well flavored. Place drained meat on broiling pan; in preheated broiler or over hot coals, set meat about 5 inches from source of heat; broil for 10 minutes or until surface is deeply browned and crusty and charred; turn steak and broil other side until equally done. With sharp knife cut perpendicularly into ¹/₄-inch slices. Edges of slices will be crusty and well done; center will be rare. Serve with drippings that have been heated with remaining teriyaki sauce. Makes 8 to 10 servings.

Note: Some pot roasts may be used for Teriyaki Steak: round bone, arm bone, or chuck. They will have the same delicious flavor but will not cut into such perfect slices.

See menus for March, 2nd week.

Beef Pot Pie

3 cups (1 pound) cubed
  cooked beef
2 to 3 cups leftover gravy or
  2 packages (.87 ounces)
  brown gravy mix
3 cups cooked carrots,
  potatoes, and onions, cut
  in bite-size pieces
Salt and pepper
¹/₂ recipe Rich Flaky Pastry
  (p. 284)

In medium saucepan combine beef, gravy, carrots, potatoes, and onions; bring to boil. Season to taste with salt and pepper. Transfer hot beef mixture to deep pie dish or 1¹/₂-quart casserole. Make pastry; roll out and place over top of meat mixture; crimp edges and cut small vent in top. Bake at 375 degrees F. for 20 to 30 minutes or until mixture is bubbling and crust is golden. Makes 4 servings.

Note: In place of homemade pastry, a prepared pastry stick or pastry mix may be used, or refrigerated biscuits may be used as topping.

See menus for December, 1st week.

Greek Cabbage Casserole

½ large head cabbage
¾ pound lean ground beef, crumbled
⅓ cup uncooked rice
1 medium onion, chopped
¾ teaspoon fennel seed
¾ teaspoon dried dill weed
1½ teaspoons dried parsley
¾ teaspoon dried mint leaves
¾ teaspoon salt
¼ teaspoon pepper
1 lemon, juiced (¼ cup)
1½ cups chopped fresh tomatoes or canned tomatoes
¾ cup rich bouillon*

Shred cabbage coarsely. In 3-quart casserole, mix all ingredients together. Cover and bake at 350 degrees F. for 1 hour. Makes 8 servings.

Note: To make rich bouillon, dissolve 1 bouillon cube in ¾ cup boiling water.

See menus for May, 2nd week; July, 3rd week; November, 2nd week.

Corned Beef Hash

4 medium potatoes (about 1½ pounds)
¼ cup (½ stick) butter or margarine
1 large onion, chopped
½ small cabbage, shredded (about 2 cups)
½ cup water
1 teaspoon salt
1 can (12 ounces) corned beef, cubed

Scrub or pare potatoes, as desired. Cook, covered, in small amount boiling water until tender; drain and cube. In large heavy skillet melt butter, add onion; cook until soft, about 3 minutes. Add potatoes; cook and stir about 5 minutes. Add cabbage, water, and salt. Cook, uncovered, over medium high heat until liquid is absorbed and hash is browned, about 10 minutes. Add corned beef; turn mixture with spatula. Cook about 3 minutes longer or until meat is heated through. Makes 4 servings.

See menus for June, 4th week.

Ground Beef Fricassee

¹/₂ cup chopped onion
1 cup sliced celery
3 tablespoons diced green
  pepper
1 tablespoon vegetable oil
1 pound lean ground beef
2 tablespoons all-purpose
  flour
1¹/₂ cups hot water
1 beef bouillon cube or 1
  teaspoon beef granules or
  beef soup base
¹/₂ cup coarsely grated
  carrots
¹/₈ teaspoon pepper
¹/₂ teaspoon onion salt
¹/₂ teaspoon garlic salt
Mashed potatoes, cooked
  rice, parsleyed noodles,
  toast points, or baked
  potatoes

In large skillet cook onion, celery, and green pepper in oil until softened. Add ground beef; cook and stir until red color has disappeared. Blend in flour; add hot water in which bouillon cube or granules have been dissolved; cook and stir until thickened. Add carrots and seasonings. Cover skillet, turn heat to low, and simmer for 15 to 20 minutes or until carrots are tender. Serve over mashed potatoes, cooked rice, parsleyed noodles, toast points, or baked potatoes. Makes 4 servings.

See menus for April, 3rd week.

Pizza Hamburger

1 pound lean ground beef
¹/₂ teaspoon salt
¹/₈ teaspoon pepper
1 large tomato, chopped, or
  1 cup well-drained canned
  tomatoes
¹/₂ cup shredded Cheddar
  cheese
1 tablespoon chopped parsley
¹/₄ teaspoon dried sweet basil
  or oregano
2 tablespoons chopped onion

Mix ground beef with salt and pepper. Pat mixture into an 8-inch pie or cake pan. Spread tomatoes over hamburger; sprinkle with remaining ingredients. Bake at 375 degrees F. for 15 to 20 minutes or until bubbling hot. Cut in quarters to serve. Makes 4 servings.

See menus for March, 1st week.

Meatballs and Gravy on Colcannon

1½ cups boiling water
4 beef bouillon cubes or 4
  teaspoons instant beef
  bouillon granules
2 tablespoons cornstarch
⅓ cup cold water
½ recipe Quick Meatballs
  (see below)
2 cups (1 pound) hot
  potatoes, mashed
2 cups hot cooked shredded
  cabbage (¼ medium
  cabbage)
¼ cup sliced green onions

In medium saucepan, dissolve bouillon cubes in boiling water. Blend together cornstarch and cold water; stir into hot bouillon; cook and stir until thick and clear. Or make gravy from 2 packages (¾ ounce each) brown gravy mix, according to package directions. Add meatballs; heat through. Serve over mounds of colcannon, a mixture of hot mashed potatoes, hot drained cabbage, and green onions, seasoned to taste. Makes 4 servings.

See menus for March, 4th week.

Quick Meatballs

1 pound lean ground beef
1 cup dry bread crumbs
½ cup milk
½ teaspoon salt
½ teaspoon Worcestershire
  sauce

Combine all ingredients. Shape mixture by level tablespoonfuls into 1-inch meatballs. Arrange in single layer in large unheated skillet. Set over medium heat; brown, loosening and turning with spatula as necessary. Makes 40 meatballs or enough for 6 to 8 servings.

Note: For delicious appetizers, omit Worcestershire sauce and add ½ package (0.7 ounces) blue cheese salad dressing mix.

Variation

Make-Ahead Meatballs: In large mixing bowl prepare 4 times the recipe to make 160 meatballs. Arrange in single layer in large dripper pan. Bake at 400 degrees F. for 12 to 15 minutes, loosening and turning with spatula once or twice, until nicely browned. To freeze, arrange meatballs on large cookie sheet; freeze for 30 to 60 minutes. Divide into meal-size portions; store in freezer containers (1 pound browned meatballs will fill 1½-pint freezer container) or in heavy plastic bags; seal tightly. To thaw, place in refrigerator for 24 hours. Use in Meatballs and Gravy on Colcannon (see above) and Sweet and Sour Meatballs (p. 109.)

See menus for March, 4th week.

Sweet and Sour Meatballs

1 can (8 ounces) pineapple chunks, packed in juice
$1/4$ cup brown sugar, packed
$1^1/2$ tablespoons cornstarch
$1/2$ cup water
3 tablespoons vinegar
$1^1/2$ teaspoons soy sauce
$1/4$ teaspoon dry mustard
$1/8$ teaspoon ground cloves
1 beef bouillon cube or 1 teaspoon instant beef bouillon granules
$1/2$ recipe Quick Meatballs (p. 108)
$1/2$ green pepper, cut into strips
1 can (5 ounces) water chestnuts, drained and thinly sliced (optional)
3 cups cooked rice (1 cup uncooked)

Drain pineapple chunks, saving syrup. Combine pineapple syrup, brown sugar, cornstarch, water, vinegar, soy sauce, mustard, cloves, and bouillon cube or granules. Cook and stir until thick. Add meatballs, pineapple chunks, green pepper, and water chestnuts. Cover; simmer until all ingredients are hot, stirring occasionally. Serve over hot cooked rice with additional soy sauce, if desired. Makes 4 servings.

See menus for March, 4th week.

Porcupine Meatballs

$1^1/2$ pounds lean ground beef
$3/4$ cup uncooked rice
2 tablespoons finely chopped onion
$1^1/2$ teaspoons salt
$3/4$ teaspoon celery salt
$3^3/4$ cups tomato juice
6 whole cloves
$3/4$ teaspoon ground cinnamon
2 tablespoons sugar
1 tablespoon Worcestershire sauce

Combine ground beef, rice, onion, salt, and celery salt. Form into balls $1^1/2$ inches in diameter. In large saucepan combine and heat remaining ingredients to boiling. Drop in meatballs. Lower heat, cover tightly and simmer 50 minutes. Makes 8 servings.

See menus for December, 4th week.

Beef, Lamb, Pork, Poultry, and Fish **109**

Hamburger Scramble

½ pound lean ground beef
½ cup uncooked long grain
  rice
1 medium onion, sliced
  (½ cup)
1 cup sliced celery
2 carrots, sliced (1 cup)
¼ pound mushrooms, sliced
  (1¼ cups)
1 teaspoon salt, divided
¼ teaspoon pepper
½ teaspoon crushed mixed
  dried herbs
1 can (1 pound) whole
  tomatoes, blended
½ cup water
½ cup shredded Cheddar
  cheese (optional)

In large cold skillet, crumble ground beef over bottom. Sprinkle rice over meat, then layer vegetables and seasonings in order given. Add water. Cook, covered, over medium low heat for 30 to 40 minutes or until rice is cooked and vegetables are tender. If desired, sprinkle cheese over top and allow to melt before serving. Makes 4 servings.

See menus for May, 4th week; September, 2nd week.

Stuffed Green Peppers

4 large green peppers
½ pound lean ground beef
1 medium onion, chopped
1 can (12 ounces) whole
  kernel corn, drained
2 slices bread, crumbled
1 teaspoon salt
⅛ teaspoon pepper
1 can (15 ounces) tomato
  sauce
½ cup (2 ounces) shredded
  Cheddar or other cheese

Cut thin slice from stem end of each pepper. Remove seeds and membranes; rinse. Cook peppers 5 minutes in enough boiling water to cover; drain. Cook ground beef and onion in skillet until meat loses its color and onion is transparent. Combine with drained corn, bread crumbs, salt, pepper, and 1 cup tomato sauce; heat through. Stuff each pepper with ground beef mixture; stand upright in ungreased 9-inch round baking dish. Pour remaining sauce over peppers. Cover; bake at 350 degrees F. for 45 minutes. Uncover; cook 15 minutes longer. Sprinkle with cheese. Makes 4 servings.

Note: Other fillings may be used to stuff peppers, following above recipe. Stuffings may include leftover chili, meat, and/or rice mixtures, vegetables, tuna, or chicken mixtures. Follow above recipe, omitting tomato sauce from filling, if desired. One cup water or other liquid may be added to green peppers in place of tomato sauce.

See menus for February, 3rd week; September, 4th week.

Haystacks

1 pound lean ground beef
1 medium onion, finely chopped
1 clove garlic, minced (optional)
3¼ cups water
1 can (8 ounces) tomato sauce
1 can (6 ounces) tomato paste
2 teaspoons sugar
1 teaspoon crushed dried oregano
1 teaspoon ground cumin seed
1 teaspoon chili powder
3 dashes Tabasco sauce
¼ cup uncooked long grain rice
1 package (11½ ounces) corn chips
Assorted garnishes: sour cream, grated Monterey Jack or Cheddar cheese, sliced ripe olives, sliced green onion, diced avocado, diced green pepper

In large skillet cook together ground beef, onion, and garlic until beef loses its color and onion is soft; drain off excess fat. Add remaining ingredients except corn chips; cover and simmer 20 minutes. Serve over corn chips with any desired garnishes. Makes 6 to 8 servings.

See menus for June, 3rd week.

Spaghetti Squash, Italian Style

1 large spaghetti squash
2 tablespoons vegetable oil
2 cloves garlic, minced
1 pound lean ground beef
½ pound seasoned bulk pork sausage
1 can (29 ounces) tomatoes or 3½ cups chopped fresh tomatoes
1 can (6 ounces) tomato paste
1 cup beef stock or bouillon
½ teaspoon oregano
Salt and pepper

Prick squash with a long-tined fork so that it won't burst. Bake whole spaghetti squash at 350 degrees F. for 1 hour or longer, until skin begins to give and squash is tender. Meanwhile, in heavy saucepan or skillet, sauté garlic and ground meats in hot oil until cooked but not brown. Add remaining ingredients; simmer over low heat for 45 minutes. When squash is tender, halve lengthwise and remove seeds. Fluff up fibrous content with fork until it resembles strands of spaghetti; remove from shell onto serving plate. Top with Italian sauce and serve immediately. Makes 8 servings.

Note: Recipe may be halved, using 1 medium squash.

See menus for October, 1st week.

Beef Tacos

²/₃ pound lean ground beef
¹/₂ cup chopped onion
   (¹/₂ medium onion)
1 clove garlic, minced
1 teaspoon chili powder, or
   to taste
8 corn tortillas
1 large tomato, chopped
³/₄ cup (3 ounces) shredded
   sharp Cheddar cheese
Shredded lettuce
Taco Sauce*
Sour cream (optional)

Combine ground beef, onion, and garlic in medium skillet; cook over medium heat until meat loses its color and onion is soft. Drain fat, if any. Stir in chili powder. Heat tortillas in 350 degree F. oven just until warm. Fill each of the taco shells with meat mixture, tomatoes, cheese, and lettuce. Serve with Taco Sauce and sour cream. Makes 4 servings.

Taco Sauce: Combine in saucepan 2 cups chopped fresh tomatoes, ¹/₂ cup chopped onion, ¹/₂ cup chopped green pepper, 2 cloves minced garlic, 2 tablespoons chopped parsley, ¹/₂ can (2 ounces) drained and chopped green chilies, 1¹/₂ teaspoons red wine vinegar, and salt to taste. Bring to boil. Simmer 30 minutes. Chill. Makes 2 cups.

Note: For hotter sauce, add ¹/₂ finely chopped jalapeño pepper.

See menus for February, 3rd week.

Cheesy 'Chilada Casserole

1 pound lean ground beef
   or pork
1 medium green pepper,
   diced
1 medium onion, chopped
1 clove garlic, minced
2 cups drained, cooked pinto
   beans (³/₄ cup dry) or 1 can
   (16 ounces) pinto beans,
   drained
1 can (15 ounces) tomato
   sauce
1 cup Picante Sauce*
1 teaspoon ground cumin
¹/₂ teaspoon salt
12 corn tortillas
2 cups (8 ounces) shredded
   Monterey Jack or Cheddar
   cheese
Shredded lettuce, sour cream,
   and chopped tomato
   (optional)

Brown meat with green pepper, onion, and garlic in 10-inch skillet; drain. Add beans, tomato sauce, Picante Sauce, cumin, and salt; simmer 15 minutes. Spoon small amount of meat mixture into 9x13x2-inch baking dish or pan, spreading to coat bottom of dish. Top with 6 tortillas, overlapping as necessary. Top with half remaining meat mixture; sprinkle with 1 cup cheese. Cover with remaining tortillas, overlapping to cover cheese; top with remaining meat mixture. Cover tightly with aluminum foil; bake at 350 degrees F. for 20 minutes. Remove foil; top with remaining cheese. Continue baking, uncovered, 5 minutes. Let stand 10 minutes before cutting. Top with lettuce, sour cream, and tomato, if desired, and serve with additional Picante Sauce. Makes 8 servings.

Picante Sauce: In blender or food processor, combine 2 large tomatoes, ¹/₂ cup chopped onion, 2 cloves garlic, and 1 to 2 canned pickled jalapeño chilies (for hot sauce) or 1 can (4 ounces) whole green chilies (for mild sauce). Blend until pureed. Heat 2 teaspoons vegetable oil in small saucepan. Add tomato mixture, 1 teaspoon liquid from canned chilies, ¹/₂ teaspoon crushed dried leaf oregano, and

½ teaspoon salt. Bring to boil; cook gently, 10 minutes. Remove from heat. Let stand 2 hours. Makes about 1½ cups.

Note: Use as many pickled jalapeño chilies as your taste desires.

See menus for March, 3rd week.

Spanish Beef and Rice

2 tablespoons vegetable oil
1 cup uncooked rice
1 pound lean ground beef or 2 cups diced cooked meat, fish, or poultry
1 clove garlic, minced
¼ cup chopped onion
¼ cup diced celery
½ green pepper, diced
2 cups cooked or 1 can (1 pound) tomatoes
½ bay leaf
1 teaspoon salt
½ teaspoon chili powder
1 cup hot water
1 can (10½ ounces) beef bouillon, undiluted

Heat oil in heavy skillet. Add rice; cook and stir until grains brown slightly. Add ground beef, garlic, onion, celery, and green pepper; cook until meat browns slightly and vegetables soften. Add remaining ingredients and cook, covered, until mixture boils. Reduce heat; simmer 30 minutes or until rice is tender and has absorbed liquid. Remove bay leaf. Makes 6 servings.

Note: 1 can (6 ounces) tomato paste may be added for richer flavor.

See menus for February, 2nd week.

Meat Loaf

⅔ cup dry bread crumbs
1 cup milk
1½ pounds lean ground beef
2 eggs, slightly beaten
¼ cup chopped onion
1 teaspoon salt
⅛ teaspoon pepper
½ teaspoon ground sage
Catsup Sauce*

Combine all ingredients except sauce. Spoon into 7½x3½x2½-inch meat loaf pan; press to make even. Bake at 350 degrees F. for 1¼ hours. Makes 6 servings.

Catsup Sauce: Combine 3 tablespoons brown sugar, ¼ cup catsup, ¼ teaspoon nutmeg, and 1 teaspoon Dijon mustard.

See menus for September, 3rd week.

Lamb

Baked Lamb Chop Dinner

8 shoulder lamb chops
1 large onion, sliced
1¼ cups (4 ounces) fresh
  mushrooms, sliced
1 can (10½ ounces) beef
  broth
Salt and pepper
8 potatoes, scrubbed or
  peeled, and halved

Brown lamb chops in skillet, using shortening as needed; remove chops. In same drippings, cook sliced onions and mushrooms until soft. Add broth and cook slightly until all drippings are gathered into mixture. Arrange 4 lamb chops in bottom of Dutch oven or casserole. Season with salt and pepper to taste. Add potatoes; season again. Top with remaining lamb chops. Pour broth, onions, and mushrooms over all. Cover and bake at 350 degrees F. for 1 to 1½ hours or at 250 degrees F. for 2 to 4 hours. Makes 8 servings.

Variation

Baked Pork Chop Dinner: Use pork shoulder chops in place of lamb chops.

See menus for July, 4th week.

Lamb Shish Kabobs

2 to 3 pounds boneless lamb
  shoulder or leg, cut in
  1½-inch cubes
1 teaspoon ground ginger
1 teaspoon dry mustard
1 teaspoon monosodium
  glutamate (optional)
2 teaspoons sugar or
  molasses
½ cup soy sauce
¼ cup vegetable oil
3 cloves garlic, minced
½ cup pineapple juice
Rice Pilaff (optional)

Combine all ingredients but lamb in glass or pottery bowl. Add lamb cubes; marinate in refrigerator for 6 to 8 hours. Arrange meat cubes on skewer, allowing space between every two pieces. Broil over hot coals or 3 inches from preheated oven broiler for about 15 minutes, turning frequently. If desired, thread whole canned mushrooms and small onions onto skewer alternately with pieces of lamb; add cherry tomatoes for last 5 minutes of cooking, if desired. Serve immediately with Rice Pilaff (p. 258), if desired. Makes 8 servings.

See menus for August, 2nd week.

Roast Leg of Lamb

1 leg of lamb, about 5 pounds
1½ cups fine dry bread
  crumbs
1 teaspoon thyme
½ teaspoon basil
1 teaspoon salt
¼ teaspoon pepper

Combine bread crumbs, thyme, basil, salt, and pepper; rub onto surface of lamb. Place lamb on rack in roasting pan. Roast at 325 degrees F. for 3 hours or until meat thermometer registers 175 to 180 degrees, depending upon desired degree of doneness. Do not overcook. Serve very hot or chilled. Makes 8 servings.

See menus for October, 2nd week.

Pork

Sausage Gravy

½ to 1 pound bulk pork
  sausage
4 tablespoons flour
2 cups milk
Ground sage
Pepper
Baked or mashed potatoes

Brown sausage in medium skillet. Stir flour into meat and blend well; add milk, and cook and stir until thick and blended. Season to taste with sage and pepper. Serve over baked or mashed potatoes. Makes 4 servings.

See menus for March, 3rd week.

Pan-Fried Sausage Links

1 pound pork sausage links
⅓ cup water

In medium to large skillet, arrange sausage links to cover bottom of pan. Add water and bring to boil over medium heat. Immediately lower heat, cover pan, and steam 5 to 10 minutes. Remove lid; continue to cook until water cooks away, then cook and turn until sausage links brown on all sides. Serve hot. Makes 4 to 5 servings.

See menus for February, 1st week.

Pork Chop Skillet

4 well-trimmed pork chops
1 can (10³/₄ ounces)
 condensed chicken broth
³/₄ cup water
1 can (1 pound) tomatoes,
 chopped
2¹/₂ cups (scant ¹/₂ pound)
 fine noodles, broken in
 pieces
Salt and pepper

In skillet brown pork chops using shortening if necessary; drain off fat. Add chicken broth and water. Cover pan; simmer 15 minutes. Add tomatoes and noodles; season to taste with salt and pepper. Cover; cook 15 minutes longer or until noodles are tender, stirring often. Makes 4 servings.

See menus for August, 1st week; November, 2nd week.

Pigs in Blankets

12 pork sausage links
 (³/₄ pound)
1 package (8 ounces)
 refrigerated dinner
 crescent rolls

Simmer pork sausage links in small amount water covered, for 5 minutes. Drain; cut links in half; set aside. Separate crescent rolls into two rectangles; pinch together perforations and pat dough to make two 4x10-inch rectangles. Cut each rectangle into 12 long thin triangles. Lay sausage piece on base of triangle; roll up sausage in dough and place on baking sheet with point tucked underneath, spacing rolls about 1 inch apart. Bake at 375 degrees F. for 5 to 7 minutes, or until biscuits are golden brown. Makes 2 dozen.

See menus for February, 4th week; March, 1st week; July, 4th week.

Oven Pork Chops

8 rib or loin pork chops,
 1-inch thick
2 tablespoons vegetable oil
1 tablespoon all-purpose flour
1 package (1¹/₂ ounces)
 Dehydrated Onion Soup
 Mix*
1¹/₄ cups boiling water
Celery leaves or parsley for
 garnish (optional)
1 cup dairy sour cream

Preheat oven to 325 degrees F. Brown chops in oil in hot skillet. Remove chops to baking pan. Pour fat from skillet, leaving about 1 tablespoon in pan. Add flour and Dehydrated Onion Soup Mix. Blend in water. Pour over chops. Cover with foil; bake in preheated oven for 1 to 1¹/₂ hours or until tender. Remove from oven. Place chops on serving plate. Garnish with celery leaves or parsley. To make gravy, blend sour cream into pan liquid; heat. Makes 8 servings.

*Dehydrated Onion Soup Mix: If preferred, homemade soup mix can be made by combining ¹/₄ cup dried minced onion, 2 tablespoons instant beef bouillon, and ¹/₂ teaspoon onion powder.

See menus for January, 4th week.

Sweet and Sour Pork

2 pork chops, boned and cut
  into small pieces
Cornstarch
⅓ cup vegetable oil
¼ cup catsup
⅓ cup cider vinegar
⅓ cup sugar
2 tablespoons soy sauce
1 cup water
3 cups prepared vegetables
  (any combination of diced
  carrots, green pepper,
  celery, onion, water
  chestnuts, mushrooms,
  bamboo shoots, or bean
  sprouts, each kept in
  separate units before
  cooking)
1½ tablespoons cornstarch
2 tablespoons cold water
Cooked rice

Roll small pieces of pork in cornstarch; allow to stand until juices of pork dissolve cornstarch coating. Heat oil in wok or heavy skillet over medium high heat. Add pork pieces; cook and stir with chopsticks or wooden spoon until meat is evenly browned. With slotted spoon, remove pork from pan and drain on paper toweling.

In large saucepan combine catsup, vinegar, sugar, soy sauce, and 1 cup water; bring to boil. Add hard vegetables (carrots, celery, water chestnuts, bamboo shoots); simmer 10 minutes. Then add soft vegetables (onions, bean sprouts, mushrooms, green pepper); simmer 2 minutes more. Blend together cornstarch and 2 tablespoons water; add to sauce; cook and stir until thick and translucent. Stir in meat; heat. Serve immediately with unsalted cooked rice. Makes 4 large servings.

See menus for October, 3rd week.

Orange-Glazed Pork Roast

30 min/lb

5 pounds blade end or "rib
  end" pork roast
1½ teaspoons ground
  ginger
¼ cup frozen orange juice
  concentrate, thawed
¼ cup honey

Have meat dealer cut bones from roast, then tie them back on with string for roasting. (Bone adds flavor to roast while cooking.) Rub surface of roast with 1 teaspoon ginger. Place roast on rack in shallow roasting pan. Insert meat thermometer so bulb is in center of thickest part of roast. Roast, uncovered at 325 degrees F. for about 2½ hours or until meat thermometer registers 170 degrees F. Meanwhile, combine orange juice concentrate, honey, and remaining ½ teaspoon ginger. Bring to boil; boil 1 minute. Cool slightly. Brush sauce over roast several times during last 30 minutes of cooking. Remove roast from oven; discard strings and bones. Allow to stand 15 minutes before slicing. Makes 12 servings.

See menus for April, 1st week.

Maple-Glazed Baked Ham

4-pound portion of boneless
  fully cooked ham
½ cup brown sugar
2 tablespoons maple-flavored
  syrup (or honey or cider
  vinegar)
1 teaspoon dry mustard
Whole cloves

Place ham on rack in shallow pan, fat side up. Bake at 325 degrees F. for 1¾ hours or until thermometer registers 140 degrees F. After first hour of roasting, remove ham from oven and score top, if desired, into a diamond pattern. Combine brown sugar with syrup (or honey or vinegar) and mustard; mix well and spread over outside of ham. Stud with whole cloves set into center of each diamond. Return to oven to finish baking. After removing meat from oven, allow it to stand for 15 minutes before carving. Makes 12 to 14 servings.

See menus for April, 3rd week.

Broiled Ham with Baby Limas and Cheese

4 slices ham, serving size,
  ¼ inch thick
1 package (10 ounces) frozen
  baby lima beans, cooked
  according to package
  directions
2 cups (8 ounces) Cheddar
  cheese

Arrange ham slices in shallow baking pan. Broil on one side; turn slices over. Spoon drained hot lima beans onto unbroiled side. Sprinkle cheese over top. Broil until hot and cheese is melted. Serve at once. Makes 4 servings.

See menus for April, 3rd week.

Sausage-Stuffed Acorn Squash

2 medium acorn squash
Dash salt
1 package (12 ounces) bulk
  pork sausage
1 cup (4 ounces) sliced fresh
  mushrooms
½ cup thinly sliced celery
¼ cup thinly sliced green
  onions
½ cup dairy sour cream
¼ cup Parmesan cheese
1 egg

Cut acorn squash in half; remove seeds. Place squash cut side down in 12x8-inch baking dish. Bake at 375 degrees F. for 45 minutes or until just tender. Turn squash cut side up; season with salt. In meantime, in large skillet, combine sausage, mushrooms, celery, and onions. Cook until tender; drain well. In small bowl, combine remaining ingredients; blend well and stir into sausage mixture. Spoon evenly into squash halves; continue to bake for 20 to 25 minutes longer or until thoroughly heated. Makes 4 servings.

    Note: To extend stuffing to fill 6 squash halves, add 1 to 1½ cups cooked white or brown rice to sausage mixture.

See menus for December, 3rd week.

Pork Pineapple Bake

1 can (12 ounces) pork
   luncheon meat
2 teaspoons Dijon mustard
1 can (8 or 9 ounces) sliced
   pineapple (4 slices), drained
   (save juice for other use)
Whole cloves (optional)
2 tablespoons brown sugar

Leaving luncheon meat whole, cut meat slightly more than half through loaf into 8 part-slices. Place in ungreased baking dish. Spoon ¹/₂ teaspoon mustard between every other cut. Cut pineapple slices in half. Insert half-slice in each cut; top loaf with remaining half-slice. Insert whole cloves in pineapple, if desired. Sprinkle brown sugar over pork. Bake at 375 degrees F. for 20 minutes. Makes 4 servings.

See menus for July, 3rd week; November, 1st week.

Pork 'N' Cabbage

1 can (12 ounces) pork
   luncheon meat
2 tablespoons vegetable oil
1 head (2 pounds) cabbage,
   quartered, sliced crosswise
   in 1-inch wide pieces
1 tablespoon soy sauce
¹/₂ teaspoon salt
¹/₄ teaspoon pepper

Cut luncheon meat into 1x2x¹/₄-inch pieces. In large skillet, brown meat in hot oil over high heat for 2 minutes, stirring. Add cabbage; cook about 5 minutes, uncovered, stirring occasionally as cabbage cooks down. Add soy sauce, salt, and pepper; simmer 1 minute longer. Makes 6 to 8 servings.

See menus for July, 2nd week; September, 1st week.

Lunch Kabobs

¹/₂ can (6-ounces) luncheon
   meat or 1 can (5 ounces)
   Vienna sausages
1 can (8 ounces) pineapple
   chunks
¹/₂ green pepper, seeded and
   cut into ³/₄-inch cubes
1-inch cubes Cheddar, Swiss,
   Monterey Jack, or other
   hard cheese

Cut luncheon meat into ³/₄-inch cubes or cut Vienna sausages in half. Thread meat, pineapple, green pepper, and cheese alternately onto wooden skewers or round toothpicks. Serve with bread and butter sandwiches. Makes 4 servings.

Note: Other items such as pickled onions, chunk pickles, cherry tomatoes, pitted ripe or stuffed green olives can also be used.

See menus for March, 2nd week.

Barbecued Frankfurters

1 pound frankfurters
2 cups Barbecue Sauce
  (p. 123)
Hot dog buns or cooked rice

In heavy saucepan cover frankfurters with barbecue sauce; heat to boiling. Lower heat, cover, and simmer 5 minutes or until frankfurters are heated through. Serve in hot dog buns or over cooked rice. Makes 4 servings.

See menus for July, 1st week.

Potato Frankfurters

1 pound frankfurters (8 to 10)
3 cups mashed potatoes
  (1½ pounds)
2 tablespoons grated onion
Salt and pepper
1 cup (4 ounces) Cheddar
  cheese, shredded
Dried or chopped fresh
  parsley

Prepare mashed potatoes, or instant mashed potatoes as directed on package; add onions; salt and pepper to taste. Cut frankfurters almost in half lengthwise; spread open. Spoon mashed potatoes on cut surfaces of frankfurters. Sprinkle with grated cheese and parsley. Bake at 400 degrees F. for about 8 minutes or broil until potatoes are hot and cheese is melted. Makes 4 servings.

See menus for January, 1st week.

Barbecued Pork Luncheon Meat

1 can (1 pound) sliced cling
  peaches
1 can (8 ounces) tomato sauce
¼ cup (packed) brown sugar
3 tablespoons cider or other
  vinegar
½ teaspoon salt
½ teaspoon Worcestershire
  sauce
1 teaspoon Dijon or other
  prepared mustard
¼ cup finely chopped onion
½ teaspoon chili powder
1 can (12 ounces) chopped or
  pork luncheon meat

Drain peaches, reserving juice for another purpose. Set aside 8 peach slices; cut remaining slices into 2 or 3 pieces. In large saucepan or skillet, combine peach pieces with remaining ingredients except luncheon meat. Bring to boil; simmer over low heat 5 minutes. Drain drippings from luncheon meat. Make 8 cuts, almost but not quite, through bottom of loaf, providing 9 slices. Insert 1 reserved peach slice into each cut. Place sliced meat with peaches into sauce. Cover saucepan; simmer until meat is hot, about 15 minutes. To serve, place luncheon meat on small platter. Spoon ½ cup sauce over meat. Serve remaining sauce in separate bowl. Makes 6 servings.

Variation

Sweet and Sour Luncheon Meat: Omit tomato sauce.

See menus for November, 3rd week.

Poultry

Oven-Fried Chicken

3-pound broiler-fryer
  chicken, cut into parts
⅓ cup all-purpose flour
1 teaspoon paprika
1 teaspoon salt
⅛ teaspoon pepper
¼ cup (½ stick) butter or
  margarine

Wash chicken pieces; pat dry; remove skin, if desired. Combine flour and seasonings in paper bag. Shake 2 to 3 pieces at a time in flour mixture. Arrange chicken pieces in greased shallow pan in single layer. Pour melted butter or margarine over chicken. Bake, uncovered, at 350 degrees F. for 60 minutes or until chicken is brown and tender. Makes 4 servings.

Chicken Gravy: For every 2 tablespoons drippings, stir in 2 tablespoons all-purpose flour and 1 cup chicken broth; cook and stir until smooth and thick.

Cream Gravy: Pour drippings from baking pan into measuring cup. Measure ½ cup fat (fat rises to top) back into baking pan; add ⅓ cup flour (leftover from coating chicken plus more flour as needed). Stir over low heat, loosening brown bits from baking pan, until smooth. Stir in 1 cup water or chicken broth; add 1½ cups half-and-half. Cook, stirring until thickened. Season. If gravy becomes too thick, stir in a little water. Serve with chicken.

Note: For an oven dinner, bake potatoes and carrots along with the chicken. Scrub potatoes and rub with oil. Pare carrots and cut into 2-inch chunks; place in loaf pan, dot with butter, season with salt and pepper and cover with foil. Bake for 1 hour at 400 degrees F.

See menus for January, 2nd week; April, 4th week; June, 1st week; October, 3rd week.

Easy Baked Tarragon Chicken

1 broiler-fryer chicken, cut
  into parts
½ cup lemon juice
1 cup fine unseasoned bread
  crumbs
2 to 3 teaspoons crushed
  dried tarragon
2 teaspoons crushed dried
  parsley flakes

Wash chicken pieces; dry with paper towel. Remove chicken skin, if desired. Dip chicken pieces into bowl containing lemon juice, then into bowl containing mixture of remaining ingredients, coating thoroughly. Place in shallow baking pan. Bake at 375 degrees F. for 45 minutes to 1 hour or until done. Makes 4 servings.

See menus for March, 2nd week; November, 2nd week; December, 2nd week.

Sesame Baked Chicken Breasts

1/3 cup (2/3 stick) butter or margarine
1 large egg, slightly beaten
1 1/2 tablespoons water
1 1/2 tablespoons soy sauce
1 1/4 teaspoons salt
1/8 teaspoon pepper
8 large chicken breast halves, boned and skinned
1/3 cup all-purpose flour
1/4 cup sesame seeds
Mushroom Sauce*

Preheat oven to 400 degrees F. Place butter in 8x12-inch baking pan; melt in oven as it preheats. In meantime blend egg, water, soy sauce, salt, and pepper. Dip chicken into flour, then into egg mixture. Arrange chicken breasts in pan, turning to coat with butter. Sprinkle generously with sesame seeds. Bake at 400 degrees F. for 40 to 45 minutes or until tender and golden brown. Serve with Mushroom Sauce. Makes 8 servings.

Mushroom Sauce: In medium saucepan melt 1/4 cup (1/2 stick) butter or margarine. Stir in 1/3 cup all-purpose flour. Remove from heat. Add 1 can (10 3/4 ounces) chicken broth; stir until smooth. Cook and stir until thick. Add 1/2 cup heavy cream, few grains pepper, 1 can (4 ounces) sliced mushrooms, and 2 tablespoons chopped fresh parsley (2 teaspoons dried).

See menus for May, 4th week; November, 1st week.

Baked Chicken with Sauerkraut

3-pound broiler-fryer chicken
1 quart (32 ounces) sauerkraut
1 small dried red chili pepper, crushed
1/2 teaspoon dried rosemary, crumbled
Juice of 1 lemon
2 teaspoons vegetable oil
Salt and pepper

Preheat oven to 375 degrees F. Cut chicken into serving pieces; wash and pat dry with paper towel; set aside. In strainer rinse sauerkraut with cold water; press with back of spoon until all moisture has been pressed out. Toss with ground pepper and rosemary and spread evenly in oiled 9-inch square baking dish. Arrange chicken, skin side up, over top of sauerkraut. Brush with lemon juice and oil; sprinkle lightly with salt and pepper to taste. Cover loosely with aluminum foil and bake in preheated oven for 1 1/2 hours. Remove foil during last half of baking to allow chicken to brown. Makes 4 servings.

See menus for January, 3rd week.

Barbecued Chicken Thighs

8 chicken thighs (about 2 1/2 pounds)
1 cup commercial or homemade Barbecue Sauce*

Wash thighs, pat dry, and remove skin and excess fat, if desired. Arrange thighs, meaty side up, in single layer in oiled 8 1/2x11-inch baking dish. Spoon Barbecue Sauce evenly over chicken. Bake at 350 degrees F. for 1 hour, spooning sauce over chicken two or three times. Makes 8 servings.

Quick Barbecue Sauce: Combine 2 tablespoons vinegar, 1¹/₂ tablespoons sugar, ²/₃ cup catsup, ¹/₃ cup water, ¹/₄ cup minced onion, and ¹/₈ teaspoon dry mustard. Simmer ingredients for 5 minutes. Makes 1¹/₂ cups sauce.

See menus for February, 1st week; April, 1st week; August, 2nd week.

Hot Chicken Salad

1¹/₂ cups (¹/₂ pound) diced cooked chicken breast
1¹/₂ cups sliced celery
³/₄ cup toasted bread cubes
¹/₂ cup mayonnaise
¹/₃ cup toasted slivered almonds
2 teaspoons lemon juice
2 teaspoons grated onion
¹/₂ teaspoon salt
Dash chili powder
¹/₃ cup shredded Cheddar cheese
2 teaspoons crushed dried parsley

Combine all ingredients except cheese. Pile lightly into 4 individual ramekins or 1-quart baking dish. Sprinkle with grated cheese and parsley. Bake at 450 degrees F. for 10 to 15 minutes or until bubbling hot. Makes 4 servings.

See menus for December, 2nd week.

Chicken a la King

¹/₄ cup (¹/₂ stick) butter or margarine
3 tablespoons all-purpose flour
1 cup chicken broth*
1 cup milk
³/₄ teaspoon salt
¹/₄ teaspoon white pepper
2 cups diced cooked chicken
Biscuits or toast

In medium saucepan melt butter or margarine; blend in flour. Add chicken broth and milk; cook and stir constantly over low heat until sauce is thick. Season to taste. Add chicken. If desired, add 1 can (2 ounces) mushroom stems and pieces, drained, and ¹/₄ cup chopped pimiento. Heat through. Serve over hot biscuits or toast. Makes 4 to 5 servings.

Note: To make chicken broth, dissolve 1 chicken bouillon cube in 1 cup boiling water.

See menus for January, 2nd week.

Oriental Chicken

4 chicken breast halves,
  skinned and boned
2 tablespoons all-purpose
  flour
1/2 teasoon salt
1/8 teaspoon pepper
2 tablespoons butter or
  margarine
3 tablespoons soy sauce
2 tablespoons honey
1/4 teaspoon ground ginger
  or gingerroot
2 grapefruit, sectioned
1 cup scallions or green
  onions, cut in 2-inch
  lengths

Cut chicken into 1x1x1/4-inch pieces. Combine flour, salt, and pepper; dredge chicken in flour mixture. In large skillet melt butter or margarine; add chicken, a small amount at a time; stir-fry until chicken has turned white all the way through. Combine soy sauce, honey, ginger or gingerroot, and juice from grapefruit sections; pour over chicken. Add scallions or onions and grapefruit sections. Toss gently. Cook until just heated through; *do not overcook.* Serve immediately. Makes 4 servings.

To section grapefruit: With an up-and-down motion, peel whole grapefruit with sharp or serrated knife, going round and round as you might for an apple and cutting deeply enough to remove white membrane. To extract sections, cut close to membrane on each side of grapefruit section and carefully slip it out. Squeeze juice from remaining membrane into bowl with fruit.

See menus for June, 3rd week; September, 2nd week.

Quick Chow Mein

2 cups cooked meat (beef,
  pork, venison, chicken), cut
  into 1/2-inch strips or cubes
2 tablespoons chopped or
  slivered onion
1/2 green pepper, cut in strips
  lengthwise
1 1/2 cups celery, diagonally
  sliced
2 tablespoons shortening
1 teaspoon salt
1 cup boiling water
1 bouillon cube or 1 teaspoon
  instant bouillon granules
2 tablespoons cornstarch
2 teaspoons (or more)
  soy sauce
1/4 cup cold water
Cooked rice

Prepare meat and vegetables; set aside in separate piles. In hot shortening in wok or heavy skillet, stir-fry meat and onion until lightly browned. Add salt and boiling water in which bouillon has been dissolved. Lower heat, cover mixture, and cook 10 minutes. Add green pepper and celery; cover and cook 5 minutes. Blend cornstarch, soy sauce, and cold water. Add to meat and cook, stirring until thick. Serve immediately on cooked rice. Makes 4 servings.

See menus for January, 3rd week; April, 1st week.

Kung Po Chicken

1 tablespoon pineapple (or other fruit) juice
1 tablespoon cornstarch
1/2 teaspoon salt
1/8 teaspoon pepper
2 uncooked chicken breast halves, skinned, boned, and cut into bite-size pieces
4 tablespoons vegetable oil
Cooking Sauce*
4 to 6 small dry hot chili peppers (found in spice section of market)
1/2 cup salted peanuts
1 clove garlic, minced
1 teaspoon grated fresh ginger
2 green onions, including stems, sliced

In medium bowl combine pineapple juice, cornstarch, salt, and pepper. Add chicken; stir to coat, then stir in 1 tablespoon oil; let stand 15 minutes to marinate. Prepare Cooking Sauce and set aside. Heat wok or large frying pan over medium heat. When pan is hot, add 1 tablespoon oil. Add whole dry hot chili peppers and peanuts, stirring until peppers begin to char. Immediately remove peppers and peanuts from pan and set aside. (If peppers become completely black, discard; remove peanuts from pan and repeat with new peppers.) Add remaining 2 tablespoons oil to pan; increase heat to high. When oil begins to heat, add garlic and ginger. Stir once, then add chicken and stir-fry until chicken becomes opaque, about 3 minutes. Add peppers, peanuts, and onion to pan. Stir Cooking Sauce, add to pan and cook, stirring until sauce bubbles and thickens. Makes 4 servings.

Cooking Sauce: In bowl combine 2 tablespoons soy sauce, 1 tablespoon white wine (or other) vinegar, 1/4 cup chicken broth or water, 2 teaspoons sugar, and 2 teaspoons cornstarch.

See menus for August, 3rd week.

Chicken with Herb Sauce

6 chicken breast halves, boned and skinned
1/3 cup (2/3 stick) butter, margarine, or shortening, melted
1/4 pound fresh mushrooms, sliced
1/2 cup chopped fresh parsley or 3 tablespoons dried parsley
1/4 cup chopped onion
1/3 cup all-purpose flour
3 cups chicken stock*
3/4 cup light cream
Pinch each of sage, rosemary, and basil
1 bay leaf
1/4 teaspoon salt
Cooked rice

Brush chicken breasts with melted butter, margarine, or shortening. Place in shallow pan and bake at 375 degrees F. for 45 minutes. In meantime, sauté mushrooms in medium skillet in 2 tablespoons butter or margarine; empty mushrooms and juice from pan; set aside. In same skillet in 3 tablespoons melted butter or margarine stir parsley, onion, and flour. Blend in chicken stock, cream, and seasonings. Cook and stir until thick and smooth; simmer 20 to 30 minutes. Add drained mushrooms. Pour sauce over chicken at end of 45 minute period; bake 15 to 20 minutes longer. To serve, placed cooked rice in center of platter. Arrange chicken around rice; pour sauce over rice. Makes 6 servings.

Note: To make chicken stock, dissolve 3 chicken bouillon cubes in 3 cups boiling water.

See menus for March, 3rd week.

Curried Chicken

3-pound broiler-fryer chicken, cut into parts
4 cups water
Sliced carrots, onion, celery or celery leaves, and black peppercorns
1/3 cup (2/3 stick) butter or margarine
1 cup chopped onion (1 large onion)
1 cup diced celery
4 to 5 cloves garlic, minced (optional)
1 to 2 tablespoons curry powder, or to taste
1/2 cup all-purpose flour
1 teaspoon dry mustard
1/2 teaspoon salt
1/4 teaspoon pepper
1 teaspoon paprika
Dash cayenne
1 1/4 cups strong beef broth or bouillon or 1 can (10 1/2 ounces) beef broth
1 cup light cream
3 tablespoons catsup
Cooked rice

In large kettle cover chicken with water; add sliced carrots, onion, celery or celery leaves, and black peppercorns; cook until tender. Remove chicken (saving stock for use in other cooking); skin, bone, and cut chicken meat into bite-size pieces; set aside. Melt butter or margarine in large skillet. Add 1 cup onion, 1 cup celery, garlic, and curry powder; cook and stir over low heat until onion is soft.

Combine remaining dry ingredients and add to onion mixture, stirring over low heat until blended. Slowly add beef stock and cream, stirring until thick and smooth. Add catsup. Cook for 2 minutes, then add chicken and heat to boiling point. Serve over cooked rice. May be served with any or all of the following condiments: chopped hard-cooked eggs, chopped onion or sliced green onion, shredded coconut, chopped salted peanuts, sweet pickle relish, chutney, chopped green pepper, chopped green or ripe olives, orange marmalade, chopped cooked crisp bacon, raisins, crushed pineapple. Curry is best if made a day ahead and reheated. Makes 6 to 8 servings.

See menus for February, 3rd week.

Chicken Cashew

1 cup diced celery
1/3 cup chopped onion
1/2 cup diced green pepper
1 tablespoon butter or margarine
1 can (10 3/4 ounces) condensed cream of mushroom soup
1/2 cup milk
2 cups diced cooked chicken
1 can (3 ounces) chow mein noodles
1 cup (4 ounces) salted cashews

Sauté celery, onion, and green pepper in butter or margarine. Mix soup with milk. Stir into celery mixture along with chicken, 1 1/2 cups of the noodles, and cashews. Pour into buttered 1 1/2-quart casserole. Sprinkle with remaining chow mein noodles. Bake at 350 degrees F. for 30 minutes. Makes 4 to 6 servings.

Variation

Tuna Cashew: In place of chicken use 1 can (6 1/2 ounces) chunk-style tuna fish, drained.

See menus for April, 4th week.

Chicken Crisp

3-pound broiler-fryer
 chicken
¼ cup minced onion
2 teaspoons instant beef
 bouillon
⅛ teaspoon onion powder
1 cup dairy sour cream
1 can (3 ounces) chow mein
 noodles

Disjoint chicken. Set wings, necks, and giblets aside for another use. Rinse chicken pieces in cold water; pat dry. For fewer calories, remove skin. Arrange chicken pieces (if not skinned, arrange with skin side up) in 7½x11¾-inch baking dish. Combine onion, instant beef bouillon, onion powder, and dairy sour cream. Spread over chicken. Bake at 350 degrees F. for 50 minutes. Sprinkle noodles over top of chicken and bake 10 minutes longer. Makes 4 servings.

Note: Two tablespoons dried onion soup mix may be used in place of mixture of dried minced onion, instant beef bouillon, and onion powder. Also, casserole may be prepared the night before and kept chilled until ready to bake.

See menus for May, 1st week.

Chicken Divan

4 chicken breast halves
1 cup water
1 bay leaf
1 small onion, sliced
⅛ teaspoon pepper
1 pound fresh broccoli or 1
 package (10 ounces) frozen
 broccoli
1 can (10¾ ounces) cream of
 chicken soup
½ cup mayonnaise, dairy
 sour cream, or plain yogurt
1 teaspoon lemon juice
½ teaspoon curry powder
1 cup (4 ounces) shredded
 sharp Cheddar cheese

In large skillet place chicken breasts. Add water, bay leaf, onion, and pepper. Cover and simmer for 30 minutes or until breasts are tender when pierced with sharp knife. Skin, bone, and cut meat into 2x4-inch pieces; set aside. Cook broccoli until crisp-tender. Arrange on bottom of 9x9x2-inch baking dish. Place chicken over broccoli. Mix together chicken soup, mayonnaise or sour cream or yogurt, lemon juice, and curry powder. Pour over chicken and broccoli. Sprinkle cheese over top. Cover with foil. Bake at 350 degrees F. for 30 to 35 minutes or until bubbling hot. Do not overbake. Makes 4 servings.

Note: Fresh or frozen asparagus or frozen or canned artichoke hearts may be used in place of broccoli. Cooked turkey breast may be used in place of chicken.

Variation

Chicken Divan with Rice: Use one 3-pound broiler-fryer, cut in pieces, in place of chicken breasts; cook as directed. In bottom of buttered 9x13-inch casserole, spread 3 cups cooked rice. Arrange cooked broccoli over rice, then top with chicken pieces. Dot soup mixture over top and spread lightly to cover casserole; top evenly with cheese. Makes 8 servings.

See menus for April, 2nd week.

Chicken Asparagus Stir-Fry

2 chicken breast halves
2 tablespoons vegetable oil
1 cup sliced celery
1/2 cup sliced green onion
4 cups diagonally sliced
   1-inch asparagus pieces
2 tablespoons vegetable oil
1 clove garlic, minced
1 tablespoon grated fresh
   gingerroot
2 teaspoons grated orange
   rind
3 tablespoons soy sauce
1 tablespoon cornstarch
1/2 cup water
1/3 cup orange juice
1/2 cup cashew nuts
Cooked rice

Skin and bone chicken breasts; cut into 1/2x1-inch pieces; set aside. Heat 2 tablespoons oil in wok or large frying pan; add celery; stir-fry for 1 minute. Add green onion and asparagus; stir-fry 3 to 5 minutes, until asparagus is bright green. Transfer cooked vegetables to bowl; set aside. In same skillet, heat 2 tablespoons oil. Add chicken, garlic, gingerroot, orange rind, and soy sauce. Stir-fry until chicken is barely cooked, about 5 minutes. In small bowl combine cornstarch, water, and orange juice, set aside. Return vegetables to chicken in wok or skillet. Add cashews and toss. Add cornstarch mixture; reheat, stirring quickly, until sauce thickens, about 3 minutes. Serve hot over cooked rice. Makes 4 to 6 servings.

Variation

Chicken Vegetable Stir-Fry: In place of asparagus, use thinly sliced or coarsely shredded celery, cabbage, or broccoli.

See menus for April, 3rd week; May, 3rd week.

Quick and Easy Cassoulet

1 to 2 chicken breast halves
1 large onion, chopped
1 clove garlic, minced
2 tablespoons vegetable oil
2 cans (1 pound each) great
   northern or other white
   beans, drained, or 4 cups
   drained cooked navy or
   white beans (1 cup
   uncooked)
1/2 pound fully cooked
   smoked sausage, cut in
   1/2-inch pieces
1 can (8 ounces) tomato sauce
1/2 teaspoon dried thyme,
   crushed
Salt to taste
1/8 teaspoon pepper

Skin and bone uncooked chicken breast(s); cut into 1-inch pieces. (Two chicken breasts will yield 2 cups of boneless chicken pieces.) Sauté chicken, onion, and garlic in oil in heavy saucepan until onion is tender and chicken lightly browned. Stir in remaining ingredients, cover and simmer 15 minutes or longer. Makes 8 servings.

Note: If desired, use 2 cans (1 pound each) pork and beans, undrained, and omit tomato sauce.

See menus for May, 3rd week; August, 4th week; December, 1st week.

Chicken and Rice Casserole

3-pound broiler-fryer
  chicken, cut into parts
1 large onion, sliced
1 tablespoon salt
2 cups water
1 teaspoon salt
1 cup uncooked long grain
  rice
1/2 cup (1 stick) butter or
  margarine
1 cup (4 ounces) sliced fresh
  mushrooms
1/2 cup all-purpose flour
3 cups chicken broth*
1 cup heavy cream
1 teaspoon salt
1/4 teaspoon pepper
1/4 teaspoon turmeric
1/4 teaspoon crushed dried
  oregano
2 tablespoons sliced green
  onion
1 cup (4 ounces) shredded
  Cheddar cheese

Wash chicken parts. In large kettle cook chicken parts in enough water to barely cover chicken; add sliced onion and 1 tablespoon salt. When chicken is tender, drain; save broth. Remove bone and skin from chicken pieces; cut into pieces and set aside. In medium saucepan bring 2 cups water to boil, add 1 teaspoon salt; stir in rice, reduce heat; cover and cook 25 minutes.

Meanwhile, in medium saucepan melt butter or margarine over medium heat; add sliced mushrooms; cook and stir until lightly browned. Sprinkle flour over mushrooms and gently stir. Add 3 cups reserved chicken broth; cook and stir until smooth and thick. Add cream and seasonings. Spoon cooked rice into 3-quart casserole; top with chicken, then with sauce. Sprinkle with sliced green onions and cheese. Bake at 400 degrees F. for 20 to 30 minutes. Makes 8 to 10 servings.

*Note: To make chicken broth, dissolve 3 bouillon cubes in 3 cups boiling water.

Variation

Quick Chicken and Rice Casserole: Prepare 1 package (7 ounces) quick-cooking rice according to package directions. Spoon into 2-quart casserole. Arrange two 5-ounce cans chunk chicken over top. Combine 1 can (10 3/4 ounces) cream of chicken soup with 1 can (10 3/4 ounces) chicken broth and 3/4 cup heavy cream. Season as above with turmeric and oregano. If desired, add 1 can (4 ounces) mushrooms stems and pieces, drained. Pour sauce over casserole. Top with green onions and cheese; bake as above. Makes 6 to 8 servings.

See menus for November, 3rd week.

Hamburgers

1 pound lean ground beef

Shape beef into four half-inch-thick patties. Place on broiler pan, and broil 3 inches from source of heat to desired doneness, turning once. Allow about 8 minutes total time for rare, 10 minutes for medium, 12 minutes for well-done. Season and serve. Makes 4 patties.

See menus for February, 4th week; August, 3rd week; October, 1st week.

8- to 12-pound turkey (for family of 4)

Turkeys may be purchased fresh or fresh frozen, allowing ½ to ¾ pounds (ready-to-cook weight) per serving. (Leftover cooked turkey can be stored in freezer for 1 to 2 months to be used for sandwiches or casseroles.)

1. To thaw frozen turkey, leave bird in original bag and use one of the following methods:

    a. Place on tray in refrigerator for 2 to 4 days, allowing 24 hours of thawing time for each 5 pounds of turkey weight.

    b. Immerse turkey in cool water; allow 30 minutes per pound of turkey weight for thawing time; change water frequently. Turkey should be thoroughly defrosted before roasting.

   Refrigerate or cook turkey as soon as it is thawed. If turkey is to be stuffed, do so just before roasting. Follow instructions on bag for commercially-stuffed turkey. Refreezing uncooked turkey is not recommended.

2. To prepare turkey, remove plastic covering from around bird; remove neck and giblets from cavities; rinse turkey and wipe dry. Cook neck and giblets in water to cover until tender; use giblets or broth or both for flavoring stuffing and for giblet gravy. Follow recipe for Old-Fashioned Sage Stuffing (p. 132).

   The National Turkey Federation recommends that turkeys be roasted unstuffed; they are easier to prepare and require less roasting time. If turkey is not to be stuffed, rub salt generously into cavities, and if desired, insert pieces of celery, carrots, onion, and parsley for flavor. Roast according to time and temperature chart accompanying this recipe. Prepared stuffing can be baked, covered, in casserole or shallow dripper pan at 375 degrees F. for 20 to 40 minutes or until hot. This can be done after turkey is removed from oven and before or while it is being carved.

   If turkey is to be stuffed, allow ¾ cup stuffing per pound of ready-to-cook weight. Extra stuffing may be baked on side as described above.

3. To roast:

   a. Fasten down legs either by tying or tucking under skin band. Neck skin should be skewered to back, and tip of wings can be tucked under back of turkey.

   b. Place turkey, breast up, on rack in shallow roasting pan. Brush with melted butter, margarine, or vegetable oil, if desired. If thermometer is to be used, insert into thickest part of inside thigh. Bulb must not touch bone. Roast in preheated 325 degree F. oven. The time chart, which follows the recipe, is a guide to the length of roasting time. A "tent" of foil placed loosely over turkey will eliminate the need to baste, although turkey may be basted, if desired. Remove foil last half hour for final browning.

   c. If turkey is lightweight enough for convenient handling, it can be roasted, breast-side down, in V-shaped rack for first half of roasting time. Insert thermometer into turkey after it is turned breast-side up. The breast-down method results in juicier white meat.

4. Turkey is done when thermometer registers from 180 to 185 degrees F. and when juices run clear after long-tined fork is pierced into deepest part of thigh and puncture area is pressed firmly.

5. Allow turkey to stand 15 to 20 minutes after removal from oven, then remove stuffing (if used)and carve. Store leftover stuffing in separate container in refrigerator or freezer; do not leave in bird. Refrigerate turkey within 2 hours and refrigerate or freeze.

See menus for February, 2nd week; November, 4th week.

Regardless of size, turkeys roasted using meat thermometer should be cooked until thermometer reads from 180 to 185 degrees F.

Ready-to-Cook Weight	Approximate Cooking Time
4 to 6 pounds	1¹/₂ to 2¹/₄ hours
6 to 8 pounds	2¹/₄ to 3¹/₄ hours (unstuffed) 3 to 3¹/₂ hours (stuffed)
8 to 12 pounds	3 to 4 hours (unstuffed) 3¹/₂ to 4¹/₂ hours (stuffed)
12 to 16 pounds	3¹/₂ to 4¹/₂ hours (unstuffed) 4¹/₂ to 5¹/₂ hours (stuffed)
16 to 20 pounds	4 to 5 hours (unstuffed) 5¹/₂ to 6¹/₂ hours (stuffed)
20 to 24 pounds	4¹/₂ to 5¹/₂ hours (unstuffed) 6¹/₂ to 7 hours (stuffed)
24 to 28 pounds	5 to 6¹/₂ hours (unstuffed) 7 to 8¹/₂ hours (stuffed)

Because turkeys vary in conformation, variety, and degree to which they have been thawed, cooking times can be only approximate. Because of this, it would be well to allow an extra half hour of roasting time in case turkey needs extra cooking.

Old-Fashioned Sage Stuffing

1¹/₂ cups diced celery
¹/₂ cup chopped onion
¹/₄ cup (¹/₂ stick) melted butter
1¹/₂ quarts (9 ounces) dried bread cubes
1 teaspoon salt
1 teaspoon dried sage, crushed
¹/₂ teaspoon poultry seasoning
¹/₄ teaspoon pepper
Hot broth or water

Cook celery and onion in butter or margarine over medium heat until onion is transparent but not brown, stirring occasionally. Combine with bread cubes and seasoning; toss lightly. Add enough broth to moisten as desired. Add additional seasoning to taste. Makes 4 servings or enough dressing to stuff 8- to 10-pound turkey.

Variations

Giblet Stuffing: Add chopped, cooked giblets; use giblet broth as liquid.

Raisin Stuffing: Add ³/₄ cup seedless raisins; add ¹/₄ cup chopped nuts also, if desired.

Chestnut Stuffing: Add 2 cups boiled chestnuts, chopped; use milk for liquid.

Mushroom Stuffing: Add one 6-ounce can broiled, sliced mushrooms, drained. Or cook 1 cup sliced, fresh mushrooms in a little butter before adding to dressing.

See menus for February, 2nd week; November, 4th week.

Stuffed Cornish Game Hens

2 frozen Rock Cornish game hens
½ pound sage-seasoned pork sausage
½ tablespoon butter or margarine
⅓ cup minced fennel bulb or celery
⅓ cup chopped onion
1 clove garlic, minced
1 tablespoon butter
½ cup coarse dry bread crumbs
½ teaspoon crushed fennel seed
½ teaspoon crushed dried sage
Salt and pepper

Thaw game hens. Remove neck, liver, and gizzards; use for making stock or in some other way. Wash game hens, pat dry and set aside. In large skillet cook pork sausage in ½ tablespoon butter or margarine over medium heat, stirring until meat is crumbled and no longer pink; transfer drained sausage to large bowl. In skillet cook minced fennel bulb or celery, onion, and garlic in 1 tablespoon butter over medium heat until soft; add bread crumbs, crushed fennel seed, and sage. Combine with cooked sausage. Season to taste.

Salt game hens inside and out. Fill cavities loosely with stuffing. With clean string, tie legs together and wings close to body. Arrange, breast side up, on rack in shallow roasting pan; brush with melted butter. Bake at 400 degrees F. for 20 minutes, basting twice with pan juices; reduce heat to 350 degrees and continue roasting for 25 minutes more or until juices run clear when fleshy part of thigh is pricked with skewer. Baste once or twice more. Transfer hens to cutting board, remove trussing strings, and cut hens in half with kitchen shears; arrange, cut side down, on heated platter. Garnish as desired. Makes 4 servings.

Note: Any favorite stuffing can be used for game hens; or they can be roasted unstuffed.

See menus for March, 4th week.

Turkey Dressing Casserole

2 to 3 cups leftover dressing
2 cups or more slices or pieces of turkey
½ cup (1 stick) butter or margarine
¼ cup all-purpose flour
2 cups chicken or turkey broth*
½ cup milk
2 eggs, beaten
1 teaspoon salt
½ cup buttered bread crumbs

In 2-quart casserole, layer dressing and leftover turkey. In saucepan melt butter or margarine, stir in flour; add broth, milk, and salt; cook and stir until thick and smooth. Add a little hot mixture to beaten egg, stirring; stir egg mixture back into heated sauce. Pour over casserole. Sprinkle buttered crumbs evenly over top. Bake at 350 degrees F. for 30 to 40 minutes, or until bubbly hot. Makes 4 servings.

Note: To make broth, dissolve 2 chicken bouillon cubes in 2 cups boiling water.

See menus for November, 4th week.

Fish

Sweet and Sour Tuna

2 cans (6½ ounces each) tuna, drained
3 tablespoons butter or margarine
1 large green pepper, cut in strips
1½ cups celery, diagonally sliced
2 tablespoons cornstarch
½ teaspoon fresh grated ginger
3 tablespoons vinegar
3 teaspoons soy sauce
1 can (20 ounces) pineapple chunks
2 chicken bouillon cubes or 2 teaspoons instant bouillon
6 cups cooked rice (2 cups uncooked)

Drain tuna fish; if packed in oil, oil may be used in place of butter or margarine. Heat butter or tuna oil in skillet. Add green pepper and celery; cook over high heat about 2 minutes. Measure cornstarch and ginger into 2-cup measure. Add vinegar, soy sauce, and syrup drained from pineapple; add enough water to make 1½ cups. Add liquid to skillet along with tuna, pineapple, and bouillon. Cook, stirring constantly, until bouillon cube is dissolved and mixture is thick and hot. Serve over cooked rice. Makes 8 servings.

See menus for January, 4th week.

Tuna Loaf

2 cans (6½ ounces each)
chunk-style tuna, packed
in water
1 cup soft (not dry) bread
crumbs
1 egg
½ cup milk
1 medium onion, chopped
(about ½ cup)
¼ cup chopped fresh parsley
or 1½ tablespoons dried
parsley
2 teaspoons lemon juice
1 teaspoon salt
¼ teaspoon pepper
¼ teaspoon crushed dried
thyme

Mix together all ingredients. Bake in greased 8x4x2-inch loaf pan at 350 degrees F. for 50 minutes or until firm. Cool in pan 10 minutes. Cut into slices and serve. Makes 6 to 8 servings.

Note: If desired, 1 can (8 ounces) tomato sauce can be heated and served over slices of tuna loaf.

See menus for June, 4th week.

Tuna Rice Skillet

1 cup chopped onion
½ green pepper, diced
2 tablespoons butter or
margarine
1⅓ cups uncooked long
grain rice
1 can (16 ounces) tomato
sauce
2½ cups water
½ teaspoon salt
¼ teaspoon dried marjoram
2 cans (6½ ounces each)
chunk-style tuna, drained
1 cup (4 ounces) coarsely
shredded Cheddar cheese
1 can (2¼ ounces) sliced
ripe olives (optional)

In large skillet cook onion and green pepper in butter or margarine until soft. Add rice; stir. Add tomato sauce, water, salt, and marjoram. Bring to boil, cover and turn heat to low. Cook 30 minutes or until rice is tender. Remove cover. Fold in drained and flaked tuna. Sprinkle cheese over top, then sliced olives. Cover; heat gently until cheese is melted. Makes 8 servings.

See menus for June, 1st week; December, 1st week.

Creamed Tuna Fish

3 tablespoons butter or
  margarine
2 tablespoons chopped onion
$\frac{1}{4}$ cup all-purpose flour
2 cups milk
Salt, pepper, paprika to taste
1 can (6$\frac{1}{2}$ ounces) tuna fish,
  chunk style
Crackers, toast, cooked rice,
  baked potato, or parsleyed
  noodles

In medium saucepan melt butter, sauté onion, then stir in flour until blended. Add milk; cook and stir until mixture is smooth and thick. Season to taste. Stir in tuna and heat. Serve over crackers, toast, cooked rice, baked potato, or parsleyed noodles. Makes 4 servings.

Note: Pimiento, sautéed green pepper, and mushrooms may be added to mixture as desired.

Variation

Creamed Chipped (or Dried) Beef: Make white sauce as above, omitting salt. Use 1 jar (4$\frac{1}{2}$ ounces) chipped or dried beef in place of tuna; tear beef into bite-size pieces.

See menus for January, 4th week; October, 4th week; December, 4th week.

Fish Zucchini Bake

1 pound fish fillets (such as
  cod, perch, sole, haddock),
  frozen or fresh
2 tablespoons chopped
  onion
2 teaspoons vegetable oil
2 cups ($\frac{1}{2}$ pound) diced,
  unpeeled, young zucchini
1 can (8 ounces) tomato sauce
$\frac{1}{2}$ cup (2 ounces) sliced
  mushrooms
$\frac{1}{4}$ teaspoon crushed leaf
  basil
$\frac{1}{8}$ teaspoon pepper
Salt

Thaw fillets, if necessary. Cut into four serving-size pieces; arrange in single layer in greased shallow baking pan. Sauté onion in oil; add zucchini; cook until barely tender, about 5 minutes. Place $\frac{1}{4}$ zucchini-onion mixture on each fillet. Combine tomato sauce, mushrooms, basil, pepper, and salt to taste; pour over fish. Bake at 350 degrees F. for 20 minutes or until fish flakes easily when tested with fork. Makes 4 servings.

See menus for July, 3rd week.

Herb-Broiled Fish Fillets

1 pound fish fillets (such as haddock, cod, halibut)
2 tablespoons melted butter or margarine
2 tablespoons chopped onion or sliced green onion
1 cup (3 ounces) fresh mushrooms, sliced
1 cup tomatoes, chopped
1/8 teaspoon crushed dried basil
3/4 teaspoon salt
Dash pepper
Tartar Sauce*
Lemon wedges (optional)

Cut fish into serving pieces and arrange in buttered 8x8x2-inch baking dish. Brush with melted butter or margarine; broil 3 to 4 minutes. Turn fillets over and top with vegetables. Sprinkle with seasonings. Broil for an additional 5 to 7 minutes or until fish flakes easily with fork. Serve with lemon wedges and Tartar Sauce. Makes 4 servings.

Tartar Sauce: In mixing bowl, mix together 1 cup mayonnaise (or part plain yogurt); 1 tablespoon capers, drained and chopped fine; 1 teaspoon Dijon mustard; 2 tablespoons finely-chopped gherkins; 2 teaspoons lemon juice; 1/2 teaspoon grated onion; 1 1/2 tablespoons chopped fresh parsley. Serve at room temperature. Makes 1 1/4 cups.

See menus for February, 2nd week; June, 3rd week; September, 2nd week.

German Fish Skillet

1 pound fresh or frozen fish fillets (such as haddock, perch, cod)
1/4 pound (about 5 slices) bacon, diced
1/2 cup all-purpose flour
1/2 teaspoon paprika
1/2 teaspoon salt
1/8 teaspoon pepper
1 1/2 pounds medium potatoes, cooked and sliced
1 tablespoon vegetable oil
3/4 cup chopped onion
1 1/2 tablespoons all-purpose flour
3/4 cup water
3/4 cup vinegar
1/4 cup sugar
1/4 teaspoon salt
1/8 teaspoon pepper
2 tablespoons parsley, chopped or 2 teaspoons dried parsley

Thaw fish if frozen. In large skillet fry bacon until brown and crisp; remove from skillet and set aside, reserving drippings. Combine 1/2 cup flour, paprika, salt, and pepper; dip fish fillets in flour mixture to coat. Fry fish in bacon drippings, adding additional vegetable oil, if needed. Keep fried fish warm while peeling and slicing potatoes. Scrape skillet clean; add 1 tablespoon oil and sauté onion. Blend in 1 1/2 tablespoons flour; gradually add water and vinegar. Stir in sugar, salt, and pepper. Heat mixture to boiling, stirring constantly; boil for 1 minute. Stir in potatoes and parsley; heat. To serve, place potato mixture in warmed serving dish with fillets arranged on top. Sprinkle with bacon pieces. Makes 4 servings.

See menus for March, 1st week.

Baked Cod with Tomato-Caper Sauce

1 tablespoon vegetable oil
1 small onion, finely chopped
1 clove garlic, minced
2 cups chopped fresh tomato
or 1 can (16 ounces) whole
tomatoes, chopped
1½ to 2 pounds cod fillets,
fresh or frozen
Salt and pepper
2 tablespoons chopped capers
2 tablespoons white wine
vinegar or other vinegar
diluted in ⅓ cup water

To make sauce, heat oil in large skillet. Add onion and garlic; sauté. Add tomatoes; cook over medium low heat for 15 minutes, stirring occasionally. Season to taste with salt and pepper to taste. Stir in capers. Keep warm. In meantime, heat oven to 425 degrees F. Lay fillets side by side in buttered baking dish. Sprinkle lightly with salt and pepper to taste. Add diluted white wine vinegar, cover with wax paper, and bake 10 to 15 minutes or until fish flakes easily. Spoon 2 tablespoons sauce over each fillet; serve remaining sauce on the side. Makes 8 servings.

Note: Since capers are somewhat expensive, chopped dill pickle may be used in their place, but the results are not as tasty.

See menus for May, 1st week; October, 4th week.

Broiled Swordfish Steaks with Cumin

1 teaspoon curry powder
4 cloves garlic, minced
2 tablespoons ground cumin
Salt to taste
2 tablespoons white wine
vinegar diluted with ¼
cup water
¼ cup vegetable oil
¼ cup fresh lemon juice
1½ pounds swordfish (or
other fish) steaks, ½ to ¾
inches thick
4 tablespoons chopped fresh
coriander or parsley

Preheat broiler. Mix together curry powder, garlic, cumin, salt, water, vinegar, oil, and lemon juice. Place in wide bowl. Add fish, and marinate in mixture for 15 minutes, turning from time to time. Remove fish from marinade and broil for 5 minutes on each side, basting once. Meanwhile, place marinade in small saucepan; heat to simmering. When fish is done, arrange on serving plate, pour marinade over fish, and sprinkle with chopped coriander or parsley. Makes 4 servings.

See menus for May, 3rd week.

Baked Stuffed Fish

3 to 4 pounds whole fish,
dressed for stuffing
Salt and pepper
1 package (5 ounces)
seasoned stuffing mix
¼ cup (½ stick) butter or
margarine, melted
1 tablespoon lemon juice

Preheat oven to 450 degrees F. Rinse fish and wipe dry. Cut fish inside along each side of backbone; remove bone, but leave skin uncut. Sprinkle inside and out with salt and pepper to taste. Prepare stuffing mix according to package directions. Stuff fish with mixture. Close stuffed area with toothpicks. Arrange fish in greased baking dish; spoon on melted butter or margarine and lemon juice. Bake fish on top shelf of oven, allowing 10 minutes of cooking time per inch of depth for fresh fish, measuring stuffed fish at its deepest point. Makes 8 servings.

Note: Any favorite stuffing may be used, allowing about 1 to 2 cups bread crumbs, rice, or other base ingredient.

See menus for October, 1st week.

Baked Halibut

1 pound halibut fish fillets
4 tablespoons (½ stick) butter or margarine
½ small onion, finely grated
2 tablespoons fresh lemon juice
Paprika
Fresh chopped parsley (optional)
Lemon wedges (optional)
Tartar Sauce (p. 137)

Preheat oven to 450 degrees F. In baking pan large enough to hold fillets, place butter or margarine; set into oven just long enough to melt butter. Dip fillets in melted butter, turning to coat all sides. Spread grated onion evenly over each fillet; squeeze fresh lemon juice over top of fillets; sprinkle liberally with paprika. Bake in preheated oven, allowing 10 minutes of cooking time for each 1 inch of thickness in fillets. When done, fish will flake at thickest portion. Sprinkle with chopped fresh parsley. Serve immediately with lemon wedges or Tartar Sauce. Makes 4 servings.

See menus for May, 2nd week; December, 4th week.

Halibut au Gratin

2 pounds fresh or frozen halibut (or turbot)
1 small onion, sliced
2 bay leaves
¼ cup (½ stick) butter or margarine
4 tablespoons all-purpose flour
2 cups milk
2 cups (½ pound) sharp or medium sharp Cheddar cheese, shredded
¾ teaspoon salt
Pepper
½ cup buttered bread crumbs

Arrange halibut on rack in skillet with a little water; top with onion slices and bay leaves. Cover; steam for 30 minutes. In meantime, melt butter or margarine in medium saucepan, stir in flour and add milk. Add salt, and pepper to taste. Stir and cook until sauce thickens and becomes smooth. Add cheese; stir until melted. (If mild Cheddar cheese is used, add a pinch of mustard and a little more salt to bring out cheese flavor.) Separate fish into serving-size pieces; place in buttered 2-quart casserole. Pour over cheese sauce; sprinkle with buttered crumbs. Bake at 350 degrees F. for 30 minutes or until bubbling hot. Makes 8 servings.

See menus for January, 2nd week; December, 4th week.

Easy Shrimp Newberg

¹/₂ cup sliced green onion
1 tablespoon butter or
    margarine
1 can (10³/₄ ounces) cream
    of shrimp soup
1 cup dairy sour cream
2 cans (4¹/₂ ounces each)
    small deveined shrimp,
    drained and rinsed or ¹/₂
    pound fresh or frozen baby
    shrimp
Pastry shells, puff paste
    shells, or cooked rice

In medium saucepan cook onion in butter or
margarine until soft. Stir in soup, sour cream, and
shrimp. Barely heat through, stirring constantly.
Serve immediately in pastry shells, puff paste shells,
or cooked rice. Makes 4 servings.
    Note: May be made with 1 can of shrimp, but protein
content will be lower.

See menus for February, 4th week.

Frozen Shrimp Cocktail

1 quart tomato juice
1 cup Cocktail Sauce*
¹/₂ cup catsup
2 teaspoons fresh horseradish
2²/₃ cups finely diced celery
1 can (4¹/₂ ounces) broken
    shrimp

Combine all ingredients; freeze. Remove from freezer
1 or 2 hours before time to serve. Spoon into dishes;
serve immediately. Makes about 10 servings.
    Cocktail Sauce: To make 1 cup cocktail sauce,
combine ³/₄ cup chili sauce, 2 tablespoons lemon juice,
1 tablespoon prepared horseradish, 2 teaspoons
Worcestershire sauce, ¹/₂ teaspoon finely chopped
onion, and a few dashes bottled Tabasco sauce; mix
well. Cover and chill several hours. Good to serve
with fish or seafood. Commercial cocktail sauce may
be used if preferred.

See menus for September, 3rd week.

Broiled Salmon with Cucumber Sauce

4 salmon steaks or fillets
¹/₄ cup (¹/₂ stick) butter,
    melted
2 tablespoons lemon juice
1 medium cucumber, pared
    and diced
¹/₂ teaspoon salt
Dash pepper
1 tablespoon chopped chives
    or green onion tops
¹/₂ cup dairy sour cream
2 teaspoons lemon juice

Brush both sides of salmon steaks or fillets generously
with mixture of melted butter and 2 tablespoons
lemon juice. Place steaks about 6 inches from source
of heat (hot coals or preheated broiler); broil 7 to 10
minutes on each side, until fish flakes easily, brushing
occasionally with butter and lemon juice mixture.
Serve hot with Cucumber Sauce, made by mixing
together cucumber and remaining ingredients. Makes
4 servings.
    Note: If desired, additional steaks may be broiled
to use later in salad, casserole, or sandwich filling for
another meal.

See menus for February, 1st week.

Salmon Tetrazzini

1 can (15½ ounces) or
 2 cans (7¾ or 7½ ounces
 each) salmon
½ pound mushrooms, sliced
½ cup sliced green onions
2 cloves garlic, minced
¼ cup (½ stick) butter or
 margarine
¼ cup all-purpose flour
1¼ cups chicken broth*
1½ cups half-and-half
½ teaspoon salt
⅛ teaspoon pepper
¼ cup grated Parmesan
 cheese
1 pound hot, cooked, and
 drained spaghetti
Lemon slices, parsley, and
 additional cheese (optional)

Drain salmon, reserving liquid. Remove bones and skin, if desired but not necessary; flake salmon; set aside. Sauté mushrooms, green onions, and garlic in butter or margarine; blend in flour. Gradually add reserved salmon liquid, chicken broth, and half-and-half. Cook and stir until thickened and smooth. Add seasonings, Parmesan cheese, and flaked salmon; heat thoroughly. Combine with cooked spaghetti. Garnish with lemon and parsley; serve with additional cheese. Makes 8 servings.

Note: To make chicken broth, dissolve 1¼ chicken bouillon cubes in 1¼ cups boiling water.

See menus for March, 4th week; November 1st week.

Jellied Salmon Loaf

2 envelopes (2 tablespoons)
 unflavored gelatin
½ cup cold water
½ cup boiling water
2 tablespoons vinegar or
 lemon juice
1 cup mayonnaise or plain
 yogurt or half of each
½ teaspoon salt
¼ teaspoon pepper
2 tablespoons catsup
1 can (15 ounces) red or
 pink salmon
2 hard-cooked eggs,
 shelled and diced
12 stuffed green olives, sliced
Fresh parsley
Lemon wedges

Soften gelatin in cold water; dissolve in boiling water; cool. Add vinegar, mayonnaise or yogurt (or combination), salt, pepper, and catsup; chill until mixture begins to thicken. Drain salmon; discard skin and bones; flake. Fold into thickened gelatin mixture along with diced eggs and sliced olives. Chill until set. Unmold and slice to serve. Garnish with fresh parsley and lemon wedges. Makes 8 servings.

See menus for July, 1st week.

Super Salmon

1 can (7³/₄ ounces) salmon or
    ½ pound fresh salmon
Milk
¼ cup sliced green onion or
    2 tablespoons chopped
    onion
½ cup sliced water chestnuts
½ cup diced celery
2 tablespoons butter or
    margarine
1 tablespoon all-purpose flour
¼ teaspoon each salt,
    crushed dried thyme,
    Tabasco sauce
1 cup (4 ounces) sharp
    Cheddar cheese
4 slices warm, buttered toast

Drain salmon, saving cooking liquid, and flake. Or cook fresh salmon in small amount boiling water for 10 minutes or until it flakes easily; drain salmon, saving liquid. Add milk to salmon liquid to make ³/₄ cup. Sauté green onion, water chestnuts, and celery in butter. Blend in flour. Add combined milk and salmon liquid. Cook, stirring, until thick and smooth. Add salmon, ¼ teaspoon salt, thyme, Tabasco sauce, and cheese. Serve hot over warm toast. Makes 4 servings.

Note: Salmon mixture is delicious served over an omelet, rice, or pasta.

See menus for April, 2nd week; August, 3rd week; September, 3rd week.

Salmon in Parchment

Pinch dried dill weed
Pinch crushed dried thyme
1 teaspoon salt
½ teaspoon pepper
2 pounds fresh or frozen
    salmon, cut into 6 fillets
2 tablespoons butter or
    margarine, melted
1 lemon, thinly sliced
6 sprigs fresh parsley or
    2 teaspoons dried parsley
6 pieces 8x8-inch parchment
Tartar Sauce (p. 137)

Combine dill, thyme, salt, and pepper; set aside. Liberally coat each salmon fillet with butter. Sprinkle with herb mixture. Place one or two lemon slices and 1 sprig parsley on each piece of parchment; top each with one salmon fillet. Fold parchment to seal in ingredients. Place parchment bundles on baking tray so lemon and parsley are on top. Bake at 400 degrees F. for 15 minutes. Place on serving plate and cut paper on top; drip more butter over top, if desired. Serve in parchment with Tartar Sauce on side. Makes 6 servings.

See menus for October, 3rd week.

Salmon Fondue

1 can (1 pound) red or pink
  salmon
¼ cup chopped onion
½ teaspoon pepper
1 tablespoon lemon juice
2 tablespoons melted butter
  or margarine
10 slices day-old bread
4 eggs
2 cups milk
¼ teaspoon salt

Casserole should be chilled several hours before baking.

Drain salmon, reserving liquid. Remove and discard skin and bones; flake meat. To salmon add onion, pepper, lemon juice, and melted butter or margarine. Trim crusts from bread; reserve for some other use. Arrange five slices of bread in greased 9x13x2-inch baking dish. Cover with salmon. Arrange remaining bread slices over top. Beat eggs with milk, salt, and salmon liquid. Pour over contents of casserole. Cover and refrigerate several hours or overnight. Bake at 350 degrees F. for 40 to 50 minutes or until puffed and brown. Makes 8 servings.

See menus for July, 2nd week.

Lazy Susan Dinner

This is an adventuresome end-of-the-week dinner that uses up all the dabs of food remaining from the week's meals. Family members enjoy it because they get to choose which foods they want to eat. A lazy Susan is an ideal vehicle for serving the variety of foods, or a series of small bowls can hold the delicious portions. A last remaining hard-cooked egg can be halved and garnished with pickle or pimiento, or deviled and cut into quarters, or made into sandwich filling and served on crackers.

Tag ends of cranberry sauce are tasty and colorful in the center of leftover peach or pear halves. Grated hard cheese mixed with mayonnaise or remnants of cottage cheese can be used to stuff celery. Cucumber slices on buttered bread, cut into rounds or small squares, make tasty open-faced sandwiches. Leftover tuna can stuff tomatoes big or little. Diced cooked vegetables mixed with small amounts of soup can be extended with milk, broth, or leftover vegetable juices to make soup enough for all. Meat, potatoes, and gravy combine to make great hash.

Lazy Susan dinners will be among your favorite meals. They provide practically a free meal and help to clear out the refrigerator, making room for another week of food buying and meal preparation.

See menus for March, 1st week; April, 2nd week; August, 2nd week.

SOUPS, SANDWICHES, AND BEVERAGES

Soups

Fresh Mushroom Soup

1 pound fresh mushrooms, sliced
1 small onion, thinly sliced
1 clove garlic, minced
3 tablespoons chopped fresh parsley
3 tablespoons butter or margarine
1/2 teaspoon salt
1 teaspoon paprika
3 tablespoons all-purpose flour
2 cans (10³/₄ ounces each) condensed chicken broth
1³/₄ cups water

In heavy saucepan brown mushrooms, onion, garlic, and parsley in butter. Stir in salt, paprika, and flour. Add chicken broth. Bring to boil, stirring constantly, and cook until thick and smooth. Simmer 5 minutes. Add water; heat to boil and serve. Makes 4 servings.

See menus for July, 4th week; September, 4th week; November, 1st week.

Creamy Cauliflower Soup

1 medium head cauliflower
1¹/₂ cups water
¹/₄ cup (¹/₂ stick) butter or margarine
²/₃ cup chopped onion
2 tablespoons all-purpose flour
2 cups chicken broth*
1 cup liquid drained from cauliflower
2 cups half-and-half
¹/₂ teaspoon Worcestershire sauce
³/₄ teaspoon salt
1 cup shredded Cheddar cheese
Chopped chives or parsley

Wash cauliflower; cut into tiny flowerets. Cook in 1¹/₂ cups boiling, salted water until barely tender. Drain, reserving liquid; set both cauliflower and liquid aside. In medium saucepan melt butter or margarine. Add onion; cook until soft. Blend in flour. Add chicken broth. Cook and stir until mixture comes to boil. Stir in liquid drained from cauliflower, half-and-half, Worcestershire sauce, and salt. Add cauliflower. Heat to boiling. Stir in cheese. Serve sprinkled with chopped chives or parsley. Makes 6 servings.
   *Note: To make chicken broth, dissolve 2 chicken bouillon cubes in 2 cups boiling water.

See menus for November, 2nd week.

Cream of Tomato Soup

3 cups tomato juice
4 tablespoons (½ stick) butter or margarine
⅓ cup all-purpose flour
3 cups milk
1½ teaspoons salt, or to taste
½ teaspoon crushed dried basil
¼ teaspoon pepper

Heat tomato juice to simmering. Meanwhile, in another saucepan melt butter or margarine, stir in flour; add milk and stir; cook until thick. Just before serving, slowly add hot tomato juice to hot white sauce, stirring constantly. Season to taste with salt, basil, and pepper. Serve immediately. Makes 4 servings.

Variation

Cream of Fresh Tomato Soup: Use 4 cups pureed fresh tomatoes in place of tomato juice.

See menus for February, 1st week; May, 1st week; August, 2nd week.

Cream of Zucchini Soup

2 medium onions
2 tablespoons butter or margarine
4 medium zucchini
3 cups chicken broth*
⅛ teaspoon salt
⅛ teaspoon nutmeg
⅛ teaspoon pepper
Pinch cayenne
½ cup half-and-half
Cheddar cheese, shredded

Clean, chop, and cook onions in butter until soft and transparent but not browned. Wash and slice zucchini. In large saucepan combine onion, zucchini, and chicken broth. Bring to boil; reduce heat and simmer 15 minutes or until squash is tender. Add seasonings. Puree mixture in blender or food processor until smooth; return to saucepan. Add half-and-half; adjust seasonings to taste. Reheat, but do not boil. Serve hot, garnished with shredded Cheddar cheese. Makes 8 servings.

Note: To make chicken broth, dissolve 3 chicken bouillon cubes in 3 cups boiling water.

See menus for May, 4th week; June, 1st week.

Broccoli Cheese Soup

5½ cups milk
2 cups (½ pound) chopped fresh broccoli or 1 package (10 ounces) frozen chopped broccoli
3 tablespoons chopped onion
2 tablespoons butter or margarine
1 tablespoon all-purpose flour
2 cups (8 ounces) shredded Cheddar or Swiss cheese
¼ teaspoon salt, or to taste

Heat milk in large saucepan until simmering. Cook broccoli and onion in milk until tender, about 10 minutes. Cream together butter or margarine and flour until smoothly blended. Add butter and flour mixture to milk, stirring with wire whisk until blended in. Cook and stir 3 minutes. Remove from heat and add shredded cheese and salt. Stir until cheese is melted. Serve immediately. Makes 8 servings.

See menus for February, 1st week; May, 2nd week; August, 1st week.

Broccoli Light Soup

6 cups raw broccoli,
   cut into pieces
1/2 cup chopped onion
1 baking potato (8 ounces),
   peeled and cubed
3 chicken bouillon cubes or
   1 tablespoon instant
   bouillon granules
3 cups water
1/2 cup evaporated milk
   (regular or low-fat) or
   light cream

Combine all ingredients but evaporated milk in large saucepan. Bring to boil; reduce heat; cover and simmer for 15 minutes or until vegetables are tender. Process vegetables in food processor or blender for 5 minutes or until velvety smooth. Combine with evaporated milk; heat and serve. Makes 4 servings.

Variation

End-of-Week Soup: Use any vegetables desired, either raw or cooked, in place of broccoli. It is best to use all green vegetables or all yellow, so that the final color is appetizing.

See menus for March, 4th week.

Cream of Corn Soup

1/2 cup diced bacon
1/4 cup chopped onion
1/4 cup all-purpose flour
4 cups milk
1 can (15 ounces) cream-style
   corn
1 teaspoon salt
1/4 teaspoon pepper
1/4 teaspoon celery salt
   (optional)

Cook bacon in heavy saucepan over medium heat until almost crisp. Add onion; cook until soft. Blend in flour, add milk; cook and stir until thick and smooth. Add corn, bring to boiling point, season with salt and pepper, and serve. Makes 4 servings.

   Note: Soup may be served with a spoonful of spiced whipped cream by combining 1/2 cup heavy cream and 1/2 teaspoon ground cinnamon and whipping until stiff.

See menus for January, 1st week.

Squash Bisque

3 tablespoons butter or
   margarine
1 medium onion, chopped
1 small carrot, finely grated
2 medium potatoes, peeled
   and cubed
2 acorn squash, peeled and
   cubed
4 cups chicken stock
1 cup half-and-half
Salt and pepper
Chopped chives (optional)

In large saucepan, melt butter or margarine; sauté onion and carrot until tender. Add potatoes, squash, and chicken stock. Simmer soup, covered, over low heat for 25 minutes or until vegetables are very tender. Puree mixture in blender. Return to saucepan; add half-and-half. Season to taste with salt and pepper. Heat and garnish with chopped chives, if desired. Makes 4 to 6 servings.

See menus for October, 2nd week.

Hamburger Vegetable Soup with Cheese

½ to 1 pound lean ground beef
2 onions, chopped
4 cups water
1 can (29 ounces) or 1 quart canned tomatoes
5 medium potatoes, pared and cubed
3 large carrots, cleaned and cubed
1 teaspoon salt
1 bay leaf
2 cups (8 ounces) Monterey Jack or other cheese, cubed

In 8-quart kettle brown ground beef with onion. Add water, tomatoes, potatoes, carrots, salt, and bay leaf. Simmer, partially covered, until vegetables are tender, about 1 hour. Just before serving, stir in cheese cubes. Makes 8 servings.

See menus for January, 1st week; April, 4th week.

Chicken Vegetable Soup

2 quarts Chicken Broth (p. 151)
1 can (16 ounces) tomatoes, cut up
1 tablespoon instant chicken bouillon granules (or 3 bouillon cubes)
1½ teaspoons crushed dried oregano
1 teaspoon dried crushed thyme
¼ teaspoon salt
⅛ teaspoon pepper
4 cups fresh vegetables (any combination of uncooked sliced or chopped celery, carrot, onion, rutabaga, mushrooms, broccoli, or cauliflower)
2 cups cooked chicken, coarsely chopped
1½ cups uncooked medium noodles

In large heavy saucepan combine broth, undrained tomatoes, bouillon granules, oregano, thyme, salt, pepper, and fresh vegetables. Bring to boiling; reduce heat. Cover and simmer for 45 minutes or until vegetables are tender. Add chicken and uncooked noodles. Simmer, uncovered, for 8 to 10 minutes or until noodles are tender. Season to taste with salt and pepper. Makes 10 servings.

Variation

Turkey Vegetable Soup: Use Turkey Broth (p. 151) and turkey meat in place of chicken.

See menus for February, 2nd week.

Chicken or Turkey Broth

Meat bones from chicken or
turkey
Cold water
1 onion, sliced
1 carrot, sliced
Celery leaves or fresh parsley
6 peppercorns
1 bay leaf
2 teaspoons salt

Strip all meat possible from chicken or turkey bones and save for soup, sandwiches, or casseroles, storing it in refrigerator for 1 or 2 days, or in freezer for a longer time. In large saucepan, cover bones with cold water. Add onion, carrot, celery leaves, peppercorns, bay leaf, and salt. Bring slowly to boil; reduce heat and cover kettle; simmer 2 hours. (Broth will not be as clear if boiled vigorously.) Strain broth through fine strainer or cheese cloth; discard bones and vegetables. Use broth at once or keep in closed jar in refrigerator for 1 or 2 days; freeze for longer storage.

See menus for February, 2nd week.

Minestrone

³/₄ pound mild bulk pork
sausage
4 cups water
2 beef bouillon cubes
1 large onion, chopped
2 medium carrots, sliced
2 medium celery ribs, diced
1 can (16 ounces) tomatoes,
pureed
2 cans tomato sauce (8 ounces
each)
2 teaspoons crushed dried
parsley flakes
¹/₂ teaspoon crushed dried
basil
¹/₂ teaspoon crushed dried
oregano
Salt and pepper to taste
Garlic salt to taste
1 can (1 pound) garbanzo
beans, drained
1 can (8 ounces) cut green
beans, undrained
²/₃ cup uncooked wide
noodles or other pasta

Brown pork sausage in heavy kettle; drain. Dissolve bouillon cubes in water. Add onions, carrots, celery, tomatoes, tomato sauce, parsley, and seasonings. Simmer, covered, for 4 to 6 hours. Thirty minutes before serving time, add beans and noodles. Simmer until noodles are tender. Makes 8 servings.

See menus for October, 3rd week.

Split Pea Soup with Sausage Balls

1 pound (2¼ cups) dried
  green split peas
3 quarts water
2 teaspoons salt
½ teaspoon pepper
¼ teaspoon dried marjoram,
  crushed (optional)
1 pound bulk pork sausage
All-purpose flour
1 cup diced celery
1 cup diced potatoes
1 cup diced onion
Salt

Wash split peas and sort. In large saucepan combine water and seasonings and bring to a boil. Add peas gradually so water does not stop boiling. Shape sausage into 1-inch balls (about 28 of them) and roll in all-purpose flour. Drop into soup; cover and simmer until sausage is cooked and peas are tender, about 2½ hours. Add vegetables and cook until tender. Add salt to taste. Makes 12 servings.

See menus for January, 3rd week; April, 2nd week; December, 2nd week; .

Gazpacho

1 can (1 pound) tomatoes,
  undrained
1 large cucumber, peeled,
  seeded and diced
¼ large green pepper,
  seeded and diced
1 clove garlic, minced (or ¼
  teaspoon garlic powder),
  optional
2 tablespoons finely chopped
  onion
2 tablespoons red wine
  vinegar
Few drops Tabasco sauce
1½ cups tomato juice
1 cup diced raw vegetables
  (such as tomatoes,
  cucumbers, celery, or
  peppers)
Croutons, sour cream
  (optional)

Combine first seven ingredients in blender or food processor; process until smooth. Add tomato juice; cover and chill several hours. Serve in bowls. Pass raw vegetables, croutons, sour cream. Makes 4 servings.

See menus for March, 3rd week.

White Gazpacho

1 chicken bouillon cube or
  1 teaspoon instant bouillon
  granules
1 cup boiling water
1 large cucumber
1 small clove garlic
1/2 pint (1 cup) dairy sour
  cream
1 teaspoon salt
1 teaspoon white vinegar
2 fresh tomatoes, diced
1/2 cup fresh parsley,
  washed, dried, and
  chopped
1 cup slivered almonds,
  toasted and salted*

Dissolve bouillon in boiling water; set aside to cool. Peel and halve cucumber; remove large seeds and cut into 8 or 10 pieces. In blender combine cucumber and garlic with a little broth; process until smooth. Combine with remaining broth; chill. When ready to serve, spoon sour cream into large bowl and stir with wooden spoon until smooth. Gradually add broth mixture, blending with wire whisk. Add salt and vinegar; chill. Serve in cups or soup plates, garnished with diced tomatoes, chopped fresh parsley, and toasted, salted almonds. Makes 5 to 6 servings.

Toasted Almonds: To toast almonds, spread in thin layer in shallow metal baking pan. Set pan on center rack of 350 degree F. oven. Bake for 5 minutes or until almonds show first sign of browning. Remove from oven. Toss with few drops of cooking oil and sprinkle lightly with salt.

See menus for July, 1st week.

Cheesy Potato Soup

4 medium potatoes, diced
1 large onion
1 quart water
1/4 cup (1/2 stick) butter or
  margarine
3 tablespoons all-purpose
  flour
1/2 cup milk
1 1/2 cups (6 ounces)
  shredded sharp Cheddar
  cheese
1 teaspoon salt
1/4 teaspoon seasoned salt
  (optional)
1/4 teaspoon paprika
1/8 teaspoon pepper
Chopped chives or parsley

Combine potatoes, onion, and water in heavy saucepan. Bring to boil; reduce heat; and simmer until tender, about 20 minutes. In heavy skillet melt butter; add flour; cook and stir until mixture bubbles. Remove from heat; stir in milk. Return to heat; cook and stir until thickened. Stir mixture slowly into potatoes; cook and stir until thick. Add cheese and seasonings. Serve with chopped chives or parsley. Makes 4 servings.

See menus for February, 1st week; December, 1st week.

Lentil Soup, Gypsy Style

1 cup dried lentils
5 cups water
1 can (15 ounces) tomato
  sauce
1 cup finely diced carrots
1/2 cup chopped onion
1 1/2 cups (8 ounces) ham
  scraps or pieces
1 1/2 teaspoons salt
1/2 teaspoon marjoram
Dairy sour cream (optional)
Ground nutmeg (optional)

Combine all ingredients except sour cream and nutmeg in 3-quart kettle. Bring to boil; reduce heat and simmer, covered, about 2 hours or until lentils are very tender. Top each serving with dollop of sour cream and sprinkling of nutmeg, if desired. Makes 8 servings.

See menus for April, 3rd week.

Chili

3 cups (1 pound) dry small
  red or pinto beans
6 cups water
2 or 3 bay leaves
1 pound lean ground beef
1/2 pound bulk pork sausage
3 large onions, chopped
3 garlic cloves, minced
1 can (29 ounces) or 1 quart
  tomatoes
1 tablespoon chili powder
2 small dried red chili
  peppers, crushed
3/4 teaspoon curry powder
1 tablespoon ground cumin
  (cominos)
1 tablespoon salt
1/4 teaspoon Tabasco sauce

Wash and pick over chili beans. Put into large kettle with water and bay leaves. Bring to boil; simmer, covered, 1 to 2 hours or until tender. In skillet brown meat, onions, and garlic. Add to drained beans along with remaining ingredients. Simmer for 1 hour. Serve hot. Makes 12 servings.

Variation

Meatless Chili: Omit meat. May be served on steamed rice to make a complete protein meal even though there is no meat.

See menus for January, 2nd week; June, 2nd week; September, 4th week.

Quick Chili

½ to 1 pound lean ground beef
½ cup chopped onion
1 can (16 ounces) kidney beans, undrained
1 cup water
½ cup prepared barbecue sauce
1 tablespoon chili powder
½ teaspoon salt
Shredded Cheddar cheese, green onion slices, crumbled bacon, sour cream, chopped chili, or avocado slices (optional)

In large skillet or heavy saucepan brown meat. Add onion; cook until tender; drain off drippings. Stir in remaining ingredients. Simmer 20 minutes, stirring occasionally. If desired, top with shredded Cheddar cheese, green onion slices, crumbled bacon, sour cream, chopped chili peppers, or avocado slices. Makes 4 servings.

See menus for January, 1st week; August, 2nd week.

Chili Wheat

1½ cups whole wheat
3 cups water
3 beef or chicken bouillon cubes
1 pound lean ground beef
1 package (1¾ ounces) chili seasoning mix
2 cans (29 ounces each) whole tomatoes, chopped
1 can (8 ounces) tomato sauce
1 cup (4 ounces) sliced fresh mushrooms or 1 can (4 ounces) mushroom stems and pieces

In large saucepan simmer wheat, water, and bouillon cubes 1 hour. In heavy saucepan brown beef. Add remaining ingredients; simmer 30 minutes. Combine with wheat; simmer 30 minutes. Makes 6 to 8 servings.

Variation

Vegetarian Chili Wheat: Omit ground beef. Top each serving with shredded cheese to make this dish a complete protein.

See menus for November, 3rd week.

Tomato Corn Chowder

2 slices bacon, diced, or
  2 tablespoons butter or
  margarine
1 small onion, diced
1 can (1 pound) cream-style
  or whole kernel corn
2 cups diced potatoes
1 can (1 pound) tomatoes
1 tablespoon sugar
1 teaspoon salt
1/4 teaspoon pepper
4 cups boiling water
1 cup half-and-half or
  undiluted evaporated milk

In heavy saucepan fry bacon until golden brown or melt butter or margarine. Add onion and cook without browning for 5 minutes. Add vegetables, sugar, and seasonings. Add water and cook slowly until potatoes are tender. Remove from heat and slowly stir in milk. Reheat slightly, if necessary. Makes 8 servings.

See menus for February, 2nd week.

Zucchini Corn Chowder

3 ears fresh corn or 1 can
  (12 ounces) whole kernel
  corn, drained
4 strips bacon
1 pound zucchini (or other
  summer squash), sliced
  (3 cups)
1 cup finely chopped onion
3/4 cup finely diced green
  pepper
1 clove garlic, minced
1 cup water
1/4 teaspoon crushed dried
  basil leaves
1/4 teaspoon crushed dried
  tarragon leaves
1 teaspoon salt
1/4 teaspoon paprika
1/8 teaspoon pepper
1/4 teaspoon sugar
2 cups cold milk
1/4 cup all-purpose flour

Cut uncooked corn kernels from cobs; set aside. In heavy saucepan sauté bacon until crisp; remove bacon, crumble, and set aside. To bacon drippings add zucchini, onion, green pepper, and garlic; sauté. Add corn, water, and seasonings. Bring mixture to boil. Reduce heat; simmer 10 minutes. Blend together milk and flour until smooth. Add to corn mixture gradually; cook and stir until thickened. Serve hot, sprinkled with bacon bits. Makes 6 servings.

See menus for July, 1st week.

New England Fish Chowder

½ pound salt pork or bacon
2 large onions, peeled and
chopped
3 large ribs celery, trimmed
and diced
3 large potatoes, peeled and
diced
1½ cups diced carrots
2½ cups water
1½ bay leaves
1¼ teaspoons salt
Pepper to taste
5 cups milk
3 tablespoons soft butter
3 tablespoons all-purpose
flour
1½ pounds lean fish fillet
(such as cod, haddock,
perch, sole, or turbot), cut
in bite-size pieces
Chopped parsley

In large, heavy kettle, cook salt pork or bacon over medium heat until golden and crisp. With slotted spoon remove it to absorbent paper; set aside. In fat, cook onion until golden. Add celery, potatoes, and carrots, stirring to coat them well. Add water and seasonings. Bring liquid to boil, reduce heat, and simmer vegetables, covered, for 10 minutes. Meanwhile, scald milk.

In small mixing bowl, combine butter and flour, blending with a fork until mixture is smooth. Add to milk, stirring constantly until mixture is slightly thickened and smooth; set aside. Bring contents of large kettle (vegetables) to boil. Add fish, reduce heat and simmer, uncovered, for 10 minutes, or until fish flakes easily. Add milk, stirring to blend chowder. To serve soup, garnish with salt pork and generous sprinkling of parsley. Makes 8 servings.

Note: If desired, canned fish, crab, or shrimp may be used in place of fresh or frozen fillets, but should be added last so it won't overcook.

See menus for March, 2nd week.

Clam Chowder

1 cup finely chopped onion
1 cup finely diced celery
2 cups finely diced potato
2 cans (6½ ounces each)
clams, undrained
½ cup (1 stick) butter or
margarine
¾ cup all-purpose flour
1 quart half-and-half (or milk
for less rich chowder)
1½ teaspoons salt
¼ teaspoon pepper

Combine vegetables in small saucepan. Drain clams; pour juice over vegetables; add enough water to barely cover. Cook, covered, until tender, about 15 minutes. In meantime, melt butter or margarine in large heavy saucepan. Stir in flour until blended and bubbly. Remove from heat; stir in cream until smooth and blended. Return to heat; cook and stir with wire whip until thick and smooth. Add undrained vegetables and clams; heat through. Season with salt and pepper. Makes 8 servings.

See menus for March, 3rd week; December, 3rd week.

Lamb Stew

1½ pounds boneless lamb
  stew meat
All-purpose flour
4 medium onions, quartered
6 medium potatoes, peeled
  and quartered
6 large carrots, peeled and
  sliced
1½ teaspoons salt
1 can (10½ ounces) beef
  broth (bouillon)
2 teaspoons lemon juice
3 tablespoons all-purpose
  flour and ¼ cup water
  (optional)

Roll lamb cubes in flour. Arrange meat and remaining ingredients (except lemon juice) in 3-quart casserole or Dutch oven. Cover with tight-fitting lid. Bake at 325 degrees F. for 2 hours or until meat is fork tender. Remove lid, stir with spoon, and add lemon juice. If desired, thicken with 3 tablespoons flour blended smoothly with ¼ cup cold water. Makes 6 servings.

Variation

Lamb Pie: Cut up leftover lamb and vegetables into 1-inch pieces; combine with any leftover gravy. Add water or beef broth, if necessary, to make enough gravy for moistness; if gravy is too thin, add a little flour and water thickening (2 tablespoons flour to 3 tablespoons cold water, blended until smooth). Pour stew mixture into 1½-quart casserole. Top with layer of pastry that has been slashed for venting (made from pastry mix or 1 cup flour, ½ cup shortening, ¼ teaspoon salt, and about 2 tablespoons of ice water); or use homemade or packaged refrigerated baking powder biscuits. Bake at 375 degrees F. for 20 to 30 minutes or until filling is bubbly hot and topping is browned.

See menus for September, 1st week.

Frankfurter Vegetable Stew

6 slices bacon (⅓ pound),
  cut into 1-inch lengths
1 cup sliced onion
1 clove garlic, minced
4 small to medium zucchini,
  sliced (about 4 cups)
2 cups sliced raw cauliflower
1 can (1 pound) tomatoes
½ teaspoon crushed dried
  basil leaves
1 teaspoon salt
½ teaspoon sugar
1 can (10¾ ounces)
  condensed tomato soup
1 pound frankfurters, cut in
  thirds
1 medium green pepper, cut
  into 1-inch squares

Fry bacon crisp. Drain bacon pieces on absorbent paper; save 2 tablespoons drippings. Sauté onion and garlic in drippings until onion is limp. Add zucchini, cauliflower, tomatoes, basil, salt, and sugar. Cover; cook until vegetables are almost tender, about 15 minutes. Blend in soup. Add frankfurters and green pepper; heat well. Sprinkle bacon over top. Makes 4 to 6 servings.

See menus for February, 4th week.

Chicken Stew with Dumplings

3-pound broiler-fryer
  chicken
4 cups water
3 stalks celery with leaves
1 small carrot, sliced
1 small onion, cut up
1 teaspoon salt
Pepper to taste
2 medium potatoes, cubed
  (about 2 cups)
1 medium turnip, cubed
  (about 1 cup)
3 medium carrots, cut into
  1-inch pieces (about 2 cups)
2 medium stalks celery, cut
  into 1-inch pieces
  (about 1 cup)
1 small onion, chopped
1½ teaspoons salt (or to
  taste)
½ teaspoon crushed
  rosemary leaves
2 chicken bouillon cubes
⅔ cup cold water
⅓ cup all-purpose flour
Dumplings*

Start this early in the morning.

Early in the morning or the day before serving, place cut-up chicken in large heavy kettle and cover with cold water (about 4 cups). Add next five ingredients. Cover; bring to boil. Reduce heat; simmer about 1 hour or until chicken is tender when pierced with point of sharp knife. Remove chicken; strain broth. Let chicken and broth cool. When chicken is cool enough to handle, remove meat, discarding skin and bones. (This may be done ahead of time, storing chicken meat and broth separately in tightly covered containers in refrigerator for no longer than 2 days.)

To make stew, heat broth to boiling, add chicken meat and remaining vegetables, 1½ teaspoons salt, rosemary, and bouillon cubes. Reduce heat, cover and simmer until vegetables are tender, about 30 minutes. Blend ⅔ cup cold water and flour until smooth; stir gradually into simmering stew. Cook and stir about 1 minute, until thick; reduce heat. Prepare Dumplings. Drop dough by 10 to 12 spoonfuls onto hot stew. Cover tightly, reduce heat, and cook 12 to 15 minutes without lifting lid. Serve Dumplings topped with hot stew. Makes 8 servings.

Dumplings: Stir and measure 1½ cups all-purpose flour; mix together flour, ¾ teaspoon salt, and 2 teaspoons baking powder; add ¾ cup milk and 3 tablespoons melted fat or vegetable oil. If desired, add 3 tablespoons chopped fresh parsley or 1 tablespoon dried parsley.

Note: One package refrigerated biscuits may be used in place of dumplings.

See menus for January, 4th week.

Skier's Stew

2 pounds stew beef, cut in
   1½-inch cubes
8 medium potatoes,
   quartered
8 large carrots, cut in fourths
2 bay leaves
1 package (1½ ounces) dried
   onion soup
1 can (10¾ ounces) cream
   of mushroom soup
1 can (10¾ ounces) cream
   of celery soup
1 can (8 ounces) tomato sauce

In large Dutch oven or heavy pan with tight-fitting lid make a layer of beef, then the vegetables. Top with bay leaves, soups, and tomato sauce. Bake at 325 degrees F. for 3 hours, at 275 degrees F. for 6 hours, or at 250 degrees F. for 8 hours. Makes 8 servings.

See menus for November, 4th week.

Chicken Cider Stew

1 cup apple cider or apple
   juice
1 cup water
2 tablespoons catsup
2 slices bacon, cut up
1½ teaspoons salt
¼ teaspoon crushed dried
   savory
¼ teaspoon crushed dried
   basil
⅛ teaspoon pepper
8 chicken thighs (2½
   pounds)
4 carrots, thinly sliced
2 medium sweet potatoes,
   peeled and quartered
1 medium onion, finely
   chopped (about 1 cup)
1 rib celery, cut into 1-inch
   pieces
1 apple, peeled, cored, and
   chopped (about 1 cup)
3 tablespoons all-purpose
   flour and ¼ cup cold
   water (optional)

In large kettle or Dutch oven stir together first eight ingredients. Add chicken thighs. Bring to boiling. Reduce heat; cover and simmer 45 minutes. Stir in carrots, sweet potatoes, onion, celery, and apple. Cover; simmer 30 minutes more or until meat and vegetables are tender. If desired, thicken with 3 tablespoons flour mixed with ¼ cup cold water. Makes 6 servings.

Note: Chicken Cider Stew contains chicken pieces with bone in, a favorite kind of stew in Spain and Mexico, where they think the bones cooked in give added flavor.

See menus for September, 2nd week.

Sandwiches

Peanut Butter Sandwich Combinations

Peanut butter can be combined with many other foods to make tasty sandwiches. For some of these sandwiches (such as those that use raisins, sliced bananas, or grated carrot), spread both slices of bread with peanut butter, then press the other ingredient in the center and close the sandwich. A few suggestions for possible sandwiches are as follows:

Peanut butter and honey
Peanut butter and jelly, jam, or marmalade
Peanut butter and bacon
Peanut butter and ham or chicken
Peanut butter and pickle slices or relish
Peanut butter and sliced hard-cooked egg
Peanut butter and raisins or chopped dates
Peanut butter, mayonnaise, and lettuce
Peanut butter and sliced bananas
Peanut butter and sliced oranges, alfalfa sprouts may
    be added
Peanut butter and applesauce
Peanut butter and sliced fresh fruit (such as apples,
    peaches, pears, pineapple, strawberries)
Peanut butter and grated or sliced carrot
Peanut butter and diced celery
Peanut butter and thinly sliced raw zucchini or
    cucumber
Peanut butter and drained crushed pineapple
Peanut butter and cheddar, cottage, or cream cheese
Peanut butter and sliced tomatoes
Peanut butter and alfalfa sprouts
Peanut butter and sunflower seeds
Peanut butter and avocado

See menus for June, 3rd week; Oct, 1st week.

Five-Minute Pizzas

4 English muffins or
  hamburger buns
1/2 cup catsup or chili sauce
1 tablespoon grated onion
1/2 teaspoon dried oregano
  leaves, crushed
2 packages (2 1/2 ounces)
  pastrami or spiced beef
8 thin slices (4 ounces)
  Mozzarella or Monterey
  Jack cheese
Sliced mushrooms, olives,
  pepperoni, green pepper,
  or other toppings (optional)

Split English muffins or hamburger buns open. If desired, lightly toast English muffins. Combine catsup or chili sauce, onion, and oregano. Spread lightly over open sandwiches, using only part of sauce. Top with pastrami or spiced beef slices, then with cheese. Garnish with mushrooms, olives, pepperoni, green pepper, or other toppings, then top with remaining pizza sauce. Broil about 5 inches from source of heat until cheese is bubbly hot and melted. Serve at once. Makes 4 servings.

See menus for March, 3rd week.

Pizza-by-the-Yard

1 pound lean ground beef
1/4 cup finely chopped onion
1/3 cup grated Parmesan
  cheese
1/4 cup sliced ripe olives
1 teaspoon salt
1/2 to 1 teaspoon crushed
  oregano
Dash pepper
1 can (6 ounces) tomato paste
1 long loaf French bread,
  sliced lengthwise into two
  layers
2 large tomatoes, sliced
1/2 pound sharp Cheddar
  cheese, sliced

In medium skillet cook ground beef and onion until meat loses its pink color and onion is transparent. Combine with Parmesan cheese, olives, seasonings, and tomato paste. Spread on cut surfaces of bread. Top with tomato and cheese slices. Broil 12 minutes or until cheese is melted and bread is crusty. While hot, slice and serve. Makes 8 servings.

See menus for October, 3rd week.

Ground Nut and Raisin Sandwich Filling

1/2 cup walnuts
1/2 cup raisins, rinsed in hot
  water to soften
1 1/2 tablespoon mayonnaise
Few drops lemon juice

Grind or process walnuts and raisins together. Moisten with mayonnaise and lemon juice. Makes enough filling for 4 sandwiches.

See menus for March, 1st week; August, 2nd week; October, 3rd week.

Olive Nut Filling

2 cans (2¼ ounces each)
  chopped ripe olives
½ cup chopped walnuts or
  pecans
Mayonnaise
8 slices whole wheat bread

Combine olives, nuts; add mayonnaise to moisten.
Spread on bread. Makes 4 servings.

See menus for April, 4th week; July, 2nd week; November, 1st week.

Pimiento Cheese Spread

½ pound sharp Cheddar
  cheese, shredded
¼ cup light cream or
  evaporated milk
1 jar (2 ounces) pimientos,
  drained and very finely
  chopped
Salt

In small heavy saucepan combine cheese and
evaporated milk; cook, stirring constantly, over
medium heat until cheese is melted and mixture is
blended. Or microwave, using *medium* power, until
melted, stirring every minute. Stir in pimiento; season
to taste. Refrigerate in covered jar. Makes enough
filling for 4 sandwiches.

See menus for July, 1st week; November, 1st week.

Cream Cheese Sandwiches

1 package (8 ounces) cream
  cheese
1 tablespoon milk, cream,
  or dairy sour cream
8 slices whole wheat or raisin
  bread

Cream together cream cheese and cream or dairy sour
cream, and add any of the following: 1 teaspoon
chopped onion or chives; 1 tablespoon finely chopped
parsley; ¼ cup chopped ripe or pimiento-stuffed
olives; 3 tablespoons chopped crisp bacon, minced
chopped beef, or ground cooked ham; ½ cup chopped
salted almonds or other nuts; 4 or 5 chopped dates or
¼ cup raisins; ⅓ cup drained crushed pineapple;
finely diced raw vegetables such as celery, green
pepper, radishes, cucumbers, zucchini, spinach, or
drained tomatoes.

See menus for March, 3rd week; July, 3rd week; July, 4th week.

Broiled Cheese Sandwiches

4 slices whole grain or
  enriched bread
4 slices (1 ounce each)
  Cheddar cheese

Arrange bread slices on baking sheet and top each
slice of bread with a slice of cheese. Just before
serving, slip sandwiches under broiler for 2 to 3
minutes, until cheese is bubbly and melted. Serve
immediately. Makes 4 servings.

See menus for April, 1st week; November, 2nd week; December, 4th week.

Carrot Raisin Sandwiches

1 cup finely shredded carrot
1 cup raisins, finely chopped
Salad dressing or mayonnaise
Lemon juice (optional)

Combine carrots and raisins; moisten as desired with salad dressing or mayonnaise. If desired, add a few drops of lemon juice. Makes enough filling for 4 sandwiches.

Note: Carrots and raisins may be ground together rather than shredded and chopped. For variety, celery or nuts may be ground with the raisins.

Variation

Carrot Peanut Sandwiches: Use peanuts in place of raisins.

See menus for August, 1st week.

Broiled Cheese and Tomato Sandwiches

4 slices whole wheat bread
  or 4 English muffins
2 tablespoons mayonnaise
1 teaspoon Dijon mustard
Tomato slices
6 ounces medium sharp
  Cheddar cheese slices

If desired, toast bread on one side or lightly toast English muffins. Spread untoasted side of bread or English muffins with mayonnaise, then mustard. Top with tomato, then cheese slices. Broil until cheese is melted and bubbling. Makes 4 servings.

Note: Many variations can be made on this, such as the addition of green onion slices, zucchini slices, or ham slices.

See menus for January, 1st week; March, 1st week; May, 4th week

Hoagie (or Hero) Sandwiches

4 6-inch French rolls
Butter or margarine
4 tablespoons mayonnaise
4 teaspoons prepared
  mustard
4 to 6 ounces Swiss or
  Cheddar cheese, sliced
4 to 6 ounces cooked meat
  (such as salami, pastrami,
  ham), sliced
Tomato slices
Dill pickle slices
Onion slices (optional)
Lettuce

Split rolls lengthwise. Butter each half and spread with mayonnaise and mustard. Arrange cheese and meat slices, overlapping, along the length of one half of roll. Add generous quantities of any of remaining ingredients.

See menus for May, 3rd week.

Broiled Shrimp Buns

1 cup finely chopped celery
1 cup (8 ounces) shredded
  sharp Cheddar cheese
1/3 cup sliced green onions
3 hard-cooked eggs, chopped
1 can (4 1/2 ounces) broken
  shrimp, drained
2 to 4 tablespoons
  mayonnaise or salad
  dressing
4 hamburger buns

Mix all filling ingredients. Spread on split hamburger buns. Just before serving, place on baking sheet and broil until cheese melts. Makes 4 servings.

See menus for March, 3rd week; July, 4th week; December, 1st week.

Chopped Pork Sandwich Filling

1 can (12 ounces) pork
  luncheon meat
4 hard-cooked eggs, chopped
1 cup (4 ounces) shredded
  Cheddar cheese
1 cup finely diced celery
1/2 cup chopped pickle or
  relish
1/2 cup mayonnaise or salad
  dressing or enough to
  moisten
1 teaspoon Dijon mustard
1/2 teaspoon salt

Grate or chop luncheon meat; combine with eggs, cheese, celery, pickles, mayonnaise, and seasonings. Makes 5 cups filling or enough for 12 sandwiches.

Variation

Hot Ham Sandwiches: Fill hot dog or hamburger buns with Chopped Pork Filling, wrap in foil and bake at 350 degrees F. for 20 minutes or until heated through.

See menus for February, 4th week.

Deviled Pork Sandwich Filling

1 can (12 ounces) pork
  luncheon meat, coarsely
  grated
4 hard-cooked eggs, chopped
1/3 cup chopped sweet pickle
  or pickle relish
1/4 cup sliced green onion
1 cup (4 ounces) shredded
  Cheddar or Swiss cheese,
  coarsely grated
1/2 cup mayonnaise or salad
  dressing
1/2 teaspoon Dijon mustard

Combine all ingredients, using just enough mayonnaise to moisten. Store in refrigerator in covered jar. Use within 3 days or freeze. Makes enough filling for 12 sandwiches.

See menus for August, 4th week; November, 2nd week.

Tuna Bunwiches

½ pound nippy Cheddar
   cheese, coarsely grated
¼ cup chopped onion
¼ cup chopped green
   pepper
⅓ cup sweet pickle relish or
   chopped sweet pickle
¼ cup sliced stuffed green
   olives
3 hard-cooked eggs, chopped
¾ cup mayonnaise or salad
   dressing
1 can (6½ ounces) chunk
   tuna fish, drained
8 potato rolls or hamburger
   buns, split open

Combine all ingredients. Spread on split rolls or buns. Broil until cheese melts and edges of buns are toasted. Serve immediately. Makes 16 open face sandwiches or 8 servings.

See menus for July, 3rd week; August, 3rd week; December, 4th week .

Tuna Burgers on Buns

1 egg
1 can (6½ ounces) tuna fish,
   chunk style, drained
1 cup fresh bread crumbs or
   ½ cup dry bread crumbs
½ cup mayonnaise
2 tablespoons chopped onion
2 tablespoons sweet pickle
   relish or chopped sweet
   pickle
1 tablespoon butter or
   margarine, melted
4 hamburger buns
Lettuce
4 tomato slices

Beat egg. Stir in tuna, bread crumbs, mayonnaise, onion, and pickle relish. Shape into four patties. Brown on both sides in butter in skillet. Serve between toasted bun halves, topping each patty with lettuce and tomato slices. Makes 4 servings.

See menus for September, 3rd week.

French Dip Sandwiches

4 to 8 thin slices cooked roast
   beef (about 8 ounces)
4 hoagie buns
2 cups beef juice or 2
   packages (.87 ounce each)
   au jus mix

Slice beef thinly and cut into pieces that will fit into hoagie buns. Heat beef slices in ½ cup of beef juice; arrange on buns. Heat remaining beef juice. Serve with sandwiches for dipping. Makes 4 servings.

See menus for December, 3rd week.

Reuben Sandwiches

8 slices cooked turkey breast
or corned beef
4 slices Swiss, Muenster, or
Monterey Jack cheese
8 slices dark rye or
pumpernickel bread
1 cup sauerkraut, drained
½ cup Quick Thousand
Island Dressing*
½ cup (1 stick) butter or
margarine

For each sandwich, put 1 slice turkey breast or corned beef and 1 slice Swiss cheese on each of 4 pieces of bread. Heap on sauerkraut and spread dressing over it. Put on second slice of turkey breast or corned beef, then top with second slice of bread. Spread outside of sandwiches with soft butter or margarine. Grill, butter side down, on both sides in hot skillet and cook until cheese melts. Serve hot. Makes 4 sandwiches.

Quick Thousand Island Dressing: Combine 1 cup thick commercial Thousand Island dressing with ¼ cup buttermilk; blend thoroughly and refrigerate.

Variation

Deviled-Ham Reubens: Use 1 can (6½ ounces) deviled ham in place of turkey or corned beef. Use 8 slices of cheese. Arrange 4 slices cheese on 4 bread slices; spread with deviled ham; top with sauerkraut, then with remaining cheese and bread slices. Grill as for Reuben Sandwiches.

See menus for February, 2nd week; October, 4th week.

Fried Egg Sandwiches

4 eggs
2 teaspoons butter or
margarine
Salt and pepper
8 slices buttered whole grain
bread
Catsup or chili sauce

For each sandwich, heat ½ teaspoon butter or margarine in medium skillet. Crack one egg into melted fat; break yolk with edge of eggshell. When egg has cooked on bottom, turn over with spatula; cook remaining side. Season with salt and pepper to taste. Place hot fried egg on slice of bread; add catsup or chili sauce as desired; top with second slice of bread. Serve hot. Makes 4 sandwiches.

Variation

Fried Egg Sandwich with Lunch Meat: After breaking yolk, lay 2 or 3 thin slices or 1 thick slice lunch meat over broken yolk, pressing it into raw egg. When egg has cooked on bottom, turn over with spatula and cook remaining side. Continue as above.

See menus for February, 3rd week; August, 1st week; December, 4th week.

Egg Salad Sandwiches

4 Hard-Cooked Eggs,*
  shelled and chopped
1/4 cup mayonnaise or salad
  dressing
1 tablespoon minced onion
1/2 teaspoon prepared
  mustard
1/4 teaspoon salt
Dash Tabasco sauce
2 tablespoons chopped
  pickle, if desired
8 slices enriched whole wheat
  or rye bread

Mix all ingredients. Makes enough filling for 4 sandwiches.

Hard-Cooked Eggs: To hard-cook eggs, place eggs in large saucepan. Add cold water to 1 inch above eggs. Bring eggs barely to boil over medium heat, turn heat to low, cover pan and cook 15 minutes. Plunge eggs immediately into cold water for 5 minutes. Crack shells and peel under cold running water.

Variation

Quick Egg Salad Sandwich: Scramble eggs until dry, rather than hard-cook them, and combine with remaining ingredients.

See menus for January, 4th week; February, 4th week; October, 1st week.

Spoonburgers

1 can (8 ounces) tomato sauce
1/4 cup catsup
1 tablespoon vinegar
1 tablespoon brown sugar
1 1/2 teaspoons
  Worcestershire sauce
1 teaspoon salt
1/2 teaspoon chili powder
1/4 teaspoon curry powder
1/8 teaspoon pepper
1 pound lean ground beef
1/4 cup chopped green
  pepper (optional)
1/4 cup finely diced celery
1/2 cup chopped onion
8 to 10 hamburger buns

In medium saucepan combine first nine ingredients; simmer 10 minutes. In skillet cook together ground beef, green pepper, celery, and onion until meat loses its pink color and vegetables are soft. Combine with sauce; simmer 5 minutes. Makes enough filling for 8 to 10 hamburger buns.

Note: Flavor of Spoonburgers improves the second day.

See menus for May, 3rd week; June, 1st week.

Barbecued Hamburgers

1½ pounds lean ground
  beef
1 egg, slightly beaten
¾ cup dry bread crumbs or
  quick-cooking oats
¾ cup evaporated milk
1½ teaspoons salt
⅛ teaspoon pepper
3 tablespoons coarsely grated
  onion
3 tablespoons vinegar
2 tablespoons sugar
1 cup catsup
½ cup water
¼ teaspoon dry mustard

Combine beef, egg, crumbs, milk, salt, pepper, and 3 tablespoons chopped onion. Shape mixture into 12 patties, allowing ¼ cup mixture per patty. Brown in hot skillet, using a little oil, if necessary. (Or patties may be quickly browned under the broiler; do not overcook, however.) Combine remaining ingredients in large heavy saucepan; simmer 5 minutes. Put drained patties carefully into barbecue sauce, making sure sauce is spooned over all of them. Simmer for 30 minutes. Serve each patty in a bun with 1 teaspoon sauce over top. Makes 12 patties.

Note: One of the advantages of these tasty hamburgers is that they may be prepared ahead of time, refrigerated, then heated slowly just before serving.

See menus for June, 1st week.

Asparagus Melt

2 onion rolls or English
  muffins or 4 French bread
  slices
4 teaspoons butter or
  margarine, softened
Mayonnaise
16 to 20 fresh asparagus
  spears (about 1 pound) or
  1 package (10 ounces)
  frozen asparagus spears,
  cooked and drained
8 tomato slices
¼ teaspoon basil, crushed
1 cup (4 ounces) shredded
  Cheddar cheese

Split rolls or English muffins; spread with butter, then with mayonnaise. On each half, place 4 to 5 cooked asparagus spears. Top each with 2 tomato slices; sprinkle with basil; top with cheese. Broil about 6 inches from heat until vegetables are hot and cheese melts, about 2 minutes. Serve immediately. Makes 4 servings.

Variation

Broccoli Melt: Broccoli, cooked until crisp-tender, can be used in place of asparagus. Other vegetables, such as spinach or zucchini, can also be used.

See menus for April, 1st week.

Turkey Stack Sandwiches

4 slices rye bread
4 slices (4 ounces) Swiss
  cheese
4 large lettuce leaves
8 tomato slices
4 generous slices cooked
  breast of turkey
8 slices bacon, cut in half and
  fried crisp
Thousand Island Dressing
  (p. 223)

For each sandwich, place 1 slice rye bread on dinner plate. Top with slice of Swiss cheese, then lettuce, tomato slices, breast of turkey, and bacon slices. Smother with Thousand Island Dressing. Makes 4 sandwiches.

Note: For Quick Thousand Island Dressing, see p. 167.

See menus for November, 4th week.

Beverages

Hot Spiced Tomato Juice

1 can (24 ounces) tomato juice
  (3 cups)
3 tablespoons brown sugar
4 whole cloves
1 full stick cinnamon, broken
4 slices lemon

Combine all ingredients in heavy saucepan; bring to boil. Lower heat; simmer 5 minutes. Strain and serve. Makes 4 servings (6 ounces each).

See menus for March, 2nd week.

French Chocolate

2½ squares (1 ounce each)
  unsweetened chocolate
½ cup water
¾ cup sugar
Dash salt
½ cup heavy cream,
  whipped
6 cups hot milk
Cinnamon (optional)

Combine chocolate and water in saucepan; cook over low heat, stirring until chocolate melts and mixture is blended. Add sugar and salt; boil 4 minutes, stirring constantly. Cool. Fold in whipped cream and chill. To serve, spoon 1 rounded tablespoon chocolate mixture into each cup; pour in hot milk. Stir to blend. Garnish with dash cinnamon, if desired. Makes 8 cups.

See menus for December, 4th week.

Orange Juice Pick-Up

2 eggs
2 cups orange juice
1½ teaspoons honey

Combine all ingredients in blender or shaker container. Cover and blend or shake until frothy and well blended. Pour into juice glasses. Makes 4 servings.

See menus for April, 4th week; June, 2nd week; July, 4th week.

Orange Julius

⅓ cup (½ 6-ounce can) frozen orange juice concentrate
½ cup milk
½ cup water
¼ cup sugar
5 or 6 ice cubes

Combine all ingredients in blender or food processor. Cover and blend or process until smooth. Serve immediately. Makes 4 servings (6 ounces each).

See menus for January, 3rd week; April, 4th week; June, 1st week.

Eggnog

4 egg yolks
¼ cup sugar
Few grains salt
1 teaspoon vanilla
1 quart milk
4 egg whites, stiffly beaten

In large bowl beat egg yolks until light. Slowly beat in sugar, salt, and vanilla. Stir in milk. Fold in egg whites; serve immediately.
    Note: When eggs are to be used without cooking, select eggs that have no cracks in the shells.

See menus for June, 3rd week.

Banana Nog

2 medium bananas, fully ripe
2 cups milk
1 cup evaporated milk
2 eggs
2 teaspoons vanilla
Dash nutmeg

Combine all ingredients in blender or food processor and blend or process until mixture is thick and smooth. Pour into glasses. Top with additional nutmeg, if desired. Makes 4 glasses.

Variation

Orange Nog: Omit bananas; decrease milk to 1½ cups; omit evaporated milk; add 2 cups orange juice and 1 teaspoon orange extract (optional). Proceed as above.

See menus for January, 3rd week.

Banana Shakes

2 cups milk
2 to 3 large ripe bananas, peeled, frozen, broken into pieces

Place milk in blender or food processor. With blender or processor in action, slowly add frozen banana pieces to milk until shake is as thick and creamy as desired. Makes 4 glasses.

Variations

Chocolate Banana Shakes: Add 2 to 4 tablespoons or more Chocolate Syrup (see below).

Fruit Shakes: One or 2 tablespoons frozen orange juice concentrate is a nice addition to Banana Shakes. Or pineapple juice may be used instead of milk, along with sliced peaches, fresh strawberries, yogurt, or nuts. The principle of freezing fruit and blending with milk, lemon juice, and sugar to taste offers limitless possibilities for nutritious quick drinks.

See menus for March, 3rd week; June, 3rd week; September, 2nd week.

Chocolate Syrup

½ cup unsweetened cocoa
1½ cups sugar
⅛ teaspoon salt
1 cup water
½ teaspoon vanilla

In medium saucepan combine all ingredients but vanilla. Bring to boil; lower heat and simmer 5 minutes. Add vanilla. Store in covered jar in refrigerator to use for making cocoa or chocolate milk.

Variations

Hot Chocolate: Stir 1 or 2 tablespoons chocolate syrup into each cup of hot milk or according to taste.

Chocolate Milk: Stir 1 to 2 tablespoons chocolate syrup into each glass of cold milk or according to taste.

See menus for February, 1st week; July, 3rd week; August, 2nd week.

Black Cows

2 cups rootbeer
2 cups rich milk or light cream

Combine equal parts of rootbeer and milk. Chill. Makes 4 cups.
   Note: Any flavor carbonated beverage may be substituted for rootbeer.

See menus for May, 3rd week.

FRUITS AND VEGETABLES

Fruits

Sour Cream Fruit Topping

1 cup dairy sour cream
2 tablespoons brown sugar
1/8 teaspoon ground
cinnamon
Dash allspice
Fresh fruit such as sliced
peaches, nectarines, grapes,
apples, or bananas

Mix together sour cream, brown sugar, cinnamon, and allspice. May be used immediately, but is better if covered and chilled at least 2 hours to allow flavors to blend. Spoon over fresh fruit. Makes enough for 4 servings.

See menus for May, 4th week; October, 3rd week; November, 2nd week.

Broiled Grapefruit

2 grapefruit
4 teaspoons butter or
margarine
4 tablespoons brown sugar,
packed

Cut grapefruit into halves; remove seeds. Cut around edges and sections to loosen; remove centers. Dot each half with 1 teaspoon butter or margarine; sprinkle with 1 tablespoon brown sugar. Set oven control to broil. Broil grapefruit 4 to 6 inches from heat until juice bubbles and edges of peels turn light brown. Serve hot. Makes 4 servings.

See menus for February, 1st week; October, 2nd week; December, 4th week.

Fresh Fruit Cup

1/3 cup sugar
1/2 cup warm water
1 tablespoon lemon juice
1 tablespoon orange juice or
1 teaspoon frozen orange
juice concentrate
1 teaspoon grated orange
rind (optional)
4 cups diced fresh fruit, any
combination (such as
apples, peaches, pears,
melons, bananas, or grapes)

Combine sugar and water in small saucepan. Bring to boil; remove from heat immediately. Stir in lemon and orange juice and grated rind, if used; chill. Prepare fruit. Stir into chilled syrup so all fruit is coated. Makes 8 servings.

Variation

Citrus Fruit Cup: Use any combination of oranges, grapefruit, pineapple.

See menus for January, 1st week; February, 1st week; December, 1st week.

Ambrosia

4 cups sliced oranges
1 cup flaked coconut

Sprinkle orange slices with coconut and chill well. Makes 8 servings.

Note: Sliced bananas may be added at the last, but it is not then strictly ambrosia.

See menus for March, 2nd week; August, 1st week; September, 1st week.

Hawaiian Fruit Cup

1 can (20 ounces) pineapple chunks or tidbits, chilled
1 can (11 ounces) mandarin oranges, chilled and drained
1 or 2 bananas, peeled and sliced
1 cup (3 ounces) shredded coconut

In large bowl combine pineapple and juice, drained mandarin oranges, and banana slices. Stir until all banana pieces have been covered with juice. Sprinkle coconut over top and serve in small dishes. Makes 6 servings.

See menus for October, 1st week; November, 2nd week.

Sautéed Apple Slices

2 large tart apples
2 teaspoons butter or margarine
½ teaspoon grated lemon or orange rind (optional)
1 teaspoon lemon juice
Nutmeg or mace
Sugar to taste

Quarter washed apples, core and slice; do not peel. Melt butter in medium skillet. Add apple slices; sauté over medium heat for 10 to 15 minutes until apples are tender and transparent. Sprinkle with lemon juice; add lemon rind, if desired; add nutmeg or mace and sugar to taste. Serve warm. Makes 4 servings.

See menus for March, 2nd week; March, 3rd week; May, 2nd week.

Applesauce

4 to 5 tart apples, 4 cups sliced
1 or 2 tablespoons water
1 tablespoon sugar, or to taste
¼ teaspoon ground cinnamon (optional)
⅛ teaspoon ground cloves (optional)

Cut apples in quarters, core, pare, and slice into large saucepan; add small amount of water, sugar, and spices, if desired. Cover and cook slowly until apples are tender, 15 to 20 minutes. Mash apples with fork or potato masher or put through food mill or chop to desired degree in food processor. Season and sweeten to taste. Makes 4 servings, ½ cup each.

See menus for April, 2nd week; July, 3rd week; October, 2nd week.

Applesauce 'N' Dumplings

1 can (1 pound) or 2 cups
  applesauce
½ teaspoon cinnamon
¼ teaspoon nutmeg
½ teaspoon vanilla
1 tablespoon butter
1 package (7.5 ounces)
  refrigerated biscuits
Cream or evaporated milk
  (optional)

In 9-inch skillet or saucepan, combine applesauce with spices, vanilla, and butter; heat barely to boiling. Arrange biscuits over top, cover and reduce heat to simmer. Cook 15 to 18 minutes, until biscuits have puffed up and are done. Serve biscuits with applesauce spooned over them. Pour cream over top, if desired. Makes 10 dumplings or about 8 servings.

Note: One-half recipe for Baking Powder Biscuits (p. 249) may be used in place of 1 package refrigerated biscuits.

See menus for January, 2nd week.

Frosty Fruit

1 cup sugar
1 cup water
1 can (1 pound) grapefruit
  sections in juice, undrained
1 can (1 pound 4 ounces)
  pineapple tidbits in juice,
  undrained
2 bananas, diced
⅓ pound seedless green
  grapes

Combine sugar and water; bring to boil, stirring to dissolve sugar. Cool. Add grapefruit, pineapple, bananas, and grapes. Freeze to a thick slush. Serve fruit in sherbet dishes. If fruit is frozen hard, remove from freezer 1 hour before time to serve. Makes 8 servings.

Note: Ginger ale may be poured over fruit just before serving, if desired, but not necessary.

See menus for May, 1st week.

Stewed Fresh Plums

1 pound plums
½ cup water
Sugar

Wash plums and pit, if desired. Place them in medium saucepan along with water. Bring to boil, turn to low, cover and cook plums until tender, about 10 minutes, adding more water if needed. Add sugar to taste and serve, hot or cold, with juices poured over. Good served over ice cream. Makes 4 servings.

See menus for July, 3rd week; August, 1st week.

Parsleyed New Potatoes

1½ pounds new potatoes or regular potatoes, quartered
Water
¼ cup (½ stick) butter or margarine, melted
2 tablespoons chopped fresh parsley or 2 teaspoons crushed dried parsley

Cook unpeeled new potatoes in small amount of boiling salted water in covered saucepan for 20 to 30 minutes or until just tender; peel. Drain and gently coat with melted butter or margarine. Sprinkle with parsley. Makes 4 servings.

Variation

New Potatoes with Sesame: Cook potatoes as above. Cook ⅓ cup sliced green onions, including green ends, in ¼ cup (½ stick) butter until soft. Spoon over hot drained potatoes; sprinkle with toasted sesame seeds. Serve immediately. To toast sesame seeds, spread in shallow layer in baking dish. Bake at 350 degrees F. 5 to 8 minutes or until lightly browned.

See menus for January, 3rd week; May, 2nd week; December, 4th week.

Creamed New Potatoes and Peas

8 new potatoes (about 1¼ pounds) or regular potatoes, quartered
Water
1 package (10 ounces) frozen peas
2 tablespoons butter or margarine
¼ cup all-purpose flour
2 cups rich milk or half-and-half
Salt and pepper
Paprika

If using new potatoes, scrub and cook without peeling in small amount boiling water until barely tender, about 12 minutes. Drain and peel. If using regular potatoes, peel before cooking and quarter potatoes. Drain thoroughly. Cook peas according to package directions; drain thoroughly. In medium saucepan, melt butter or margarine; blend in flour. Add milk or cream and cook, stirring until mixture thickens and is smooth. Season to taste. Pour over potatoes and peas in serving bowl. Sprinkle with paprika. Makes 4 servings.
    Note: White sauce can be made quickly and easily in microwave.

See menus for June, 4th week; October, 3rd week; October, 4th week.

Baked Potatoes with Seafood Sauce

¼ cup (½ stick) butter or
   margarine
1 cup (4 ounces) sliced
   mushrooms
¼ cup sliced green onions
1 clove garlic, minced
3 tablespoons all-purpose
   flour
1 can (10¾ ounces)
   condensed chicken broth
½ cup milk or cream
¼ teaspoon ground nutmeg
½ pound crab or imitation
   crab or 1 can (7½ ounces)
   crabmeat
2 tablespoons chopped fresh
   parsley or 2 teaspoons
   crushed dried parsley
4 to 6 hot baked potatoes

In 10-inch skillet, melt butter over medium heat; add mushrooms, green onions, and garlic; cook and stir until vegetables are tender. Blend in flour. Remove pan from heat; gradually stir in chicken broth, milk, and nutmeg. Add crab (or other cooked seafood of your choice) and parsley. Reduce heat to low. Cover and heat through. Using fork, make X in top of potatoes and with thumbs and index fingers push potato to open it up. Spoon sauce over potatoes. Serve immediately. Makes 3 cups sauce or enough for 4 to 6 servings.

See menus for August, 2nd week; October, 1st week.

Stuffed Baked Potatoes

4 medium-size baking
   potatoes
2 tablespoons butter or
   margarine
Hot milk
Salt and pepper
¼ cup shredded Cheddar
   cheese
1 teaspoon crushed dried
   parsley

Scrub potatoes and, if desired, rub with oil. Bake at 375 degrees F. for 1 hour or until potatoes are tender. With mitts or towel gently roll hot potatoes between palms of hands to soften centers. Carefully cut top off long side of each potato; empty contents into medium bowl. With potato masher or electric beater, mash or whip hot potato centers with butter or margarine and enough hot milk to make fluffy. Season to taste with salt and pepper. Pile mixture back into potato cases. Sprinkle with shredded cheese and parsley. Potatoes may be refrigerated or frozen at this point to be baked later at 375 degrees F. for 30 minutes or until hot and cheese is melted. Or they may be baked immediately at 350 degrees F. for 20 minutes. Makes 4 servings.

Note: Two slices diced bacon, cooked crisp, may be added to potato filling. Also sautéed sliced green onions or shredded cheddar cheese or both may be added for extra flavor. If cheese is added to the potato, then sprinkle top with parsley and paprika.

See menus for December, 4th week.

Baked Potatoes with Mushroom Topping

4 large baking potatoes
1 cup (¼ pound) sliced fresh mushrooms
2 tablespoons sliced green onions
⅛ teaspoon crushed dried savory or tarragon
3 tablespoons butter
½ cup plain yogurt or sour cream (optional)
2 tablespoons grated Parmesan cheese
½ teaspoon salt
⅛ teaspoon pepper

Scrub potatoes, prick with fork, and, if desired, rub with oil or shortening. Bake at 375 degrees F. for 1 hour or until soft. Roll between mitted hands to soften centers. In the meantime, sauté mushrooms, onion, and savory or tarragon in butter for 1 minute. Remove from heat; stir in yogurt or sour cream (if used), cheese, salt, and pepper. To serve, slit potatoes and press open. Sprinkle lightly with salt; spoon 2 tablespoons topping into each potato. Makes 4 servings.

Variations

Baked Reuben Potatoes: Combine 2 cups diced cooked corned beef or 1 can (12 ounces) corned beef, shredded, with 2 cups (1 pound) drained sauerkraut, 1 cup (4 ounces) shredded Swiss cheese, and ¼ teaspoon caraway seed (optional). Pile onto opened baked potatoes; broil until cheese is slightly melted. Makes 4 servings.

Nacho Potatoes: Combine 2 cups (8 ounces) shredded sharp Cheddar cheese, 1 can (4 ounces) chopped green chilies, and 1 can (4½ ounces) sliced or chopped ripe olives, drained. Pile onto opened baked potatoes; broil until topping melts. If desired, serve with crisp bacon bits, sliced green onion, chopped fresh tomato or sour cream or both. Makes 4 servings.

See menus for January, 2nd week; February, 1st week; July, 1st week.

Hashed Brown Potatoes

6 tablespoons bacon fat or shortening
4 cups finely diced potatoes, raw or cooked (about 1½ pounds)
1 tablespoon finely chopped onion
Salt and pepper

Heat fat or shortening in large skillet. Arrange potatoes evenly over bottom of skillet and top with onion, salt, and pepper. Cook over low heat until bottom side is golden brown, allowing more time if potatoes are raw. (Raw potatoes will cook faster if skillet is covered for a short time.) When potatoes have browned on bottom, flip over with spatula, cutting portion in half if necessary to facilitate turning potatoes over. Continue cooking until potatoes have browned on second side. Season to taste. Serve hot. Makes 4 servings.

See menus for February, 2nd week.

Oven-Fried Potatoes

3 to 4 medium potatoes
3 tablespoons vegetable oil
Salt and pepper

Preheat oven broiler to 450 degrees F. Peel and thinly slice enough potatoes to make about 3 cups. Toss oil into sliced potatoes until all slices are coated. Rub oil generously into shallow baking dish and arrange potatoes evenly over bottom of dish so that potatoes are only about 2 slices deep. Broil potatoes about 6 inches from source of heat for 5 to 7 minutes, until potatoes are golden brown. With spatula, turn potatoes over, sprinkle with salt and pepper to taste and continue to broil until potatoes are tender and golden brown. Makes 4 servings.

Note: Oven-Fried Potatoes are convenient to prepare and cook with other broiled foods, such as steak, hamburgers, or salmon.

See menus for September, 1st week; November, 2nd week.

Scalloped Potatoes

4 cups (1⅓ pounds) thinly
  sliced potatoes
½ cup sliced onion
⅓ cup all-purpose flour
Salt and pepper
4 tablespoons (½ stick)
  butter or margarine
1⅔ cups milk
Paprika

Peel and slice potatoes into ⅛-inch slices; drop into cold water. Peel and slice onion. Butter 2-quart casserole. Drain and pat potatoes dry with paper towel. Divide ingredients into fourths. In following order, layer potatoes, season with salt and pepper, add onion, sprinkle with flour, and dot with butter. Repeat this layering three times. Pour milk over potatoes. Sprinkle with paprika. Bake, covered, at 350 degrees F. for 45 minutes; remove lid and continue baking another 45 minutes or until potatoes are tender and lightly browned. Makes 4 servings.

Note: Scalloped potatoes can have any of the following added: corned beef, meat loaf, diced ham, sausage, or sliced frankfurters. Vegetables such as carrots, broccoli, turnips, cauliflower, green tomatoes, or seeded red tomatoes can also be added.

Variation

Potatoes au Gratin: Using 2 cups shredded cheese, layer cheese along with other ingredients, finishing off with cheese.

See menus for March, 1st week; September, 3rd week.

Pan-Roasted Potatoes

8 small whole potatoes or
   potato chunks
Vegetable oil
Salt and pepper

Peel potatoes. Rub with oil and place alongside roast
or in a separate greased shallow pan. Bake with roast
for last hour, turning occasionally. Season with salt
and pepper to taste. Makes 4 servings.

See menus for April, 4th week; October, 2nd week.

Potato Pancakes

2 tablespoons all-purpose
   flour
1½ teaspoons salt
¼ teaspoon baking powder
⅛ teaspoon pepper
2 eggs, well beaten
2 tablespoons chopped onion
1 tablespoon chopped fresh
   parsley or 1 teaspoon
   crushed dried parsley
3 cups potatoes, grated
¼ cup shortening or
   vegetable oil

Combine flour, salt, baking powder, and pepper;
combine with eggs, onion, and parsley. Peel potatoes,
grate coarsely, and squeeze dry in towel. *Immediately*
stir potatoes into egg and flour mixture until well
mixed. In skillet, heat shortening or oil until drop of
water sizzles in it. Spoon 2 tablespoons batter into fat;
press flat with spatula for each pancake, leaving 1-
inch space between pancakes. Cook over medium
heat until golden brown and crisp; turn carefully and
brown other side. Drain on absorbent paper. Keep
warm in 200 degree F. oven until all pancakes are
cooked. Serve with Sauerbraten (p. 104) or as main
dish with applesauce. Makes 10 to 12 medium
pancakes.

See menus for February, 3rd week.

Stuffed Celery

1 package (3 ounces)
   cream cheese and 1
   tablespoon   Roquefort or
   blue cheese OR
Cheddar, Swiss, or other
   cheese, and cream or
   mayonnaise

Clean and cut 3- to 4-inch lengths of tender celery; set
aside. Blend cream cheese with Roquefort or blue
cheese, softening with a little milk or cream. Use
mixture to fill celery pieces. Or a filling may be made
by blending finely grated cheddar, Swiss, or other
cheese with a little cream or mayonnaise to soften;
season as desired.

Variation

Stuffed Dates: The same cheese mixtures can be used
to stuff dates or prunes.

See menus for April, 1st week; August, 4th week; December, 1st week.

Stir-Fried Celery

1 stalk celery
3 tablespoons vegetable oil
Salt and pepper
$1/3$ cup water or broth
Soy sauce (optional)

Wash celery well, separating ribs and saving leaves for other recipes. Cut celery into $1/4$-inch diagonal slices. Heat oil in wok or large skillet, add celery and stir rapidly, coating with oil. Season with salt and pepper to taste; cook, tossing constantly for 2 to 3 minutes. Add water or broth, turn heat to medium-low, cover and cook for 2 minutes longer. Remove cover, turn heat to high and reduce liquid until thickened. Add soy sauce to taste. Makes 4 servings.

Note: Other vegetables, such as carrots and/or mushrooms, may be added.

See menus for November, 1st week.

Fresh Snap Green or Wax Beans

1 pound fresh snap beans OR 1 package (10 ounces) frozen green or wax beans OR 1 can (1 pound) cut green or wax beans

Trim fresh beans and, if desired, snap into $1\frac{1}{2}$-inch lengths. Cover with water and bring to boil; simmer 5 to 20 minutes, until barely tender. Or cook frozen beans as directed on package. Or heat canned beans. Drain off and save liquid to use in soups. Season beans in any of the ways listed below. Makes 4 servings.

Variations

Buttered Beans: Toss beans with 1 tablespoon melted butter or margarine. Season to taste with salt and pepper.

Dilly Beans: Add $1/2$ teaspoon dill weed to Buttered Beans.

Beans and Onions: Lightly brown 2 tablespoons chopped onions in 1 tablespoon butter or margarine; toss with cooked, drained beans until well mixed.

Beans with Almonds: Brown 2 tablespoons slivered almonds in 1 tablespoon butter; add cooked, drained beans; toss.

Beans with Bacon: Cook 2 strips bacon, diced, until crisp; toss bacon and drippings with drained beans until they are coated.

Beans and Mushrooms: Sauté $1/4$ pound sliced mushrooms in 1 tablespoon butter. Toss with cooked, drained green beans; heat through.

See menus for February, 3rd week; March, 4th week; June, 1st week.

Stir-Fried Asparagus

1½ cups fresh asparagus
3 tablespoons olive or
  vegetable oil
1 clove garlic, minced
¼ cup slivered almonds
Soy sauce

Wash asparagus thoroughly, peel stalks and cut into ½ inch diagonal slices. Heat oil in wok or large frying pan. Add garlic and nuts. Stir-fry until well coated. Add sliced asparagus; stir-fry until asparagus is crisp-tender, 3 to 5 minutes. Season to taste with soy sauce. Serve immediately. Makes 4 servings.

See menus for March, 3rd week.

Buttered Asparagus

1½ pounds fresh asparagus
2 tablespoons butter
Salt and pepper

Wash asparagus thoroughly. Cut asparagus or leave stalks whole, as desired. In large amount boiling salted water (1 teaspoon salt per 1 quart water) plunge asparagus and partially cover until water boils again, then uncover. Reduce heat and cook 4 minutes. Test for tenderness by piercing asparagus with sharp knife point. When asparagus tests barely tender, remove from heat; with slotted spoon lift asparagus out of water, drain on clean towel and arrange on serving platter. Top hot asparagus with pats of butter and season to taste with salt and pepper. Makes 4 servings.

Variations

Asparagus with Lemon Mayonnaise: With wire whisk, beat 1 tablespoon fresh lemon juice into ¼ cup mayonnaise until smooth. Pour over cooked asparagus.

Asparagus with Butter and Cheese: Top warm asparagus with Parmesan cheese, melted butter, and lemon juice to taste. If desired, place under broiler to slightly melt cheese.

Asparagus Polonaise: Chop 3 hard-cooked eggs; combine with 3 tablespoons chopped parsley; set aside. Melt 2 tablespoons butter or margarine; sauté ¼ cup bread crumbs. Toss with egg and parsley; sprinkle over cooked asparagus.

Creamed Asparagus: In medium saucepan melt ¼ cup (½ stick) butter or margarine; stir in ¼ cup all-purpose flour. Add 2 cups milk; cook and stir until thick and smooth. Season to taste with salt, pepper, and paprika. Gently stir in well-drained cooked asparagus. Serve over toast.

See menus for March, 3rd week; June, 4th week.

Glazed Onions

4 to 6 medium peeled onions
Salt and pepper
¼ cup honey
3 tablespoons butter or
　margarine
Ground cloves

Cook whole onions in small amount salted water, covered, until barely tender, about 20 minutes. Arrange in well-buttered baking dish; season with salt and pepper to taste. Heat together honey and butter; pour over onions. Sprinkle lightly with ground cloves. Bake at 400 degrees F. for 20 to 25 minutes or until golden brown. Makes 4 servings.

Note: These may be baked at a lower temperature for a longer time to adjust to an oven meal.

See menus for March, 4th week.

Mushroom Patties

1 pound fresh mushrooms
2 cups soft (not dry) bread
　crumbs
½ cup chopped walnuts
¼ cup chopped onion
¼ cup chopped fresh parsley
4 eggs, slightly beaten
¾ teaspoon salt
¼ teaspoon pepper
¼ cup vegetable oil

Rinse, pat dry, and finely chop mushrooms to make about 4 cups. In large bowl combine mushrooms with all remaining ingredients except oil; mix well. Shape into patties about 4 inches in diameter. In large skillet heat oil. Add patties; fry over medium low heat until patties are set and golden, about 5 minutes on each side. Makes 8 patties.

See menus for June, 2nd week.

Gingered Parsnips

½ cup water
3 cups diced parsnips
　(3 medium)
1 tablespoon butter
⅛ teaspoon salt
⅓ cup orange juice
½ teaspoon grated orange
　rind (optional)
1 teaspoon grated fresh
　gingerroot

In large skillet heat water; add parsnips; cover and simmer 5 minutes or until parsnips are barely tender. Remove lid and continue cooking until water has disappeared. Add butter, salt, orange juice, orange rind, and gingerroot. Heat and serve. Makes 4 servings.

See menus for January, 4th week.

Spinach Apple Toss

2 bunches (³/₄ pound) fresh
  spinach, trimmed and
  washed thoroughly
1 tart red apple, sliced
4 slices bacon, diced and
  fried crisp
¹/₄ cup salad dressing or
  mayonnaise
2 tablespoons frozen orange
  juice concentrate

Dry trimmed and washed spinach leaves; tear into
bite-size pieces. Combine spinach, apples, and bacon.
Mix salad dressing and orange juice concentrate; pour
over spinach-apple mixture; toss lightly. Makes 4
servings.

See menus for April, 4th week; August, 3rd week; December, 3rd week.

Sautéed Spinach with Bacon

2 bunches (³/₄ pound) fresh
  spinach, trimmed and
  washed thoroughly
6 slices bacon, cut into
  ¹/₂-inch pieces
1 large clove garlic, minced
  (optional)
1¹/₂ tablespoons lemon juice
Salt and coarsely ground
  pepper

Dry trimmed and washed spinach leaves. In 10-inch
skillet, cook bacon until crisp; add garlic and sauté 1
minute. Add greens and toss to coat. Add lemon juice
and cover. Cook, stirring occasionally, until greens
are limp, 3 to 7 minutes. Season to taste with salt and
pepper. Makes 4 servings.
  Note: Turnip greens, beet greens, mustard greens,
chard, or collards may be used in place of spinach.

See menus for June, 3rd week.

Parsleyed Carrots

1 pound carrots
2 tablespoons water
¹/₄ teaspoon sugar
¹/₈ teaspoon salt
1 tablespoon butter or
  margarine
1 tablespoon chopped fresh
  or dried parsley

Peel carrots and slice, dice, julienne, or grate into
medium saucepan. Add water, sugar, and salt. Bring
to boil, cover and reduce heat; cook 2 to 3 minutes for
grated carrots; or 4 to 7 minutes for sliced or diced
carrots, until barely tender. Remove lid, cook off
liquid and toss with butter or margarine and parsley
until coated. Serve immediately. Makes 4 servings.

Variations

Basil Carrots: Place ³/₄ pound thinly sliced or diced
carrots with 1 tablespoon butter into medium
saucepan. Add several sprigs of fresh basil, finely
chopped, or 1 teaspoon crushed dried basil. Cook,
stirring, over medium heat until butter melts. Cover

saucepan, turn heat to low, and cook for 10 to 12 minutes or until carrots are barely tender. Other herbs that can be used with carrots in place of basil include anise, chives, caraway, cinnamon, nutmeg, ginger, allspice, mint, curry, cilantro, thyme, rosemary, or mustard. Makes 4 servings.

See menus for January, 1st week; June, 3rd week; July, 1st week.

Glazed Carrots: Sauté drained, cooked carrots in 1 tablespoon butter along with enough maple-flavored syrup, honey, brown sugar, light corn syrup, concentrated orange juice, or apple juice to glaze.

See menus for February, 2nd week; April, 4th week; December, 1st week.

Oven-Cooked Carrots

1 pound carrots
2 tablespoons butter or
  margarine
1 teaspoon sugar
¼ teaspoon salt
2 tablespoons water

Peel carrots; cut into pieces 2 to 3 inches long and ½ inch thick. Place into baking dish along with remaining ingredients. Cover and bake at 350 degrees F. for 30 to 45 minutes or until fork tender. Especially good to prepare with an oven dinner. Makes 4 servings.

    Note: These may be baked in microwave on full power for 6 minutes or until tender.

See menus for February, 1st week.

Turnip Carrot Puree

½ pound carrots
  (3 medium)
½ pound turnips (2 large)
1½ tablespoons butter
Salt and pepper

Wash and peel carrots and turnips; cut into 1-inch pieces. Cook in vegetable steamer or small amount of salted water for 10 to 12 minutes or until barely tender. Drain and puree together in food processor or blender or mash together with potato masher. Blend in butter or margarine and seasonings to taste. Serve with one last grind of pepper. Makes 4 servings.

See menu for November, 4th week.

Sweet 'N' Sour Carrots

1 pound (7 medium) carrots
2 tablespoons butter or
  margarine
¼ teaspoon salt
1 tablespoon lemon juice
½ tablespoon honey
Chopped parsley

Peel or scrape carrots; slice thinly. In medium saucepan melt butter; add carrots and salt; cover pan; turn heat to low. Cook until carrots are crisp-tender, 15 to 20 minutes. Add lemon juice and honey; stir until all carrots are coated. Serve hot, garnished with chopped parsley. Makes 4 servings.

See menus for October, 3rd week; November, 4th week; December, 4th week.

Broiled Tomato Halves with Crumbs

4 teaspoons butter or
  margarine
¼ cup dry bread crumbs
¼ cup Parmesan cheese
¼ teaspoon crushed dried
  mixed herbs (such as
  oregano, thyme, or basil)
4 large tomatoes
Salt and pepper

Melt butter or margarine and toss with dry bread crumbs, cheese, and herbs; set aside. Wash and half tomatoes. Arrange, cut side up, on oiled baking pan; brush with oil and sprinkle with salt and pepper to taste. Place pan under broiler; broil for 4 to 5 minutes or until tomatoes are lightly colored and heated through. Sprinkle with crumb mixture and set in lower part of oven to keep warm until time to serve. Makes 4 servings of two halves each.

Variation

Baked Tomatoes: Prepare tomatoes as above, topping with crumbs. Bake at 350 degrees F. for 20 to 30 minutes.

See menus for February, 1st week; May, 1st week; August, 3rd week.

Stewed Tomatoes

4 large tomatoes, peeled, or
  1 can (1 pound) tomatoes
2 tablespoons butter
⅓ cup chopped onion
½ cup diced celery
½ teaspoon sugar
Chopped fresh or crushed
  dried basil
Salt and pepper
1 to 2 slices day-old bread,
  torn in pieces

Cut tomatoes into eighths; set aside. Melt butter in small saucepan; add onion and celery; cook over medium heat until vegetables are soft. Add tomatoes, seasonings to taste, and bread; cover and simmer 15 minutes. Makes 4 servings.

See menus for June, 4th week; September, 3rd week.

Zucchini Italiano

3 tablespoons olive or
vegetable oil
2 small onions, chopped
1 clove garlic, minced
1 pound firm medium-size
zucchini, cut into 1/4-inch
slices
1/2 teaspoon seasoned salt,
or to taste
1/4 teaspoon oregano

In 10-inch skillet, heat oil; add onion and garlic; cook
3 minutes, stirring. Add zucchini; season with salt
and oregano. Cover; cook 3 to 5 minutes, stirring
once. Remove from heat; allow to stand 2 or 3 minutes
to mingle flavors before serving. Makes 4 servings.

See menus for September, 1st week.

Baked Stuffed Zucchini

4 medium zucchini squash
6 slices day-old bread
3/4 teaspoon salt
1/4 teaspoon pepper
1/2 teaspoon crushed dried
leaf thyme or sage
1/3 cup chopped onion
1 egg, beaten
2 tablespoons butter or
margarine, melted
1 cup (4 ounces) shredded
Cheddar cheese

Wash squash; cut off both ends. Blanch in boiling
salted water until tender but still firmly shaped,
approximately 10 minutes. Remove, cool in cold water
and drain. Halve lengthwise and scoop out flesh,
leaving a thick enough edge to hold stuffing; set
zucchini shells aside. Chop scooped-out zucchini; put
into strainer to drain excess water. In food processor
or blender, crumble bread. Toss with salt, pepper,
thyme, onion, egg, butter or margarine, and squash
meat; mix thoroughly. Place squash shells into well-
oiled baking pan; fill with stuffing mixture. Top with
shredded cheese. Bake at 375 degrees F. for 20
minutes or until tender and brown. Makes 4 servings,
allowing 2 halves per serving.
   Note: Any stuffing mixture may be used.

See menus for July, 2nd week.

Baked Winter Squash

Winter squash
Vegetable oil
Butter or margarine
Salt and pepper

Cut squash in half, clean out seeds, brush cut surfaces
with oil, and bake cut side down on greased cookie
sheet at 350 degrees F. for 30 minutes. Turn squash
cut side up and continue baking until squash is tender
when pierced with pointed knife. Baking time ranges
from 45 minutes for small squash, to 1 hour or longer
for larger squash. Cut through skin into serving size
pieces and serve with butter or margarine and salt and
pepper to taste.

See menus for October, 4th week.

Mashed Winter Squash

1½ pounds unpeeled winter
squash (such as banana,
acorn, hubbard, butternut,
or buttercup)
¼ cup (½ stick) butter or
margarine
Salt and pepper

Peel squash and steam until tender. Or bake squash
(see directions for Baked Winter Squash p. 189) until
tender; scrape tender meat into bowl. Mash cooked
squash with butter and season to taste with salt and
pepper.

Variation

Baked Mashed Squash: Spoon mashed squash into
buttered 1-quart baking dish. Dot with 1 tablespoon
butter; bake at 350 degrees F. for 30 minutes. If
desired, casserole may be sprinkled with 1 tablespoon
brown sugar and ¼ cup chopped nuts before baking.
Or it may be topped with 1 cup shredded Swiss or
Cheddar cheese, then with ½ cup buttered bread
crumbs before baking.

See menus for October, 4th week.

Honey-Glazed Acorn Squash

2 medium or large acorn
squash
Vegetable oil
¼ cup (½ stick) butter or
margarine
¼ cup honey or maple-
flavored syrup
Salt and pepper

Cut squash lengthwise from stem to base. Scoop out
seeds and stringy portions and cut a small slice off
bottoms of squash halves so they will sit securely.
Brush cut surfaces with oil and arrange cut side down
on baking sheet. Bake at 400 degrees F. for 30 minutes.
Melt butter and combine with honey. Turn squash cut
sides up. Continue to bake until tender, 15 to 20
minutes longer, basting frequently with honey and
butter mixture. Season with salt and pepper to taste,
and serve with pork sausage links or patties. Makes
4 servings.
   Note: These may be baked, covered loosely with
plastic wrap, in microwave on *full power* for 9 to 11
minutes, or until tender, turning once.

See menus for January, 3rd week; February, 1st week.

Tasty Peas

2 cups fresh, shelled peas
(1½ pounds in pod) or 1
package (10 ounces) frozen
peas

Cook fresh peas in small amount boiling water for 2
to 4 minutes or until barely tender; if desired, add
sprinkle of sugar or salt to water. Or cook frozen peas
according to package directions. Do not overcook.
Drain off and store any remaining liquid for use later

in soups. Season hot cooked peas in any of the ways listed below. Makes 4 servings.

Variations

Buttered Peas: Season drained peas with 2 tablespoons butter or margarine.

Herbed Peas: Add a pinch of tarragon, mint, chives, basil, or thyme to buttered peas; toss and serve immediately.

Gourmet Peas: Sprinkle hot peas with 1/4 teaspoon beef or chicken bouillon mix; stir lightly until bouillon granules dissolve. Or use double-strength bouillon as cooking liquid. Add 1/4 cup dairy sour cream or plain yogurt. Stir and heat quickly; serve immediately.

Peas and Onions: Add 1 cup tiny boiled onions to peas; sauté quickly in 1 to 2 tablespoons butter or margarine.

Minted Peas: Add 1 tablespoon butter and 1 tablespoon chopped fresh mint (or 1 teaspoon dried mint); toss with cooked drained peas.

Mushrooms and Peas: Sauté 1/2 cup sliced fresh mushrooms (about 2 ounces) in 1 tablespoon butter or margarine; stir gently into cooked drained peas; heat through.

See menus for February, 2nd week; May, 1st week; October, 2nd week.

Broccoli Stir-Fry

2 tablespoons vegetable oil
2 cloves garlic, minced (optional)
1/2 teaspoon grated fresh gingerroot
4 cups broccoli flowerets and julienne-cut stems
2 tablespoons water
2 teaspoons soy sauce

Heat oil in wok or skillet. Add garlic and ginger, then broccoli. Stir-fry to coat with oil. Add water and soy sauce. Continue to stir-fry until broccoli is bright green and crisp-tender, about 3 to 4 minutes. Serve at once. Makes 4 servings.

See menus for August, 3rd week; October, 1st week.

Broccoli with Orange Sauce

1 pound broccoli
1 cup water
¼ teaspoon salt
1 tablespoon butter
1 tablespoon all-purpose flour
Pinch salt
½ cup orange juice

Wash and trim broccoli. Separate stem from flowerets; cut stem lengthwise into 3 or 4 pieces, then cut in half crosswise. Separate branches of flowerets. In large saucepan bring 1 cup water and ¼ teaspoon salt to boil; add broccoli, lower heat and cover. Simmer 5 to 7 minutes or until broccoli stems are barely tender when pierced with paring knife. In meantime, in small saucepan melt butter; stir in flour and pinch salt; add orange juice. Cook and stir until thick and smooth. Serve over hot drained broccoli. Makes 4 servings.

Note: Sauce can be made quickly and easily in microwave.

See menus for February, 4th week; September, 1st week; November, 2nd week.

Tasty Broccoli

1 pound broccoli, trimmed and cut into desired pieces

Cover broccoli with water, add ½ teaspoon salt, and bring to boil. Simmer 4 to 5 minutes or until broccoli stalks are barely tender when pierced with sharp pointed knife. Drain, saving cooking liquid to use in soups. Season broccoli in any of the ways listed below. Makes 4 servings.

Variations

Buttered Broccoli: Arrange hot broccoli on serving platter. Dot with butter or margarine; sprinkle lightly with salt and pepper. Parmesan cheese or crumbled bacon may be added, if desired.

Broccoli with Lemon Sauce: Arrange hot broccoli on serving platter. Blend together ¼ cup mayonnaise and 1 tablespoon lemon juice. Spoon over broccoli. Dust with paprika.

Broccoli with Buttered Crumbs: Melt ¼ cup butter or margarine. Toss with ¾ cup fine dry bread crumbs until evenly mixed. One teaspoon dried mixed herbs may be added, if desired. Spoon crumbs over hot broccoli that has been arranged on serving tray.

See menus for February, 2nd week; April, 2nd week; May, 4th week.

Broccoli Onion Casserole

1½ pounds fresh broccoli or
  2 packages (10 ounces each)
  frozen cut broccoli
4 medium onions, quartered,
  or 1 can (1 pound) small
  onions
¼ cup (½ stick) butter or
  margarine
3 tablespoons all-purpose
  flour
½ teaspoon salt
Dash pepper
1½ cups milk
1 package (3 ounces) cream
  cheese
1½ cups (6 ounces)
  shredded Cheddar cheese

Wash and trim broccoli; cut pieces lengthwise into 2 or 3 pieces, then crosswise into 1-inch pieces. Cook in a small amount of boiling salted water until barely tender, about 15 minutes. Drain (saving juice to use later in a soup or sauce); set broccoli aside. Cook onions in boiling salted water to cover until tender; drain. In medium saucepan melt butter; blend in flour, salt, and pepper. Add milk; cook and stir over medium heat until thick and bubbly. Reduce heat; blend in cream cheese till smooth. Place vegetables in 2-quart casserole. Pour sauce over. Top with grated cheese. Bake, covered, at 325 degrees F. for 30 minutes; remove lid; continue baking 15 minutes longer. Makes 8 servings.

Note: If desired, buttered bread crumbs may be sprinkled around edge during last 15 minutes of baking.

See menus for December, 2nd week.

Broccoli with Cheese Sauce

1 pound broccoli, trimmed
  and split
½ cup Cheese Sauce*
½ teaspoon Dijon mustard
¼ teaspoon paprika
Pimiento pieces (optional)

Cook trimmed broccoli in small amount of boiling salted water until crisp-tender, 7 to 10 minutes; drain. In meantime, make Cheese Sauce; season with mustard and paprika. Serve hot over drained hot broccoli. Garnish with pimiento, if desired. Makes 4 servings.

Cheese Sauce: Melt 2 tablespoons butter or margarine in small saucepan; blend in 2 tablespoons all-purpose flour. Remove from heat. Stir in 1 cup milk until smooth and blended. Return to heat; cook and stir until thick. Remove from heat; add 1 cup (4 ounces) sharp Cheddar cheese. Allow to stand until cheese is partially melted; stir to blend. Season to taste. Makes 2 cups.

See menus for June, 2nd week.

¾ pound brussels sprouts
½ cup water

Trim off outer leaves of brussels sprouts to tight, firm heads. With tip of paring knife, mark an X on stem end to help make cooking more even. If desired, cut large brussels sprouts in halves or quarters lengthwise. Bring water to boil, add sprouts and cook 3 to 5 minutes, until texture is just slightly crunchy to the bite. The color of the brussels sprouts should remain bright green. Serve immediately with melted butter and fresh lemon juice. Makes 4 servings.

Variations

Orange-Glazed Brussels Sprouts: Combine 1 tablespoon frozen orange juice concentrate, 1 tablespoon butter, and pinch of salt in small skillet; bring to simmer. Add hot drained sprouts; toss quickly to coat until glazed; serve immediately.

See menus for January, 2nd week; March, 1st week.

Brussels Sprouts with Cream: Drain cooked brussels sprouts and coat with heavy cream. Sprinkle with paprika and serve immediately.

Sautéed Brussels Sprouts: Washed and trimmed sprouts, especially small ones or halves, may be sautéed (rather than cooked in water) in skillet with butter for 10 to 15 minutes until crisp-tender. For added flavor, sprinkle with any of the following: caraway seeds or ground or crushed cumin, cardamom, basil, dill, oregano, sage, or marjoram.

Cheesy Brussels Sprouts: Cook brussels sprouts as above; drain, toss with shredded sharp Cheddar cheese and buttered crumbs. Serve immediately.

Saucy Brussels Sprouts: Thin mayonnaise with fresh lemon juice and serve over cooked and drained brussels sprouts. Sprinkle very lightly with curry powder and serve immediately.

See menus for April, 4th week; September, 2nd week; November, 4th week.

Stir-Fried Brussels Sprouts

1 pound brussels sprouts
  (choose the smallest
  possible)
2 tablespoons vegetable oil
1 tablespoon butter
1 small clove garlic, minced
2 tablespoons water or broth
1/8 teaspoon sugar
1/8 teaspoon grated fresh
  gingerroot or ground ginger
1/2 lemon, juiced
Salt and pepper

Wash and trim brussels sprouts; slice into thirds or fourths. Heat oil and butter over medium heat in medium wok or skillet. Add brussels sprouts and garlic; stir-fry for 5 to 10 minutes, until brussels sprouts are barely tender. Add water or broth; cover and steam for 3 to 4 minutes; remove lid and let liquid cook off. Add sugar, ginger, lemon juice, and salt and pepper to taste. Serve at once. Makes 4 servings.

See menus for April, 1st week; July, 3rd week.

Cooked Cauliflower

5-inch head cauliflower
Boiling salted water
Lemon juice (optional)

Trim and core whole cauliflower; cauliflower may be cooked whole or separated into individual flowerets. Drop into rapidly boiling salted water (1 to 2 teaspoons salt per quart of water). If desired, add a little lemon juice to water to keep cauliflower white. Whole head cooks to crisp-tender in 10 to 15 minutes; individual flowerets cook in 3 to 6 minutes. Makes 4 servings.

Variations

Cauliflower with Browned Butter: Melt butter (no substitute) in small saucepan; then continue cooking over medium heat until butter becomes a nut brown color; watch so that it doesn't burn. Pour over cooked and drained cauliflower. Sprinkle with chopped fresh parsley.

Cauliflower with Crumbs: Top cooked cauliflower with 1/3 cup bread crumbs that have been tossed with 2 tablespoons melted butter or margarine and 1 teaspoon crushed dried parsley.

Cauliflower with Parmesan Crumbs: Prepare buttered crumbs as described and toss in 1 tablespoon grated Parmesan cheese.

See menus for November, 1st week.

Sautéed Cauliflower

5-inch head cauliflower
¼ cup butter or margarine
  or vegetable oil
Thyme, rosemary, savory,
  marjoram, or basil

Trim and core cauliflower; and cut into small flowerets and dice the stems. Heat butter or margarine or oil in wok or skillet. Toss cauliflower in pan until coated with oil. Cover pan, reduce heat to low and cook 3 to 5 minutes or until crisp-tender, stirring occasionally. Sprinkle with one or more of the following herbs: thyme, rosemary, savory, marjoram, or basil. Add additional butter, if desired. Makes 4 servings.

Note: A clove of minced garlic may be added to pan, if desired.

See menus for November, 1st week.

Beet Greens

Steamed:
1 pound beet greens
Butter or bacon fat
Vinegar or lemon juice

Stir-fried:
1 pound beet greens
2 tablespoons butter
Salt and pepper
Wine vinegar
Lemon juice

Beet greens may be steamed or stir-fried.

To steam, wash beet greens thoroughly, discarding any that are fried or have thick stalks. Rinse and drain lightly. Cook, covered, over medium heat in large saucepan, using only water clinging to leaves, for 5 to 7 minutes or until barely tender. Drain, season with butter or bacon fat and vinegar or lemon juice. If desired, cook small beets separately and slice into cooked greens; heat and serve with vinegar or lemon juice.

To stir-fry, prepare beet greens as above; drain, spin, or pat dry. Cut leaves and small stalks diagonally into ½-inch slices, or if very small leave whole. In wok or frying pan, heat butter and vegetable oil. Add beet greens and sauté for 2 to 3 minutes, stirring, until they wilt and become tender. Season with salt and pepper to taste; set aside. If desired, add sliced cooked beets the last minute to reheat. Serve with a little wine vinegar or lemon juice. Makes 4 servings.

See menus for May, 3rd week.

Cabbage Stir-Fry

2 tablespoons vegetable oil
4 cups (1 pound) coarsely
  shredded cabbage
1 or 2 dried hot red peppers,
  crushed (optional)
1 teaspoon freshly grated
  gingerroot
¹/₂ teaspoon sugar
¹/₂ teaspoon salt
2 tablespoons water or broth
Soy sauce (optional)

Heat oil in wok or large frying pan. Add cabbage and peppers; cook, stirring constantly, for 2 minutes, lowering heat if cabbage begins to brown. Stir in gingerroot, sugar, and salt. Add water or broth, cover and cook 2 or 3 minutes or until cabbage is barely tender. Season with a few drops of soy sauce, if desired. Serve immediately. Makes 4 servings.

See menus for January, 1st week; May, 1st week; September, 2nd week

Butter-Braised Cabbage

8 cups finely sliced green
  cabbage
¹/₂ cup chicken or beef broth*
Salt and pepper to taste
2 tablespoons butter or
  margarine

In large saucepan, combine all ingredients. Bring to boil, cover. Cook over medium heat for 7 minutes or until just tender, stirring or tossing occasionally. Makes 4 servings.
  Note: To make broth, dissolve ¹/₂ bouillon cube in ¹/₂ cup boiling water.

See menus for December, 3rd week.

Scalloped Spring Cabbage

2 tablespoons butter or
  margarine
¹/₄ cup all-purpose flour
2 cups milk
2 cups shredded Cheddar
  cheese (medium or sharp)
1 tablespoon vinegar
Salt and pepper
¹/₂ medium head green
  cabbage (4 cups)
¹/₂ cup buttered bread
  crumbs

In medium saucepan melt butter or margarine; blend in flour. Add milk; cook and stir until thick and smooth. Add shredded cheese; stir until smooth. Add vinegar; season to taste with salt and pepper. Set aside. Cut cabbage into small wedges. Cook in small amount boiling salted water until crisp-tender, about 7 minutes. Drain thoroughly. Arrange in buttered 1 1/2 quart casserole. Top with cheese sauce. Cover with buttered crumbs. Bake at 350 degrees F. for 20 minutes or until crumbs are browned lightly and sauce is bubbling. Makes 4 to 6 servings.
  Note: Drained cooked cabbage may be mixed with hot cheese sauce, sprinkled with buttered bread crumbs and served immediately.

See menus for May, 4th week; June, 4th week.

Spiced Red Cabbage

4 cups shredded red cabbage
2 onions, thinly sliced
1 medium apple, peeled,
 cored and sliced
1 small potato, sliced
2 tablespoons vinegar
1/4 cup sugar
1/4 teaspoon cloves
1/2 teaspoon salt
1/8 teaspoon pepper
1 tablespoon shortening

Combine cabbage, onion, apple, and potato in small amount boiling salted water; simmer until tender. Drain and combine with remaining ingredients. Makes 4 servings.

See menus for August, 2nd week.

Fluffy Sweet Potatoes with Orange

2 1/2 pounds sweet potatoes
 (yams)
1/2 can (3 ounces) frozen
 orange juice concentrate
1/4 cup (packed) brown sugar
Grated rind of 1 orange
1/4 cup (1/2 stick) butter or
 margarine

Wash sweet potatoes. Cook in 2 inches boiling salted water until tender. Peel. Mash with remaining ingredients. Makes 8 servings.

See menus for November, 1st week; December, 3rd week.

Sweet Potato Balls

1 pound sweet potatoes
 (yams)
2 2/3 tablespoons (1/3 stick)
 butter or margarine
1 1/2 tablespoons brown
 sugar
1/8 teaspoon salt
6 marshmallows
2 cups corn flakes (not
 crushed)

Wash and scrub sweet potatoes thoroughly. Cook, covered, in small amount boiling salted water until tender, 30 to 40 minutes. Drain, peel, and mash to make 2 cups. Season with butter, brown sugar, and salt. Cool slightly. With tablespoon, scoop up about 1/4 cup of mixture; shape around marshmallow, using more sweet potato mixture as needed to make ball. Roll each ball in uncrushed corn flakes. Place on buttered baking dish; refrigerate until ready to bake. Bake at 325 degrees F. for 20 to 30 minutes or until hot and marshmallow begins to ooze out. Makes 6 sweet potato balls.

Note: Recipe may be doubled or tripled. Sweet potato balls may be frozen, but if frozen they need to bake about 40 minutes.

See menus for December, 2nd week.

Baked Sweet Potato Chips

2 medium sweet potatoes or
  yams
Ice water
1 teaspoon vegetable oil
Salt

Peel sweet potatoes or yams. Cut into thin slices; soak in ice water for 15 minutes; drain and pat dry. Spread in single layer on oiled or nonstick baking sheet. Spread oil lightly over slices and sprinkle lightly with salt to taste. Bake at 350 degrees F. for 8 to 10 minutes or until tender and lightly browned. Makes 4 servings.

See menus for September, 3rd week.

Baked Sweet Potatoes

4 medium sweet potatoes
3 tablespoons melted butter
  or margarine

Scrub potatoes and bake at 350 degrees F. for 1 hour or until tender. Before serving, roll potatoes between hands to loosen flesh. Split open and serve with melted butter or margarine. Makes 4 servings.

Variation

Baked Sweet Potatoes with Herb Butter: Mix melted butter or margarine with 1 tablespoon minced fresh herbs or 1 teaspoon crushed dry herbs: tarragon, summer savory, sage, marjoram, oregano, thyme, basil, parsley, or any combination.

See menus for January, 1st week; April, 1st week; April, 3rd week.

Stir-Fried Vegetables

2 slices lean bacon
1½ cups finely shredded
  cabbage
⅔ cup celery, thinly sliced
  diagonally
1 small onion, thinly sliced
1 small to medium carrot, cut
  into matchstick-size strips
½ green pepper, cut
  lengthwise into thin strips
1 cup (4 ounces) sliced fresh
  mushrooms
1 teaspoon sugar
Salt and pepper

Prepare all vegetables; set aside. Cut bacon into ½-inch pieces; fry quickly in hot skillet until barely crisp. Immediately add all vegetables; sprinkle with sugar, salt and pepper to taste. Stir-fry until barely tender, 4 or 5 minutes. Serve immediately. Makes 4 servings.

  Note: If desired, 2 tablespoons oil may be used in place of bacon.

See menus for January, 4th week; June, 1st week; August, 2nd week.

Vegetables with Dill Dressing

½ pound fresh mushrooms, cleaned and halved
¼ cup (½ stick) butter
1½ cups carrots, thinly sliced diagonally
1½ cups pearl onions or onion wedges
1½ cups zucchini, thinly sliced
2 tablespoons lemon juice
¼ teaspoon salt
⅛ teaspoon pepper
¼ leaf marjoram, crushed
Dill Dressing*

Sauté fresh mushroom halves in butter. Add carrots, onions, zucchini, lemon juice, and seasonings. Cover; simmer gently for 15 minutes or until vegetables are crisp-tender. Turn into serving bowl, spoon juices over vegetables and top with Dill Dressing. Makes 6 servings.

Dill Dressing: Blend together ½ cup mayonnaise, ½ cup sour cream, 2 tablespoons chopped onion, ¾ teaspoon dried dill weed, ⅛ teaspoon salt, ¼ teaspoon onion powder, dash monosodium glutamate (optional), and ¼ teaspoon crushed celery seed.

See menus for February, 2nd week; May, 2nd week.

Gingered Vegetables

1 pound small carrots (1-inch or less in diameter)
1 tablespoon butter
Pinch sugar
Pinch salt
⅛ pound (2 ounces) sugar peas
¼ pound Tokay grapes, halved and seeded if necessary
½ teaspoon fresh grated gingerroot or ground ginger

Peel carrots; cut diagonally into ½-inch slices. Sauté carrots in melted butter; sprinkle with sugar and salt. Cover pan and cook over lowest heat for 15 to 20 minutes or until crisp-tender. For the last few minutes, add sugar peas that have been washed, trimmed, and drained. Just before serving, add grapes and ginger and toss to heat through. Serve immediately. Makes 4 servings.

See menus for March, 2nd week; September, 2nd week; December, 4th week.

Marinated Fresh Vegetables

2 tomatoes
2 ribs celery
1 small unpeeled zucchini
1 carrot
1 onion (optional)
1 green pepper
½ cup sugar
½ cup cider vinegar
½ teaspoon salt
⅛ teaspoon pepper

Peel tomatoes, scrape out seeds, and dice in ½-inch squares. Clean and dice remaining vegetables; toss together. Combine sugar, vinegar, salt, and pepper. Stir into vegetables. Refrigerate several hours. Drain and serve. Makes 8 servings.

Note: Raw vegetable sticks or bite-size pieces of vegetables such as celery, carrots, zucchini, broccoli, or cauliflower may also be marinated, drained, and served as relishes.

See menus for April, 2nd week.

Vegetables in Puff Pancake

1 recipe Puff Pancake
(p. 254)
1 pound fresh mushrooms,
quartered
3 medium (½ pound)
carrots, pared and thinly
sliced
1 medium zucchini, washed,
trimmed, and thinly sliced
2 tablespoons vegetable oil
½ teaspoon dill weed
1 teaspoon crushed dried
summer savory
½ teaspoon salt
1 cup (4 ounces) shredded
Gouda, Gruyère, or
Monterey Jack cheese
Additional shredded cheese

Prepare all vegetables; set aside. Bake Puff Pancake in 9-inch pie dish. Meanwhile, in large skillet, sauté mushrooms, carrots, and zucchini in hot oil for about 5 minutes. Add seasonings. Lower heat; stir in 1 cup cheese. Cook, stirring, until cheese melts and coats vegetables, about 2 minutes. Spoon vegetable mixture into baked pancake, sprinkle with additional shredded cheese. Cut in wedges; serve immediately. Makes 4 to 6 servings.

See menus for June, 4th week.

Garden Scramble

¼ cup vegetable or peanut oil
2 large garlic cloves, minced
2 cups broccoli flowerets, cut
in ½-inch slices
2 cups cauliflowerets, cut in
½-inch slices
⅓ cup water
1 cup carrots, cut diagonally
into ½-inch slices
1 bell pepper, red or green,
cut in ½-inch slices
1 large onion, cut in half
lengthwise, then cut
lengthwise into strips
Soy sauce
Salt and pepper
Whole roasted cashews or
sesame seeds

All ingredients should be prepared and ready to use. (This can be done ahead of time with vegetables refrigerated in separate baggies.) Place wok or large skillet over high heat. When wok is hot, add 1 tablespoon of oil. When oil is hot, add garlic; stir-fry for 30 seconds. Add broccoli and cauliflower; stir-fry for 1 minute. Add 4 tablespoons of the water; cover and cook, stirring occasionally, for about 3 minutes.

Remove vegetables from wok and set aside. Add remaining oil to wok. When oil is hot, add carrots, red pepper, and onion. Stir-fry for 1 minute. Add remaining water; cover and cook, stirring occasionally, for about 2 minutes or until vegetables are crisp-tender. Return broccoli and cauliflower to wok; stir-fry until heated through, about 1 minute. Add soy sauce, salt, and pepper to taste; garnish with cashews or sesame seeds. Makes 4 to 6 servings.

Note: Any vegetables in season may be used.

See menus for August, 1st week.

Ratatouille

2 small eggplants, peeled and cubed
6 tomatoes, peeled and chopped
2 green peppers, seeded and finely diced
4 small zucchini, sliced
2 medium onions, chopped
2 cloves garlic, minced
$\frac{1}{2}$ cup chopped fresh parsley or 2 tablespoons crushed dried parsley
5 tablespoons vegetable oil
1 tablespoon salt, or to taste
$\frac{1}{8}$ teaspoon pepper
$\frac{1}{2}$ teaspoon crushed rosemary
$\frac{1}{2}$ cup water

Combine vegetables in large heavy saucepan or Dutch oven. Add oil, seasonings, and water. Cover and cook over low heat for $1\frac{1}{2}$ hours or until all vegetables are tender. Stir occasionally to prevent scorching and to baste vegetables with delicious juices as they collect. Serve hot, cold, or reheated. Makes eight 1-cup servings.

See menus for October, 2nd week.

Mashed Potatoes

4 large baking potatoes
$\frac{1}{2}$ cup hot milk
3 tablespoons butter
Salt
Pepper

Peel potatoes and cut into quarters. In saucepan, cover potatoes with cold water. Bring to boil and cook gently, 20-25 minutes, until tender when pierced with fork. Drain well. Add hot milk and butter, and mash with potato masher or fork until smooth. Makes 4 servings.

See menus for February, 2nd week.

SALADS AND SALAD DRESSINGS

Salads

Fruit and Cottage Cheese Salad

2 tablespoons honey
2 tablespoons orange juice
1 cup (8 ounces) dairy sour cream
Lettuce leaves
2 cups (8 ounces) cottage cheese
4 cups fresh fruit of your choice (such as apple slices, grapes, sliced bananas, pineapple slices, pears, peaches, or strawberries)

Several hours before serving, combine honey and orange juice until blended; gently fold in dairy sour cream; chill. To make salad, line large serving platter or individual serving plates with washed crisp lettuce leaves. Fill center of plate with cottage cheese. Wash and dry fruit; arrange around outer edge of cottage cheese. Serve with Honey and Orange Dressing. Makes 4 servings.

See menus for November, 3rd week.

End-of-the-Week Fruit Salad

Assorted fruits (fresh, canned, or frozen)
Mayonnaise or salad dressing
Lemon juice or cream or evaporated milk
Lettuce cups

Prepare an assortment of fruits (fresh, canned, or frozen) that are left at the end of the week. Moisten with a little mayonnaise or salad dressing that has been thinned with lemon juice or cream or evaporated milk and sweetened slightly; spoon into lettuce cups. Or arrange assorted fruits on greens and serve with French dressing. Such a salad can be the mainstay of a meal if served with a scoop of cottage cheese, a broiled cheese sandwich, or any leftover meat dish.

See menus for November, 2nd week.

Apple Pomegranate Salad

1 small head romaine lettuce, torn into small pieces
1 red apple, diced
1 pomegranate, seeded
2 tablespoons vinegar
2 tablespoons vegetable oil
3 tablespoons sugar
Dash salt

In medium bowl combine lettuce, diced apple, and pomegranate. In small jar combine remaining ingredients; shake thoroughly. Pour over salad; toss until lettuce is completely coated. Makes 4 servings.

See menus for November, 2nd week.

Waldorf Salad

3 firm ripe red apples,
  unpeeled
1 tablespoon lemon juice
1 cup diced celery
½ cup coarsely chopped
  walnuts
⅓ cup mayonnaise
1 teaspoon honey (optional)
Salt
Salad greens

Core and quarter apples, but do not peel. Dice and toss in bowl with lemon juice. Add celery and walnuts. Cover and chill. Mix mayonnaise with honey until smooth and toss with apple mixture; season to taste with salt. Serve on bed of salad greens. Makes 4 servings.

Note: One-half cup seedless green grapes, halved, or ½ cup raisins, or both, may be added. Also ¼ cup heavy cream, whipped and slightly sweetened, may be folded in just before serving.

See menus for January, 3rd week; April, 2nd week; December, 2nd week.

Avocado Grapefruit Salad

2 large yellow or pink
  grapefruit
2 large avocados
Salad greens
½ cup Catalina Dressing
  (p. 223) or Celery Seed
  Dressing (p. 224)

With sharp knife cut flat piece off top of grapefruit, cutting barely into flesh. With an up and down motion, pare grapefruit as you would an apple, going round and round, cutting into the fruit and cutting away the outer membrane. Cut down on both sides of membranes to extract grapefruit sections that are free of membrane; set aside. Cut avocados in half, remove stone and peel. Cut into wedges the size of grapefruit sections. On individual beds of salad greens, arrange alternate sections of grapefruit and avocado so that a striped effect is reached. Serve with Catalina or Celery Seed Dressing. Makes 4 servings.

Variations

Avocado, Grapefruit, and Apple Salad: Alternate wedges of unpeeled red apple with avocado and grapefruit sections.

Pomegranate Salad: Make Avocado Grapefruit Salad. Sprinkle generously with pomegranate seeds. This is good to serve at Christmastime.

Avocado, Grapefruit, and Crab Salad: Arrange grapefruit and avocado sections on salad greens. Top with crabmeat. Serve with Catalina Dressing.

See menus for May, 3rd week; June, 3rd week; December, 3rd week.

Pear Swiss Waldorf Salad

2 winter pears, diced (2 cups)
1 tablespoon lemon juice
1/2 cup diced Swiss cheese
1/3 cup sliced celery
1/3 cup raisins
1/3 cup coarsely chopped
  walnuts
1/4 to 1/3 cup mayonnaise
Salt
Salad greens

Toss diced pears with lemon juice. Add Swiss cheese, celery, raisins, and walnuts; toss. Stir in enough mayonnaise to moisten. Season to taste with salt. Chill, if desired. Serve on salad greens. Makes 4 servings.

See menus for March, 3rd week; October, 1st week; October, 2nd week.

Grape Pecan Salad

1 pound seedless green
  grapes
1 package (3 ounces) cream
  cheese
2 tablespoons sugar
2 tablespoons orange juice
1 cup chopped pecans
Salad greens

Wash and stem grapes; dry with paper toweling. Blend together cream cheese and sugar until smooth, then blend in enough orange juice to make mixture the consistency of heavy cream. Gently combine grapes, cream cheese mixture, and pecans. Chill until cheese mixture forms a white coating on grapes. Serve on crisp salad greens. Makes 4 servings.

Note: This mixture of cream cheese, sugar, and orange juice is delicious used as a salad dressing on molded or other fruit salads.

See menus for July, 3rd week; October, 2nd week; November, 4th week.

Frozen Fruit Salad

1 package (3 ounces) cream
  cheese, softened
1 can (8 ounces) crushed
  pineapple in juice,
  drained, reserving juice
1 cup heavy cream, whipped
1/2 pound marshmallows,
  cut up
4 large bananas, diced
1 small bottle maraschino
  cherries, drained and
  quartered
Salad greens

Soften cream cheese; add pineapple juice gradually and beat until smooth and creamy. Stir in drained pineapple. Combine with whipped cream. Fold in remaining ingredients; freeze until firm. Cut and serve on crisp salad greens. Makes 8 servings.

See menus for June, 1st week.

Cider Fruit Salad Mold

1 envelope (1 tablespoon) unflavored gelatin
¼ cup cold cider or apple juice
2 cups cider or apple juice, heated just to boiling
2 tablespoons sugar
2 tablespoons fresh lemon juice
1 cup diced unpeeled red apple
¾ cup diced celery
Salad greens
Cream Cheese Dressing* (optional)

In medium bowl, sprinkle gelatin over ¼ cup cold juice; allow to soften. Stir in boiling juice; add sugar; add lemon juice; stir until gelatin and sugar are dissolved. Chill until mixture is consistency of unbeaten egg white, about 1 hour. Add apples and celery. Chill until firm. Serve on salad greens. Serve with Cream Cheese Dressing, if desired. Makes 6 servings.

Cream Cheese Dressing: Cream together 2 tablespoons mayonnaise or salad dressing, 1 package (3 ounces) softened cream cheese, and a pinch of salt. Stir in ½ cup sour cream, 1 teaspoon grated orange rind, and 1 tablespoon orange juice. May be kept covered in refrigerator for several days.

Note: Any combination of fruits may be used. Children seem to prefer peeled, coarsely grated apple stirred into the gelatin mixture rather than the diced apple and celery. It is less colorful, but certainly nutritious for children.

Variation

Cran-Apple Salad Mold: Use cranberry juice in place of apple juice. Any combination of fruit may be used, but apples and mandarin oranges are delicious.

See menus for February, 4th week; October, 3rd week; December, 1st week.

Hasty Tasty Orange Bavarian

1 can (8 ounces) crushed pineapple
1 envelope (1 tablespoon) unflavored gelatin
¾ cup boiling water
½ can (6 ounces) frozen orange juice concentrate, thawed
6 ice cubes
1 large or 2 small bananas
½ cup heavy cream

Drain ¼ cup juice from pineapple into small bowl. Sprinkle unflavored gelatin over juice; allow to soften, then add to boiling water; stir to dissolve. Add thawed orange juice concentrate and ice cubes. Stir until gelatin begins to thicken; remove any remaining ice cubes. Stir in drained pineapple and bananas. Whip cream; fold into gelatin mixture. Pour into serving bowl or 8 individual bowls; cover and chill. Makes 8 servings.

See menus for April, 4th week.

Sour Cream Fruit Salad

1 can (11 ounces) mandarin
   oranges, drained
1 can (1 pound) pineapple
   tidbits, drained (save juice
   for other use)
1 cup (8 ounces) dairy sour
   cream
1¼ cups (3½ ounces)
   flaked coconut
1 cup small or cut up
   marshmallows
Salad greens

Make ahead of time and chill.

Combine all ingredients. Chill in covered container
for several hours. Serve on crisp salad greens. Makes
5 to 6 servings.
   Note: Recipe may be doubled or tripled.

See menus for July, 3rd week.

Raw Cranberry Salad

3 cups (12 ounces) raw
   cranberries
1 orange
1¼ cups sugar
1 package (3 ounces) lemon
   or orange flavor gelatin
1 cup boiling water
½ cup pecans, coarsely
   chopped
½ cup finely diced celery
Mayonnaise

Chop or grind cranberries and whole orange to
medium degree of coarseness, catching all juice to
pour back into cranberries. Add sugar to fruit; set
aside. Dissolve gelatin in boiling water. Stir in
cranberry and orange mixture, nuts and celery. Pour
into 6-quart salad mold. Chill until set. Serve with dab
of mayonnaise. Makes 8 servings.

See menus for November, 3rd week.

Molded Grape Salad

1 envelope (1 tablespoon)
   unflavored gelatin
¼ cup cold water
1 cup boiling water
2 tablespoons sugar
Dash salt
1 can (6 ounces) frozen grape
   juice concentrate
3 tablespoons lemon juice
¾ cup halved and seeded
   Tokay grapes or red
   seedless grapes
2 medium bananas, sliced
Salad greens

Soften gelatin in cold water. Add boiling water, sugar,
salt; stir until gelatin dissolves. Blend in grape juice
concentrate and lemon juice. Chill until slightly thick,
then fold in grapes and bananas. Pour into lightly
oiled 1-quart mold. Chill until set. Serve on crisp salad
greens. Makes 4 to 6 servings.

See menus for October, 1st week.

Pineapple Shredded Cheese Salad

4 slices pineapple
1½ cups (6 ounces) medium
  Cheddar, shredded
Salad greens

Arrange pineapple slices over salad greens and top with shredded cheese. Makes 4 servings. May be made with pears, as well.

See menus for July, 3rd week.

Molded Citrus Salad

1 can (1 pound) grapefruit
  sections and juice
2 envelopes (2 tablespoons)
  unflavored gelatin
2 cans (11 ounces each)
  mandarin oranges and juice
⅓ cup sugar
1 can (6 ounces) frozen
  orange juice concentrate
Salad greens
Mayonnaise or salad dressing

Drain juice from canned grapefruit into large bowl. Sprinkle unflavored gelatin onto juice and allow to soften. Drain juice from mandarin oranges; add enough water to measure 2½ cups; bring to boil in medium saucepan. Pour over gelatin mixture; add sugar and stir to dissolve. Add frozen orange juice concentrate; stir and break up with fork until melted. Chill 15 to 30 minutes until mixture is consistency of unbeaten egg white. Fold in drained grapefruit and orange sections. Pour into 6-cup salad mold. Chill until firm. Serve on crisp salad greens with mayonnaise or salad dressing. Makes 8 servings.

See menus for February, 1st week, March, 4th week; August, 1st week.

Corned Beef Potato Salad

4 cups (1½ pounds) pared
  cooked potatoes, cubed
1 can (12 ounces) corned beef
½ cup celery, finely diced
¼ cup onion, chopped
¼ cup vegetable oil
2 tablespoons vinegar
½ teaspoon salt
¼ teaspoon garlic powder
¼ teaspoon pepper
⅔ cup dairy sour cream
2 tablespoons mayonnaise
2 tablespoons fresh
  horseradish
½ teaspoon Dijon mustard
Salad greens
Dill pickles
Tomato wedges

Combine potatoes, corned beef, celery, and onion in large bowl. In jar shake together oil, vinegar, salt, garlic powder, and pepper until well mixed. Pour over potato mixture; toss lightly. Cover and chill several hours. Just before serving, mix sour cream and mayonnaise with horseradish and mustard. Toss carefully into salad. Season to taste. Serve on salad greens, garnish with dill pickles and tomato wedges, if desired. Makes 4 to 6 servings.

See menus for August, 4th week.

Hot Potato Salad

6 large baking potatoes
1/2 cup vinegar
2 teaspoons salt
1/4 teaspoon pepper
1 pound bacon (or a little
  less) cut into 1/2-inch pieces
6 eggs
3/4 cup sliced green onions
  and tops
Salad greens
Frankfurters

Cook potatoes in boiling water; peel and dice. Add vinegar and seasonings. Fry bacon until crisp. Drop eggs into boiling water and cook just 4 minutes; remove and cool slightly. Combine potatoes, bacon, 1 tablespoon bacon fat, onion, and soft-cooked eggs. Mix well, sprinkle with bacon and serve on salad greens with big frankfurters. Makes 8 servings.

See menus for August, 3rd week.

Potato Salad

6 medium potatoes
1/2 medium onion, finely
  chopped
8 hard-cooked eggs
3 to 4 tablespoons Dijon
  mustard
1 cup salad dressing or
  mayonnaise
1 tablespoon sugar
1 teaspoon salt
1/2 to 1 teaspoon celery
  seed (optional)

Cook, peel, and dice potatoes; combine with chopped onion; set aside. Shell eggs; separate yolks and whites. Dice egg whites; set aside. Mash yolks with mustard; stir into salad dressing along with sugar, salt, and celery seed, if desired. Combine dressing with potatoes and onions. Stir in egg whites carefully. Season to taste. Cover bowl and chill for several hours before serving. Makes 8 servings.

See menus for May, 2nd week; July, 2nd week.

Tomato Aspic Salad

4 cups tomato juice
1/3 cup chopped onion
1/4 cup chopped fresh celery
  leaves
2 tablespoons brown sugar
1/2 teaspoon salt, or to taste
1 teaspoon crushed dried
  basil
2 envelopes (2 tablespoons)
  unflavored gelatin
1/4 cup cold water
3 tablespoons lemon juice
1 cup finely diced celery

In large saucepan, combine tomato juice, onion, celery leaves, brown sugar, salt, and basil; simmer 5 minutes. Strain. Soften gelatin in cold water; add to hot juice along with lemon juice; stir until dissolved. Chill until partially set, about 1 hour. Stir in celery. Pour into 8- or 9-inch square dish or pan, or into 5-cup ring mold and fill center with Shrimp Salad (p. 221) or Cole Slaw (p. 214). Makes 8 servings.

See menus for December, 1st week.

Three Bean Salad

1 can (8 ounces) garbanzo
 beans, drained
1 can (8 ounces) cut green
 beans, drained
1 can (8 ounces) red kidney
 beans, drained
1/2 cup finely diced onion
1/4 cup sugar
1/2 cup vinegar
1/3 cup vegetable oil
1/2 teaspoon salt
1/8 teaspoon pepper

In large bowl combine beans and onion. In screw-top jar combine remaining ingredients; cover and shake until sugar is dissolved. Pour over vegetables and stir lightly. Cover and refrigerate at least 6 hours or overnight, stirring occasionally. Drain vegetables before serving. Makes 8 servings.

See menus for May, 4th week; November, 2nd week.

Crisscross Salad

1 pound (2 stalks) broccoli
1/2 red onion, chopped
2 tomatoes, diced
1 can (8 ounces) red kidney
 beans, drained
1 cup (4 ounces) shredded
 medium to sharp Cheddar
 cheese
2/3 cup Italian or French
 dressing (p. 223)

Wash broccoli; trim leaves and tough tips from stalk. Peel remaining stalks; dice stalk and flowers into pieces about the size of kidney beans. Toss with remaining ingredients until all vegetables are well coated with dressing. Cover and refrigerate 24 to 48 hours. Makes 2 quarts or 10 to 12 servings.

See menus for March, 1st week; April, 1st week; December, 1st week.

Lentil Salad

1 cup dried lentils
1 quart water
1 teaspoon salt
1/2 cup vegetable oil
1/4 cup vinegar
1 teaspoon salt
1/2 teaspoon dry mustard
1/2 teaspoon paprika
1/4 teaspoon pepper
1/4 cup sweet relish or
 chopped sweet pickle
1/2 cup sliced green onion

Rinse lentils in cold water. In large saucepan cover lentils with 1 quart water and 1 teaspoon salt. Bring to boil; simmer 20 to 30 minutes or until tender; drain. Combine remaining ingredients in large bowl. Add hot, drained lentils to dressing mixture; toss until lentils are well coated. Refrigerate for at least 2 hours. Makes 6 servings.

Note: For Lentil and Tomato Salad, wash and trim medium tomatoes and section partly through. Open up as for petaled flowers and serve lentil salad inside.

See menus for June, 2nd week.

Ham Salad

1½ cups diced cooked ham
2 hard-cooked eggs, finely
  diced
½ cup diced celery
¼ cup diced green pepper
2 tablespoons chopped pickle
  or pickle relish
¼ cup mayonnaise or salad
  dressing
Salad greens
Tomato or avocado slices

Combine all ingredients, using just enough mayonnaise to moisten. Serve on crisp salad greens with tomato or avocado slices. Makes 4 servings.

Variations

Ham Salad Sandwiches: Butter 8 slices rye, pumpernickel, or whole wheat bread. Spread Ham Salad on four slices of the bread, top with lettuce leaves and remaining 4 bread slices. Makes 4 servings.

Ham Salad in Pita Bread: Cut two large pita bread loaves or rounds in half; fill each half with ½ cup filling. Makes 4 servings.

See menus for April, 3rd week.

Chicken Pineapple Salad

¼ cup chicken broth
¾ cup mayonnaise or salad
  dressing
2 chicken breast halves,
  cooked, skinned, boned,
  and diced (2 cups) or
  2 cans (5 ounces each)
  chunk chicken, well
  drained
1½ cups diced celery
¼ cup coarsely chopped
  pecans
¼ cup sliced stuffed green
  olives
¾ teaspoon salt
Pinch curry powder
  (optional)
Pepper to taste
4 slices pineapple, fresh
  or canned
Salad greens
Additional mayonnaise or
  salad dressing

Gradually add chicken broth to mayonnaise or salad dressing, blending well after each addition. Lightly toss together chicken, celery, pecans, olives, and seasonings. Add mayonnaise or salad dressing mixture, blending it in lightly. For each serving, place a pineapple slice on crisp lettuce. Mound chicken salad on top. Garnish with additional mayonnaise or salad dressing, if desired. Makes 4 servings.

Variation

Turkey Pineapple Salad: Use turkey in place of chicken.

See menus for September, 1st week.

Chicken Oriental Salad

2 chicken breast halves
2 tablespoons slivered
  almonds, toasted or not,
  as desired*
¹/₂ head cabbage, finely
  chopped (about 4 cups)
2 green onions, sliced
1 package (3 ounces) Ramen
  oriental noodles, chicken
  flavor
2 tablespoons toasted sesame
  seeds*
1 tablespoon sugar
¹/₂ cup vegetable oil
1 teaspoon salt
¹/₄ teaspoon pepper
3 tablespoons vinegar
¹/₂ teaspoon monosodium
  glutamate (optional)
Salad greens
Tomato wedges

Chill 2 to 24 hours before serving.

Cook chicken in small amount of water, covered, until tender, about 20 to 30 minutes; skin, debone, and dice chicken to make 2 cups. Combine chicken with almonds, cabbage, green onions, and uncooked noodles that have been broken up with envelope of seasonings; set aside. In glass jar combine sugar, oil, salt, pepper, vinegar, and monosodium glutamate, if desired; shake until blended. Pour over salad; toss. Add more salt and pepper as needed. Cover and refrigerate for at least 2 hours or for as long as 24 hours. Serve on crisp salad greens garnished with tomato wedges. Makes 8 to 10 servings.

Toasted Sesame Seeds and Almonds: To toast sesame seeds, spread in shallow pan in single layer; bake at 350 degrees F. for 2 to 3 minutes, stirring occasionally. To toast slivered almonds, spread in single layer in shallow pan; bake at 350 degrees F. for about 5 minutes.

See menus for July, 1st week; August, 4th week; December, 1st week.

Cabbage Slaw

2 cups (¹/₂ pound) shredded
  cabbage
¹/₄ cup mayonnaise or salad
  dressing
¹/₂ tablespoon vinegar or
  lemon juice
1 teaspoon sugar
Dash salt

Place cabbage in medium bowl. For dressing, blend together mayonnaise or salad dressing, vinegar or lemon juice, sugar, and salt. Pour over cabbage; toss lightly to coat vegetables. Chill. Makes 4 servings.

Variations

Cabbage Tomato Slaw: Add 1 medium diced tomato.

Cabbage Pineapple Slaw: Add ¹/₂ cup drained crushed pineapple.

Vegetable Slaw: Add ¹/₄ cup shredded carrot, 1 tablespoon chopped onion, 2 tablespoons diced green pepper, and ¹/₄ cup diced celery. Stir ¹/₄ teaspoon dry mustard or ¹/₂ teaspoon prepared mustard into dressing.

Cabbage Peanut Slaw: Add ¹/₂ cup salted peanuts to salad.

Cabbage Apple Slaw: Add 1/2 to 1 diced unpeeled apple.

Cabbage Raisin Slaw: Add 1/4 to 1/2 cup raisins to salad. Or cut-up dates may be used in place of raisins.

Cabbage Shrimp Slaw: Add 1 can (4 1/2 ounces) small deveined shrimp. Omit sugar.

See menus for January, 1st week; September, 1st week; December, 1st week.

Skillet Cabbage Salad

4 slices bacon
1/4 cup vinegar
1 tablespoon brown sugar
1 teaspoon salt
1 tablespoon finely chopped onion
4 cups shredded cabbage
1/2 cup chopped fresh parsley or 1 tablespoon dried parsley

Cook bacon until crisp. Remove from skillet; crumb and set aside. To bacon drippings in skillet add vinegar, brown sugar, salt, and onion. Add crumbled bacon; heat thoroughly. In large bowl pour hot dressing over cabbage and parsley; toss until vegetables are thoroughly coated. Makes 4 servings.

See menus for August, 2nd week.

Sunshine Cabbage Salad

2 cups shredded red cabbage
2 cups shredded green cabbage
1/3 cup chopped walnuts
1/2 cup canned pineapple tidbits, drained
1/4 cup dark or white raisins
Dressing*

Combine all ingredients for salad, plumping raisins in a little hot water if they are hard. Combine all ingredients for Dressing and toss into salad. Makes 4 servings.

Dressing: Combine 1/4 cup mayonnaise or salad dressing with 1/2 tablespoon honey.

See menus for August, 2nd week.

Simple Carrot Slaw

4 medium carrots, shredded (2 cups)
1/3 cup mayonnaise or salad dressing
Salt

Toss grated carrot with mayonnaise, season to taste; chill. Makes 4 servings.

Variations

Carrot Pineapple Slaw: Add 1/2 cup drained crushed pineapple.

Carrot Peanut Slaw: Add ½ cup peanuts.

Carrot Raisin Slaw: Add ⅓ cup raisins.

Carrot Apple Slaw: Add ½ cup diced, unpeeled apple. If desired ½ cup diced celery, and 1 tablespoon minced onion may also be added.

Carrot Sandwiches: Use any of these slaws as sandwich fillings, using whole grain bread. Makes 4 sandwiches.

See menus for January, 2nd week; June, 3rd week; August, 3rd week.

Salmon Salad

½ cup diced celery
¼ cup chopped pickle
½ cup mayonnaise or salad
  dressing
½ teaspoon salt
Dash pepper
2 cups (more or less) canned
  or cooked salmon, flaked
Salad greens
Lemon wedges

Combine celery, pickle, mayonnaise or salad dressing, and seasonings. Add salmon and toss lightly. Serve on salad greens with additional mayonnaise, if desired, and a wedge of lemon. Makes 4 servings.

Variation

Salmon Salad Sandwiches: Butter 8 slices bread. Spread salmon salad mixture on four slices; top with lettuce; cover with remaining bread slices. Makes 4 sandwiches.

See menus for February, 1st week; February, 3rd week.

Salmon Dinner Salad

1 small head cauliflower
1 pound broccoli
1 can (1 pound) red or pink
  salmon
4 cups shredded iceberg
  lettuce
4 green onions, sliced
1 package (10 ounces) frozen
  peas, defrosted and drained
½ cup mayonnaise
1 cup plain yogurt
1½ teaspoons curry powder
¾ cup salted peanuts

Needs to be chilled 4 to 24 hours.

Wash and trim cauliflower; break into flowerets; cut stems into ¼-inch slices. Peel broccoli stems and slice ¼ inch thick; cut large broccoli flowers into halves or thirds. Cook cauliflower and sliced broccoli stems in small amount boiling salted water, covered, until barely tender, about 5 minutes; add broccoli flowerets the last 1 or 2 minutes. Drain and plunge into cold water to cool; drain well; set aside. Drain salmon and break into chunks. Place lettuce in a 3- or 4-quart glass serving bowl. Sprinkle with ⅓ of the onions. Top with broccoli and ½ of remaining onions, then cauliflower and last of onions. Arrange salmon over top, then cover with frozen peas. Blend mayonnaise, yogurt, and curry; spread evenly over top. Cover and chill 4 to 24 hours. Sprinkle with peanuts and serve. Makes 6 to 8 servings.

See menus for August, 4th week.

Tuna Fish Salad

1 can (6½ ounces) tuna fish, drained
1½ tablespoons finely chopped pickle or pickle relish
¼ cup finely diced celery
¼ cup mayonnaise, salad dressing, or yogurt
1 teaspoon lemon juice
2 cups (packed) shredded lettuce
Salt, pepper, other seasonings as desired

Flake tuna and combine with pickle, celery, mayonnaise, and lemon juice. Toss with lettuce; season to taste. Makes 4 servings.

Note: Many different vegetables such as green pepper, chopped onion, grated carrot, radishes, cucumbers, tomatoes, or avocado may be added to salad. Or fruits such as chopped or drained crushed pineapple, grapes, or apple, or nuts (toasted almonds or pecans) may be added.

Variations

Chicken or Turkey Salad: Use 1 cup diced cooked chicken or turkey in place of tuna fish. Use any of suggested variations.

Tuna Salad Sandwiches: Makes enough filling for 4 sandwiches. Any desired variations may be used in the sandwiches.

Grilled Tuna Sandwiches: Omit lettuce. Spread tuna filling evenly onto four slices of bread; top with four more slices of bread. Butter outside of bread generously and sauté on both sides on medium hot griddle or skillet or cook in sandwich grill. Serve hot.

Chicken or Turkey Salad Sandwiches: Recipe for chicken or turkey salad makes enough filling for 4 sandwiches. Any desired ingredients may be added.

See menus for February, 1st week; May, 1st week; October, 1st week.

Mexicali Salad

1 large head iceberg lettuce, shredded
2 cups (8 ounces) shredded sharp Cheddar cheese
1 can (1 pound) chili beans without meat, undrained
1/2 cup sliced green onions
1/2 cup Catalina Dressing (p. 223)
1 package (11 1/2 ounces) corn chips

In large bowl combine all ingredients but corn chips; toss. Just before serving, toss in corn chips. Makes 4 servings.

See menus for August, 4th week; December, 2nd week.

Caesar Salad

1/4 cup olive or vegetable oil
1 clove garlic, minced
4 quarts salad greens, washed and chilled with no excess moisture
2 teaspoons Worcestershire sauce
Pepper to taste
2 tablespoons grated Parmesan or Romano cheese
1/4 cup (1 ounce) crumbled blue cheese
1 egg, broken onto greens
1 lemon, juiced (about 1/4 cup)
1 cup croutons

Combine 1/4 cup oil with minced garlic; set aside in covered jar. Combine all remaining ingredients but croutons in order given, covering unbeaten egg with lemon juice. Toss all together lightly from bottom to top until greens are coated with a light dressing. Remove garlic from oil; pour oil over croutons, tossing until they are evenly covered. Toss croutons into greens just before serving. Serve immediately. Makes 4 servings.

See menus for August, 2nd week; October, 2nd week.

Raw Vegetable Salad

3 cups prepared raw vegetables
1/2 cup Catalina Salad Dressing (p. 223)

In a medium wooden bowl toss together prepared raw vegetables, using any combination of the following: shredded green cabbage, shredded red cabbage, diced celery, thinly sliced carrots, sliced radishes, sliced green onions, raw cauliflower flowerets, sliced zucchini, shredded lettuce, tomato wedges, diced green pepper, broccoli flowerets, diced avocado, tender asparagus tips, sliced cucumbers, fresh garden peas, raw spinach leaves, or chopped tomatoes. Chill until ready to serve. Just before serving toss with enough Catalina Salad Dressing to coat all vegetables. The salad will need no further seasoning. Makes 4 servings.

See menus for March, 3rd week; July, 2nd week; September, 4th week.

Spinach Bacon Salad

6 cups (2 bunches) fresh spinach leaves
1/2 cup sliced green onions
Pepper
3 slices bacon
2 teaspoons white wine (or other) vinegar
1 1/2 teaspoons lemon juice
1/2 teaspoon sugar
1/8 teaspoon salt

Wash and trim spinach leaves; drain well and pat or spin dry; chill. Tear spinach leaves into bite-size pieces and place in large bowl; add sliced green onion. Grind a generous amount of pepper over torn greens. Cut uncooked bacon into small pieces. In medium-size skillet, cook bacon till crisp; do not drain off drippings. Stir in vinegar, lemon juice, sugar, and salt. Remove from heat; pour immediately over spinach, tossing until all leaves are coated. Serve immediately. Makes 4 servings.

Variation

Spinach Egg Salad: Chop two hard-cooked eggs; toss into salad with other ingredients.

See menus for March, 2nd week; September, 2nd week.

Spinach Salad with Mandarin Oranges

1 bunch spinach
1 can (11 ounces) mandarin oranges, well drained
4 green onions, sliced
1/4 pound fresh mushrooms, sliced
1 medium avocado, diced
1/4 pound cherry tomatoes, washed and stemmed, or 1 tomato, seeded and diced
1 small cucumber, thinly sliced (optional)
Orange French Dressing*

Wash and trim spinach leaves; drain well and pat or spin dry. Tear spinach into bite-size pieces. Toss gently with remaining ingredients. Makes 4 servings.

*Orange French Dressing: Combine in blender 1/4 teaspoon grated orange rind, 1/4 cup frozen orange juice concentrate (thawed), 1/4 cup oil, 1 tablespoon sugar, 1 tablespoon wine vinegar, 1 1/2 teaspoons lemon juice, and 1/4 teaspoon salt. Blend thoroughly; chill.

See menus for June, 4th week.

Spinach Orange Salad

6 cups (8 ounces) fresh
 spinach leaves
2 oranges, sectioned and cut
 in thirds, or 1 can
 (11 ounces) mandarin
 oranges, drained
3 tablespoons vegetable oil
1 tablespoon lemon juice
1 teaspoon sugar
½ teaspoon poppy seeds
¼ teaspoon salt

Wash and trim spinach leaves; drain well and pat or spin dry. Tear spinach leaves into bite-size pieces and place into large salad bowl. Add well-drained orange sections and toss lightly; cover and chill, if desired. For dressing, combine salad oil, lemon juice, sugar, poppy seeds, and salt in screw-top jar. Cover and shake well. Pour over salad; toss lightly. Serve immediately. Makes 4 servings.

Note: If desired, toasted slivered almonds may be sprinkled over salad before serving.

Variation

Spinach Grapefruit Salad: Use 1 large or 2 small grapefruit, sectioned, in place of oranges.

See menus for January, 1st week; March, 1st week; December, 2nd week.

Tabboulah Salad

1 head romaine lettuce
1 small bunch fresh parsley
½ to 1 cup bulgur wheat
1 large tomato, finely diced
1 large cucumber, peeled and
 finely diced
1 medium onion, finely
 chopped
¼ cup vegetable oil
½ cup lemon juice
 (2 lemons)
Salt and pepper

Wash lettuce; drain thoroughly and dry; cover and chill. Wash, shake dry, and stem parsley. With sharp knife shred lettuce and parsley finely together; cover and chill. Thirty minutes before assembling salad, set bulgur wheat to soak in a little more than an equal amount of water; let stand until all water has been absorbed. Combine greens with softened bulgur. At this point salad may be covered tightly and refrigerated. When time to serve, add finely diced vegetables, salad oil, and lemon juice. Toss until well mixed, using hands as the Lebanese do, if desired. Season to taste with salt and pepper. Be sure to add enough lemon juice and salt to get characteristic flavor. Makes 8 servings.

Note: If tightly covered and refrigerated, Tabboulah Salad will stay fresh for 2 or 3 days. Bulgur wheat may be purchased in Middle Eastern markets or in most specialty food shops.

See menus for March, 1st week.

Luncheon Meat Salad

1 large head romaine lettuce, shredded
2 medium tomatoes, diced
1 small dill pickle, chopped
1 cup (4 ounces) shredded cheese (Cheddar, Monterey Jack, Swiss, or a combination)
1/2 can (6 ounces) pork luncheon meat, coarsely grated
French dressing
1 can dried onion rings

Toss together all ingredients except onion rings, using any kind and amount of French dressing desired. Sprinkle dried onion rings over top; serve immediately. Makes 6 servings.

See menus for July, 4th week.

Shrimp Salad with Herbs

2 cans (4 1/2 ounces each) small deveined shrimp
2 tablespoons lemon juice
3/4 cup mayonnaise or plain yogurt or combination
2 tablespoons tarragon vinegar
2 tablespoons cream or evaporated milk
2 tablespoons finely chopped parsley or 2 teaspoons dried parsley
2 tablespoons finely chopped onion or 2 teaspoons dried minced onion
1/2 teaspoon celery seed
1/2 teaspoon sweet basil
1/2 teaspoon salt
1/2 teaspoon monosodium glutamate (optional)
1/4 teaspoon pepper
2 cups shredded cabbage
1 cup diced celery
Avocado halves or tomato cups
Salad greens

Drain shrimp; rinse. Place in bowl; cover with ice-filled water; add lemon juice; chill 20 minutes. In meantime, blend mayonnaise (or yogurt), vinegar, cream, and all herbs and spices; refrigerate in covered jar. To serve, combine drained shrimp, cabbage, celery, and herb dressing. Toss to mix evenly. If desired, serve in avocado halves or tomato cups on crisp salad greens. Makes 8 servings.

Note: If desired, use plain vinegar and a pinch of tarragon in place of tarragon vinegar. Leftover shrimp salad may be extended with shredded lettuce and eaten in pita bread.

See menus for April, 1st week; June, 1st week.

Crab Salad in Avocados

³/₄ pound crab or imitation crab or 2 cans (7¹/₂ ounces each) crabmeat
4 green onions, thinly sliced
Sour Cream Dill Dressing (see below)
4 avocados, halved and seeded
Salad greens

Flake crabmeat; combine with onions and mushrooms. Arrange avocado halves, two per serving, cut side up on salad greens. Mound crab salad over avocados. Serve with Sour Cream Dill Dressing. Makes 4 servings.

Variation

Crab Salad Sandwiches: Crab and green onions moistened with mayonnaise may be used as sandwich filling.

See menus for August, 1st week; December, 3rd week.

Shrimp and Cucumber Salad

1 cup small shrimp, cooked, peeled, and cleaned or
1 can (4¹/₂ ounces) small deveined shrimp, drained and rinsed
3 large cucumbers
1 tablespoon salt
1 small head leaf lettuce, shredded
¹/₂ cup Sour Cream Dill Dressing*

Prepare shrimp. Refrigerate in covered bowl. If canned shrimp are used, cover with ice water to which 1 tablespoon lemon juice has been added. Halve cucumbers lengthwise; slice very thin. Put into bowl, sprinkle with salt, and let stand 30 minutes. Drain cucumbers, pressing out excess liquid. Combine cucumbers with Sour Cream Dill Dressing in clean bowl; cover and chill for 2 hours. Just before serving, stir drained shrimp into cucumbers. Serve over bed of shredded lettuce. Makes 4 servings.

Sour Cream Dill Dressing: Combine ¹/₂ cup dairy sour cream, 1 tablespoon mayonnaise, 1¹/₂ teaspoons lemon juice, pinch dry mustard, dash salt, and ¹/₄ teaspoon dried dill weed. Cover; chill several hours. Makes ¹/₂ cup.

See menus for April, 3rd week.

Salad Dressings

Cottage Cheese Dip

1 cup cream-style cottage cheese
¹/₄ teaspoon garlic salt
¹/₄ teaspoon onion salt
1 teaspoon chopped chives or chopped or dried parsley

Blend or mash together all ingredients and serve with vegetable sticks. Makes 1 cup.

See menus for January, 2nd week.

French Dressing

½ cup vegetable oil
⅓ cup red wine or other
  vinegar
1 teaspoon crushed dried
  basil
½ teaspoon salt
½ teaspoon Dijon-type
  mustard
¼ teaspoon sugar
¼ teaspoon paprika
¼ teaspoon garlic salt

Combine ingredients in jar; shake thoroughly. Makes
¾ cup.

See menus for March, 3rd week; April, 1st week; July, 2nd week.

Catalina Dressing

½ cup vinegar
½ cup vegetable oil
½ cup sugar
½ cup catsup
1 teaspoon salt
½ teaspoon garlic salt
½ teaspoon onion salt

Combine all ingredients in quart jar and shake
thoroughly. Chill. Shake again before using.
Especially good on raw vegetable or grapefruit salads.
Makes 1½ cups.

See menus for March, 3rd week; July, 2nd week; November, 1st week.

Thousand Island Dressing

1 egg
¼ teaspoon dry mustard
⅛ teaspoon salt
1½ tablespoons sugar
1 tablespoon vinegar
Few grains paprika
Few grains cayenne
1 cup vegetable oil
¾ cup catsup
½ small onion, grated
3 to 4 sweet gherkin pickles,
  chopped
1 jar (2 ounces) pimientos,
  drained and chopped

In medium bowl beat egg until thick; add mustard,
salt, sugar, vinegar, paprika, and cayenne. Gradually
add oil, beating constantly. Add catsup gradually. Stir
in onion, pickles, and pimientos. Store, covered, in
jar in refrigerator for several hours before using.
Makes 1 pint.

See menus for November, 4th week.

Celery Seed Dressing

¹/₂ cup sugar
³/₄ teaspoon salt
1 teaspoon paprika
1 teaspoon celery salt
1 teaspoon prepared mustard
1 teaspoon onion juice or
  onion salt
¹/₄ cup vinegar or lemon
  juice or a combination
  of both
1 cup vegetable oil
1 teaspoon celery seed

Combine all ingredients but salad oil and celery seed in medium mixing bowl; beat together. While continuing to beat, add salad oil drop by drop at first; then increase amounts very slowly until all oil is added. Dressing should be thick. Stir in celery seed. Delicious on both fruit and vegetable salads. Makes 1¹/₂ cups.

See menus for March, 4th week.

Italian French Dressing

1 teaspoon salt
¹/₂ teaspoon white pepper
¹/₂ teaspoon celery salt
¹/₄ teaspoon cayenne
¹/₄ teaspoon dry mustard
¹/₄ cup red wine vinegar
1 cup vegetable oil
1 clove garlic, minced
Dash Tabasco sauce

Combine ingredients in jar; cover and shake vigorously. Makes 1¹/₄ cups.

See menus for January, 2nd week.

Poppy Seed Dressing

³/₄ cup sugar
1 teaspoon dry mustard
1 teaspoon salt
¹/₃ cup vinegar
1¹/₂ teaspoons finely grated
  onion
1 cup vegetable (not olive) oil
1¹/₂ teaspoons poppy seeds

In small mixing bowl combine all ingredients but oil and poppy seeds; mix thoroughly. While beating, add oil, almost drop by drop at first, then increasing to a small stream. When all oil is added and dressing is thick, add poppy seeds; beat one minute more. Delicious on fresh fruit salad or as a dip for pieces of fresh fruit. Makes 2 cups dressing.

See menus for July, 4th week; August, 3rd week.

PASTA, EGG, AND CHEESE DISHES

Pasta Dishes

Tuna Pasta Salad

4 ounces vermicelli or
  spaghetti
1 can (6 ounces) tuna fish
1 small zucchini, cut into thin
  strips
1 cup (4 ounces) sliced fresh
  mushrooms
2 tomatoes, peeled, seeded
  and chopped
2 tablespoons chopped fresh
  parsley
Dressing*

Break vermicelli or spaghetti into 1½-inch lengths; and cook according to package instructions. Drain; rinse with cold water; drain thoroughly. Combine with remaining ingredients; toss lightly. Cover; chill until time to serve. Makes 4 servings.

Dressing: In glass jar, combine together ⅓ cup vegetable oil; ¼ cup red wine vinegar; 1 tablespoon fresh basil, finely chopped, or 1 teaspoon dried basil, crushed; ¼ teaspoon salt; ½ teaspoon Dijon mustard; ¼ teaspoon sugar; ¼ teaspoon paprika; ¼ teaspoon garlic salt. Shake thoroughly. Makes ¾ cup.

See menus for February, 3rd week; August, 1st week; December, 2nd week.

Lemon Clam Spaghetti

1 pound spaghetti
½ cup (1 stick) butter or
  margarine, divided
3 tablespoons olive or
  vegetable oil
2 tablespoons chopped onion
2 cloves garlic, minced
Clam liquid, drained from
  clams
3 tablespoons lemon juice
1 tablespoon chopped parsley
  or 1 teaspoon crushed
  dried parsley
2 teaspoons grated lemon
  peel
¼ teaspoon pepper
1 bay leaf
2 cans (6½ ounces each)
  minced clams, drained
1 cup grated Parmesan
  cheese
8 lemon wedges

Cook spaghetti according to package instructions. Drain and keep warm while making sauce. Heat 3 tablespoons butter or margarine and 3 tablespoons oil in heavy pan. Sauté onion and garlic until tender. Add clam liquid, lemon juice, parsley, lemon peel, pepper, and bay leaf. Simmer until liquid is reduced to about 1 cup. Remove bay leaf. Stir in clams; add remaining butter or margarine; heat and stir until melted. Pour sauce over spaghetti. Sprinkle with Parmesan cheese; serve with lemon wedges. Makes 8 servings.

See menus for October, 2nd week.

Zucchini Mushroom Pasta

1 pound medium zucchini
1 pound medium mushrooms
2 tablespoons vegetable oil
1 cup thinly sliced scallions
  or green onions
2 cloves garlic, minced
1 tablespoon minced fresh or
  1 teaspoon dry basil
1/2 teaspoon salt
1/2 teaspoon pepper
1 pound noodles
1 tablespoon butter, softened
2 tablespoons finely minced
  fresh parsley or 2 teaspoons
  dry parsley
Freshly grated Romano or
  Parmesan cheese

Wash zucchini. Trim ends and cut lengthwise into 2-inch matchstick-size pieces; set aside. Wipe mushrooms clean, trim ends, and slice thinly; set aside. In large skillet heat oil over medium heat. Stir-fry scallions until barely tender, about 1 minute. Add garlic; stir-fry 30 seconds. Add zucchini; cook until crisp-tender, about 2 minutes, while stirring. Add mushrooms and sauté, stirring constantly, until tender, about 1 minute. Add basil, salt and pepper; mix well and remove from heat. In meantime, cook pasta according to package instructions. Drain in colander, transfer to bowl. Stir in butter. Add half of vegetables to pasta and toss to blend. Spoon remaining vegetables over top of pasta. Garnish with minced parsley and serve with freshly grated Romano or Parmesan cheese. Makes 8 servings.

See menus for January, 1st week.

Skillet Macaroni and Cheese

1/4 cup (1/2 stick) butter or
  margarine
1³/4 cups (7 ounces)
  uncooked elbow macaroni
1 large onion, chopped
1 medium green pepper,
  chopped
1/2 teaspoon salt
1/2 teaspoon garlic salt
1/8 teaspoon pepper
1/2 teaspoon oregano
1/8 teaspoon dry mustard
2 cups water
1 tablespoon all-purpose flour
1 can (13 ounces) evaporated
  milk
2 tablespoons pimiento, diced
2 cups (8 ounces) sharp
  Cheddar cheese, shredded

In large skillet melt butter or margarine over low heat. Add uncooked macaroni, onion, green pepper, and seasonings. Cook, stirring occasionally, over medium heat for 7 minutes, or until onion becomes transparent. Add water; bring to boil. Cover; simmer 20 minutes or until macaroni is tender. Sprinkle flour over mixture; blend well. Stir in evaporated milk, pimiento, and shredded cheese. Simmer 5 minutes longer, stirring occasionally, until cheese melts. Serve hot. Makes 6 servings.

See menus for March, 1st week; June, 3rd week; November, 3rd week.

Macaroni and Cheese

1½ cups (6 ounces) elbow
  macaroni
3 tablespoons butter or
  margarine
¼ cup finely chopped onion
3 tablespoons all-purpose
  flour
1½ cups milk
½ teaspoon salt
Dash pepper
3 cups (12 ounces) shredded
  sharp Cheddar cheese
¼ teaspoon paprika
Tomato slices, if desired

Cook macaroni according to package instructions. Drain; set aside. In medium saucepan melt butter or margarine. Add onion; cook until soft. Blend in flour, then milk; cook and stir until thick and smooth. Add salt, pepper, and cheese, heat and stir until cheese is melted. Mix sauce with macaroni. Pour into greased 1½-quart casserole. Sprinkle with paprika; then top, if desired, with an arrangement of tomato slices that have been sprinkled with salt. Bake at 350 degrees F. for 30 minutes or until bubbly and lightly browned on top. Makes 6 servings.

See menus for September, 2nd week.

Vegetarian Lasagne

10 lasagne noodles (6 ounces)
1 pound fresh spinach
1 tablespoon butter
1 cup grated carrot (about 1
  carrot)
½ cup chopped onion
¼ pound sliced fresh
  mushrooms
1 can (15 ounces) tomato
  sauce
1 can (6 ounces) tomato paste
1 can (2¼ ounces) sliced
  ripe olives, drained
1 teaspoon crushed dried
  oregano
1 teaspoon crushed dried
  sweet basil
2 cups (1 pound) cream-style
  cottage cheese
1 egg, beaten
2 cups (8 ounces) Monterey
  Jack cheese, shredded

Cook lasagne noodles according to package instructions. Drain, rinse, and set aside in fresh clear water. In meantime, wash and trim spinach; rinse several times, then drain and place spinach leaves, without shaking off excess water, into large saucepan. Cover and cook over medium heat until steam forms, then reduce heat and cook 5 minutes. Drain well; set aside.

In large heavy saucepan, melt butter and sauté carrots, onion, and mushrooms until tender but not brown. Stir in tomato sauce, tomato paste, ripe olives, oregano, and basil; set aside. Combine cottage cheese and beaten egg.

In greased 13x9x3-inch pan, layer half each of noodles, spinach, sauce, cottage cheese mixture, and Monterey Jack cheese. Repeat layers ending with shredded cheese. Bake at 375 degrees F. for 30 minutes. Let stand 15 minutes before serving. Makes 8 servings.

Note: If desired, lasagne may be assembled as described, using uncooked noodles and allowing casserole to stand in refrigerator for several hours before baking. Cover with double thickness of aluminum foil and bake for 1 hour. Or casserole may be baked in microwave at *full power* for 15 to 20 minutes, turning every 5 minutes.

See menus for June, 2nd week.

Tomato Vegetable Spaghetti

1 pound spaghetti or pasta
  shells
2 tablespoons vegetable oil
2 cloves garlic, minced
2 large onions, chopped fine
1/2 cup finely diced celery
1/2 green pepper, finely diced
1 small zucchini, finely diced
3/4 teaspoon salt
1/2 teaspoon crushed dried
  oregano
2 teaspoons crushed dried
  basil
1 can (29 ounces) tomatoes,
  pureed
1/2 teaspoon sugar

Cook spaghetti or pasta shells according to package instructions. Drain and keep warm while making sauce. In large saucepan, heat oil; sauté garlic for 1 to 2 minutes. Add onions, celery, green pepper, and zucchini; sauté until vegetables soften. Add seasonings, tomatoes, and sugar. Bring to boil, lower heat and simmer, uncovered, for no longer than 30 minutes, stirring occasionally. Add a little water, if necessary, for right consistency. Season to taste. Serve over freshly cooked pasta, allowing 2 ounces uncooked pasta per serving. Makes 8 servings.

See menus for February, 4th week.

Red Snapper with Pasta

8 ounces rotelle (little pasta
  wheels) or other pasta
3 tablespoons vegetable oil
1 large green or red pepper
1 medium onion, sliced thinly
1 clove garlic, minced
3 cups peeled, seeded, and
  chopped fresh or canned
  tomatoes
Pepper
1 pound red snapper fillets
1 teaspoon lemon juice
2 tablespoons butter or
  margarine

Cook pasta according to package instructions. Drain and keep warm while preparing fish sauce. In heavy saucepan, heat oil; add green or red pepper, onion, and garlic. Cook and stir until vegetables are limp. Add tomatoes and a robust amount of pepper. Cook 10 minutes. Add fish and lemon juice; cook just until fish is tender and flaky, 5 minutes or less. Toss cooked pasta with butter or margarine and arrange on large warm platter. Top with Red Snapper Sauce. Makes 4 servings.

See menus for April, 3rd week.

Irish-Italian Spaghetti

1 pound lean ground beef
1 cup chopped onion
¹/₂ teaspoon salt
¹/₂ teaspoon chili powder
¹/₂ teaspoon Tabasco sauce
¹/₈ teaspoon pepper
1 can (10³/₄ ounces) cream
  of mushroom soup
1 can (10³/₄ ounces) cream
  of tomato soup
8 ounces spaghetti
Parmesan cheese

In large skillet or heavy saucepan, cook ground beef and onion until meat is brown and onion is transparent. Add seasonings; simmer 10 minutes. Add soups; cover and simmer 30 minutes. Cook spaghetti according to package instructions. Drain and serve hot with hot sauce spooned over. Sprinkle with Parmesan cheese. Makes 4 to 6 servings.

See menus for December, 3rd week.

Egg Dishes

Scrambled Eggs

6 eggs
¹/₄ cup milk, light cream, or
  evaporated milk
¹/₄ teaspoon salt
¹/₈ teaspoon pepper
2 tablespoons butter or
  margarine

With fork or wire whip, beat together eggs, milk, salt and pepper. In 10-inch skillet, melt butter or margarine over low heat; pour in egg mixture. Cook, without stirring, until eggs begin to set on bottom and around edges. Gently stir mixture, lifting up and over from bottom as it thickens. Continue to stir intermittently until eggs are cooked throughout but still glossy and moist. Remove from heat immediately. Eggs thicken and dry out towards end of cooking, so for soft moist eggs, remove from heat a little before they reach desired texture. Makes 4 servings.

Variations

Scrambled Eggs with Bacon or Ham: Add 4 slices bacon, fried crisp and crumbled, or ¹/₂ cup finely chopped cooked ham, to egg mixture.

Scrambled Eggs with Herbs: Add to egg mixture 1 teaspoon crushed dried parsley or 1 tablespoon chopped fresh parsley and ¹/₈ teaspoon crushed dried tarragon or ¹/₃ teaspoon chopped fresh tarragon.

Scrambled Eggs with Cream Cheese: As scrambled eggs begin to cook and thicken in skillet, add 1 package (3 ounces) cream cheese, cut into small cubes, and 1¹/₂ teaspoons chopped chives or ¹/₂ teaspoon freeze-dried chives.

Scrambled Eggs with Cheese: As scrambled eggs begin to cook and thicken in skillet, add 1/2 cup shredded Cheddar or Swiss cheese. Continue cooking until eggs are firm and cheese melts. If desired, sprinkle with 1 teaspoon chopped chives or 1 tablespoon finely sliced green onion tops.

Scrambled Eggs with Mushrooms: In melted butter, cook 1 tablespoon chopped onion and 3/4 cup (2 ounces) sliced fresh mushrooms until soft. Add beaten egg mixture that has been seasoned with 1/4 teaspoon Worcestershire sauce. Continue cooking as directed.

Scrambled Eggs with Sausage Slices: In skillet brown 4 to 6 sausage links that have been cut into 1/4-inch slices. Decrease butter or margarine to 1 tablespoon. Add egg mixture; continue to cook as directed.

See menus for April, 4th week; June, 1st week; August, 4th week.

Deviled Eggs

4 eggs
2 tablespoons mayonnaise
1/8 teaspoon onion salt
3/4 teaspoon Dijon mustard
1/2 teaspoon vinegar
Dash Tabasco sauce
Dash paprika
Salt and pepper

Arrange eggs in single layer in medium saucepan. Add cold water to cover 1 inch above eggs. Bring to boil; cover pan; remove from heat; allow to stand 20 minutes. Plunge eggs into cold water immediately; crack and remove shells. Cut cooled eggs in half lengthwise. Carefully remove yolks into small mixing bowl. Mash yolks with remaining ingredients, seasoning to taste. Pile mixture into egg halves. Sprinkle with additional paprika. Makes 8 deviled egg halves.

See menus for March, 3rd week.

Cheesy Egg Cups

2 tablespoons fine bread crumbs
4 small slices Cheddar cheese
4 eggs
Additional shredded cheese
Salt and pepper

Grease four custard or muffin cups. Put 1/2 tablespoon bread crumbs on bottom of each cup, then top with cheese slice. Break one egg into each cup; sprinkle eggs with shredded cheese; salt and pepper to taste. Bake at 325 degrees F. for 12 to 18 minutes. Serve immediately. Makes 4 servings.

See menus for May, 1st week; June, 4th week; December, 2nd week.

Creamed Hard-Cooked Eggs

6 Hard-Cooked Eggs (p. 168)
¼ cup (½ stick) butter or margarine
¼ cup all-purpose flour
2 cups milk
½ teaspoon salt
¼ teaspoon paprika
Few drops Tabasco sauce
Pepper
Toast or cooked rice

In medium saucepan melt butter or margarine; stir in flour. Add milk; cook and stir over medium heat until thick. Season with salt, paprika, Tabasco sauce, and pepper to taste. Add sliced hard-cooked eggs; heat through. Serve over toast or cooked rice. Makes 4 servings.

See menus for January, 1st week.

Egg Casserole

1 can (10½ ounces) cream of celery or chicken soup
2 tablespoons milk
1 small onion, grated
1 teaspoon Dijon mustard
1 cup (4 ounces) shredded Cheddar cheese
6 hard-cooked eggs, peeled and cut in half lengthwise
½ teaspoon crushed dried parsley
Cooked rice or toast

Combine soup, milk, onion, and mustard in saucepan. Cook and stir until smooth and heated through. Remove from heat, add cheese and stir until melted. Pour 1 cup sauce into 2x6x10-inch baking dish. Place eggs, cut side down, into sauce. Spoon remaining sauce around eggs. Bake at 350 degrees F. for 15 minutes. Sprinkle with parsley. Serve over cooked rice or toast. Makes 6 servings.

Variation

Curried Egg Casserole: Season sauce with 1 teaspoon (or to taste) of fine quality curry powder.

See menus for September, 4th week; November, 3rd week.

Western Omelet

8 slices bacon
2 tablespoons chopped onion
¼ cup diced green pepper
6 eggs, slightly beaten
⅓ cup milk
⅓ cup mayonnaise
¼ cup diced pimiento
4 slices whole grain bread, toasted and buttered on one side
2 tomatoes, peeled and sliced

Fry bacon until crisp; drain and crumble into medium bowl. In drippings, cook onion and green pepper until soft. Stir in eggs, milk, mayonnaise, and pimiento. Pour into greased 8x8x2-inch baking dish. Bake at 350 degrees F. for 20 to 25 minutes or until knife inserted in center comes out clean. Serve on buttered toast. Top with tomato slices. Makes 4 servings.

See menus for March, 4th week.

Omelet

1 tablespoon butter or
  margarine
6 eggs
1 tablespoon cold water
1 teaspoon salt
Dash pepper

In medium skillet or omelet pan, melt butter over low heat, tipping skillet back and forth to grease bottom and lower sides. With fork or wire whip, beat eggs with water, salt, and pepper just long enough to blend; pour into skillet. As mixture begins to set, gently lift up edges of omelet, allowing uncooked egg mixture to flow to bottom. Repeat until omelet is lightly set but creamy on top. With spatula, loosen around edge of omelet. With skillet in left hand, spatula in right, carefully roll up omelet from skillet handle toward opposite side. If desired, increase heat; brown bottom of omelet lightly. Hold skillet in left hand, heated platter in right, so that bottom edge of skillet rests on edge of platter. Slowly tip the two together until omelet rolls onto platter. Makes 4 servings.

Variations

Cheese and Tomato Omelet: When omelet is cooked, arrange 1 small tomato, chopped, and 1/3 cup shredded medium or sharp Cheddar cheese over half of omelet opposite skillet handle. With spatula, loosen around edge and roll omelet as described above.

Mushroom Omelet: Sauté 1 1/4 cups (1/4 pound) sliced mushrooms or 1 can (4 ounces) mushrooms in 1 tablespoon butter. Spoon over half of cooked omelet and continue as above. Sautéed sliced green onions, crisp bacon pieces, cooked sausage slices, or finely chopped fresh spinach may be used in any combination.

Corned Beef Omelet: Use 1/3 can (4 ounces) corned beef, shredded, over omelet. Continue as above.

See menus for April, 2nd week; September, 2nd week.

Poached Eggs on Toast

4 eggs
1 teaspoon vinegar (optional)
$^1/_2$ teaspoon salt
4 slices buttered toast

Fill medium or large skillet two-thirds full of water. Add vinegar and salt. Bring water to simmer. Working with each egg separately, break carefully into saucer without breaking yolk. Slide egg into water, placing each egg in different spot in skillet. Spoon simmering water over eggs for 2 to 3 minutes until they are set; or turn off heat, cover pan and let eggs stand in water for 5 to 6 minutes. Eggs are done when whites become opaque and yolks lose their shine. Remove one by one with slotted spoon. Serve hot over warm toast. Makes 4 servings.

See menus for February, 1st week; March, 1st week; November, 4th week.

Mixed Vegetables with Poached Eggs

2 tablespoons vegetable oil
1 can (8 ounces) stewed tomatoes or 1 cup stewed fresh tomatoes
1 beef bouillon cube or 1 teaspoon instant beef bouillon granules
2 cups sliced unpeeled zucchini
$^3/_4$ cup coarsely diced green pepper
$^1/_2$ cup fresh, frozen, or canned whole kernel corn, drained
$^1/_2$ cup sliced carrots
$^1/_2$ cup diced potatoes
$^1/_2$ cup coarsely chopped onion
$^1/_2$ teaspoon dried oregano leaves, crushed
1 teaspoon salt
$^1/_8$ teaspoon pepper
4 eggs

In 10-inch skillet, combine all ingredients except eggs. Cover; simmer until crisp-tender, about 20 minutes. With slotted spoon, remove vegetables to serving dish; keep warm. Bring vegetable juice in skillet to a boil. (If necessary, add water to make liquid 1 inch deep.) Crack eggs into vegetable juice, taking care not to break yolks and keeping eggs separated. Cover skillet and cook 2 to 4 minutes or until eggs are cooked to desired doneness. Serve over hot vegetables for a whole meal. Or omit eggs and serve vegetables as a side dish. Makes 8 servings.

See menus for June, 1st week.

Zucchini Egg Scramble

Cheese Sauce*
1 medium zucchini, sliced
  (about 4 ounces)
1 small onion, sliced
1 tablespoon butter
8 eggs
1/2 cup milk
1/2 teaspoon salt
1/2 teaspoon basil leaves,
  crushed
1/4 teaspoon pepper

Prepare Cheese Sauce. In 10-inch skillet over medium heat, cook zucchini and onion in butter until lightly browned, about 5 minutes. In large bowl mix eggs, milk, salt, basil, and pepper. Pour over zucchini and onion. As mixture begins to set, gently draw an inverted pancake turner completely across bottom and sides of pan, forming large soft curds. Continue until eggs are thickened but still moist. Do not stir constantly. Serve immediately with Cheese Sauce. Makes 4 servings.

Note: It is better to remove scrambled eggs from pan when they are slightly underdone. Heat retained in eggs completes the cooking.

Cheese Sauce: In small saucepan melt 1 tablespoon butter; blend in 1 tablespoon flour; cook and stir until mixture is smooth and bubbly. Stir in 1/2 cup milk. Cook and stir until mixture boils and is smooth and thick. Remove from heat. Stir in 1/4 cup shredded Swiss or Cheddar cheese and, if desired, 1 tablespoon Parmesan cheese. Blend in 1 tablespoon lemon juice. Serve warm.

See menus for August, 3rd week.

Zucchini Frittata

8 eggs
3 tablespoons cream or water
1/4 teaspoon salt
Pepper
2 tablespoons grated
  Parmesan or Romano
  cheese
4 tablespoons vegetable oil
1 clove garlic, minced or
  pressed (optional)
1 pound tender young
  zucchini, washed, unpared,
  and thinly sliced
4 green onions, sliced, using
  part of green stems

With fork lightly blend eggs, cream or water, salt, pepper to taste, and cheese; set aside. In 10- or 11-inch skillet, combine 3 tablespoons of the oil with garlic. Cook and stir just until garlic is golden. Add zucchini and onion slices and cook lightly for 3 to 4 minutes; spread evenly over bottom of pan. Pour egg mixture over vegetables and cook, without stirring, until eggs begin to set.

With wide spatula, loosen and lift egg mixture around outer edge of pan, allowing uncooked egg to flow down onto bottom of pan. Continue cooking until bottom is lightly browned and eggs are almost set but top of center is still moist and creamy. Invert frittata onto plate, add remaining 1 tablespoon oil to skillet, then slide frittata back into skillet, uncooked side down. Cook about 2 minutes more until bottom is lightly browned, then invert onto serving plate. Cut into wedges and serve hot or at room temperature. Makes 4 servings.

Note: Other vegetables such as spinach, chard, or asparagus may be used in place of zucchini. Firm vegetables may need to be partially cooked and drained before placing in skillet.

See menus for January, 4th week.

Mushroom Quiche

1 9-inch unbaked pastry shell
½ pound fresh mushrooms, sliced
¼ cup sliced green onions with tops
1 tablespoon butter or margarine
1 cup (4 ounces) shredded Swiss cheese
4 eggs
1 cup half-and-half
¼ cup grated Parmesan cheese
½ teaspoon salt
⅛ teaspoon pepper

In large omelet pan or skillet over medium heat, cook mushrooms and onions in butter or margarine until mushrooms are lightly browned, 6 to 8 minutes. Spread mushroom mixture evenly over bottom of unbaked pie shell. Sprinkle Swiss cheese over mushroom mixture. Beat together remaining ingredients until well blended. Pour over mushroom mixture and cheese. Bake on lowest shelf of oven at 375 degrees F. for 40 minutes or until quiche is slightly puffed and appears set when gently shaken. Allow to stand 10 minutes before serving. Makes 6 servings.

See menus for April, 4th week; September, 4th week; December, 4th week.

Cheese Dishes

Cheese Soufflé

¼ cup (½ stick) butter or margarine
¼ cup all-purpose flour
1 teaspoon salt
Dash cayenne pepper
1½ cups milk
2 cups (8 ounces) shredded Cheddar cheese
6 egg yolks, beaten
6 egg whites, stiffly beaten

In medium saucepan, melt butter or margarine; stir in flour; salt, and cayenne; add milk and blend. Cook over medium heat, stirring constantly, until sauce is thick and smooth. Add cheese; stir until melted. Remove from heat. Add beaten egg yolks; mix well. Cool mixture slightly, then pour slowly over stiffly beaten egg whites, cutting and folding mixture gently until mixed. Pour into ungreased 2-quart casserole. With teaspoon, draw line around casserole 1 inch in from edge. (When baked, center of soufflé rises to form a top hat.) Bake at 300 degrees F. for 1¼ hours. Serve at once. Makes 4 generous servings.

See menus for October, 2nd week.

Cheese Rarebit

4 tablespoons (1/2 stick)
  butter or margarine
1/4 cup all-purpose flour
1/2 teaspoon dry mustard
2 cups milk
2 cups shredded sharp
  Cheddar cheese
1/2 teaspoon Worcestershire
  sauce
Toast or crackers

In medium saucepan melt butter, stir in flour and mustard, then add milk; cook and stir until smooth and thick. Add cheese and Worcestershire sauce; stir until cheese melts. Serve hot over toast or crackers. Makes 4 servings.

See menus for March, 3rd week; May, 3rd week; October, 1st week.

Cheese Strata

12 slices (1-pound loaf)
  enriched white bread
2 cups (8 ounces) shredded
  medium or sharp Cheddar
  cheese
4 eggs
2 1/2 cups milk
1 teaspoon dry mustard
1 tablespoon chopped onion
1 1/2 teaspoons salt
1/4 teaspoon pepper

Remove crusts from bread. Arrange 6 slices of trimmed bread in bottom of well-buttered 12x7x2-inch baking dish. Cover with cheese, then with remaining slices of trimmed bread. Beat eggs; add milk, mustard, onion, salt, and pepper; pour over bread and cheese. Cover with plastic wrap; refrigerate several hours or overnight. Bake at 350 degrees F. for 60 minutes or until done. Serve immediately. Makes 6 to 8 servings.

Variations

Sausage Strata: Cook 1 pound (approximately 16) pork sausage links until brown. Cut into thirds and arrange over cheese. Continue as above.

Cheese and Spinach Strata: Clean and chop 1 bunch of spinach or use 1/2 bag (5 ounces) of frozen spinach. Toss with cheese. Continue as above.

Shrimp Strata: Arrange 2 cans (4 1/2 ounces each) broken shrimp, drained, over cheese before covering with top layer of bread slices.

Salmon Strata: Drain 1 can (1 pound) pink or red salmon, saving liquid to use in place of equal amount of milk. Remove skin and bones, if desired, but not necessary. Break salmon into pieces. Arrange over bottom layer of bread slices. Reduce cheese to 1 cup; sprinkle over salmon. Continue as above.

See menus for May, 1st week; October, 4th week.

Swiss Fondue

1 cup chicken broth or white grape juice
1 clove garlic, bruised
2¹/₂ cups (10 ounces) shredded Swiss cheese
2 tablespoons cornstarch
¹/₂ teaspoon salt
¹/₄ teaspoon Worcestershire sauce
¹/₈ teaspoon white pepper
¹/₄ teaspoon nutmeg
¹/₃ cup cold chicken broth or white grape juice
1 small loaf French bread

In top of double boiler but over direct heat, heat 1 cup broth or grape juice with garlic until very hot; remove garlic. Place pan over boiling water. Add Swiss cheese; stir constantly until cheese is melted. (At this point, cheese may not be thoroughly combined with liquid.) Combine cornstarch, salt, Worcestershire sauce, white pepper, and nutmeg with ¹/₃ cup cold chicken broth or grape juice. Stir into cheese mixture. (When cornstarch is added, cheese will combine with liquid for smooth blend.) Continue heating and stirring until smooth and hot. Serve over slices of French bread or from chafing dish with cubes of French bread to dip into it. Makes 4 servings.

See menus for July, 4th week.

Ringtum Diddy

4 tablespoons butter or margarine
1¹/₂ cups (6 ounces) shredded sharp Cheddar cheese
¹/₂ cup all-purpose flour, stirred and measured
1¹/₂ cups hot milk
1¹/₂ cups cooked fresh or heated canned tomatoes
¹/₂ teaspoon dried mustard
¹/₂ teaspoon paprika
¹/₂ teaspoon salt
Dash cayenne
Pepper
Crackers, toast, or cooked rice

Melt butter or margarine in heavy skillet. Add cheese. Sprinkle flour over cheese and cover pan. Cook over low heat until cheese melts and bubbles up through flour. Stir in milk slowly. Blend thoroughly. Stir hot tomatoes into cheese mixture. Add seasonings to taste. Simmer only a few minutes to blend. Do not overcook. Serve on crackers, toast, or cooked rice. Makes 4 servings.

See menus for April, 2nd week; September, 4th week.

BREADS AND CEREALS

Breads

Gingerbread

½ cup boiling water
½ cup shortening
½ cup brown sugar, packed
½ cup light molasses
1 egg, beaten
1½ cups all-purpose flour, stirred and measured
½ teaspoon salt
½ teaspoon baking powder
½ teaspoon soda
¾ teaspoon ground ginger
¾ teaspoon ground cinnamon

Brush 8-inch baking pan with oil, line with waxed or parchment paper, and oil paper lightly. Pour water over shortening; add brown sugar, molasses, and egg; beat well. Add sifted dry ingredients; beat until smooth. Spread batter evenly in prepared pan. Bake at 350 degrees F. for 35 minutes. Serve warm or cold with butter. Makes 8 servings.

Variation

Gingerbread with Lemon Sauce: Split cooled gingerbread into two layers and fill between layers with 1 package (8 ounces) cream cheese that has been blended until fluffy with a little milk or cream. Serve in squares with hot Lemon Sauce.

Lemon Sauce: Mix ½ cup sugar, 1 tablespoon cornstarch, ⅛ teaspoon salt, and ⅛ teaspoon nutmeg. Gradually add 1 cup boiling water; cook over low heat until thick and clear. Add 2 tablespoons butter or margarine, 1 teaspoon grated lemon rind, and 1½ tablespoons lemon juice; blend thoroughly. Makes 1⅓ cups.

Note: Lemon Sauce may be made quickly and easily in microwave.

See menus for January, 3rd week; August, 1st week.

Apple Banana Bread

1 small banana
Applesauce
½ cup shortening
¾ cup sugar
2 eggs
3 tablespoons buttermilk or sour milk (3 tablespoons milk plus 1 teaspoon vinegar)
2 cups all-purpose flour, stirred and measured
1 teaspoon soda
½ teaspoon salt

Mash bananas; add enough applesauce to measure 1 cup; set aside. Cream together shortening and sugar. Add eggs; beat well. Add buttermilk or sour milk and banana and applesauce mixture. Sift or mix together dry ingredients; add to creamed mixture; blend well. Pour into greased 8½x2½x4½-inch loaf pan. Bake at 350 degrees F. for 45 minutes or until done. Makes 1 loaf.

See menus for May, 2nd week.

Banana Nut Bread

1 cup shortening
2 cups sugar
4 eggs
5 large, ripe bananas, mashed
3½ cups all-purpose flour,
  stirred and measured
2 teaspoons soda
1 teaspoon salt
1 cup walnuts, coarsely
  chopped

In large bowl cream together shortening and sugar until fluffy; add eggs and beat well; blend in mashed bananas. Stir sifted dry ingredients into creamed mixture along with walnuts. Bake in two well-greased 8½x4½x2½-inch loaf pans at 300 degrees F. for 75 minutes or until bread tests done when inserted toothpick comes out clean. Cool 10 minutes; turn out onto rack to cool. Makes 2 loaves.

See menus for February, 4th week; October, 2nd week.

Easy French Bread

2¼ cups warm water
  (115 degrees)
2 tablespoons sugar
2 packages (2 tablespoons)
  active dry yeast
1 tablespoon salt
2 tablespoons soft shortening
  or vegetable oil
6 cups all-purpose flour,
  stirred and measured
1 beaten egg with 1
  tablespoon water (optional)
Sesame or poppy seeds
  (optional)

In large mixing bowl combine warm water and sugar. Sprinkle yeast over top; allow to soften. Add salt, shortening, and 3 cups flour; beat well with heavy spoon. Add enough remaining flour so that dough pulls away from side of bowl. Leave spoon in batter and allow dough to rest 10 minutes; stir down with spoon; allow dough to rest 10 minutes; stir down again. Repeat until dough has been stirred down five times.

Turn dough out onto floured board; knead two or three times to coat dough with flour so dough can be handled. Divide dough into two parts. Roll each portion of dough into rectangle 9x12 inches. Roll dough up, starting from long side; pinch edge of loaf to seal. Arrange seam side down on large baking sheet that's been greased or sprinkled with cornmeal, allowing room for both loaves. Repeat with second portion of dough.

Cover lightly; allow to rise 30 minutes. With very sharp knife, cut three gashes at an angle in top of each loaf; brush entire surface with egg wash (1 egg beaten slightly with 1 tablespoon water). If desired, sprinkle with sesame or poppy seeds. Bake at 400 degrees F. for 25 minutes or until brown. Cool on racks. Makes 2 loaves.

See menus for February, 2nd week; April, 2nd week; May, 1st week.

Garlic French Bread

1 loaf long French bread
1 clove garlic or ¼ teaspoon garlic powder
½ cup (1 stick) butter or margarine, softened

Slash bread in even 1½-inch slices, making cuts on the bias without cutting clear through. In small bowl mash garlic thoroughly; remove garlic. In same bowl, cream softened butter or margarine so that it absorbs the garlic juice that is left in bowl. (Or blend ¼ teaspoon garlic powder into butter or margarine.) Spread mixture generously between slices. Wrap loaf in aluminum foil. Bake at 375 degrees F. for 30 minutes or until hot. Makes 20 slices.

See menus for December, 3rd week.

Easy Bread Sticks

1 package (1 tablespoon) active dry yeast
1 tablespoon honey or sugar
1½ cups warm (115 degrees F.) water
1 teaspoon salt
3 to 4 cups all-purpose flour, stirred and measured

In large mixing bowl, soften yeast and honey or sugar in warm water; allow to stand 5 minutes. Stir in salt. Gradually add flour, blending with wooden spoon until dough pulls away from sides of bowl to form a ball. Divide dough into 12 pieces. Roll each piece between hands or stretch and roll on floured pastry board or cloth to make sticks about 10 to 12 inches long. Place lengthwise on large (14x16-inch) greased baking sheets, allowing six sticks to each sheet. Brush with beaten egg; sprinkle with desired seasonings: coarse salt, poppy or sesame or caraway seeds, Parmesan cheese, crushed dried parsley, salad seasonings, or any combination. Allow to rise 10 to 15 minutes, if desired, but not necessary. Bake at 400 degrees F. for 15 minutes or until golden brown.

Note: If desired, this dough may be shaped into 24 smaller bread sticks. Bake 10 minutes.

See menus for February, 3rd week; March, 2nd week; April, 3rd week.

Corn Bread

1 cup all-purpose flour, stirred and measured
¼ cup sugar
4 teaspoons baking powder
¾ teaspoon salt
1 cup yellow cornmeal
2 eggs
1 cup milk
¼ cup soft shortening

Stir together flour, sugar, baking powder, salt, and cornmeal. Add eggs, milk, and shortening. Beat with electric beater until just smooth, about 1 minute. Pour into greased 9x9x2-inch pan. Bake at 425 degrees F. for 20 to 25 minutes.

Variation
Corn Sticks: Spoon batter into preheated greased corn stick pans, filling ⅔ full. Bake 12 to 15 minutes.

See menus for April, 3rd week; September, 4th week; November, 3rd week.

Three-Grain Peanut Butter Bread

½ cup quick-cooking oats
1 cup all-purpose flour,
    stirred and measured
½ cup yellow cornmeal
½ cup nonfat dry milk
    powder
½ cup sugar
3 teaspoons baking powder
1 teaspoon salt
⅔ cup cream-style peanut
    butter
1 egg
1½ cups milk

In mixing bowl combine oats and dry ingredients. Cut in peanut butter as for pastry. Blend egg and milk and add to peanut butter mixture; mix well. Spoon into greased and floured 9x5-inch loaf pan; spread batter evenly. Bake at 325 degrees F. for 1 hour and 10 minutes or until toothpick inserted into center comes out clean. Cool 10 minutes and remove from pan. Makes 1 loaf.

See menus for September, 1st week.

Grilled Sweet Rolls

4 day-old sweet rolls
4 teaspoons butter or
    margarine

With sharp knife split sweet rolls in half and rearrange so that top and bottom of rolls are pressed together with the two cut surfaces exposed on top and bottom. Spread both surfaces of each roll with softened butter or margarine and place onto medium hot griddle or skillet. When one side is golden brown, turn roll over and grill other side. Serve warm. Makes 4 servings.
    Note: A good way to serve day-old sweet rolls.

See menus for January, 4th week; April, 2nd week; October, 4th week.

Frozen Wheat Bread Rolls

1 loaf frozen bread
½ cup (1 stick) butter or
    margarine, melted

Allow bread to thaw in refrigerator overnight. Cut in half lengthwise, then crosswise into six pieces, making 12 pieces in all. Roll pieces of bread in melted butter or margarine and arrange 1½ inches apart on baking sheet. Cover lightly and allow to rise for 2 to 4 hours. Bake at 375 degrees F. 20 minutes or until golden brown and crusty. Makes 12 rolls.

Variation
Bundt Rolls: One-half cup (1 stick) butter or margarine, melted, 2 loaves frozen whole wheat or white bread, almost but not quite thawed. Pour melted butter or margarine into a 10-inch Bundt pan; brush butter or

margarine over entire inside of pan. On lightly floured board, cut partially frozen bread into ¹/₂-inch slices. Dip both sides of bread slices into melted butter, then stand slices up on end, one against the other, around the pan, accordian fashion. Cover lightly and allow to rise about 2 hours or until dough rises nearly to top of pan. Bake at 375 degrees F. for 30 minutes or until golden brown. Turn out immediately and serve hot, pulling roll slices out with fingers. Makes 8 servings.

See menus for February, 1st week; April, 1st week; August, 4th week.

Cinnamon Rolls

2 packages (2 tablespoons) active dry yeast
¹/₄ cup warm water (115 degrees)
²/₃ cup instant nonfat dry milk
1³/₄ cups hot water
³/₄ cup melted shortening or vegetable oil
¹/₂ cup sugar
2 teaspoons salt
5¹/₂ cups all-purpose flour, scooped and leveled
4 eggs, beaten
¹/₂ cup (1 stick) butter or margarine, melted
6 tablespoons sugar
2 tablespoons cinnamon
¹/₃ to ¹/₂ cup raisins (optional)
Powdered Sugar Frosting*

Soften yeast in ¹/₄ cup warm water; allow to stand for 5 minutes. In large mixing bowl, combine nonfat dry milk, 1³/₄ cups hot water, and shortening. Add sugar and salt; cool to lukewarm. Blend in 2 cups flour. Add yeast mixture and eggs; stir thoroughly. Stir in remaining 3¹/₂ cups flour to make a soft dough. Cover and refrigerate for 8 hours or overnight. Turn dough (it will be sticky) onto well-floured board, turning to coat so it can be handled.

Divide dough into two parts. Roll each portion into an 8x15-inch rectangle. Spread with half the melted butter or margarine; sprinkle generously with sugar that has been mixed with cinnamon and with raisins. Beginning on long side, roll up as for jelly roll. Pinch edges. With sharp knife cut into 1-inch pieces; set 2 to 3 inches apart onto ungreased baking sheets. Cover lightly with clean towel; allow to rise 1¹/₂ to 2 hours or until double in size. Bake at 400 degrees F. for 8 to 10 minutes. Frost hot rolls generously with Powdered Sugar Frosting. Makes 2 to 2¹/₂ dozen cinnamon rolls.

Powdered Sugar Frosting: Cream together 4 cups confectioners' sugar and ¹/₂ cup (1 stick) softened butter or margarine. Add 2 teaspoons vanilla and enough hot water to make spreadable.

See menus for February, 4th week; March, 2nd week.

Butterhorns

1 package (1 tablespoon) active dry yeast
¹/₄ cup warm water (115 degrees)
¹/₂ cup (1 stick) butter or margarine
³/₄ cup milk, scalded
¹/₂ cup sugar
³/₄ teaspoon salt
3 eggs, beaten
3¹/₂ to 4¹/₂ cups all-purpose flour, scooped
¹/₂ cup (1 stick) butter or margarine, melted

Soften yeast in warm water. Combine melted butter or margarine and scalded milk. Stir in sugar, salt, and eggs. Cool. Stir in softened yeast and enough flour to make a soft dough. Cover; allow to rise until double in bulk, 2 to 3 hours. Turn out onto lightly floured board; knead just to coat dough with flour. Dough is very soft and should remain so. Divide dough. Roll each half into 14-inch circle. Spread each circle with ¹/₄ cup melted butter or margarine. Cut pie-fashion into 16 pieces. Roll each piece loosely from large end to small. Place on greased cookie sheet, allowing about an inch between rolls. Let rise at room temperature for 2 to 3 hours or until double in bulk. Bake at 375 degrees F. for 12 to 15 minutes or until golden brown. Makes 32 rolls.

Note: If it is more convenient, rising time for dough and rolls may be stretched out to as long as 6 hours by keeping them in a cool place.

Variations

Orange Rolls: Prepare dough as above. After first rising, divide dough in half and roll each portion of dough into 8x14-inch rectangle. Spread each rectangle with half of orange filling, made by creaming together ¹/₂ cup (1 stick) butter or margarine with ¹/₂ cup sugar and grated rind of 1 orange. Roll loosely, starting from long side, and pinch edge closed. Slice into 12 pieces; place each piece, cut side down, in buttered muffin pan. Cover lightly; allow to rise 2 to 3 hours or until double in bulk. Bake as above. As soon as rolls come out of oven, brush hot rolls with frosting, made by combining 1 cup confectioners' sugar with 1 tablespoon hot water and ¹/₂ teaspoon rum extract. Remove rolls from pan to cool. Makes 24 rolls.

Freeze-Ahead Rolls: Rolls may be frozen ahead of time by shaping as desired, then immediately placing rolls close together onto baking sheet and quick-freezing. Remove frozen rolls from baking sheet; place in heavy plastic freezer bag. Secure bag so it is airtight. Keep rolls frozen for no longer than 2 weeks. Three hours before time to bake, remove from freezer and arrange on greased baking sheet, allowing 1 inch between rolls, or place into greased muffin tins, according to recipe. Allow to thaw and rise for about 3 hours; bake as directed.

See menus for May, 4th week; November, 4th week.

Cinnamon Stack Biscuits

2 cups all-purpose flour,
  stirred and measured
3 teaspoons baking powder
½ teaspoon cream of tartar
½ teaspoon salt
3 tablespoons sugar
½ cup shortening
⅔ cup milk
¼ cup (½ stick) butter or
  margarine, melted
¼ cup sugar
1 tablespoon cinnamon

In large mixing bowl, stir together flour, baking powder, cream of tartar, salt, and 3 tablespoons sugar. Cut in shortening until mixture forms coarse crumbs. Add milk; stir until mixture forms ball. Turn onto lightly floured board; knead gently 4 or 5 times. Roll dough into 16x10-inch rectangle. Brush with melted butter; sprinkle with mixture of ¼ cup sugar and cinnamon. Cut lengthwise into five 2-inch strips. Stack the five strips; cut into 12 pieces. Place cut side down in 12 greased muffin tins. Bake at 425 degrees F. for 12 to 15 minutes. Makes 12 biscuits.

See menus for February, 2nd week; March, 2nd week.

Baking Powder Biscuits

2 cups all-purpose flour,
  stirred and measured
3 teaspoons baking powder
½ teaspoon cream of tartar
½ teaspoon salt
2 teaspoons sugar
½ cup shortening
⅔ cup milk

In large mixing bowl stir together flour, baking powder, cream of tartar, salt, and sugar. Cut in shortening until mixture forms coarse crumbs. Add milk all at once; stir until dough follows fork around bowl. Turn out onto lightly floured surface. Pat or roll dough ½ inch thick; cut with biscuit cutter. Bake on ungreased baking sheet at 425 degrees F. for 10 to 12 minutes or until golden brown. Makes 16 medium biscuits.

Note: Leftover biscuits can be split, buttered, and toasted for another meal.

Variation

Rich Shortcake for Strawberries or Other Fruit: Increase sugar to 2 tablespoons; use butter or margarine in place of shortening; add 1 beaten egg to ½ cup milk; proceed as above. Split hot or cold shortcakes in half and serve with crushed sweetened strawberries or other fruit and slightly sweetened whipped cream.

See menus for January, 2nd week; April, 1st week; June, 1st week.

Cornmeal Muffins

⅓ cup shortening
⅓ cup sugar
1 egg, beaten
1¼ cups milk
1 cup all-purpose flour,
  stirred and measured
½ teaspoon salt
4 teaspoons baking powder
1 cup yellow cornmeal

Grease 12 muffin cups. Cream together shortening and sugar; add egg and beat until smooth. Mix in milk alternately with sifted flour, salt, and baking powder. Add cornmeal, stirring only enough to mix. Fill greased muffin pans ⅔ full. Bake at 425 degrees F. for 25 minutes or until done. Makes 1 dozen muffins.

See menus for January, 1st week; July, 1st week; August, 4th week.

Bran Muffins

1¼ cups all-purpose flour,
  stirred and measured
3 teaspoons baking powder
¼ teaspoon salt
2 tablespoons sugar
1 cup fortified whole-bran
  cereal
1 cup milk
1 egg
3 tablespoons vegetable oil or
  melted shortening

Grease twelve 1½-inch muffin-pan cups; set aside. Stir together flour, baking powder, salt, and sugar; set aside. Measure bran cereal and milk into large mixing bowl. Stir to combine, then allow to stand until cereal is softened, 1 to 2 minutes. Add egg and oil; beat well. Add flour mixture and stir only enough to combine. Divide batter evenly among prepared muffin cups. Bake at 400 degrees F. for 25 minutes or until lightly browned. Makes 12 muffins.

See menus for January, 4th week.

Oatmeal Muffins

1 cup buttermilk or sour
  milk*
1 cup rolled oats
1 egg, unbeaten
½ cup (packed) brown
  sugar
1 cup all-purpose flour,
  stirred and measured
½ teaspoon salt
1½ teaspoons baking
  powder
½ teaspoon soda
¼ cup vegetable oil
Raisins or dates (optional)

Pour buttermilk over oats. Let stand 5 minutes. Add egg and brown sugar to oats; mix well. Add sifted dry ingredients and oil; mix thoroughly. Spoon into 12 greased muffin tins or cupcake liners. Raisins or dates may be added, if desired. Bake at 400 degrees F. for 18 minutes or until done. Makes 12 large muffins.

Sour Milk: Sour milk can be substituted for buttermilk. To make sour milk, place 1 tablespoon vinegar in 1-cup measure; add milk to measure one cup; allow to stand 2 to 3 minutes.

See menus for March, 3rd week; December, 2nd week.

Whole Wheat Muffins

1 cup sifted all-purpose flour
1 cup sifted whole wheat flour
1/2 teaspoon salt
4 teaspoons baking powder
1/2 cup brown sugar, packed
1 cup milk
2 eggs, slightly beaten
1/3 cup vegetable oil or melted shortening

Grease 12 large (2 1/2 inch) muffin cups or use cupcake liners. In large mixing bowl blend all-purpose flour and whole wheat flour, salt, baking powder, and brown sugar. Combine milk, eggs, and oil; stir just until dry ingredients are moistened. Spoon batter into prepared pans. Bake at 425 degrees F. for 15 minutes or until done. Makes 12 muffins.

Note: 1/2 cup coarsely chopped raisins, dates, or nuts or a combination of these may be added, if desired.

See menus for January, 2nd week; February, 3rd week; September, 2nd week.

Twin Mountain Muffins

1/4 cup (1/2 stick) butter or margarine
1/4 cup sugar
1 egg
2 cups all-purpose flour, stirred and measured
1/2 teaspoon salt
4 teaspoons baking powder
1 cup milk

Cream together butter or margarine and sugar; beat in well-beaten egg. Add mixed dry ingredients alternately with milk. Bake in greased muffin tins at 375 degrees F. for 25 minutes. Makes 1 dozen muffins.

Variations

Bacon Muffins: Add 3 strips bacon, fried crisp and crumbled, to batter.

Blueberry Muffins: After muffin batter is in tins, divide 1 cup blueberries (fresh, frozen, or drained canned) among the 12 muffin tins; carefully push berries down into batter with back of teaspoon. This method prevents blueberries from sinking to bottom.

Cheese Muffins: Stir 1/2 cup shredded Cheddar or Swiss cheese into batter along with flour.

Cranberry Muffins: Stir 1 cup coarsely chopped raw cranberries into batter; spoon into muffin pans; sprinkle top of muffins generously with granulated sugar before baking.

Date or Raisin Muffins: Add 1/2 cup chopped pitted dates or 1/3 cup raisins to batter.

Pecan Muffins: Add 1/2 cup chopped pecans to batter. After filling cups, sprinkle with sugar, cinnamon, and more chopped nuts.

See menus for March, 1st week; April, 3rd week; June, 3rd week.

Parmesan Toast

4 slices bread
Butter or margarine
Parmesan cheese

Lightly toast bread on both sides. Spread one side generously with butter or margarine; sprinkle generously with Parmesan cheese and broil just until lightly browned. Makes 4 servings.

See menus for February, 1st week; April, 3rd week; May, 3rd week.

Thin Butter Toast

4 slices bread, chilled
3 tablespoons soft butter or
   margarine

Holding each slice of bread flat on cutting board with palm of hand, cut bread into two slices with sharp French or serrated knife. Spread each thin slice with softened butter or margarine. Just before serving, broil until golden brown and crisp. Makes 4 servings.

See menus for September, 4th week; November, 1st week.

Cinnamon Toast

4 slices bread
Butter
4 tablespoons sugar
4 teaspoons cinnamon

Butter one side of each bread slice. Sprinkle liberally with mixture of granulated sugar and cinnamon. Broil until butter, cinnamon, and sugar bubble. Serve at once. Makes 4 servings.

See menus for May, 1st week; November, 3rd week; December, 4th week.

Breakfast Cottage Cheese Special

1 cup small curd cottage
   cheese
4 teaspoons sugar
1/4 teaspoon cinnamon
4 slices whole wheat bread,
   toasted on one side

Combine cottage cheese, sugar, and cinnamon. Spread evenly on untoasted sides of toast. Broil until bubbly and hot. Makes 4 servings.

See menus for February, 2nd week.

Cheese Toast

1 loaf (1 pound) unsliced
   French bread
Softened butter or margarine
Garlic salt
Shredded sharp Cheddar
   cheese or grated Parmesan
   cheese

Cut bread into ½-inch slices. Spread generously with butter and sprinkle with garlic salt. Top each slice with desired cheese and bake at 425 degrees F. for 10 minutes or until cheese is melted. Serve hot. Makes 10 to 12 slices.

See menus for October, 4th week.

Honey Butter

½ cup butter, softened
¼ teaspoon vanilla
1 egg yolk
¾ cup honey

With electric mixer or wooden spoon, cream butter until soft. Add vanilla and egg yolk; blend thoroughly. While creaming, add honey gradually. Store in covered container in refrigerator. Makes 2 cups.

See menus for December, 2nd week; December, 4th week.

Everyday Pancakes

3 eggs
1 cup milk
3 tablespoons vegetable oil
   or melted shortening
1½ cups all-purpose flour,
   stirred and measured
3 teaspoons baking powder
½ teaspoon salt
1 tablespoon sugar

Beat eggs thoroughly; stir in milk, shortening, and sifted dry ingredients just until blended. Bake on lightly greased griddle. Makes 8 to 10 pancakes.

Variation:

Apple Pancakes: Stir in 1 cup finely chopped apple.

Blueberry Pancakes: Stir in 1 cup fresh, frozen, or canned and drained blueberries.

See menus for February, 4th week; July, 1st week; December, 2nd week.

Maple-Flavored Syrup

2 cups sugar
1 cup water
1 teaspoon maple flavoring

In small saucepan bring sugar and water to a boil; reduce heat and simmer for 5 minutes. Remove from heat; add maple flavoring. Makes 1½ cups.

See menus for February, 1st week; November, 1st week; December, 2nd week.

Whole Wheat Pancakes or Waffles

1¼ cups sifted whole wheat flour
3 teaspoons baking powder
3 tablespoons sugar, brown or granulated
¾ teaspoon salt
3 eggs, well beaten
1¼ cups milk
3 tablespoons vegetable oil

Stir together dry ingredients. Combine eggs, milk, and oil; stir into flour mixture. Bake on lightly greased griddle until golden brown, then turn. Or bake in waffle iron. Makes 12 pancakes or waffle sections.

Note: For lighter pancakes or waffles, eggs may be separated; blend egg yolks with milk and cooking oil for batter; fold stiffly beaten egg whites into batter just before baking.

See menus for January, 3rd week; March, 2nd week; August, 1st week.

Puff Pancakes

3 eggs
½ cup all-purpose flour, stirred and measured
½ cup milk
¼ teaspoon salt
2 tablespoons butter or margarine

Preheat oven to 400 degrees F. Set 9-inch clear colorless glass pie dish into hot oven on lowest oven shelf until very hot. Meanwhile, beat together eggs, flour, milk, and salt in small mixer bowl, blender, or food processor until smooth, about 3 minutes. Remove pie dish from oven; add butter or margarine and rotate pie dish until fat is melted. Add batter immediately. Bake on lowest oven shelf for 20 minutes or until golden. Serve immediately with syrup, jam, or applesauce; or fill with your favorite salad or creamed dish. Makes 4 servings.

Note: For serving a large group, triple recipe and bake in 9x13-inch baking pan.

Variation

Apple Puff Pancakes: In 9-inch clear colorless glass pie dish, melt 2 tablespoons butter in oven as it preheats to 450 degrees F. Stir in 2 tablespoons sugar and ¾ teaspoon cinnamon. Add 1 large tart apple that has been cored, peeled, and sliced; stir to coat apple slices; cook 4 minutes. In meantime, make batter as above, adding 2 tablespoons sugar and decreasing flour to ⅓ cup. Pour over apples. Bake at 450 degrees F. for 10 minutes, then reduce heat to 350 degrees F. and continue cooking for 6 minutes. Serve immediately. Makes 4 servings.

See menus for April, 2nd week; November, 3rd week; December, 1st week.

Swedish Pancakes

4 eggs
1 cup milk
1 cup all-purpose flour,
    stirred and measured
2 tablespoons sugar
1/2 teaspoon salt

Combine all ingredients in blender or large mixing bowl. Blend or beat until smooth. Batter will be thin. Heat 9-inch crepe pan or frying pan, rub with shortening and pour enough batter into center of pan to make a cake about 5 inches across. Quickly tip pan in all directions until batter completely covers bottom of pan. Pancake browns quickly; loosen edges, turn and brown slightly on other side. Spread with butter and jam or brown sugar; roll up and cut into bite-size pieces. Makes 8 to 10 pancakes.

See menus for March, 4th week; April, 4th week; May, 3rd week.

Cottage Cheese Pancakes

1 cup small curd cottage
    cheese
3 eggs
2 tablespoons melted butter
1/4 cup all-purpose flour,
    stirred and measured
1/4 cup salt

Drain cottage cheese in sieve; press down firmly until all liquid has been pressed out. In mixing bowl beat eggs until thick. Add cottage cheese, butter, flour, and salt; mix only enough to blend. Drop by large spoonfuls onto buttered, moderately hot griddle or frying pan. Turn gently with spatula when lightly browned on underside; bake on other side until light brown. Serve warm. Makes 12 pancakes.

See menus for February, 2nd week; June, 2nd week; July, 2nd week.

Favorite Waffles

2 1/2 cups all-purpose flour,
    stirred and measured
3/4 teaspoon salt
4 teaspoons baking powder
1 1/2 tablespoons sugar
2 beaten eggs
2 1/4 cups milk
1/2 cup melted shortening or
    vegetable oil

Stir together dry ingredients. Combine eggs, milk, and shortening. Combine liquid and dry ingredients just before baking; beat until smooth. Bake in hot waffle iron. Makes 12 waffles.

Variation

Nut Waffles: Sprinkle 1 tablespoon chopped pecans on batter for each waffle before closing down lid of waffle iron.

See menus for November, 4th week.

French Toast

2 eggs, lightly beaten
4 tablespoons milk
½ teaspoon sugar
Dash salt
4 slices, 1 inch thick, French
(or other) bread

Lightly beat together eggs, milk, sugar, and salt; pour egg mixture into shallow dish. Dip bread on both sides into egg mixture; cook until golden on both sides in hot skillet that has been lightly rubbed or sprayed with shortening. Serve hot with maple-flavored syrup. Makes 4 servings.

See menus for April, 1st week; August, 2nd week; December, 4th week.

Cereals

Cooked Cornmeal

1 cup yellow or white
cornmeal
1 cup cold water
3 cups boiling water
¾ teaspoon salt

Mix cornmeal with cold water. In saucepan, add cornmeal mixture to boiling salted water. Cook and stir over medium heat for 7 minutes or until thick. May be served as cooked cereal or chilled for making Fried Cornmeal Mush. Makes 6 servings.

Variation

Fried Cornmeal Mush: Cook cornmeal as described above. Spread hot cooked cornmeal in loaf pan and refrigerate. When it is thoroughly chilled, cut in ½-inch slices. Fry in hot fat or butter and oil in skillet until golden on both sides. Serve with honey or maple-flavored syrup.

See menus for November, 1st week.

Swiss Oatmeal (Muesli)

½ cup rolled oats, instant
or regular
½ cup boiling water
1 to 2 unpeeled cooking
apples, cored and grated
finely
2 tablespoons lemon juice
3 to 4 tablespoons brown
sugar, packed
Evaporated milk or light
cream

In small bowl combine rolled oats and boiling water; stir to blend well. Add apples, lemon juice, and brown sugar to taste; stir vigorously. Serve cold with evaporated milk or light cream. Makes 4 servings.

Note: Any other fresh or canned fruit, such as berries, peaches, or pears may be blended thoroughly into mixture. Also, this is a tasty idea to try with 1 cup of any cooked cereal.

See menus for March, 4th week; May, 1st week; December, 3rd week.

Steamed Rice

2 cups water
1 teaspoon salt
1 cup long grain rice

Combine water and salt in medium saucepan. Bring to boil. Stir in rice, turn heat to low, cover and cook 25 minutes. Remove from heat; allow to stand 10 to 15 minutes. Remove lid; fluff up with fork and serve. Makes 3 cups cooked rice.

Variation

Brown Rice: Follow directions for cooking rice, replacing long grain rice with brown rice. Extend cooking time to 50 minutes or until brown rice is tender.

See menus for February, 3rd week; September, 1st week; November, 3rd week.

Fried Rice

3 tablespoons vegetable oil
6 green onions, sliced, or
  ½ cup thinly sliced onion
½ green pepper, seeded and
  cut in thin strips
½ cup diced celery
2 cups day-old cooked rice,
  brown or white
½ teaspoon salt
1 tablespoon soy sauce
Chopped fresh coriander
  (cilantro), if desired

Heat 1 tablespoon oil in large skillet. Add onion, green pepper, and celery; stir-fry for 2 minutes, adding more oil as needed. Add rice and salt; toss and cook until hot and golden. Stir in soy sauce. Makes 4 servings.

Note: Thinly sliced carrots or mushrooms or both may be stir-fried along with other vegetables. One and one-half cups julienned cooked roast pork or ham or 1 cup diced cooked shrimp may be added to skillet along with rice and salt. If desired, 3 eggs may be whipped and added along with rice; cook until barely set.

See menus for March, 2nd week; April, 1st week.

Brown Rice Pilaff

1 cup regular brown rice
¼ cup (½ stick) butter or
  margarine
1 can (10¾ ounces) beef
  consommé or broth
½ can (⅔ cup) water
1 can (4 ounces) small
  button mushrooms,
  drained (optional)

Wash rice; drain. Melt butter or margarine in heavy skillet and brown rice, stirring constantly. In 1½-quart casserole combine browned rice with bouillon and water. Cover; bake at 375 degrees F. for 1¾ hours. Stir in drained mushrooms; bake, covered, 15 minutes longer. Makes 8 servings.

See menus for March, 4th week.

Rice Pilaff

2 cups uncooked long grain white rice
1 large onion, chopped
1/2 cup (1 stick) butter
3 tablespoons chopped fresh parsley or 1 tablespoon dried parsley
2 cans (11 ounces each) condensed beef broth (bouillon)
1 1/3 cups water
1 cup shelled pine nuts or toasted slivered almonds (optional)

Sauté rice and chopped onion in butter in skillet until rice is golden. Combine with parsley, consommé, and water; pour into greased 2-quart casserole. Cover; bake at 350 degrees F. for 30 minutes or until all water is absorbed. Uncover at once. To serve, fluff up rice with fork; spoon onto serving dish and sprinkle with pine nuts or almonds. Makes 8 servings.

See menus for August, 2nd week.

Barley Pilaff

1/2 cup (1 stick) butter or margarine
1 1/3 cups regular pearl barley
1 large onion, minced
1 1/4 cups (4 ounces) sliced fresh mushrooms
4 cups chicken bouillon*
3/4 teaspoon salt
1/4 teaspoon pepper
1 1/3 cups coarsely grated carrots (optional)

In large heavy saucepan melt butter or margarine over medium heat. Add onion, barley, and mushrooms; sauté until lightly browned. Add chicken bouillon, salt, pepper, and carrots. Bring to boil, then reduce heat to simmer. Cover and cook until barley and carrots are tender and bouillon has been absorbed, about 45 minutes. Makes 8 servings.

Variation

Chicken Barley Casserole: Two cups diced raw chicken (2 half breasts) may be browned along with barley, onion, and mushrooms, then cooked in casserole.

Note: To make chicken bouillon, dissolve 4 chicken bouillon cubes in 4 cups boiling water.

See menus for December, 4th week.

Creole Beans and Rice

2 tablespoons butter or
  margarine
1 clove garlic, minced
  (optional)
1 medium onion, chopped
1/2 cup finely diced green
  pepper
1 can (15 1/2 ounces)
  chili-style beans
1 can (1 pound) whole
  tomatoes, cut up
1 teaspoon chili powder
1 teaspoon brown sugar
1/2 teaspoon salt
Dash cayenne pepper
3 cups cooked rice*
  (1 cup uncooked)

In 10-inch skillet, melt butter. Add garlic, onion, and green pepper and cook, stirring occasionally, until vegetables are soft. Add all remaining ingredients except rice; simmer together 15 to 20 minutes, stirring occasionally, until flavors are blended. Serve over hot rice. Makes 6 servings.

Note: To cook rice, bring 2 cups water and 1 teaspoon salt to boil. Stir in rice, turn heat to lowest level, cover and cook 15 minutes. Fluff rice with fork and serve immediately or cover and allow to stand for 20 minutes. Makes 3 cups rice. A combination of beans and rice, served together as in this dish, provides a complete protein.

See menus for November, 1st week.

Country Baked Beans

2 1/2 cups small white or
  navy beans
Water for soaking
6 cups water
1 large onion, diced
1 cup catsup
1/2 pound lean bacon, cut
  into 1-inch pieces
3/4 cup brown sugar, packed
1/4 teaspoon garlic salt
1 1/2 tablespoons prepared
  mustard
1 tablespoon horseradish
1 1/2 tablespoons
  Worcestershire sauce

Sort and rinse beans. Soak in tepid water to cover for 6 to 8 hours. (Or bring beans and water to boil, cook 2 minutes, remove from heat and cover; let stand 1 hour.) Drain; discard soaking water. Combine soaked beans and 6 cups water. Bring to boil; reduce heat. Cover and simmer 1 1/2 hours or until beans are tender. Drain beans, saving cooking water. In 2 1/2-quart bean pot or casserole combine drained beans with remaining ingredients. Cover; bake at 300 degrees F. for 4 to 6 hours or until beans are tender, stirring occasionally. Add cooking liquid as needed to keep beans just covered with liquid. Makes 10 servings.

Note: Two cans (1 pound each) pork and beans may be used in place of cooked beans. Bake 3 to 4 hours.

See menus for March, 2nd week.

CAKES AND COOKIES

Cakes

Pumpkin Spice Cake

³/₄ cup shortening
1¹/₄ cups sugar
2 eggs
1 cup canned or cooked
  pumpkin
³/₄ cup milk
1 teaspoon soda
2 cups all-purpose flour,
  stirred and measured
¹/₂ teaspoon salt
3 teaspoons baking powder
1 teaspoon ground cinnamon
¹/₂ teaspoon ground cloves
¹/₂ teaspoon ground nutmeg
1 cup coarsely chopped nuts

In large mixing bowl cream together shortening and sugar. Add eggs; beat until light and fluffy. Combine pumpkin, milk, and soda; add alternately with sifted dry ingredients. Stir in nuts. Pour into two 8-inch layer cake pans that have been lined with waxed paper, then greased and floured. Bake at 350 degrees F. for 25 minutes or until done. Frost, if desired, with Cream Cheese Frosting (p. 267).

Note: Cake may be baked in 9x13-inch pan for 40 to 45 minutes or until done. Leftover canned pumpkin may be frozen for later use.

See menus for October, 4th week.

Upside Down Pumpkin Cake

³/₄ cup (1¹/₂ sticks) butter
  or margarine, divided
³/₄ cup (packed) brown
  sugar, divided
1 tablespoon water
1 cup toasted sliced almonds
1 cup granulated sugar
2 eggs
1 cup cooked or canned
  pumpkin
2 cups all-purpose flour,
  stirred and measured
2 teaspoons baking powder
1 teaspoon Pumpkin Pie
  Spice*
¹/₄ teaspoon baking soda
¹/₄ teaspoon salt
¹/₃ cup milk
1 cup heavy cream

Melt ¹/₄ cup (¹/₂ stick) butter or margarine in round 10x2-inch deep pan or skillet. Stir in ¹/₄ cup brown sugar and water; mix well. Sprinkle with almonds; set aside. Cream remaining ¹/₂ cup butter or margarine with remaining ¹/₂ cup brown sugar, granulated sugar, and eggs. Stir in pumpkin. Combine flour with baking powder, pumpkin pie spice, baking soda, and salt. Blend into creamed mixture alternately with milk. Carefully spoon over almonds; level top. Bake in center of oven at 350 degrees F. for 50 to 55 minutes or until cake tests done. Invert onto serving plate. Serve warm or cool with slightly sweetened whipped cream. Makes 10 servings.

*Pumpkin Pie Spice: If desired, ¹/₂ teaspoon ground cinnamon and ¹/₄ teaspoon each of ground nutmeg and ground cloves may be used in place of pumpkin pie spice.

See menus for October, 3rd week.

Thirty-Minute Cocoa Cake

1 cup (2 sticks) butter or margarine
1/4 cup unsweetened cocoa powder
1 cup water
2 cups sugar
2 cups all-purpose flour, stirred and measured
1 teaspoon soda
1 teaspoon cinnamon
1/2 cup buttermilk or sour milk*
2 eggs
1 teaspoon vanilla
Quick Cocoa Frosting**
Chopped nuts (optional)

In medium saucepan, combine butter or margarine, cocoa, and water; bring to boil over medium heat, cooking until butter is melted; set aside. In large mixing bowl, stir together sugar, flour, soda, and cinnamon. Add cocoa mixture; blend. (Save cocoa pan, unwashed, for making Quick Cocoa Frosting.) Beat together buttermilk and eggs; stir into batter. Add vanilla. Pour into ungreased 9x13x2-inch baking pan. Bake at 400 degrees F. for 20 minutes. Five minutes before cake is done, begin to make Quick Cocoa Frosting. Frost cake as soon as it comes from oven. If desired, sprinkle immediately with chopped nuts. Cool. This moist and delicious cake will stay fresh for days.

*Note: To make sour milk, measure 1/2 tablespoon vinegar into measuring cup; add enough milk to make 1/2 cup. Allow to stand for 5 minutes.

**Quick Cocoa Frosting: In medium saucepan combine 1/2 cup (1 stick) butter or margarine, 1/4 cup unsweetened cocoa powder, and 1/3 cup milk. Bring to boil; simmer 3 minutes; remove from heat. Stir in 3 1/2 cups (1 pound) confectioners' sugar and 1 teaspoon vanilla; beat until smooth. If desired, stir 1 cup broken nuts or 1 cup raisins or both into frosting before spreading over cake.

See menus for March, 3rd week; July, 3rd week.

Apricot Spice Cake

2 eggs
1 cup sugar
1/2 teaspoon salt
1/2 cup vegetable oil
2 cups apricots plus juice (or thick apricot puree)
2 cups all-purpose flour, stirred and measured
1 teaspoon ground cinnamon
1 teaspoon ground cloves
2 teaspoons soda
1 tablespoon hot water
1 cup coarsely chopped nuts

Generously grease 9x13-inch baking pan. In large mixing bowl combine eggs, sugar, salt, and oil; beat well. Stir in apricots or apricot puree. Add flour, spices, and soda mixed with hot water. Stir in nuts. Pour into prepared baking pan. Bake at 350 degrees F. for 25 to 30 minutes. Cool. Frost, if desired, with Cream Cheese Frosting (p. 267).

See menus for April, 4th week.

Oatmeal Cake

1¼ cups boiling water
1 cup quick-cooking rolled oats
½ cup (1 stick) butter or margarine
¾ cup granulated sugar
¾ cup (packed) brown sugar
2 eggs, slightly beaten
1 teaspoon vanilla
1½ cups all-purpose flour, stirred and measured
1 teaspoon soda
½ teaspoon salt
1 teaspoon cinnamon
½ teaspoon nutmeg
Broiled Coconut Topping*

Pour boiling water over rolled oats; set aside for 20 minutes. (Or 1½ cups leftover oatmeal may be used.) In large mixing bowl, cream together butter or margarine and sugars; add eggs and vanilla and blend well. Stir in oatmeal, then mixed dry ingredients. Bake in greased 9x13-inch pan at 350 degrees F. for 40 to 45 minutes or until done. Spread with Broiled Coconut Topping; broil until frosting bubbles, taking care not to burn.

Broiled Coconut Frosting: Combine 6 tablespoons (¾ stick) butter or margarine, ½ cup (packed) brown sugar, ¼ cup cream or evaporated milk, ¾ cup chopped nuts, and 1 cup (3½ ounces) coconut. Mix well. Spread over cake; broil until frosting bubbles and is slightly brown.

See menus for October, 2nd week.

Sponge Cake

6 eggs, separated
¾ teaspoon cream of tartar
½ cup plus 2 tablespoons sugar
1½ cups all-purpose flour, stirred and measured
½ cup plus 2 tablespoons sugar
¾ teaspoon baking powder
½ teaspoon salt
½ cup orange juice, apricot nectar or water
1 tablespoon grated orange rind (optional)
1 teaspoon lemon or vanilla extract

Separate eggs, placing whites in large mixing bowl, yolks in small mixing bowl. (If egg whites are brought to room temperature before beating, they will give greater volume.) Add cream of tartar to egg whites. Beat at high speed until foamy. Gradually add ½ cup plus 2 tablespoons sugar, continuing to beat until stiff peaks form; set aside. To egg yolks, add flour, remaining sugar, baking powder, salt, orange juice or water, orange rind, and flavoring. Blend at low speed until moistened; beat 1 minute at medium speed, scraping bowl occasionally. Pour over egg whites. By hand, fold carefully just until well blended. Pour batter into ungreased 10-inch tube pan. Bake at 375 degrees F. for 35 to 40 minutes or until top springs back when lightly touched. Invert and cool thoroughly. Remove cooled cake from pan. If desired, frost with Lemon Butter Fluff Frosting (p. 267) or brush with Lemon Glaze.

Lemon Glaze: In bowl, combine 2 cups confectioners' sugar, 1 teaspoon grated lemon peel or lemon extract, and enough lemon juice to give mixture a glaze consistency. Makes 1½ cups.

See menus for February, 4th week.

Ginger Cakes

⅓ cup melted shortening
  or vegetable oil
½ cup sugar
½ cup molasses
1 egg
1 teaspoon soda
2 cups all-purpose flour,
  stirred and measured
1 teaspoon ground ginger
½ teaspoon ground
  cinnamon
¼ teaspoon ground cloves
½ cup sour milk* or
  buttermilk
½ cup nuts, coarsely
  chopped
½ cup raisins
Caramel Frosting**

In large mixing bowl combine melted shortening, sugar, molasses, egg, and soda; beat until well blended and light. Add sifted dry ingredients and sour milk or buttermilk; mix until well blended. Stir in nuts and raisins. Spoon batter into muffin tins that have been greased or lined with cupcake liners, filling about ⅔ full. Bake at 350 degrees F. for 20 to 25 minutes. If desired, frost with Caramel Frosting. Makes 18 large cupcakes.

*Note: To sour milk, put ½ tablespoon vinegar into measuring cup; add enough milk to make ½ cup; allow to stand for 5 minutes.

**Caramel Frosting: In small heavy skillet or saucepan place 2 tablespoons granulated sugar over medium heat until sugar melts and is caramel brown in color, shaking skillet as needed to keep sugar from burning. Add 2 tablespoons water; cook and stir until sugar is dissolved. Remove from heat; set aside. In medium bowl, cream together 2 tablespoons butter or margarine, 2 cups confectioners' sugar, pinch salt, and enough caramel syrup to make spreadable.

See menus for August, 4th week.

Streusel Coffee Cake

Streusel*
1½ cups all-purpose flour,
  stirred and measured
2 teaspoons baking powder
½ teaspoon salt
⅔ cup sugar
¼ cup soft shortening
1 egg, beaten
¾ cup milk

Prepare Streusel; set aside. In medium mixing bowl, combine all ingredients and beat on medium speed of mixer for 1 minute or until ingredients are mixed. Spread half of batter in greased and floured 8-inch square baking dish; sprinkle with half of Streusel. Spread remaining batter over top and sprinkle with remaining Streusel. Bake at 375 degrees F. for 25 to 35 minutes. Makes 8 servings.

*Streusel: Combine ½ cup brown sugar, 2 tablespoons flour, 2 teaspoons cinnamon, 2 tablespoons melted butter or margarine, and ½ cup finely chopped nuts.

See menus for July, 1st week.

Carrot Cake

2 cups brown sugar, packed
1 cup vegetable oil
3 eggs
3 cups (3/4 pound) finely grated carrots
3 cups all-purpose flour, stirred and measured
1 teaspoon salt
1 teaspoon soda
1 teaspoon ground cinnamon
2 teaspoons vanilla
1 cup raisins
1 cup walnuts, broken

Grease and flour 9x13-inch baking pan or spray 10-inch Bundt pan with vegetable cooking spray (or grease heavily) and coat thoroughly with granulated sugar. Beat together brown sugar, oil, and eggs. Stir in carrots. Blend together dry ingredients; stir into batter thoroughly. Add vanilla, raisins, and nuts. Pour into prepared pan. Bake at 350 degrees F. for 30 to 35 minutes for 9x13-inch cake or 1 hour for Bundt cake or until cake tests done. If desired, frost with Lemon Butter Fluff Frosting or Cream Cheese Frosting.

Note: One cup drained crushed pineapple may be substituted for 1 cup of the grated carrots and 1 cup coconut may be added. Also, whole wheat flour may be used in place of all-purpose flour.

Cream Cheese Frosting: In large bowl, cream together 1 package (3 ounces) softened cream cheese and 2 tablespoons softened butter or margarine until smooth. Gradually beat in 3 cups confectioners' sugar and 1 teaspoon vanilla. Beat until spreading consistency, adding cream or evaporated milk as needed. Frosts 9-inch layer cake or 10-inch Bundt cake.

Lemon Butter Fluff Frosting: In above recipe, increase butter or margarine to 1/2 cup, increase confectioners' sugar to 4 cups, add in place of vanilla 1 tablespoon lemon juice and 2 teaspoons grated lemon rind. Beat in 2 tablespoons cream.

See menus for February, 1st week.

Applesauce Cupcakes

2 cups all-purpose flour, stirred and measured
1 teaspoon soda
1/4 teaspoon salt
1 teaspoon cinnamon
1/2 teaspoon cloves
1/2 cup seedless raisins
1/2 cup chopped nuts
1/3 cup (2/3 stick) butter or margarine
1 cup sugar
1 egg
1 cup applesauce

Line 24 cupcake pans with cupcake liners; set aside. In large bowl stir together flour, soda, salt, and spices; stir in raisins and nuts. In separate bowl cream together butter or margarine and sugar; add egg and beat until mixture is fluffy. Stir in applesauce alternately with dry ingredients. Fill prepared muffin pans 2/3 full. Bake at 375 degrees F. for 20 to 25 minutes. Cool and serve frosted or unfrosted, as desired. Makes 2 dozen cupcakes.

See menus for January, 3rd week.

Fresh Apple Cake

⅓ cup boiling water
2 cups finely chopped pared apples (2 medium)
2 cups all-purpose flour, stirred and measured
1¼ cups sugar
1¼ teaspoons baking soda
1 teaspoon salt
1 teaspoon ground cinnamon
1 teaspoon ground nutmeg
1 teaspoon ground cloves
½ cup vegetable oil
3 eggs
1 teaspoon vanilla
1 cup coarsely chopped nuts

Grease and flour 9x13-inch or 9x9x2-inch pan; set aside. Pour boiling water over apples. In large mixing bowl combine dry ingredients. Add oil, eggs, vanilla, and apple and water mixture. Beat together on medium speed until well blended, about 1 minute. Stir in nuts. Pour batter into prepared pan. Bake at 350 degrees F. for 35 to 40 minutes or until wooden pick inserted in center comes out clean. Cool. If desired, frost with 1/2 recipe of Cream Cheese Frosting or Lemon Butter Fluff Frosting (p. 267).

See menus for September, 4th week.

Pineapple Upside Down Cake

4 pineapple slices
2 tablespoons butter or margarine
½ cup brown sugar, packed
1 tablespoon pineapple juice
4 maraschino cherries, halved
2 eggs, separated
¼ teaspoon cream of tartar
¼ cup sugar
¾ cup all-purpose flour, stirred and measured
¼ cup sugar
¼ teaspoon salt
½ teaspoon baking powder
½ cup pineapple juice
½ teaspoon lemon extract
¼ teaspoon vanilla
Cream, whipped and sweetened to taste (optional)

Drain pineapple, reserving liquid; cut slices in half. Melt butter in 8-inch round baking pan. Stir in brown sugar and 1 tablespoon reserved pineapple liquid. Arrange pineapple and cherries in pan. Add cream of tartar to egg whites; beat at high speed until foamy. Gradually add ¼ cup sugar, beating until stiff peaks form; set aside. To egg yolks, add flour, remaining sugar, salt, baking powder, pineapple juice, and flavorings. Blend at low speed until moistened; beat 1 minute at medium speed. Pour over egg whites. By hand, fold carefully just until well blended. Pour batter over pineapple slices. Bake at 350 degrees F. for 25 to 30 minutes or until top springs back when lightly touched. Let stand 5 minutes, then invert onto plate and serve warm or cold, plain or with whipped cream. Makes 8 servings.

Variation

Apple Upside Down Cake: Prepare butter and brown sugar mixture in bottom of pan, using 1 tablespoon lemon juice in place of pineapple juice. Arrange 1½ cups peeled sliced apples in circular pattern in pan. Prepare batter as above, using orange juice or water in place of pineapple juice. Continue as above.

See menus for March, 2nd week.

Cookies

Soft Ginger Cookies

³/₄ cup (1¹/₂ sticks) butter
  or margarine
1 cup sugar
2 eggs
1 cup molasses
4 cups all-purpose flour,
  stirred and measured
¹/₂ teaspoon salt
1 teaspoon soda
2 teaspoons cinnamon
2 teaspoons ginger
¹/₃ teaspoon cloves
³/₄ cup water

Cream together butter or margarine and sugar. Add eggs and beat well. Stir in molasses. Mix together dry ingredients and add alternately with water. Drop from dessert spoon onto oiled cookie sheets. Bake at 350 degrees F. for 12 to 15 minutes. Cookies should be large, soft, and thick. Makes 7 dozen.

See menus for January, 1st week.

Gingersnaps

³/₄ cup (1¹/₂ sticks) butter,
  margarine, or shortening
1 cup sugar
1 egg
¹/₄ cup molasses, light or
  dark
2 cups all-purpose flour,
  stirred and measured
2 teaspoons soda
¹/₂ teaspoon salt
2 teaspoons ground ginger
³/₄ teaspoon ground
  cinnamon
¹/₄ teaspoon ground cloves

Cream butter, margarine, or shortening; add sugar gradually. Beat until fluffy. Add egg and molasses; blend. Stir or sift together flour, soda, salt, and spices; stir into dough. Roll dough into balls about size of walnuts; roll in granulated sugar. Place on ungreased baking sheet 1¹/₂ inches apart. Bake at 350 degrees F. for 8 to 10 minutes, or until cookies have melted and puffed. For crisper cookies, bake until cookies flatten down. Cookies form perfect rounds with traditional gingersnap cracks on top. Makes 5 dozen cookies.

See menus for February, 3rd week; May, 1st week; August, 3rd week.

Butterscotch Crunchies

2 packages (6 ounces each)
  butterscotch chips
¹/₂ cup peanut butter
6 cups cornflakes

Melt butterscotch chips and peanut butter together over medium heat. Stir in cornflakes. Drop from teaspoon onto waxed paper, shaping cookies with spoon. Allow to set. Makes 3 dozen cookies.

See menus for April, 3rd week.

Butterscotch Cookies

¹/₂ cup (1 stick) butter or
  margarine
1¹/₂ cups brown sugar,
  packed
2 eggs
1 teaspoon vanilla
2¹/₂ cups all-purpose flour,
  stirred and measured
1 teaspoon soda
¹/₂ teaspoon baking powder
¹/₂ teaspoon salt
1 cup dairy sour cream (or
  1 tablespoon vinegar plus
  enough evaporated milk to
  measure 1 cup)
²/₃ cup coarsely chopped
  nuts
Browned Butter Frosting*

In large mixing bowl, cream together butter and brown sugar until light and fluffy. Add eggs and vanilla; beat until blended. Stir together dry ingredients; add to dough alternately with sour cream, stirring well after each addition. Stir in nuts. Drop by teaspoonfuls onto buttered cookie sheet. Bake at 350 degrees F. for 10 minutes. Baked cookies should be soft and mounded. When cool, frost with Browned Butter Frosting. Makes 5 dozen cookies.

Browned Butter Frosting: In small saucepan melt ¹/₄ cup (¹/₂ stick) butter (no substitute); cook over medium heat until butter becomes nut brown in color and stops bubbling; do not burn. Remove from heat. Blend in 2 cups confectioners' sugar and enough boiling water (1 or 2 tablespoons) to make spreadable. Stir in ¹/₂ teaspoon vanilla. If frosting becomes too stiff, add a few more drops of hot water.

See menus for March, 4th week.

Chocolate Chews

¹/₂ cup shortening
1²/₃ cups sugar
1 teaspoon vanilla
2 eggs
2 squares (1 ounce each)
  unsweetened chocolate,
  melted
2 cups all-purpose flour,
  stirred and measured
2 teaspoons baking powder
¹/₂ teaspoon salt
¹/₃ cup milk
¹/₂ cup nuts, chopped
  (optional)
¹/₂ cup confectioners' sugar

Cream shortening, sugar, and vanilla. Beat in eggs and melted chocolate. Sift dry ingredients; add to batter alternately with milk. Stir in nuts. Chill 2 to 3 hours. Form into 1-inch balls; roll in confectioners' sugar; place on greased baking sheet 2 to 3 inches apart. Bake at 350 degrees F. for 12 minutes. Makes 3 dozen cookies.

See menus for May, 4th week.

Pepper Cookies

½ cup sugar
½ cup dark corn syrup
½ cup (1 stick) butter
1½ teaspoons vinegar
1 egg, slightly beaten
2¼ cups all-purpose flour,
    stirred and measured
½ teaspoon soda
¼ teaspoon pepper
½ teaspoon ground ginger
½ teaspoon ground cloves
½ teaspoon ground
    cinnamon

In medium saucepan combine sugar, corn syrup, butter, and vinegar; bring almost to boiling point, then cool to room temperature. Stir in egg. Add sifted dry ingredients, blending well. Cover; refrigerate several hours or overnight. Divide dough into two portions, keeping each part chilled until time to roll out. Roll dough very thinly on floured board. Cut into desired shapes. Bake on greased cookie sheet at 350 degrees F. for 7 to 8 minutes or until barely browned. Remove from baking sheet immediately. Cool. Store in loosely covered container so cookies will remain crisp. Makes 8 dozen 3-inch cookies.

Note: Recipe can be doubled. Divide dough into four portions; keep three portions refrigerated while rolling out fourth.

See menus for December, 1st week.

Raisin Nut Nibbles

1 cup water
2 cups raisins
1 teaspoon soda
1 cup shortening
2 cups sugar
1 teaspoon vanilla
3 eggs
3½ cups all-purpose flour,
    stirred and measured
1 teaspoon baking powder
1 teaspoon cinnamon
½ teaspoon nutmeg
1 teaspoon salt
½ to 1 cup chopped nuts

In small saucepan combine water and raisins; bring to boil, reduce heat, and simmer 5 minutes. Cool; stir in soda; set aside. Cream together shortening and sugar. Beat in vanilla and eggs. Stir in raisin mixture. Add sifted dry ingredients and nuts; drop by teaspoonfuls onto ungreased baking sheets, allowing room for cookies to spread. Bake at 375 degrees F. for 10 minutes or until barely done. Makes 6 dozen cookies.

See menus for January, 2nd week; June, 1st week.

Apple Oatmeal Cookies

½ cup (1 stick) butter or margarine
⅔ cup sugar
2 eggs
1 cup all-purpose flour, stirred and measured
1 teaspoon baking powder
1 teaspoon ground cinnamon
½ teaspoon ground nutmeg
½ teaspoon salt
1 cup rolled oats, quick-cooking or regular
1 cup chopped unpeeled apple
1 cup coarsely chopped walnuts

Cream butter or margarine and sugar until fluffy. Add eggs, one at a time, beating well after each addition. Sift together flour, baking powder, spices, and salt; blend into egg mixture. Stir in rolled oats, apples, and nuts. Drop by teaspoonfuls onto greased baking sheet about 1½ inches apart. Bake at 350 degrees F. for 10 to 12 minutes or until lightly browned. Makes 2 dozen medium large cookies. (Recipe may be doubled.)

See menus for March, 1st week; June, 4th week; October, 3rd week.

Oatmeal Cookies

1 cup shortening
¾ cup granulated sugar
⅓ cup brown sugar, packed
2 eggs
1 teaspoon vanilla
1½ cups all-purpose flour, scooped and leveled
½ teaspoon salt
1 teaspoon soda
1 tablespoon hot water
2 cups quick-cooking rolled oats
½ cup nuts, coarsely chopped (optional)

Cream shortening and sugars together until fluffy. Beat in eggs and vanilla. Add flour and salt. Add soda that has been dissolved in hot water; blend. Stir in rolled oats, and nuts. Drop by teaspoonfuls onto ungreased baking sheet about 1½ inches apart. Bake at 375 degrees F. for 10 minutes or until barely brown and still a little puffy. For crisper cookies bake until cookies flatten. Makes 3 dozen cookies. Recipe may be doubled.

Note: Coconut or raisins may also be added to this basic cookie dough.

Variation

Chocolate Chip Oatmeal Cookies: Add 1 package (6 ounces) chocolate chips with the oats and nuts.

See menus for January, 4th week; March, 2nd week; September, 3rd week.

Pumpkin Bars

³/₄ cup (1¹/₂ sticks) butter
  or margarine
1¹/₂ cups sugar
1 can (16 ounces) pumpkin
4 eggs
2 cups all-purpose flour,
  stirred and measured
¹/₂ teaspoon salt
¹/₂ teaspoon soda
2 teaspoons baking powder
1 teaspoon ground cinnamon
¹/₄ teaspoon ground nutmeg
1 cup chopped walnuts
Cream Cheese Frosting
  (p. 267)

In large mixing bowl cream together butter or margarine and sugar until light and fluffy. Blend in pumpkin and eggs. Add combined dry ingredients; mix well. Stir in nuts. Spread mixture into greased and floured 10x15-inch jelly roll pan. Bake at 350 degrees F. for 30 minutes or until wooden toothpick inserted in center comes out clean. Cool. Spread with Cream Cheese Frosting. Makes 24 bars.

See menus for November, 1st week.

Pumpkin Cookies

³/₄ cup shortening
1 cup sugar
1 egg
1 cup canned or cooked
  pumpkin
¹/₂ teaspoon vanilla
¹/₂ teaspoon lemon extract
2 cups all-purpose flour,
  stirred and measured
4 teaspoons baking powder
1 teaspoon ground cinnamon
¹/₂ teaspoon ground nutmeg
¹/₄ teaspoon ground ginger
¹/₂ cup shredded coconut
  (optional)
¹/₂ cup chopped nuts
Maple Frosting*

In large mixing bowl cream together shortening and sugar. Add egg, pumpkin, vanilla, and lemon extract; beat well. Sift in dry ingredients; mix thoroughly. Fold in coconut and nuts. Drop onto greased cookie sheet by teaspoonfuls. Bake at 350 degrees F. for 15 minutes or until done. Frost when cool. Makes 3 dozen cookies.

Maple Frosting: In small bowl blend together until smooth 2 tablespoons soft butter or margarine, 1 cup confectioners' sugar, 2 tablespoons milk or cream, and ¹/₂ teaspoon maple flavoring.

See menus for April, 2nd week; October, 1st week.

Refrigerator Peanut Butter Cookies

1 cup shortening
1 cup brown sugar (packed)
1 cup granulated sugar
1 cup chunky peanut butter
2 eggs
2¾ cups all-purpose flour,
   stirred and measured
2 teaspoons soda

Cream together shortening, sugars, and peanut butter; beat in eggs; add dry ingredients. Shape into rolls; chill in refrigerator or freezer. Rolls of cookies may be somewhat soft, but will slice off easily into ¼-inch slices. Bake on ungreased cookie sheet at 375 degrees F. for 8 to 10 minutes. Do not overbake. Makes 4 dozen cookies.

See menus for August, 1st week.

Snickerdoodles

1 cup soft shortening
1½ cups sugar
2 eggs
2¼ cups all-purpose flour,
   stirred and measured
2 teaspoons cream of tartar
1 teaspoon soda
½ teaspoon salt
2 tablespoons sugar
2 teaspoons cinnamon

In large mixing bowl, cream shortening and 1½ cups sugar; add eggs; beat until light and fluffy. Stir together flour, cream of tartar, soda, and salt; stir into shortening mixture until well blended. Roll dough into balls the size of small walnuts, then roll in mixture of 2 tablespoons sugar and cinnamon. Place 2 inches apart on ungreased baking sheet. Bake at 400 degrees F. for 8 to 10 minutes or until cookies have barely flattened out and are slightly browned. (Cookies puff up at first, then flatten out with crinkled tops.) Makes 5 dozen 2-inch cookies.

See menus for February, 2nd week; June, 3rd week.

Apple Peanut Butter Cookies

½ cup (1 stick) butter or
   margarine
½ cup granulated sugar
½ cup brown sugar, packed
½ cup peanut butter
2 eggs
1 teaspoon vanilla
1½ cups grated apple
1¼ cups all-purpose flour,
   stirred and measured
½ teaspoon baking powder
½ teaspoon soda
¼ teaspoon salt

Cream together butter or margarine, sugars, and peanut butter. Add eggs and vanilla; beat well. Stir in grated apple. Stir together dry ingredients; stir into shortening and apple mixture. Drop by teaspoonfuls onto greased baking sheets. Bake at 350 degrees F. for 10 minutes. Makes 4 dozen cookies.

See menus for July, 2nd week.

Celebration Cookies

1 cup (2 sticks) butter or margarine
2 cups sugar
2 eggs
1 cup dairy sour cream
1 teaspoon vanilla
1/2 teaspoon soda
4 teaspoons baking powder
4 1/2 cups all-purpose flour, scooped and leveled
1/2 teaspoon salt
Nutmeg or cinnamon and sugar

This is a soft sugar cookie.

Cream together butter and sugar. Add eggs and beat well. Add sour cream and vanilla. Sift together dry ingredients and add to creamed mixture until a soft dough forms. Roll dough on floured surface to a scant 1/2 inch thickness. Cut with large round cookie cutter, 2 to 2 3/4 inches in diameter. Place on greased cookie sheet about 2 inches apart and sprinkle with nutmeg or cinnamon and sugar. Bake at 350 degrees F. for 14 to 17 minutes or until very lightly browned. Cookies should be large, soft, and thick. Makes 2 1/2 dozen.

Note: Shortening or lard may be used in place of butter. Plain yogurt may be used in place of sour cream. Almond extract may be used in place of vanilla. Raisins, nuts, or chocolate chips may be added to dough. Cookies may be frosted or decorated as desired.

See menus for May, 3rd week.

Cut-Out Sugar Cookies

2/3 cup shortening
3/4 cup sugar
1 egg
1/2 teaspoon vanilla
1/2 teaspoon almond extract
1 3/4 cups all-purpose flour, stirred and measured
1 teaspoon baking powder
1/4 teaspoon salt
4 teaspoons milk
Butter Frosting*

Thoroughly cream shortening and sugar. Add egg; beat until mixture is light and fluffy. Add vanilla and almond; mix in thoroughly. Add sifted dry ingredients together with milk; mix until blended. Chill 1 hour for ease in handling. Roll out dough to 1/8-inch thickness. Cut into desired shapes. Arrange on greased cookie sheet. Bake at 375 degrees F. for 6 to 8 minutes or until done. Cool; if desired, frost with Butter Frosting. Makes 2 dozen cookies. Recipe may be doubled.

Butter Frosting: Blend together 2 tablespoons soft butter and 1 cup sifted confectioners' sugar. Stir in 1 tablespoon cream or evaporated milk and 1/2 teaspoon vanilla. Makes frosting for 2 dozen cookies.

See menus for October, 4th week.

Coconut Date Cookies

1 cup shortening
1/2 cup lightly packed brown sugar
1 cup granulated sugar
3 tablespoons grated orange rind (optional)
2 eggs
2 cups all-purpose flour, stirred and measured
2 teaspoons baking powder
1/2 teaspoon salt
2 cups (8 ounces) flaked coconut
1 cup (8 ounces) chopped dates
1 cup uncooked rolled oats

Cream together shortening, sugars, and orange rind, if used. Add eggs, one at a time, beating well after each addition. Sift together flour, baking powder, and salt; add to shortening; blend well. Stir in coconut, dates, and rolled oats. Drop by teaspoonfuls onto greased baking sheet. Bake at 350 degrees F. for 10 minutes. Makes 4 dozen 2-inch cookies.

See menus for July, 1st week.

DESSERTS

Desserts

Vanilla Pudding

½ cup sugar
2 tablespoons cornstarch
½ teaspoon salt
2 cups milk
1 egg or 2 yolks, slightly beaten
1 tablespoon butter or margarine
1 teaspoon vanilla

In medium saucepan blend together sugar, cornstarch, and salt. Stir in milk. Cook over medium heat, stirring, until mixture thickens and comes to full boil; turn heat down to low and continue cooking 2 minutes longer. Stir half of hot mixture into beaten egg, then combine with mixture in saucepan. Cook 2 minutes longer, stirring. Remove from heat; add butter or margarine and vanilla, stirring until butter is melted. Pour into bowl and place clear plastic wrap carefully over top so it rests directly on surface. Chill. Makes 4 servings.

Note: 1 cup evaporated milk and 1 cup water may be used place of milk for richer flavor.

Variations

Butterscotch Pudding: Prepare Vanilla Pudding as above, using brown sugar in place of granulated sugar.

Chocolate Pudding: Prepare Vanilla Pudding as above, increasing sugar to ¾ cup. Add 2 squares (1 ounce each) unsweetened chocolate, chopped, along with milk. Continue as directed.

Banana Cream Pudding: Prepare Vanilla Pudding as above. To serve, slice ½ banana into bottom of each serving dish before topping with Vanilla Pudding.

Coconut Cream Pudding: Prepare Vanilla Pudding as above, using ½ teaspoon vanilla extract and ½ teaspoon almond extract. Stir in ½ cup coconut.

Peanut Butter Pudding: Prepare Vanilla Pudding as above. While pudding is still hot, blend in ¼ cup peanut butter or more, according to taste.

Chocolate Peanut Butter Pudding: Prepare Chocolate Pudding. While pudding is hot, blend in ¼ cup peanut butter or more, according to taste.

See menus for March, 4th week; June, 4th week; August, 3rd week.

Lemon Surprise Pudding

3 tablespoons butter or
  margarine
1½ cups sugar
6 tablespoons all-purpose
  flour
¼ teaspoon salt
½ cup lemon juice (2 or 3
  lemons)
2 teaspoons grated lemon
  rind
4 large eggs, separated
2¼ cups milk, scalded

In large bowl, cream together butter and sugar. Stir in flour, salt, lemon juice, and grated rind. Add beaten egg yolks and milk; blend well. (Do not be concerned if mixture curdles.) Fold in stiffly beaten egg whites. Pour into greased 2-quart casserole. Set casserole into shallow pan of hot water. Bake at 325 degrees F. for 1 hour or until done. Serve hot or chilled. Makes 8 servings.

See menus for January, 2nd week; August, 3rd week; December, 4th week.

Banana Bavarian Pudding

2 tablespoons cold water
1 envelope (1 tablespoon)
  unflavored gelatin
6 tablespoons water
1 cup sugar
3 large ripe bananas
1 orange, juice and grated
  rind
½ lemon, juice and grated
  rind
1 cup whipping cream

Mix 2 tablespoons cold water with gelatin; soak until soft. In small saucepan, combine 6 tablespoons water with sugar; bring to boil. Stir in gelatin mixture until dissolved; set aside to cool. Mash bananas; combine with juices and grated rinds. Add to gelatin mixture; chill until consistency of egg white. Whip cream; fold into gelatin. Pour into 6-cup mold. Chill until set. Makes 6 servings.

See menus for April, 3rd week; June, 4th week; December, 1st week.

Custard Rice Pudding

2 eggs, well beaten
½ cup sugar
¼ teaspoon salt
2 cups milk, scalded
1¼ cups cooked, cooled rice
1 cup seedless raisins
1 teaspoon vanilla
Dash cinnamon
Dash nutmeg

Combine eggs, sugar, and salt. Gradually add scalded milk. Add rice, raisins, vanilla, cinnamon, and nutmeg. Pour into greased 1-quart casserole. Set in shallow pan; pour hot water into pan 1-inch deep. Bake at 325 degrees F. for 1½ hours. Makes 4 to 6 servings.

See menus for January, 4th week.

Old-Fashioned Rice Pudding

4 cups milk, scalded
$\frac{1}{3}$ cup uncooked long grain rice
$\frac{1}{3}$ cup sugar
$\frac{1}{4}$ teaspoon salt
$\frac{1}{4}$ teaspoon nutmeg or cinnamon
$\frac{1}{2}$ teaspoon vanilla
$\frac{1}{2}$ cup raisins (optional)

Combine all ingredients but vanilla and raisins in buttered $1\frac{1}{2}$-quart casserole. Bake at 325 degrees F. for $1\frac{1}{2}$ hours, stirring each half hour. Stir in vanilla and raisins. Bake, without stirring, for another half hour, or until rice is tender and milk is absorbed. Makes 8 servings.

Note: Converted rice may be used, but not quick-cooking rice.

See menus for January, 1st week.

Cranberry Pudding with Hot Butter Sauce

3 tablespoons butter or margarine
1 cup sugar
$1\frac{3}{4}$ cups all-purpose flour, stirred and measured
2 teaspoons baking powder
$\frac{1}{2}$ teaspoon salt
1 cup evaporated milk
2 cups ($\frac{1}{2}$ pound) whole raw cranberries
Hot Butter Sauce*

Cream together butter or margarine and sugar. Add sifted dry ingredients alternately with evaporated milk, beating after each addition. Fold in washed and drained cranberries. Pour into greased 8x8x2-inch baking dish. Bake at 350 degrees F. for 25 to 30 minutes. Serve with Hot Butter Sauce. Makes 8 servings.

Hot Butter Sauce: In small saucepan, combine $\frac{1}{4}$ cup ($\frac{1}{2}$ stick) butter (no substitute), $\frac{3}{4}$ cup sugar, and $\frac{1}{2}$ cup heavy cream. Bring to boil; reduce heat and simmer 10 minutes. Remove from heat. Add 1 teaspoon vanilla. Makes 1 cup.

See menus for November, 4th week.

Apple Nut Pudding

2 eggs
1 cup sugar
$\frac{3}{4}$ cup all-purpose flour, stirred and measured
1 teaspoon baking powder
$\frac{1}{2}$ teaspoon salt
$\frac{1}{2}$ teaspoon ground cinnamon
$\frac{1}{4}$ teaspoon ground nutmeg
$\frac{1}{2}$ teaspoon vanilla
$\frac{3}{4}$ cup chopped walnuts
$1\frac{1}{2}$ cups diced unpeeled raw apples
Cream, whipped and sweetened to taste (optional)

Beat eggs until fluffy. Add sugar gradually, beating thoroughly after each addition. Stir in flour that has been sifted with baking powder, salt, and spices. Fold in vanilla, nuts, and apples. Pour into well-greased 8-inch square pan. Bake at 325 degrees F. for 45 to 50 minutes. Serve with slightly sweetened whipped cream. Makes 8 servings.

See menus for June, 3rd week; November, 2nd week; December, 2nd week.

Baked Apple Tapioca

4 cups water
3 tablespoons lemon juice
4 tart apples, unpared but
  sliced
½ cup quick-cooking tapioca
1⅓ cups brown sugar,
  packed
¾ teaspoon salt
⅓ teaspoon nutmeg or mace
4 tablespoons (½ stick)
  butter or margarine
Cream, whipped and
  sweetened to taste, or
  half-and-half or evaporated
  milk (optional)

In buttered 2-quart casserole combine water and lemon juice. Add apples; cover and bake at 375 degrees F. for 15 minutes. Mix together tapioca, brown sugar, salt, and nutmeg or mace. Stir into hot apples. Add butter; stir until melted. Cover; continue baking 15 minutes longer, stirring once. Allow to stand 10 to 15 minutes before serving. Good hot or cold, with or without cream. Makes 8 servings.

See menus for January, 4th week; April, 1st week; October, 4th week.

Apple Crisp

3 large cooking apples
¾ cup brown sugar
½ cup all-purpose flour
½ cup (1 stick) butter or
  margarine
¾ cups rolled oats

Arrange sliced apples in buttered 9-inch round baking dish. Combine brown sugar and flour; cut butter into mixture as for pastry. Toss in rolled oats. Spoon mixture over apples, pressing down lightly. Bake at 350 degrees F. for 35 to 40 minutes. Makes 6 servings.
  Note: Two cans (1 pound) apple slices may be used in place of fresh apples.

Variations

Apricot Crisp: Arrange ½ to 1 pound fresh apricots, halved and seeded, in baking dish. Or use 1 can (29 ounces) apricot halves, drained. Top with streusel mixture and bake as for above.

Peach Crisp: Slice 3 large fresh peaches or thoroughly drain 1 can (29 ounces) sliced peaches. Place in baking dish, sprinkle with lemon juice and top with streusel mixture. Bake as for above.

Cranberry Crisp: Spread evenly 2 cans (1 pound each) cranberry sauce in bottom of buttered baking dish. Top with streusel mixture and bake as for above.

See menus for February, 2nd week; May, 3rd week; August, 2nd week.

Baked Apples

4 baking apples (Rome
  Beauty, Golden Delicious,
  Granny Smith, Greening,
  or Pippin)
$^1/_4$ cup brown sugar
$^1/_4$ teaspoon ground
  cinnamon
$^1/_4$ teaspoon ground nutmeg
Chopped raisins or nuts or
  both (optional)
4 teaspoons butter or
  margarine
$^1/_2$ cup boiling water

Core apples and pare $1^1/_2$ inches from top of apple to prevent splitting. Place apples upright in buttered baking dish. Blend together brown sugar and spices. Stuff evenly into apple centers along with raisins or nuts, if used. Dot with butter. Pour boiling water around apples. Bake, uncovered, at 350 degrees F. for about 1 hour or until apples are tender, basting occasionally. Serve warm with light cream or ice cream, if desired. Makes 4 servings.

Note: These may be baked in microwave on *full power* for 4 to 5 minutes or until apples are tender. Let apples stand a few minutes before serving.

See menus for February, 1st week; April, 3rd week; April, 4th week.

Apple Kuchen

1 9-inch unbaked pastry shell
  (see Rich Flaky Pastry
  p. 284)
$^1/_3$ cup nuts, finely ground
4 cups peeled thick apple
  slices
$^1/_4$ cup sugar
$^1/_2$ to 1 teaspoon cinnamon
$^1/_2$ tablespoon flour
Cream, whipped and
  sweetened to taste
  (optional)

When making pastry shell, shape and flute edge so that it is thin and low. Spread ground nuts evenly over bottom of unbaked pastry shell. Arrange apple slices overlapped in orderly fashion around outer edge of bottom of pastry shell; then arrange another circle inside that and another until entire bottom is covered. Combine sugar, cinnamon, and flour; sprinkle evenly over fruit. Bake at 375 degrees F. for 40 to 45 minutes or until fruit is tender and cooked. Serve warm topped with whipped cream.

Note: Any fresh fruit may be used. Apricots, plums, and sour cherries are especially good.

Variation

Apple Kuchen with Custard: Arrange apples in bottom of unbaked pastry shell as described above. Combine 2 eggs, pinch salt, 3 tablespoons cream or rich milk, and 3 to 4 tablespoons sugar. Pour over apples. Bake for 40 to 45 minutes or until fruit is tender.

See menus for March, 1st week.

Rich Flaky Pastry

1 cup vegetable shortening
  (do not use butter or lard)
¾ teaspoon salt
2 cups all-purpose flour,
  stirred and measured
¼ cup cold water

Measure shortening into bowl. Add salt and half of flour. Stir with spoon until ingredients cream together and mixture is smooth and satiny. Add water and remaining flour. Stir with spoon until mixture clings together in ball. Roll out as desired. Do not be afraid to handle. Makes 2 pastry shells or enough pastry for a double-crust pie.

Note: Recipe may be doubled or tripled.

See menus for March, 1st week.

Lemon Torte

4 egg whites (at room
  temperature)
¼ teaspoon cream of tartar
1 cup sugar
4 egg yolks
⅔ cup sugar
¼ cup lemon juice (1 lemon)
1 tablespoon grated lemon
  rind (2 lemons)
1⅓ cups heavy cream
2 tablespoons sugar

Needs to chill for 12 to 24 hours.

Generously butter a 9- or 10-inch pie dish; set aside. In large bowl, beat egg whites with cream of tartar until frothy. Add 1 cup sugar gradually, continuing to beat until stiff meringue is formed. Spoon meringue into prepared pie dish; spread to form a crust, pushing meringue up sides. Bake at 275 degrees F. for 1 hour. (Meringue shell will extend above rim of pie dish.) Cool.

In large bowl, beat egg yolks until creamy and thick. Gradually add ⅔ cup sugar, then lemon juice and grated rind. When thoroughly beaten, cook over low heat until very thick, stirring constantly. (Or it may be cooked in microwave at *medium* level.) Remove from heat; cool. Whip cream and sweeten with 2 tablespoons sugar. Fold half of whipped cream into cooled lemon mixture; spoon into Meringue Shell (p. 285). Top with remaining whipped cream. Cover; chill for 12 to 24 hours. Makes 8 servings.

See menus for July, 2nd week; September, 3rd week.

Traditional Pumpkin Pie

2 eggs, slightly beaten
1 can (1 pound) pumpkin
³/₄ cup sugar
¹/₂ teaspoon salt
1 teaspoon ground cinnamon
¹/₂ teaspoon ground ginger
¹/₄ teaspoon ground cloves
1 can (13 fluid ounces)
  evaporated milk
1 9-inch unbaked pastry shell
  with high fluted rim
Cream, whipped and
  sweetened to taste
  (optional)

In large bowl combine all filling ingredients in order given. Pour into pastry shell. Bake at 425 degrees F. for 15 minutes. Reduce temperature to 350 degrees F., continue baking for 45 minutes or until knife inserted into center of pie filling comes out clean. Cool. Garnish with slightly whipped cream, if desired. Makes one 9-inch pie.

Note: To double recipe for two pies, use 1 can (29 ounces) pumpkin

See menus for November, 3rd week.

Meringue Shell

3 egg whites at room
  temperature
1 teaspoon vanilla
¹/₄ teaspoon cream of tartar
Dash salt
1 cup sugar

Place egg whites in large bowl; add vanilla, cream of tartar, and salt. Beat until frothy. Gradually add sugar, beating until very stiff peaks form and sugar is dissolved. Cover baking sheet with plain ungreased paper. Using a 9-inch round cake pan as guide, draw a circle on paper. Spread meringue over circle; shape into shell with back of spoon, making bottom ¹/₂ inch thick and mounding around edge to make sides 1³/₄ inches high. Bake at 275 degrees F. for 1 hour. Turn off heat and allow to dry in unopened oven for at least 2 hours. Cool. Fill with fresh fruit and garnish with slightly sweetened whipped cream.

Note: Individual meringues may be made by shaping ¹/₃ cup meringue mixture into individual 3¹/₂-inch circles. Bake as above, allowing 1 hour for shells to dry in closed oven. Makes 8 shells.

See menus for July, 2nd week; September, 3rd week.

Baked Custard

3 slightly beaten eggs
¼ cup sugar
¼ teaspoon salt
2 cups milk, scalded
½ teaspoon vanilla
Nutmeg

Combine eggs, sugar, and salt; slowly add milk and vanilla. Pour into 1 quart casserole; sprinkle with nutmeg. Set casserole into pan of hot water so water comes up 1½ inches on side of casserole. Bake at 325 degrees F. for 45 to 50 minutes or until a silver knife blade, inserted into custard, comes out clean. Serve warm or cold. Makes 6 servings.

See menus for July, 4th week; August, 1st week.

Molded Custard Ring with Strawberries and Cream

4 cups milk
4 eggs
¾ cup sugar
⅛ teaspoon salt
2 envelopes unflavored gelatin
½ cup cold water
1 teaspoon vanilla
½ teaspoon almond extract
2 cups fresh strawberries, cleaned and hulled
1 cup heavy cream, whipped and slightly sweetened

Scald milk in heavy pan or in microwave. Beat egg yolks with sugar and salt until thick. Stir a little hot milk into egg yolk mixture, then stir egg mixture back into remaining milk. In double boiler or over lowest heat, cook egg mixture until it coats spoon, stirring constantly. Or cook mixture in microwave (50 percent power) until mixture coats spoon, stirring every minute. Remove from heat. Soak gelatin in cold water until softened; stir into hot custard mixture until dissolved. Add extracts. Pour into 5-cup ring mold; chill 7 to 8 hours or until firmly set. To serve, unmold custard ring onto serving platter. Fill center with fresh hulled strawberries; garnish with whipped cream. Makes 8 generous servings.

Note: Leftover egg whites may be used in making Chocolate Angel Pie, Meringue Shells, Coconut Macaroons, also as an egg wash on uncooked yeast rolls. Sliced fresh peaches are equally delicious served in a Molded Custard Ring.

See menus for May, 3rd week; August, 4th week.

Caramel Custard

½ cup granulated sugar
5 eggs
½ cup sugar
¼ teaspoon salt
1 teaspoon vanilla
3¼ cups milk

Sprinkle ½ cup granulated sugar over bottom of small heavy skillet. Cook over low heat, stirring with wooden spoon until sugar turns to golden syrup. Immediately remove from heat; pour into bottom of 5-cup mold, turning mold to coat sides. Cool. In large bowl, lightly beat eggs with ½ cup sugar, salt, and vanilla. Gradually stir in milk. Pour into caramel-lined mold. Set mold in pan of hot water and bake on middle rack of oven at 325 degrees F. for 55 to 60 minutes or until set. Remove mold immediately from hot water. Chill for 3 to 24 hours. Loosen sides of mold with small spatula or knife and unmold to serve. Makes 6 servings.

Note: May be baked in 5-cup ring mold and served with fresh strawberries or other fruit in center.

See menus for March, 4th week.

Apricot Soufflé

1 can (29 ounces) apricot halves
3 tablespoons butter or margarine
¼ cup all-purpose flour
1 cup milk, scalded
4 egg yolks
¼ cup sugar
⅛ teaspoon salt
4 egg whites, stiffly beaten
1 cup heavy cream, whipped and sweetened to taste
Apricot syrup, drained from apricots

Drain apricots, reserving syrup. Arrange apricot halves close together, cut side up, in bottom of buttered 2-quart casserole. In medium saucepan melt butter, blend in flour, and gradually add hot milk; cook and stir until mixture thickens and comes to boil; remove from heat. In small bowl, beat egg yolks with sugar and salt until thick; stir into white sauce, then fold into egg whites. Pour soufflé mixture over apricots. Set casserole into shallow pan of hot water. Bake at 350 degrees F. for 60 minutes until soufflé is lightly browned and cooked through. Serve warm with cold apricot syrup poured over and topped with slightly sweetened whipped cream. Makes 6 servings.

See menus for December, 2nd week.

Peach Cobbler

2 tablespoons butter or
  margarine
3 cups sliced fresh peaches
  or 1 can (29 ounces) peach
  slices, drained
$^1/_2$ cup sugar
2 tablespoons flour
$^1/_2$ teaspoon cinnamon
1 cup all-purpose flour,
  stirred and measured
2 tablespoons sugar
$^1/_4$ teaspoon salt
$1^1/_2$ teaspoons baking
  powder
$^1/_3$ cup vegetable oil or
  melted shortening
3 tablespoons milk
1 egg, slightly beaten

Preheat oven to 350 degrees F. As oven is heating, melt butter in 11$^1/_2$x7$^1/_2$-inch baking pan. Arrange sliced peaches evenly in prepared pan. Stir together $^1/_2$ cup sugar, 2 tablespoons flour and cinnamon; sprinkle evenly over fruit; set aside. Blend together 1 cup flour, 2 tablespoons sugar, salt, and baking powder in medium mixing bowl; stir in remaining ingredients that have been mixed together just until blended. Spoon evenly over fruit. Bake at 350 degrees F. for 25 to 30 minutes or until done. Makes 8 servings.

Note: Other fruits such as cherries, plums, pears, or apples (fresh, canned, or frozen) may be used in place of peaches. For fresh fruit that is somewhat tart, you may want to increase $^1/_2$ cup sugar to $^2/_3$ cup.

See menus for January, 1st week.

Stewed Rhubarb

1 pound rhubarb stalks
$^1/_2$ cup sugar
1 teaspoon grated lemon rind
$^1/_4$ cup water

Wash and trim rhubarb, peeling off tough skins. Cut into 1-inch pieces to make 3 cups. Combine with sugar, lemon rind, and water in medium saucepan. Cover and cook over medium heat for 5 minutes or until tender. Makes 4 servings.

See menus for May, 1st week; May, 2nd week.

Autumn Pears

4 fresh pears
$^1/_4$ cup ($^1/_2$ stick) butter or
  margarine
$^1/_4$ cup brown sugar
$^1/_4$ cup corn syrup
$^1/_2$ cup water
1 teaspoon lemon juice

Cut pears in half; peel and core; set aside in lightly salted water to cover. In medium saucepan, combine butter, brown sugar, corn syrup, and water. Simmer until smooth and blended. Add lemon juice. Place drained pear halves in syrup; simmer a few minutes, until tender, spooning syrup over pears occasionally. Serve warm or cold. Makes 6 to 8 servings.

Note: One can (29 ounces) pear halves may be used in place of fresh pears; use pear syrup in place of water.

See menus for September, 1st week.

Honey-Sauced Fresh Pineapple

1 fresh pineapple
1/2 cup honey
1 tablespoon lime juice
1/2 cup heavy cream
1/2 cup macadamia nuts,
  cashews, or toasted
  almonds

Cut top and bottom away from pineapple, cutting into flesh about 1/2 inch. Cut into four wedges lengthwise. With sharp knife, cut along both sides of wedge inside of shell to loosen fruit. Core and dice fruit; chill until serving time. Beat honey with electric mixer until foamy, about 1 minute. Stir in lime juice; chill. Whip cream until stiff. Fold into chilled honey mixture. cover and refrigerate. When ready to serve, stir nuts into whipped cream mixture; serve atop pineapple chunks. Makes 4 to 6 servings.

See menus for April, 1st week.

Banana Pops

8 wooden skewers
4 bananas, cut in half
  crosswise
1 milk chocolate bar
  (8 ounces)
1 1/2 cups chopped peanuts

Insert wooden skewers lengthwise into banana halves, set onto waxed paper on baking sheet and freeze. Melt chocolate in small, heavy saucepan over lowest heat. *Do not add liquid.* Remove from heat. Working quickly, roll bananas in melted chocolate, then immediately in chopped nuts. Set on baking sheet; refreeze until firm. Wrap each banana pop in plastic wrap; return to freezer. Makes 8 banana pops.

See menus for February, 1st week; May, 2nd week; September, 4th week.

Strawberry Tarts

2 pints fresh strawberries,
  divided
1 cup sugar, divided
2 tablespoons cornstarch
1/3 cup water
1 cup heavy cream, whipped
8 baked tart shells

Reserve 8 whole strawberries for garnish. Crush 1/2 of remaining cleaned and hulled berries. Combine with 1/2 cup of the sugar, cornstarch, and water. Cook over low heat until thick. Chill. Cut remaining berries in halves and quarters; sprinkle with remaining 1/2 cup sugar; let stand 15 minutes. Stir into cooked, cooled strawberry mixture. Spoon into tart shells. Top with whipped cream; garnish with whole strawberries. Makes 8 tarts.

See menus for May, 2nd week.

Frozen Strawberry Squares

1 cup all-purpose flour
1/4 cup brown sugar, packed
1/2 cup (1 stick) butter or margarine
1/2 cup pecans or walnuts, coarsely chopped
2 egg whites
1 package (10 ounces) frozen strawberries, partially defrosted
1 cup sugar
2 tablespoons lemon juice
1 cup heavy cream, whipped

Combine flour and brown sugar. Cut in butter as for pastry until mixture forms crumbs; stir in nuts. Spread in large shallow pan. Bake at 350 degrees F. for 15 minutes, stirring frequently to keep from burning. Remove from oven. Cool and crush into crumbs. Set aside.

In large bowl combine egg whites, strawberries, and sugar; beat until stiff and thick, at least 5 minutes. (Mixture looks like a big pink cloud.) Stir in lemon juice. Fold in whipped cream. In bottom 9x13x2-inch baking pan or dish, spread all but 1 cup of crumbs. Pour strawberry filling evenly over crumbs. Sprinkle remaining crumb mixture over top; cover with foil or plastic wrap and freeze for several hours. (Mixture will not freeze hard.) Cut into squares to serve. Makes 12 servings.

Variation

Mile High Strawberry Pie: Strawberry mixture may be piled *very* high into 9-inch baked pastry shell, then frozen. If desired, 1/2 recipe of crumb mixture may be sprinkled over top.

See menus for May, 4th week; September, 2nd week; December, 4th week.

Ruby Grapefruit

1 package (10 ounces) frozen red raspberries
2 to 4 tablespoons sugar, if desired but not necessary
4 large fresh grapefruit

Heat raspberries in small saucepan until completely thawed. If desired, add sugar to taste. Puree raspberries in electric blender or food processor; strain. Refrigerate raspberry sauce in covered jar. To prepare membrane-free grapefruit sections, peel whole fresh grapefruit with serrated knife, going round and round grapefruit as you might for an apple, cutting deep enough to remove white under-membrane. To extract sections, cut close to membrane on each side of a grapefruit section and slip it carefully out. Each grapefruit should yield 11 sections. Squeeze juice from remaining membrane into bowl with fruit. Arrange grapefruit sections in serving bowls; spoon raspberry sauce over top. Makes 8 servings.

Note: Ruby Grapefruit is equally delicious served as an appetizer or as a dessert.

See menus for May, 2nd week; November, 4th week; December, 4th week.

Chocolate Yule Log

5 egg yolks
1 cup sifted confectioners'
  sugar
¼ cup all-purpose flour,
  stirred and measured
½ teaspoon salt
3 tablespoons cocoa
1 teaspoon vanilla
5 egg whites, stiffly beaten
1 cup whipping cream
8 to 12 large marshmallows,
  cut up
½ recipe Chocolate Butter
  Cream Frosting*
¼ cup chopped nuts

In small bowl beat egg yolks until thick and lemon colored. Sift together confectioners' sugar, flour, salt, and cocoa 3 times; beat into egg yolks until well blended. Add vanilla. Fold in stiffly beaten egg whites. Bake at 375 degrees F. for 15 to 20 minutes in jelly roll pan (10x15x1-inch) that has been greased, lined with waxed paper, and greased again. Turn out onto towel sprinkled with confectioners' sugar. Remove waxed paper. Roll chocolate sponge and towel up together to cool. Unroll. Whip cream and sweeten slightly. Fold in marshmallows. Spread over chocolate sponge. Roll as for jelly roll. Frost. Sprinkle with chopped nuts. Chill. Slice to serve. Makes 8 servings.

Chocolate Butter Cream Frosting: In small mixing bowl, cream 2 tablespoons butter or margarine that has softened to room temperature. Add 2 cups confectioners' sugar, ⅛ teaspoon salt, 1 square (1 ounce) melted unsweetened chocolate, 1 teaspoon vanilla, and enough warm cream or evaporated milk (approximately 2 tablespoons) to make of spreadable consistency.

Note: For a richer, more satiny icing increase butter or margarine to ¼ cup (½ stick).

See menus for December, 3rd week.

Chocolate Velvet

1 package (4 ounces) sweet
  cooking chocolate
¼ cup water
¼ cup dairy sour cream
1 container (8 ounces) frozen
  whipped topping, thawed
8 maraschino cherries,
  chopped (optional)

Combine chocolate and water in saucepan; cook over low heat, stirring constantly, until melted and smooth. Slowly add chocolate mixture to sour cream in mixing bowl. Set aside ½ cup whipped topping; fold rest of topping into chocolate mixture, blending well. Spoon into 8 small serving dishes. Chill until ready to serve. Garnish with topping and cherries. Makes 8 servings.

Note: Banana slices can be placed in serving dishes before spooning in pudding to make a more nutritious dessert.

See menus for September, 4th week.

Rice in Cream with Raspberry Sauce

1 cup boiling water
1/2 teaspoon salt
1/2 cup long grain rice
1/3 cup (approximately) milk
3 tablespoons
(approximately) sugar
1/4 teaspoon almond extract
1 cup heavy cream, whipped
Raspberry Sauce*

In medium saucepan bring water to boil; add salt. Stir in rice slowly so water continues to boil. Turn heat to simmer, then cover pan and allow rice to cook for 25 minutes or until just tender. Add milk enough to barely fill and be level with top of rice. Cover pan; simmer 30 minutes longer or until all milk is absorbed. Stir in sugar to taste and almond extract. Chill. Just before serving, fold in whipped cream. Serve with chilled Raspberry Sauce or Cherry Sauce. Makes 6 servings. Recipe can be doubled.

Raspberry Sauce: Add 1/2 cup water to 1 package (10 ounces) frozen raspberries; bring to boil. Put through sieve, extracting all juice; discard seeds. To raspberry juice, add water to make 1 1/2 cups. Combine 1 1/2 tablespoons cornstarch and 1 tablespoon cold water; stir into juice; cook until mixture is thick and clear. Add pinch salt, 1 tablespoon sugar, and 1/2 tablespoon lemon juice to taste. Chill. Serve over Rice in Cream. Makes 1 1/2 cups. Recipe can be doubled.

Cherry Sauce: Combine 1 can (1 pound) undrained sour cherries and 2 tablespoons sugar; allow to stand several minutes so cherries absorb sweetness. Drain juice into small saucepan. Blend 1 1/2 tablespoons cornstarch and 1/4 cup cold water; stir into cherry juice. Cook over medium heat, stirring, until mixture is thick and clear. Reduce heat to simmer; cook another 15 minutes over low heat. Stir in cherries and 1/4 teaspoon almond extract; cool, then chill. Serve over Rice in Cream. Makes 2 cups. Recipe can be doubled.

See menus for December, 2nd week.

Instant Strawberry Ice Cream

1 package (10 ounces) frozen
strawberries
1 cup heavy cream
1 tablespoon lemon juice
Sugar

Run hot water over unopened package of frozen strawberries; empty contents into food processor or blender. Add remaining ingredients and blend until mixture is thick and smooth and well mixed. Sweeten to taste. Serve immediately or store in freezer for later use. Makes 4 servings.

See menus for November, 3rd week.

Cranberry Sherbet

2 cups (¹/₂ pound) fresh or
    frozen cranberries
1¹/₂ cups water
1 cup sugar
¹/₂ envelope (¹/₂ tablespoon)
    unflavored gelatin
¹/₄ cup cold water
¹/₄ cup lemon juice (1 lemon)

Cook washed cranberries in 1¹/₂ cups water until skins pop. Press through sieve; add sugar; stir until sugar dissolves. Soften gelatin in cold water; add to cranberries. Cool; add lemon juice. Freeze firm in shallow tray. Break into chunks; beat smooth with electric beater. Return quickly to freezer; freeze firm. Makes 4 to 6 servings.

See menus for October, 4th week.

Orange Sherbet

1 can (6 ounces) frozen
    orange juice concentrate
1 envelope (1 tablespoon)
    unflavored gelatin
³/₄ cup granulated sugar
Pinch salt
¹/₄ cup lemon juice (1 lemon)
1 teaspoon lemon rind
    (1 lemon)
1 cup half-and-half

Reconstitute orange juice with water by label directions. Soak unflavored gelatin in ¹/₂ cup of juice in small bowl for 5 minutes. Set bowl over boiling water; heat and stir until gelatin is dissolved. Combine with remaining orange juice, sugar, salt, lemon juice, lemon rind, and cream. Turn into freezing tray; freeze until half frozen. In chilled bowl beat frozen mixture until fluffy. Return to freezing tray and freeze until firm. Makes 4 servings.

See menus for February, 2nd week.

Index

About the Author

Winnifred Jardine was graduated from Iowa State University in technical journalism and foods and nutrition. As a home economics consultant, author, and lecturer, she has received numerous awards in her field. For thirty-six years, she was food editor at the *Deseret News* in Salt Lake City. She has also been a home economist in the Martha Logan Test Kitchen at Swift & Company in Chicago; director of home economics in the public relations department of the American Meat Institute in Chicago; home economics director for radio station KMBC in Kansas City, Missouri; and an instructor of foods and nutrition at the University of Utah. A past president of the Utah Home Economics Association and the Utah State Nutrition Council, she is the author of *The No Gimmick Diet, Famous Mormon Recipes, Mormon Country Cooking,* and *What Shall We Eat Today?*